SUCCESS STC W9-BSV-252

◆ ◆ ◆

Dear Jyl,

In September of 1998, I weighed 245 pounds—which I carried on a 5´5½˝ body frame. I was overweight, miserable, and for the first time in my forty-one years, my weight began tugging on my health. Then, I found your book, Recipes for *FAT FREE Living 2!*

I began trying the recipes . . . and the more I tried them, the better I felt. Boy— what a difference you have helped me make in my life!! Just in the first week because of the reduction of fat in my system, I lost 9 pounds and felt like I'd lost 100!

I have now lost a total of 50 pounds. I am just on cloud nine—my energy level is high, high, high! I am no longer miserable and unhealthy and even my skin glows! I will never again worry about weight gain, because with your help I have learned that food no longer controls my life . . . I DO!

Thank you so much for your recipes and your desire to help people like me who need a positive reinforcement in life! You've truly been an inspiration to me. With your helpful books, the love of family and encouragement of friends, I know my life will continue to be positive and I will continue to be healthy and happy! Thanks again

—Kristy Benvenuto

◆ ◆ ◆

Dear Ms. Steinback,

I am a single mother with three great kids, and I must say that when I purchased your cookbooks, my life changed forever!

When I reached forty my entire body type and metabolism began changing, especially not for the better. I knew things were going to happen, but I was shocked. I was relieved to discover your cookbooks and purchased two more for my mother. I love preparing your endless delicious recipes and have gained control of my weight, body, and life again. Best of all, my kids enjoy everything I have prepared, especially those from your dessert book.

I work as a volunteer at a women's shelter and have prepared and shared many of your recipes with them. Those leaving the shelter have purchased many of your cookbooks.

You have done more for many than you will ever know. You have helped many whom you will never meet. Thank you! I look forward to your next cookbook—I am certain it will fit in perfectly with all my others. Thank you again.   —Mary Hussong

◆ ◆ ◆

Jyl,

You are an inspiration! My husband has very high cholesterol and a family history of heart disease, diabetes, stroke, and high blood pressure. I also have diabetes on my side, so I am trying to educate myself so I can train my children to make good choices for life! It is hard in this fast-paced world, but your enthusiasm is contagious! Thank you for your commitment to making it a better world for all of us!

—Markay Ebejer

◆ ◆ ◆

more . . .

SUPERFOODS

Cook Your Way
to Health

Jyl Steinback

Published by QVC Publishing, Inc., 50 Main Street, Mt. Kisco, New York 10549

Q Publishing and colophon are trademarks of QVC Publishing, Inc.

Manufactured in Hong Kong

ISBN: 1-928998-40-2

First Edition

10 9 8 7 6 5 4 3 2 1

CONTENTS

◆ ◆ ◆

ACKNOWLEDGMENTS
◆ ◆ ◆

SUPERFOODS: Cook Your Way to Health is a dream come true. I have envisioned this cookbook for over a year now and am proud to present this wonderful gift to all of you. It is my mission in life to share my healthy ideas. It is a lifestyle that is extraordinary in so many ways. I feel life is full of choices, and you can make a change! You can make a difference! I am passionate about helping people adopt a lifestyle that improves the quality not only of their life but also that of future generations. This is not just a personal mission; it is my life's quest. I love watching people improve their lives while learning to appreciate their "specialness." Accept every moment as a gift—learn to celebrate YOU! I ask you now to take charge of your life and join me in believing in yourselves. Let's get healthy together NOW!

To my handsome husband, Gary—we just celebrated our twentieth anniversary, and it is a wonderful miracle. I must say each year gets better and better, especially since spirituality has entered both of our lives. Thanks, Gary—you are an extraordinary gift in my life, and I love you very much! You are my soul mate, my friend, my partner, and the love of my life.

Jamie—you are fifteen years old. Where have all the years gone? It's been way too quick for me! You are a beautiful person inside and out—I am so lucky to have you in my life as my daughter. Thank you for your generous heart, fabulous personality, and unconditional love—you are beautiful in every way! I do love you, Jamie, with all my heart! Lucky me!

Scott—you promised me you wouldn't grow up but you're already seven years old and entering school as a first-grader. What a handsome boy you are. You have a heart of gold! You are definitely my spiritual child and a genius, too! Thank you for your gift of being my son—a treasure I will cherish in my heart for life. I love you, Scott!

Mom and Dad—you have taught me so many wonderful qualities in my life! You are two of my most precious gifts. I am so lucky you are both here to celebrate life with the "Sunshine Kids." Thank you for surrounding my life with tremendous amounts of love and lots of fabulous family time! You two are my greatest believers and supporters! I love you both so very much! Thank you!

Jacie—you are the greatest sister and aunt! Thank you! Thank you for e-mailing great motivational stories, calling, and being a major part of our lives. I appreciate you and love you very much!

Jeff, Diane, Alex, and Casey—one of the best benefits of QVC publishing this wonderful book is that I get to see all of you more often. It has been really special and a lot of fun! Thank you for always being there for us! I love you lots—thank you for your big hearts and the special times we share.

Snooky and Harlan—I love the great e-mails, fabulous cards, and stories. Harlan, that computer of yours fits just perfectly. Thank you both very much for all of your wonderful support and love. I love you lots!

Grandma, I love you!

I am extremely thankful for the incredible opportunity to work with each and every one of you. You are a special gift in my life—I am lucky and blessed to know and work with you.

Mikki Eveloff—you are more than amazing! You are gifted in so many ways, and I thank you for sharing all of your gifts with me. Your outstanding friendship, your beautiful heart and shining soul, your loyalty and passionate devotion, your attention to details and deadlines and wonderful knack for knowing what to do and how to take charge and go for it! You truly are a blessing in my life! I love you lots! Thank you for everything! I think we are a great team!

Debbie Kohl—when I set those deadlines you came through each and every time. You are great! Thank you—for you, your time, positive energy, and special friendship. You are a gift and a treasure to work with always! (Debra Kohl is a Registered Dietitian with a master's degree in nutrition and dietetics; you can reach her services at 602-266-0324.)

Elliot Lincis—you did it! I always tell you it only takes two extraordinary shots—one for the front and one for the back. You did it again, my good friend! Thank you for the fun day in Sedona and great photographs! You're a doll!

Mike Swaine—you outdid yourself with these phenomenal front and back covers. You are a perfectionist, and I love that about you. Your eye for design is a gift—I thank you for your talent, your friendship and for working with us.

Mike Ruddy, You are a wonderful friend and I love working with you and Jumbo Jacks. Thank you!

Jim Nissen, You're the best! Thanks for always being positive and uplifting and doing fabulous work!

Jill Cohen and Karen Murgolo, you are both a special gift in my life. Thank you so much! It is an honor and a pleasure working with you both! And this is just the beginning. . .together we will change the world into a healthier place to live. Thank you!

Patrick Filley you are a saint! You are a pleasure to work with and without you "Superfoods" would have been 600 plus pages. Thanks for keeping me in line and all of your wonderful time and energy! I appreciate everything.

Matthew and Staff at the Walking Store—thanks a million for all of the beautiful camping supplies that made our front and back cover picture so colorful and perfect. It is always great working with you!

To all of my wonderful success stories—I love to hear about you! It's exciting to learn how you've taken charge of your lives and allowed me to help you become healthier. Thank you so very much for sharing and sending your great before and after shots. Please continue to write and share with me at: 15202 N. 50th Place, Scottsdale, Arizona 85254 or email: Jyl@AmericasHealthiestMom.com. My website for updated articles and information is AmericasHealthiestMom.com. As my parents have always said, "Keep those cards and letters coming!" I love all the correspondence and love working with you from the bottom of my heart. Thank you for allowing me to share in your life and successes.

INTRODUCTION
♦ ♦ ♦

What do **superfoods,** *antioxidants,* **phytochemicals,** **nutraceuticals,** **phytoestrogens,** **lycopene,** **flavonoids,** **bromelain,** **histidine,** **chromium,** **boron,** *and* **soluble fiber** *have in common?* They are . . .
(check all that apply)

(a) common cures for indigestion
(b) harmless pesticides used on vegetables and fruits
(c) costly supplements found in health food stores
(d) your best defense against heart disease, cancer, osteoporosis, arthritis, and diabetes.

The correct answer is . . . **d!**

Although such terminology sounds like mind-boggling, mystical, scientific nomenclature, you can find these natural products in some of your favorite foods! There are no magic potions or pills to ward off disease, yet research studies have found that you can benefit from increasing or decreasing your intake of certain foods. What are your choices? Scale down on fat, slash the sodium, pare down on protein, eliminate sugar, boost calcium, indulge in iron, and/or become a veritable vitamaniac! Forget the hype, the scams, and the empty promises—take charge of your body with familiar foods! It's never too late to improve your eating habits and receive all the health benefits along the way!

**What's the connection between the Big "D's"
(Diet and Disease)?**
- 1 out of every 4 American adults has high blood pressure that can be controlled by diet!
- 96.8 million Americans (51% of the population) have high cholesterol levels (over 200) that can be controlled by diet!
- Someone dies of cardiovascular disease every 33 seconds in the United States.
- Diet related cancers account for more than 360,000 deaths in the United States each year.

- The U.S. Surgeon General's report on Health and Nutrition stated that two-thirds of all deaths linked to heart disease, cancer, and associated diseases are diet related!
- Breast cancer rates are low in Japan, but high among Japanese women living in the United States; this can be attributed to higher-fat American diets.
- Stomach cancer rates are higher in Japan than in Japanese Americans due to the higher consumption of smoked, pickled, and salted foods.

Now . . . if you could reduce your risk and improve your chances for a longer and healthier life, **what would you eat?**

SUPERFOODS!

FOOD is the fuel that keeps our bodies running properly. What we eat supplies us with the nutrients we need to maintain good health. **YOU are WHAT you EAT!** According to the Health and Human Services branch of the U.S. Department of Agriculture, your primary source of vitamins and minerals should come from a variety of foods, not supplements (e.g., pills, powders, etc.)

What are SUPERFOODS a.k.a. (also known as) FUNCTIONAL FOODS and NUTRACEUTICALS?

SuperFoods, functional foods, and **nutraceuticals** are common foods with an abundance of vitamins, protein, minerals, enzymes, and special trace elements; they not only provide basic nourishment, but also enhance your body's disease-fighting capabilities. According to Chare Hasler, Ph.D., director of the University of Illinois Functional Foods for Health Program, functional foods provide health benefits that are "best realized from a wide variety of food rather than supplements." SuperFoods are the most natural way to supply your body with all it needs for peak performance, vitality, and health.

What are PHYTOESTROGENS?

Phytoestrogens are a group of phytochemicals with a structure similar in effect to estrogen. Isoflavones and lignans are the main types of phytoestrogens. These can be found in soybeans (isoflavones); flaxseeds, whole grains, and berries (lignans).

What are PHYTOCHEMICALS?

Phytochemicals are plant-chemical compounds that have been found to benefit health and aid in disease prevention. The

National Cancer Institute, John Hopkins University of Medicine, and other major medical institutions are currently studying the role of phytochemicals on human health in relation to

- preventing and slowing the development of certain cancers
- enhancing the immune system
- decreasing the effects of aging
- reducing the risk of heart disease

It's easy to incorporate these supernutrients into a daily diet by including a variety of fruits, vegetables, grains, legumes, nuts, and teas.

What are ANTIOXIDANTS?

Antioxidants are molecular compounds that help fight off disease by neutralizing free radicals (destructive oxygen by-products). Free radicals are produced not only by our bodies (*heart disease, cancer, arthritis, cataracts*), but also by the environment (*cigarette smoke, polluted air, Xrays, sunlight*). Antioxidants neutralize these free radicals and decrease their damaging effects within our bodies. The most common antioxidants include vitamins C and E, beta-carotene, and minerals selenium, zinc, and manganese. These powerful antioxidants work together to protect your body against free-radical damage.

**FUNCTIONAL FOODS = SUPERFOODS =
HEALING FOODS**
SuperFoods contain SuperNutrients for SuperHealth!

VITAMINS

Vitamin A

Function: vision; body tissues; growth and bone formation; resistance to infection

Best Sources: carrots; sweet potatoes; dark green leafy vegetables; pumpkin

Signs of Deficiency: night blindness; loss of appetite; increased susceptibility to infection; changes in skin and teeth

Vitamin D

Function: bone and teeth formation; blood clotting; calcium absorption

Best Sources: sunlight; dairy products; cod liver oil

Signs of Deficiency: rickets; osteoporosis; hearing loss

Vitamin E

Function: antioxidant; stabilizes cell membranes; protects body tissues; prevent oxidation of LDL (bad) cholesterol; improves immune function

Best Sources: vegetable oils; nuts and seeds; wheat germ

Signs of Deficiency: nerve damage; anemia; weakness

Vitamin K

Function: blood clotting; prevention of osteoporosis

Best Sources: green, leafy vegetables; cabbage; cauliflower; asparagus; broccoli; chickpeas, green tea

Signs of Deficiency: increased bleeding time

Vitamin C

Function: formation and maintenance of collagen; antioxidant; increases resistance to infection

Best Sources: orange juice; Brussels sprouts; citrus fruits; melons; broccoli; strawberries; cabbage

Signs of Deficiency: anemia, infections, muscle pain; joint pain; delayed wound healing; scurvy

Thiamine (Vitamin B$_1$)

Function: carbohydrate (energy) metabolism; nerve function

Best Sources: legumes; whole grains; enriched cereals

Signs of Deficiency: heart damage; muscular weakness; confusion; fatigue; weight loss

Riboflavin (Vitamin B$_2$)

Function: energy and protein metabolism; healthy skin; formation of red blood cells

Best Sources: dairy products; whole grains; enriched bread and cereal; green vegetables (broccoli, turnip greens, spinach, asparagus)

Signs of Deficiency: eyes sensitive to sun; skin rash, cracks at corners of mouth

Niacin (Vitamin B$_3$)

Function: carbohydrate (energy) metabolism; healthy skin; lowers blood cholesterol; maintain healthy intestinal tract

Best Sources: lean meat; dried beans and peas; brewer's yeast; poultry; tuna; whole grains; brown rice; enriched bread and cereal

Signs of Deficiency: dermatitis; dementia; loss of appetite; dizziness

Pyridoxine (Vitamin B$_6$)

Function: metabolism of protein and amino acids; manufacture antibodies, hemoglobin, and hormones

Best Sources: salmon; nuts; wheat germ; brown rice; peas; beans; nuts

Signs of Deficiency: depression; anemia; nerve inflammation

Vitamin B$_{12}$

Function: cell function; cell division; maintain normal bone marrow

Best Sources: clams; oysters; salmon; sardines; tempeh

Signs of Deficiency: anemia; nervous system damage

Pantothenic Acid

Function: energy and protein metabolism; production of fats and red blood cells

Best Sources: meats; eggs; whole-grain cereals; legumes

Signs of Deficiency: cardiovascular and digestive problems; fatigue; vomiting

Folate

Function: form new cells; maintain healthy cells; regulate cell division and maintain cell's genetic code

Best Sources: leafy green vegetables; legumes; brewer's yeast; beans; nuts; liver

Signs of Deficiency: anemia; digestive disorders; confusion; headaches; irritability

Biotin

Function: energy and amino acid metabolism; fat synthesis

Best Sources: oatmeal; soybeans; green vegetables; liver

Signs of Deficiency: dementia; depression; hair loss; fatigue; loss of appetite; muscle pain; skin inflammation

MINERALS

Magnesium

Function: bone and teeth development; nerve impulses; muscle contraction; activate enzymes

Best Sources: bananas; dried beans and peas; whole grains; dark green leafy vegetables; nuts

Signs of Deficiency: heart failure; muscle spasm; convulsions; weakness

Phosphorous

Function: strong bones and teeth; energy metabolism

Best Sources: lean meat; fish; poultry; dairy products; legumes; eggs; nuts

Signs of Deficiency: bone disease; nervous disorders; weakness

Calcium

Function: strong bones and teeth; blood clotting; blood pressure; muscle contraction and relaxation

Best Sources: dairy products; dark green leafy vegetables; broccoli; shrimp; salmon; legumes; tofu; fortified orange juice; clams

Signs of Deficiency: hypertension; osteoporosis

Potassium

Function: keeps cell fluid balanced; maintains steady heartbeat; muscle contraction

Best Sources: bananas; potatoes; spinach; broccoli; chickpeas; strawberries

Signs of Deficiency: irregular heartbeat; toxic kidneys; general weakness

TRACE MINERALS

Chromium

Function: blood sugar; protein synthesis

Best Sources: lean meat; orange juice; whole grains; brewer's yeast; vegetable oil

Signs of Deficiency: diabetes or hypoglycemia (inability to properly use glucose); high blood cholesterol

Copper

Function: production of hemoglobin; make red blood cells; assist enzyme functions

Best Sources: shellfish; whole grains; legumes; nuts

Signs of Deficiency: anemia; loss of pigment; heart disease

Fluoride

Function: bone and teeth formation; prevents tooth decay

Best Sources: fluoridated water and toothpastes; seafood

Signs of Deficiency: tooth decay

Iron

Function: produce hemoglobin, which carries oxygen from the lungs to body cells

Best Sources: lean red meat; organ meat;legumes; enriched cereals and breads; dried fruits

Signs of Deficiency: anemia; heart disease; infections; itchy skin; inability to regulate body temperature

Manganese

Function: works with enzymes to help cell processes

Best Sources: tea; spinach; raisins

Signs of Deficiency: impaired fertility; growth retardation; birth defects

Selenium

Function: antioxidant; cancer prevention

Best Sources: organ meat; seafood; whole-grains; potato with skin; turkey or chicken breast; wheat germ

Signs of Deficiency: birth defects; increased cancer risk; muscle weakness

Zinc

Function: protein and energy conversion; insulin production

Best Sources: lean meat; poultry; fish; whole-grain cereals and breads

Signs of Deficiency: altered taste; metabolic upset; anemia; dry skin; delayed wound healing

Boron

Function: helps brain function; healthy bones; increase alertness; metabolism of calcium, magnesium, and phosphorous

Best Sources: apples; dates; nuts

Fiber

In a world without fiber . . .
the incidence of heart disease; breast, colon, and other cancers; artherosclerosis; high cholesterol; high blood pressure; constipation; digestive problems; diabetes and obesity would continue to soar to sky-high proportions. While 35% of all cancers have been linked to the typical low-fiber, high-fat American diet, a 1996 report from Boston researchers stated "increasing dietary fiber intake from the average 12 grams per day to 28 grams per day resulted in a dramatic 41% reduction in heart attacks." (Murphy) The American Dietetic Association, National Cancer Institute, and other public health agencies recommend including 25 to 35 grams of fiber each day to optimize health benefits. Even though fiber itself does not contain any nutrients, foods high in dietary fiber contain powerful disease-preventing nutrients such as vitamins, antioxidants, and phytochemicals.

More you need to know . . .
In order to consume the RDA for fiber from fast food, you would have to consume more than **4,000 calories** and **200 grams of fat** each day—in a little over one year, the average person would gain more than **200 pounds!** What better reason to fiber-fill your body?

What's the difference?

Soluble Fiber	vs.	**Insoluble Fiber**
. . . allows the body to absorb carbohydrates more efficiently, contributing to stabilized blood sugar levels.		. . . keeps food moving through the colon, reducing the time that harmful substances can remain in the digestive tract.
. . . binds with cholesterol and pulls it out of the body, decreasing the risk of heart and artery disease by lowering blood cholesterol.		. . . promotes regularity, contributing to reduced risk for colon cancer and diverticulosis.
. . . includes: oats, brown rice, barley, oat bran, beans, rye, seeds, vegetables, and fruits.		. . . includes: legumes, wheat bran, whole-grain breads and cereals, vegetables and fruit.

Fabulous Fiber: Oatmeal, low-fat bran cereals, wheat bran, dried pears, cooked barley, chickpeas, kidney beans, raspberries, whole wheat, pasta, lentils, figs, apples, brown rice, whole-wheat pasta, artichokes, turnips, Brussels sprouts, and mashed sweet potatoes

SOME "FUN-WITH-FIBER" FOOD IDEAS

- Start the day with calcium-fortified orange juice
- Select fiber-rich fruit snacks: apples, pears, oranges, grapefruit, and prunes
- Satisfy hunger with broccoli and nonfat cheese-stuffed baked potatoes
- Substitute fruit smoothies or shakes for quick-fix meals (fresh or frozen fruits, nonfat yogurt, and juice)
- Serve air-popped popcorn with seasonings of choice
- Satisfy hunger with crisp bread (with whole rye listed as number one ingredient)
- Scoop up low-fat dips with raw veggies
- Score with beans added to soups, stews, salads, and dips
- Suit yourself with oatmeal topped with fruit and skim milk
- Set the breakfast table with fiber-rich cereal: Shredded Wheat, Grape Nuts, Bran Flakes
- Shape up casseroles and baked goods with added oat bran or oatmeal
- Stir up some barley in soups and stews
- Satiate a sweet tooth with fat-free fig bars and skim milk
- Spread low-fat tortilla with fat-free refried beans

♦ ♦ ♦

The Most Proclaimed Superfoods Are . . .

APPLES: high in soluble fiber, vitamin C, and pectin, which help reduce and stabilize cholesterol levels; naturally low in calories and fat; cholesterol-free; helps cleanse teeth of food debris; exercises jaw and hardens gums.
- 2 apples a day can cut cholesterol by 10%

BEANS: packed with cholesterol-lowering soluble fiber; helps control blood-sugar levels; contain polyphenolics (potent antioxidants) which keep blood from oxidizing; rich in complex carbohydrates; contain lignans, isoflavones,saponins, phytic acid, and protease inhibitors, compounds that inhibit the growth of cancer cells; excellent low-fat protein source.
- ½ cup of beans a day has been shown to lower cholesterol (study conducted by the American Heart Association).

BLUEBERRIES: contain anthocyanins and other natural compounds (cancer-fighting phytochemicals); help promote urinary tract health; may reduce eye strain and improve night vision; are powerful food in battle against aging (James Joseph, M.D., Tufts University).
- One cup of raspberries supply a third of your daily requirement of fiber. One half cup blueberries deliver as much antioxidant power as 5 servings of other fruits and vegetables. (Ronald L. Prior, Ph.D., USDA)

BREAD: (whole-wheat): good source of carbohydrates and fiber; low in fat; good source of magnesium, folic acid, and B vitamins.
- Whole wheat bread contains 4 times more fiber than white bread.

BROCCOLI: rich source of phytochemicals; good source of fiber; full of minerals, especially calcium, magnesium, phosphorous, and potassium; contains glutathione (amino acid), which may reduce the risk of arthritis, diabetes, and heart disease; rich in vitamin A and lutein, which helps guard against cataracts and macular degeneration.
- Broccoli florets have eight times as much beta-carotene as the stalks.

DRIED FRUITS (apricots, dates, raisins, prunes, cranberries): blood pressure, anemia, water retention and constipation; great source of energy.

- Prunes contain twice the antioxidants per serving than any other fruit or vegetable. Apricots have beta-carotene which helps to protect the eyes. Raisins are a number one source for iron.

FISH: great source of omega-3 fatty acids that may block the body's production of certain compounds responsible for increasing blood pressure and promoting unwanted blood clotting; reduces the production of prostaglandins that may be responsible for tumor growth

Salmon: boosts immune system; thins the blood and reduces the risk of heart disease; helps counteract effects of caffeine and alcohol; richest source of omega-3 fatty acids; rich in B vitamins

Tuna: contains omega-3 fatty acids that reduce blood cholesterol, lowering the risk of heart disease and stroke; helps prevent blood clots from forming; inhibits the growth of cancer cells; excellent source of low-cholesterol protein that provides minerals and vitamins

- Eating salmon one time a week will cut heart disease by 50%.

FLAXSEED: rich source of lignans (contains seventy-five times more than any other plant food), powerful antioxidants that may reduce the risk of breast cancer; rich source of polyunsaturated fats, including omega-3 fatty acids that limit the body's production of prostaglandins (that may speed up tumor growth); fiber-rich; lowers levels of LDL cholesterol; may aid in fighting infections.

- Flaxseed is rich in fiber, which lowers cholesterol, prevents constipation, and keeps blood sugar levels steady. The omega-3s in flaxseeds also ease inflammation and improve mood.

GARLIC: contains allacin, a sulphur compound that has antibiotic and antifungal properties and inhibits the production of cholesterol; contains diallyl sulfide, a compound that inactivates carcinogens and suppresses tumor growth; contains adenosine, a smooth muscle relaxant, shown to lower blood pressure; contains phosphorus, potassium, calcium, protein, vitamins B and C; stimulates the production of glutathione (an amino acid), a powerful antioxidant and detoxifier; helps relieve rheumatism; helps cleanse blood, prevent clots, and boost the immune system; protects against heart disease and strokes.

- The Iowa Women's Study found that those who ate garlic frequently were 30 % less likely to develop colon cancer.

GINGER: rich source of iron; combats nausea and travel sickness; stops blood cells from making thromboxane, reducing the risk of blood clots; lowers bloodcholesterol; aids digestion; may help prevent cancer.

- Research shows that it can relieve motion sickness, morning sickness and nausea caused by anesthesia.

GRAPES: phytochemical-rich; contain ellagic acid, a potential cancerfighter; contains resveratrol and quercetin, linked to lowering the risk of heart disease; have antioxidant properties that reduce the risk of cataracts.

- All grapes are really berries. Red grapes are known for their ability to prevent heart disease.

KIWIFRUIT: rich in vitamin C, potassium, calcium, fiber, and vitamin E.

- Two kiwis equal the fiber in 1 cup bran flakes. Pound for pound it provides almost as much potassium as bananas.

MANGOES: rich in iron and antioxidants (vitamins C and E, beta-carotene); good source of phytochemicals (flavonoids); packed with fiber, which helps control appetite and blood cholesterol, as well as aids in digestion.

- Mangoes contain as much vitamin C as an orange. They are the single best fruit source of cancer-fighting carotenoids. More than apricots and cantaloupe.

MEAT: important source of iron, improving the oxygen-carrying potential of blood and reducing the risk of anemia; contains heme iron, 15% more absorbable than nonheme iron found in plant foods; good source of zinc and B vitamins (B_{12}, riboflavin, B_6, niacin, and thiamin).

- Father's Day is the biggest meat-eating day of the year—over 80 million pounds are consumed.

NONFAT MILK: best source of calcium; prevents risk of osteoporosis, lowers risk of kidney stones; lowers cholesterol, reducing the risk of heart attacks or strokes.

- One 8 oz. glass of skim milk contains 300 mg of calcium, 400 mg of potassium, and .4 mg of riboflavin.

NUTS: low in saturated fat (1 gram per ounce); good source of monounsaturated fat (10 grams per ounce); cholesterol-free; contain substantial amounts of dietary fiber (3 grams per ounce); good source of calcium, copper, magnesium, zinc, vitamin E, and phytochemicals.

- Although high in fat, consuming just 1 ounce of nuts 4 to 5 times a week has been found to cut the risk of heart attacks by 40 to 50%.

OATS: can reduce blood cholesterol; help ease. constipation by adding bulk to diet; supply linoleic acid, B vitamins, vitamin E, protein, and fiber; help stabilize blood-sugar levels; help soothe nerves.

- Quick oats are a great time-saving breakfast. They provide just as many vitamins and minerals as the traditional, slower-cooking oats.

ORANGES: good source of antioxidants, beta-carotene, and vitamin C; contain bioflavonoids that help strengthen capillary walls and arm against infection; boost iron absorption from iron-rich foods we eat; good source of vitamin A.

- One glass of freshly squeezed orange juice can boost absorption of iron from a traditional American breakfast by 300%. One 4-oz glass of orange juice meets 100% of the RDA for Vitamin C.

POTATOES: high in fiber, potassium, and vitamin C; low in calories; rich source of complex carbohydrates; potato skins contain anti-oxidants and protease inhibitors (anti-oxidants that block the activation of viruses and carcinogens in the intestines).
Sweet potatoes: contain the same number of calories as white potatoes, but they contain more vitamin C and three times the beta-carotene as white potatoes.

- The average American consumes 120 lbs. of potatoes a year (mostly in the form of high-calorie, fat-saturated French fries and potato chips).

SEEDS/SPROUTS: rich in B vitamins, minerals, and complex carbohydrates; higher in protein than other plant-based foods; low in calories, cholesterol-free.

- Eating raw sunflower seeds causes the body to produce adrenaline, which generates pleasant feelings.

SOY: helps reduce cholesterol levels (particularly LDL (bad) cholesterol); may increase or maintain bone density in post-menopausal women; rich in genistein and daidzein, compounds that may fight breast, prostate, colon and endometrial cancer; rich in isoflavones, a plant version of estrogen.

- People with elevated cholesterol who add a daily 25 grams of soy protein to their diet will lower their total cholesterol by 9% and their LDL cholesterol by as much as 15%. That's alot, since every 1 % drop lowers heart disease risk by 2 to 3 %. 1/2 cup of edamane (soy beans) = 22 grams of protein.

SPINACH: major source of antioxidant vitamins C, E, and beta-carotene; contains significant amounts of riboflavin, vitamin K, dietary fiber, and folic acid; frozen spinach retains vitamins and minerals, keeping it just as nutritious as fresh.

- Boiling spinach in 1 cup of water instead of 2 will help spin-ach retain almost 50% more of its nutrients.

SWEET PEPPERS: rich in vitamin C and beta-carotene, providing potent protection against cataracts.

- Red bell peppers are number 1: they provide 3 times as much Vitamin C as oranges and they provide 20 times more than other peppers in beta carotene.

TOMATO: rich in lycopene; contains two powerful compounds (coumaric acid and chlorogenic acid) that may help block the effects of nitrosamines (cancer-causing compounds); rich in vitamin C.

- A 1995 Harvard study of 48,000 men found that those who ate more than 10 servings of tomato products a week had a 35% lower risk of prostate cancer than men who ate fewer than 1½ servings.

WATER: required by every cell for optimum health; improves overall well-being; boosts energy by relieving dehydration; improves mental alertness; helps maintain healthy weight;

reduces the risk of kidney stones; helps breathing; cleanses body from the inside out; maintains proper muscle tone; helps skin stay healthy, resilient, and wrinkle resistant; keeps you slim—eating and drinking more water-rich foods (fruits and vegetables) in place of other high-fat, high-sodium, high-calorie food choices can help cut calories.

- The human body is composed of 72.3% water; an earthworm is 80% water; a carrot 90%, and the human brain consists of 85% water.

WINTER SQUASH (hubbard, acorn, butternut): low in calories; rich in complex carbohydrates; high in beta-carotene, vitamin C, and fiber.

YOGURT (with live cultures): super source of calcium; prevents yeast infections; strengthens immune system; heals and prevents ulcers; easy-to-digest dairy alternative for lactose-intolerant people.

- Bacteria in active-culture yogurt helps prevent yeast infections. It is also excellent for soothing an upset stomach. One cup provides more than 40% of the RDA of calcium.

BOTTOM LINE:

Reduce your intake of high-fat foods, sodium, and alcohol.

Increase your intake of foods rich in antioxidants, phytochemicals, fiber, and other essential nutrients.

Exercise regularly to reduce the risk of disease associated with aging.

What you eat is important to your future health—what will you eat today?

A report recently published in the New England Journal of Medicine *on the DASH Trial (Dietary Approaches to Stop Hypertension) compared the effects of three different diets on blood pressure in patients with hypertension. The study concluded that a diet high in fiber, low in fat, and high in dietary calcium is an effective alternative approach to the treatment of high blood pressure. They suggested the following Dietary Guidelines:*

- 7 to 8 daily servings of grains and grain products
- 4 to 5 daily servings of vegetables
- 4 to 5 daily servings of fruit
- 2 to 3 daily servings of low-fat or nonfat dairy foods
- 1 to 2 daily servings of lean meat, poultry (no skin, breast meat preferable) or fish
- 4 to 5 weekly servings of legumes, nuts, and seeds
- Total daily fat intake not to exceed 30%

FOOD FOR HEALTH SAKE!

Foods That Protect Against Cancer

Highest	Modest	Some
garlic	onion	oats
soybeans	flax	barley
cabbage	citrus	mint
ginger	turmeric	rosemary
licorice	cruciferous vegetables:	thyme
carrot	(broccoli, Brussels	oregano
celery	sprouts, cabbage,	sage
cilantro	cauliflower)	basil
parsley	solanaceous vegetables:	cucumber
parsnips	tomato, peppers,	cantaloupe
	brown rice, whole-wheat grain,	berries
	orange and grapefruit	
	juice	
	tea	

Foods That Protect Against Heart Disease

soy protein	red wine	kale
flaxseed	pumpkin seeds	red grapes
flax oil	soy	broccoli
garlic	rice	cherries
onion	herbs	grain cereal
apples		

◆ ◆ ◆

SEASON and SPICE

for everything nice
Some shake it once, some shake it twice
Whatever your pleasure, whatever you like
From garlic and pepper to versatile "Spike."

The recipe for Healthy Cooking:

ingredients: One Reliable Cookbook:
SUPERFOODS: Cook Your Way to Health
Two Weeks of Patience*
Three Tasting Sessions(*sometimes more, sometimes less*)
NONFAT COOKING SPRAY**
Open willingness to experiment and have fun
Endless portions of creativity

directions: Open cookbook. Select recipe(s) of choice. Line up
ingredients. Follow directions accordingly. Serve to self
or others. Too bland? Spice it up! Too spicy? Tone it
down! The beauty of home cooking is you get to make it
just the way YOU like it!

Serves: unlimited!

*Give your taste buds time to adapt to new foods, flavors, and textures. If the world's population could trade in their Big Macs for veggie burgers and their whole dairy for nonfat products, the world would be a healthier, fitter, and happier planet! As you adjust your taste buds, take advantage of the multitude of seasonings and spices—they're basically calorie-free, fat-free, cholesterol-free, and good for you, too!

**Some recipes suggest butter- or garlic-flavored cooking sprays. Regular nonfat cooking spray can be substituted in any recipe (spice up with garlic powder or Butter Buds, if desired).

Add Spice* to Your Life!

Mix and Match your favorite

Seasonings	With . . .	Or Substitute . . .
Allspice	baked goods, puddings, fruits	cinnamon, cloves, and nutmeg
Basil	fish, salads, tomato dishes, soups, salad dressings, dips	
Cajun seasoning	poultry, lean meat, potatoes	
Chili powder	chili, meat sauce	cumin seed, chili peppers, oregano, salt, cayenne pepper, garlic, allspice
Cinnamon	cooked fruits, winter squash, baked goods	
Cloves	baked goods, puddings, soups, cooked fruits, hot tea or cider, winter squash	
Cumin seed	curry dishes, soups, chili	
Dill	baked goods, condiments, cheese	
Ginger	cooked fruits, chicken, stir-fry, sweet potatoes, pumpkin, carrot, baked goods (gingerbread, pumpkin pie)	
Marjoram	fish, meat, poultry, stuffing, soups, stews	oregano
Nutmeg	baked goods, pumpkin, sweet potatoes, carrots, soups	
Oregano	pizzas, Italian dishes (e.g., pasta), vegetables, dips, fish, salads, soups	marjoram
Parsley	soup, salad, vegetables, potatoes, or garnish for any dish	cilantro
Rosemary	fish, meat, poultry, stuffing, vegetables, potatoes, stews	
Sage	soups, stews, stuffing, salad dressings, fish, pizza sauce	
Thyme	tomato-based dishes, soups, sauces, salad dressings, poultry seasoning, herbed breads, and snacks	

*To preserve the quality of spices, store them in tightly sealed glass jars in a cool, dark place.

Top Contenders for Boosting Flavor

Pepper—Most Popular Spice in the World!: excellent "after cooking" seasoning (along with garlic powder and cayenne pepper), pepper can be used in almost every dish at one time or another

Mrs. Dash seasoning: poultry, fish, lean meat, potatoes, vegetables, eggs (regular and extra spicy), soup, salads, sandwiches, stir-fries, and MORE!

Spike: EVERYTHING!

Cajun seasoning: fish, seafood, poultry, meat, potatoes, vegetables

Garlic powder: just about anything and everything except baked goods, cereal, and ice cream!

Onion powder: same as garlic powder, just a little different flavor

Butter Buds: Boost your butter taste without calories, fat, and cholesterol!

Italian seasoning: pasta dishes, pizzas, lean meats, poultry, fish, breads, vegetables, potatoes, sandwiches, soups, tomatoes, salads, and MORE! Mix up your own blend with marjoram, thyme, rosemary, savory, sage, oregano, basil.

Crushed Red Pepper: pizzas, pastas, lean-meat dishes (burgers, meat loaf, etc.), salad dressings, salsas, soups, seafood, chicken, and MORE!

The shopping list for each recipe is listed with the typical grocery store layout in mind. Items are grouped according to fresh, frozen, canned, baking products, spices, meats, etc. Sizes suggested for purchase may differ from those in the ingredient list; this is based on the smallest package we found available. If you can't find a particular item or brand, purchase a suitable replacement; in most cases, this should not affect your results. If a certain nonfat ingredient is not available, substitute a low-fat product (the difference in calories and fat will be slightly higher).

♦ ♦ ♦

Learn to Control Your Blood Sugar

The body converts all foods with calories into glucose. This is critically important to diabetics because their body does not have the ability to place the glucose (sugar) into the cell where it is utilized as energy and then it builds up into the blood. The amount of time to convert food to blood glucose varies from 6 to 8 hours for dietary fat, 3 to 4 hours for protein; and 30 minutes for carbohydrates. Any high-carbohydrate foods will raise blood sugar levels; the amount is more important than the type of carbohydrate. High carbohydrate foods include rice, pasta, bread, cereals, and other starches; vegetables; milk and milk products; and any foods made with added sugars, such as candies, cookies, cakes, and pies. Carbohydrates, particularly complex carbohydrates, provide essential nutrients and are an extremely important part of a well-balanced diet. They should comprise approximately 50 to 60% of the daily calories. Protein should comprise 10 to 20%, and fat should be less than 25 to 30% each day.

There is no such thing as a single "diabetic diet." A nutritious diabetic meal plan focuses on attaining good blood-sugar control by evenly releasing glucose into the blood from meal to meal. The plan should provide a mixture of fats, carbohydrates, and proteins at each meal with calorie levels to promote desired body weight. In order to promote maximum compliance, the diet plan must consider the person's social and cultural needs.

There are multiple dietary tools for controlling diabetes. Some of these include the diabetic exchange system, carbohydrate counting custom, total available glucose (TAG) system, "healthy eating" guidelines, or the Food Guide Pyramid and daily menus. The goal is to use the simplest, most effective method that controls blood sugar and prevents complications associated with diabetes.

These methods can safely be used by nondiabetics who are seeking weight loss or reduction of cholesterol levels. This book lists the diabetic exchanges for each recipe to assist those using the exchange system, carbohydrate choices, and/or carbohydrate counting system.

What is the diabetic exchange system?

This method groups foods that are alike into seven categories (starches, other carbohydrates, meats, vegetables, fruits, dairy, and fat). Portions for each food is listed so that calories, carbohydrates, and other nutrients are carefully measured and controlled. You can trade or exchange foods within the same category; they are similar in nutrition content. A specific number of servings or "exchanges" from each group will be recommended by the dietitian to provide a well-balanced diet within a certain number of calories. This is the most structured of the meal-planning methods for diabetic control and must be carefully followed to attain good glycemic control. The table below shows the nutrient values for each of the exchange lists.

Groups/ Lists	Carbohydrate (grams)	Protein (grams)	Fat (grams)	Calories	Serving Size
Carbohydrates					
1 starch	15	3	1 or less	80	1 slice bread, ½ cup cereal, grain, pasta, or starch vegetable
1 fruit	15	—	—	60	1 small fruit, ½ canned fruit or juice
1 milk	12	8	0 to 3	90	1 cup skim milk
1 other carbohydrate	15	varies	varies	varies	varies
Vegetables					
1 vegetable	5	2	—	25	1 cup raw, ½ cup cooked or juice
Meat and Meat Substitute					
1 very lean meat	—	7	0 to 1	35	1 oz. or amount listed for all categories
1 lean meat	—	7	3	55	
1 medium-fat	—	7	5	75	
1 high-fat	—	7	8	100	
Fat					
1 fat	—	-	5	45	variable

If you need further information contact:
The American Diabetic Association: 1-800-232-6733 or 1-800-232-3472

What is carbohydrate counting?

Carbohydrate counting is a relatively new method used for diabetic control; it is based on the premise that all carbohydrates* are equal. Whether a person with diabetes eats 15 grams of carbohydrate from cake or 15 grams from potatoes, the results of blood sugar testing will be very similar.

A Registered Dietitian can help a person with diabetes determine the appropriate daily intake of carbohydrates. This number is based on the number of calories needed to maintain a healthy body weight. The carbohydrates should be spread out evenly throughout the day to allow for even release of blood glucose into the bloodstream. The timing of the meals and snacks will vary from person to person; this is based on the individual's nutritional needs as well as lifestyle and medication regimen.

Determining the amount of carbohydrate in foods can be accomplished in several ways. One way is to read product labels. Look for "Total Carbohydrates" on the Nutrition Facts Label. Pay attention to serving size—this is always based on one serving size. An alternative method of calculating carbohydrates is the Diabetic Exchange System; 1 exchange of starch, other carbohydrate, fruit, or milk is counted as 15 grams of carbohydrate. Nutrition books, such as *Food Values of Portions Commonly Used* by Pennington, include reference tables or charts that can be quite helpful. When following this method, protein and fat intake must be monitored in order to prevent weight gain. Refer to the table below for examples of carbohydrate counting. A single portion is equal to 15 grams of carbohydrate or 1 carbohydrate choice.

Carbohydrate Choices	Target Total Grams of Carbohydrate	Range of Total Grams of Carbohydrate
1	15	8 to 22 grams
2	30	23 of 37 grams
3	45	38 of 52 grams
4	60	53 of 65 grams

*Exchanges and carbohydrates are listed in this cookbook for your convenience. If you need a meal plan or further education to use this data, contact a Registered Dietitian in your area by logging onto the American Dietetic Association website.

◆ ◆ ◆

All recipes were analyzed using the Nutritionist IV program, Bowes & Church Food Values of Portions Commonly Used, the U.S. Department of Agriculture data base and manufacturers' nutrition labels. All nutrients are rounded to the nearest whole number.

Exchanges listed for each recipe are based on the diabetic exchange lists. One carbohydrate choice equals 15 grams of carbohydrate and is rounded to the nearest one-half of carbohydrate choice.

Use specified ingredients and measurements listed for each recipe for the most accurate nutrient composition. If a specific brand is not listed, select a low-fat products of any brand. Pay attention to the number of servings in the recipe. The nutrient analysis of each recipe is based on one serving.

AWESOME
APPETIZERS

Bagel Chips with Garlic Herb Spread

Easy — Do Ahead

Ingredients:
- 8 oz. nonfat ricotta cheese
- 1 tsp. minced garlic
- 1 tsp. dried thyme
- 1 tbsp. dried basil
- ⅛ tsp. black pepper
- mini bagel chips

Directions:
Combine all ingredients except bagel chips in food processor or blender; process until smooth. Spoon into bowl, cover and refrigerate several hours before serving. Serve dip with seasoned bagel chips, crackers, or pita crisps, etc.

Serves: 4

Shopping List:
8 oz. nonfat ricotta cheese, garlic, thyme, basil, pepper, mini bagel chips

Nutrition per serving		Exchanges
calories:	46	1 very lean meat
total fat (0%):	0 g	
carbohydrate:	4 g	carbohydrate choice: 0
cholesterol:	9 mg	
dietary fiber:	0 g	
protein:	8 g	
sodium:	110 mg	

Dairy products (such as low-fat cheese) are the most concentrated and absorbable natural sources of calcium; 3 servings can bring you close to the Recommended Daily Allowance (RDA) of 1,000 milligrams.

Chicken Flautas

Easy — Do Ahead — Freeze

Ingredients:
- ¾ lb. skinless, boneless chicken breast tenders, cooked and shredded
- ½ cup salsa
- ½ tsp. Southwest seasoning blend
- 16 corn tortillas
- 2 cups nonfat shredded Cheddar cheese

Directions:
Preheat oven to 350 degrees. Line baking sheet with foil and spray with cooking spray. Combine shredded chicken, salsa, and seasoning blend in a medium bowl; toss until mixed. Spray nonstick skillet with cooking spray and heat over medium-high heat. Add tortillas (one at a time) and cook 1 to 2 minutes to soften. Spread chicken mixture down center of each tortilla; sprinkle with cheese. Roll tortillas and place seam side down on baking sheet. Sprinkle flautas with any remaining cheese. Bake 15 to 20 minutes until tortillas are crisp and lightly browned.

Serves: 8

Shopping List:
¾ lb. low-fat chicken tenders, salsa, Southwest seasoning blend, corn tortillas, 8 oz. nonfat shredded cheddar cheese,

Nutrition per serving		Exchanges
calories:	221	2 starch
total fat (8%):	2 g	2 very lean meat
carbohydrate:	28 g	
cholesterol:	27 mg	
dietary fiber:	3 g	carbohydrate choice: 2
protein:	21 g	
sodium:	568 mg	

American consumption of poultry increased from 34 pounds in 1970 to 61 pounds in 1995. Each year 4.9 billion pounds of chicken are sold; unfortunately, they are deep fried by fast-food restaurants!

"Choke 'n' Bean" Dip

Easy — Do Ahead

Ingredients:
- 16 oz. canned black beans, rinsed and drained
- 14 oz. canned artichoke hearts
- 3 oz. nonfat cream cheese, softened
- 2 tbsp. chopped green chilies
- 1 tsp. garlic powder
- 2 tbsp. lemon juice
- 1 tsp. dried parsley

Directions:
Combine all ingredients in a food processor or blender; process until smooth. Serve with low-fat tortilla chips, crackers, or assorted vegetables (celery, cucumber, jicama, etc.)

Serves: 12

Shopping List:
16 oz. canned black beans, 14 oz. canned artichoke hearts, 3 oz. nonfat cream cheese, chopped green chilies, garlic powder, lemon juice, dried parsley

Nutrition per serving

		Exchanges
calories:	58	½starch
total fat (0%):	0 g	1 vegetable
carbohydrate:	11 g	
cholesterol:	0 mg	
dietary fiber:	2 g	carbohydrate choice: 1
protein:	4 g	
sodium:	238 mg	

Chilies are a rich source of the antioxidants vitamin C and beta-carotene, which protect your body by "neutralizing" free radicals.

Chunky Bean and Corn Salsa in Wonton Cups

Easy — Do Ahead

Ingredients:
36 whole wonton wrappers
15½ oz. can black-eyed peas, rinsed and drained
15 oz. can black beans, rinsed and drained
15 oz. canned corn, drained
½ cup chopped red onions
½ cup chopped bell pepper (red, yellow, or green)
4 oz. chopped green chilies (mild to hot, depending on taste)
28 oz. canned Mexican-style tomatoes, diced, drained, and liquid reserved
½ tsp. garlic powder

Directions:
Preheat oven to 350 degrees. Lightly spray mini-muffin tin with nonfat cooking spray. Place one wonton wrapper in each muffin cup; lightly spray with cooking spray. Bake 8 to 10 minutes until golden brown and crisp. Remove wontons from pan and cool completely. Combine all ingredients except wonton wrappers in a medium bowl and mix well. Add reserved tomato liquid as desired for consistency. Spoon mixture into wonton cups, or serve with low-fat baked tortilla chips, baked potatoes (great topping!), or pita chips.

Serves: 8

Shopping List:
15 ½ oz. can black-eyed peas, 15 oz. can black beans, 15 oz. can corn kernels, 28 oz. can Mexican-style tomatoes, 4 oz. chopped green chilies, red onion, bell pepper, garlic powder, wonton wrappers

Nutrition per serving		Exchanges
calories:	259	2 starch
total fat (3%):	1 g	4 vegetable
carbohydrate:	55 g	
cholesterol:	0 mg	carbohydrate choice: 3½
dietary fiber:	8 g	
protein:	10 g	
sodium:	1,059 mg	

Beans are packed with soluble fiber and cancer-fighting compounds.

Garlic Aioli Dip

Easy — Do Ahead

Ingredients:
    ¾ cup nonfat mayonnaise
    3 tbsp. lemon juice
    ¾ tsp. dried dill weed
    1½ tsp. minced garlic

Directions:
    Combine all ingredients in a bowl; mix until blended and smooth. Refrigerate at least one hour before serving. Great with "Oven-Fried" Artichokes (page 290) or other vegetables, pita crisps, etc.

Serves: 4

Shopping List:
    6 oz. nonfat mayonnaise, lemon juice, minced garlic, dried dill weed

Nutrition per serving

calories:	34
total fat (0%):	0 g
carbohydrate:	7 g
cholesterol:	0 mg
dietary fiber:	0 g
protein:	0 g
sodium:	316 mg

Exchanges
½ other carbohydrate

carbohydrate choice: ½

Garlic contains allicin, an antibiotic, antifungal, and possibly antiviral compound.

Ginger Dipping Sauce

Easy — Do Ahead

Ingredients:
⅔ cup nonfat mayonnaise
½ cup sweet pickle relish
2 tbsp. lemon juice
1⅓ tbsp. minced fresh ginger

Directions:
Combine all ingredients in a small bowl; mix well. Cover and refrigerate several hours before serving. Great with chicken tenders, Cajun shrimp, fish, or sweet potato chips.

Serves: 6

Shopping List:
nonfat mayonnaise, sweet pickle relish, lemon juice, fresh ginger

Nutrition per serving		Exchanges
calories:	62	1 other carb
total fat (0%):	0 g	
carbohydrate:	14 g	carbohydrate choice: 1
cholesterol:	0 mg	
dietary fiber:	0 g	
protein:	0 g	
sodium:	376 mg	

Ginger stops blood cells from making thromboxane, a substance that enables blood platelets to stick together and eventually form a possible life-threatening clot.

Hummus

Easy — Do Ahead

Ingredients:
   16 oz. can chickpeas, drained
   1½ tsp. onion powder
   ¾ tsp. garlic powder
   ½ to ¾ cup tomato sauce
   1 tbsp. lemon juice
   1 tsp. ground cumin
   ½ tsp. ground caraway
   ⅛ tsp. cayenne pepper
   2 tbsp. fresh cilantro, chopped
   pepper to taste

Directions:
   Combine all ingredients in food processor or blender and process until smooth. Cover and refrigerate several hours before serving. Great with pita crisps!

Serves: 8

Shopping List:
   16 oz. canned chickpeas, tomato sauce, lemon juice, fresh cilantro, onion powder, garlic powder, ground cumin, ground caraway, cayenne pepper, pepper

Nutrition per serving		**Exchanges**
calories:	65	1 starch
total fat (10%):	<1 g	
carbohydrate:	2 g	carbohydrate choice: 1
cholesterol:	0 mg	
dietary fiber:	3 g	
protein:	3 g	
sodium:	319 mg	

Chickpeas are an excellent source of fiber, helping to stabilize blood-sugar levels. Canned chickpeas are a good source of vitamin E and manganese.

"I Can't Believe It's NOT Guacamole!"

Easy — Do Ahead

Ingredients:
10 oz. frozen asparagus spears, thawed and drained
1 cup frozen green peas, thawed and drained
1 cup canned chopped tomatoes, drained
¼ cup salsa
1 tsp. onion powder
2 tbsp. fresh cilantro, chopped
2 tbsp. nonfat mayonnaise
1 tbsp. lime juice
½ to ¾ tsp. Tabasco pepper sauce
¾ tsp. garlic powder
¼ tsp. ground red pepper
pepper to taste

Directions:
Combine asparagus and peas in food processor or blender; process until smooth. Add remaining ingredients; blend until mixed. Cover and refrigerate several hours before serving. Serve with low-fat tortilla chips.

Serves: 4

Shopping List:
10 oz. frozen asparagus spears, 10 oz. frozen peas, canned chopped tomatoes, nonfat mayonnaise, salsa, Tabasco pepper sauce, lime juice, fresh cilantro, onion powder, garlic powder, ground red pepper, pepper, low-fat tortilla chips

Nutrition per serving
calories:	70
total fat (13%):	1 g
carbohydrate:	13 g
cholesterol:	0 mg
dietary fiber:	1 g
protein:	5 g
sodium:	156 mg

Exchanges
3 vegetable

carbohydrate choice: 1

***Asparagus is the perfect heart-healthy food—
fat-free, cholesterol-free, and sodium-free!***

Indian Chicken Curry Spread

Easy — Do Ahead

Ingredients:
　　8 oz. nonfat cream cheese, softened
　　½ cup nonfat sour cream
　　½ cup nonfat plain yogurt
　　1½ tsp. curry powder
　　⅛ tsp. garlic powder
　　¼ tsp. ground ginger
　　1 cup cooked chicken breast, finely chopped
　　1 cup chopped bell pepper
　　½ cup raisins
　　jicama, celery, kohlrabi, and apple slices

Directions:
　　Combine cream cheese, sour cream, yogurt, curry powder, garlic powder, and ginger in a medium bowl and blend until smooth. Add chicken. Spread mixture into bottom of pie plate. Sprinkle with bell pepper and raisins. Serve with jicama, celery, kohlrabi, and apple slices.

Serves: 8

Shopping List:
　　8 oz. nonfat cream cheese, 4 oz. nonfat sour cream, 4 oz. nonfat plain yogurt, chicken breast (raw or cooked) or tenders, bell pepper, raisins, jicama, kohlrabi, celery, apples, curry powder, garlic powder, ground ginger

Nutrition per serving		**Exchanges**
calories:	98	½ fruit
total fat (9%):	1 g	1 very lean meat
carbohydrate:	12 g	½ other carbohydrate
cholesterol:	13 mg	
dietary fiber:	1 g	carbohydrate choice: 1
protein:	11 g	
sodium:	209 mg	

Raisins are an excellent source of potassium, dietary fiber, and iron, providing health benefits such as lowering blood pressure, improving digestion, and creating hemoglobin in red blood cells.

Mandarin Chicken Roll-ups

Easy — Do Ahead

Ingredients:
4 low-fat flour tortillas
8 oz. nonfat cream cheese
1 lb. skinless, boneless chicken breast tenders,
    cooked and cut into bite-size pieces
8 oz. canned mandarin orange sections, drained
8 oz. canned pineapple tidbits, drained
2 tbsp. chopped green onion
½ cup diced red bell pepper
½ cup water chestnuts, chopped fine
sweet and sour sauce, optional

Directions:
Spread each tortilla with 2 tablespoons cream cheese. Top each tortilla with remaining ingredients; roll tightly and secure with toothpick, if necessary. Wrap tortillas in plastic wrap and refrigerate at least one hour before serving. Slice tortillas into 1½ to 2 inch pieces and serve with sweet and sour sauce, if desired.

Serves: 8

Shopping List:
1 lb. low-fat chicken tenders, 8 oz. nonfat cream cheese, 8 oz. can mandarin orange sections, 8 oz. can pineapple tidbits, 6 oz. can water chestnuts, red bell pepper, green onion, low-fat flour tortillas, sweet and sour sauce (optional)

Nutrition per serving		Exchanges
calories:	156	2 very lean meat
total fat (6%):	1 g	½ fruit
carbohydrate:	20 g	1 vegetable
cholesterol:	35 mg	½ starch
dietary fiber:	01 g	
protein:	17 g	carbohydrate choice: 1
sodium:	315 mg	

Heart disease kills more men and women each year than cancer, accidents, AIDS, or any other cause of death; in fact, nearly one in two deaths in the United States is the result of heart disease.

Red Hot Pepper Dip

Easy — Do Ahead

Ingredients:
7½ oz. roasted red peppers (not packed in oil), drained
½ cup nonfat sour cream
½ cup nonfat mayonnaise
1 tbsp. Dijon mustard
¾ tsp. garlic powder
1 tbsp. lemon juice
3 drops Tabasco pepper sauce

Directions:
Combine all ingredients in a food processor or mixing bowl; process until smooth. If mixing by hand, peppers will not be completely blended. Refrigerate at least one hour or overnight. Serve with toasted pita chips, low-fat crackers, or assorted vegetables (cucumber, carrot, jicama, etc.)

Serves: 6

Shopping List:
7½ oz. jar roasted peppers (not in oil), nonfat sour cream, nonfat mayonnaise, Dijon mustard, lemon juice, garlic powder, Tabasco pepper sauce; pita chips, low-fat crackers or assorted vegetables

Nutrition per serving		Exchanges
calories:	55	½ other carb
total fat (0%)	0 g	
carbohydrate:	10 g	carbohydrate choice: ½
cholesterol:	0 mg	
dietary fiber:	1 g	
protein:	2 g	
sodium:	192 mg	

Cutting just 1 teaspoon of oil, margarine, or butter from your food plan each day will leave you four pounds lighter after one year.

Strawberry-Banana Fruit Dip

Easy — Do Ahead

Ingredients:
1 cup nonfat yogurt (strawberry, strawberry-banana, or
   vanilla)
½ whole banana
1⅓ tbsp. honey
⅛ tsp. ground cinnamon

Directions:
Combine all ingredients in food processor or blender;
process until smooth and creamy. Serve as dip with fruit
kabobs or as dressing for fruit salad.

Serves: 4

Shopping List:
8 oz. nonfat yogurt (strawberry, strawberry-banana, or
vanilla), banana, honey, ground cinnamon

Nutrition per serving		Exchanges
calories:	57	1 fruit
total fat (0%)	0 g	
carbohydrate:	13 g	carbohydrate choice: 1
cholesterol:	1 mg	
dietary fiber:	<.5 g	
protein:	2 g	
sodium:	35 mg	

***Over half of the top ten killer diseases in the
United States are related to what we eat, such as
too much fat, sodium, and cholesterol.***

Touch 'o' Spice Lentil Dip

Average — Do Ahead

Ingredients:
1 cup red lentils
1 cup chopped red onion
2½ cups water
2 tsp. curry powder
1 tsp. whole cumin seeds
¾ tsp. hot pepper sauce
2 tsp. crushed garlic

Directions:
Combine lentils, onion, and water in a medium saucepan. Cover and bring to a boil over high heat. Reduce heat to low and simmer 20 to 25 minutes until lentils are soft. Place lentil mixture in food processor or blender and process until smooth (don't overprocess or it will be runny). Spray non-stick skillet with cooking spray; add curry powder and cumin seeds and cook over medium heat 1 to 2 minutes. Add hot pepper sauce and crushed garlic; cook over medium heat for 1 minute. Stir spicy mixture into lentils and serve with baked garlic pita chips or low-fat crackers.

Serves: 8

Shopping List:
red lentils, red onion, hot pepper sauce, curry powder, crushed garlic, whole cumin seeds; baked pita chips or low-fat crackers

Nutrition per serving

calories:	68
total fat (0%):	0 g
carbohydrate:	12 g
cholesterol:	0 mg
dietary fiber:	3 g
protein:	5 g
sodium:	4 mg

Exchanges
1 starch

carbohydrate choice: 1

A good source of soluble and insoluble fiber, lentils contribute to regulating blood-sugar levels, normalizing bowel functions, and lowering cholesterol levels.

Yummy Yummy Yogurt Dip

Easy — Do Ahead

Ingredients:
1 cup nonfat plain yogurt
1½ tsp. fresh parsley, chopped
1½ tsp. fresh cilantro, chopped
1½ tsp. green onion, chopped
¾ tsp. celery salt
2 tsp. chopped green chilies

Directions:
Combine all ingredients in a medium bowl and mix well. Cover and refrigerate several hours before serving with fresh vegetables or pita chips.

Serves: 4

Shopping List:
8 oz. nonfat plain yogurt, fresh parsley, fresh cilantro, green onion, canned chopped green chilies, celery salt

Nutrition per serving	
calories:	33
total fat (0%):	0 g
carbohydrate:	5 g
cholesterol:	1 mg
dietary fiber:	0 g
protein:	3 g
sodium:	56 mg

Exchanges
½ milk

carbohydrate choice: 0

Parsley is rich in iron, carotenoids, and vitamin C.

Pepper-Topped Crostini

Easy — Do Ahead

Ingredients:
½ lb. loaf French bread, cut diagonally in ½-inch slices
1½ cups frozen bell pepper, thawed and drained
½ cup red onion, sliced thin
1 tsp. minced garlic
3 tbsp. nonfat Parmesan cheese

Directions:
Preheat oven to 375 degrees. Line baking sheet with foil; arrange bread slices in single layer and bake 12 to 15 minutes until lightly browned and crisp. Cool completely; wrap airtight. Spray large nonstick skillet with cooking spray and heat over medium-high heat; add pepper, onion, and garlic. Cook, stirring frequently, until onion is lightly browned and softened. Spoon mixture into bowl, cover, and refrigerate at least 1 hour before serving. Arrange crostini on serving platter; top each bread slice with spoonful of pepper mixture. Sprinkle with Parmesan cheese and serve.

Serves: 6

Shopping List:
½ lb. loaf French bread, 10 oz. frozen bell pepper, red onion, minced garlic, nonfat Parmesan cheese

Nutrition per serving		Exchanges
calories:	64	1 starch
total fat (14%):	1 g	
carbohydrate:	12 g	carbohydrate choice: 1
cholesterol:	0 mg	
dietary fiber:	1 g	
protein:	3 g	
sodium:	116 mg	

According to a survey conducted by the Centers for Disease Control and Prevention (1998), the average consumption of fruit and vegetables each day is: 3.5% (never or less than 1 a day); 33% (1 to 2 times a day); 39.6% (3 to 4 times a day); 23.8% (5 or more times a day).

Roasted Garlic

Easy — Do Ahead

Ingredients:
4 whole garlic heads
olive oil cooking spray

Directions:
Preheat oven to 400 degrees. Line baking sheet with foil and lightly spray with cooking spray. Arrange heads of garlic on baking sheet; lightly spray with cooking spray. Bake 45 to 60 minutes, until garlic is soft. Remove from oven, let cool, and squeeze onto crusty bread, crackers, or pita chips.

Serves: 6

Shopping List:
4 garlic heads, olive oil cooking spray

Nutrition per serving		Exchanges
calories:	18	free
total fat (0%):	0 g	
carbohydrate:	4 g	
cholesterol:	0 mg	
dietary fiber:	0 g	
protein:	1 g	
sodium:	2 mg	

Garlic is a true superfood! It lowers cholesterol and triglycerides; prevents high blood pressure, heart disease, and stroke by thinning the blood; blocks the growth of cancer cells, especially in the stomach and colon; kills bacteria associated with ear infections; helps boost immunity; reduces high levels of blood sugar; and may relieve asthma.

Seafood in a "Cap"

Easy — Do Ahead

Ingredients:
- 1 lb. nonfat garden-vegetable cream cheese, softened
- 2 tbsp. chopped green onions
- 8 oz. canned crabmeat, drained
- 2 packages green onion dip (or dry onion dip mix)
- ¼ tsp. garlic powder
- paprika
- 1 lb. large white mushrooms, cleaned and stems removed

Directions:
Combine all ingredients except mushrooms in a medium bowl and mix until completely blended. Cover and refrigerate several hours or overnight. Generously spoon crab mixture into cleaned mushroom caps; sprinkle with paprika and serve.

Serves: 4

Shopping List:
1 lb. large white mushrooms, 1 lb. nonfat garden-vegetable cream cheese, 8 oz. canned crabmeat, 2 1-oz. packages green onion or dry onion dip mix, green onion, garlic powder, paprika

Nutrition per serving

calories:	172
total fat (5%):	1 g
carbohydrate:	13 g
cholesterol:	50 mg
dietary fiber:	0 g
protein:	28 g
sodium:	902 mg

Exchanges
3 very lean meat
2 vegetable
½ other carb

carbohydrate choice: 1

Mushrooms are a good source of niacin and riboflavin, important B vitamins that serve as "helper nutrients." Niacin helps your body convert sugars into energy, use fats, and keep your tissues healthy. Riboflavin helps convert other nutrients (niacin, vitamin B$_6$, and folate) into usable forms.

Seafood Stuffed in Sun-Dried Tomato Wraps

Easy — Do Ahead

Ingredients:
- 3 oz. nonfat cream cheese, softened
- 4 oz. can crabmeat, drained
- 4 oz. can baby shrimp, drained and chopped
- 1 tbsp. chopped green onions
- 1 tsp. crushed garlic
- 2 sun-dried tomato wraps
- chili sauce

Directions:
Combine all ingredients except wraps and chili sauce in a medium bowl and mix until completely blended. (You can process in food processor or blender, but the mixture will be creamy.) Divide mixture among wraps and spread down the center. Fold in sides and roll up; secure with several toothpicks. Cover with plastic wrap and refrigerate several hours or overnight. Just before serving, cut seafood wraps into 1-inch slices (secure each piece with toothpick). Serve with chili sauce.

Serves: 4

Shopping List:
4 oz. canned crabmeat, 4 oz. canned baby shrimp, 3 oz. nonfat cream cheese, sun-dried tomato wraps, green onions, crushed garlic, chili sauce

Nutrition per serving		Exchanges
calories:	159	1 starch
total fat (11%):	2 g	2 very lean meat
carbohydrate:	19 g	
cholesterol:	77 mg	carbohydrate choice: 1
dietary fiber:	2 g	
protein:	17 g	
sodium:	553 mg	

Shellfish provide generous amounts of vitamins, including vitamin B_{12} that keeps nerves healthy and makes red blood cells.

Spinach-Herb Wraps

Easy — Do Ahead

Ingredients:
  16 oz. frozen chopped spinach, thawed and
    drained
  ½ package (½ oz.) Ranch dressing mix
  ½ cup nonfat mayonnaise
  ¼ cup nonfat yogurt
  ½ cup nonfat sour cream
  ½ cup chopped water chestnuts
  1 tsp. onion powder
  10 spinach-herb wraps
  chunky-style salsa, optional

Directions:
  Combine all ingredients except wraps in a medium bowl
  and mix until blended. Divide the mixture evenly among
  wraps; roll up and secure with toothpick, if desired. Wrap
  in plastic wrap and refrigerate several hours or overnight.
  Just before serving, slice wraps into 1-inch slices, and
  arrange on serving tray. Serve with chunky salsa, if desired.

Serves: 10

Shopping List:
  16 oz. package frozen chopped spinach, 1 oz. package
  Ranch dressing mix, nonfat mayonnaise, nonfat yogurt,
  nonfat sour cream, 6 oz. water chestnuts, spinach-herb
  wraps (or low-fat tortillas), onion powder, chunky salsa (optional)

Nutrition per serving

calories:	203
total fat (4%):	1 g
carbohydrate:	41 g
cholesterol:	0 mg
dietary fiber:	4 g
protein:	9 g
sodium:	691 mg

Exchanges

1½ starch
2 vegetable
½ other carb

carbohydrate choice: 3

**Spinach is an excellent source of folate,
vitamin B$_6$ and heart-healthy minerals (magnesium,
potassium, and calcium). It is the number one source
of carotenoids (¹/₂ cup spinach provides
1 milligram of beta-carotene).**

"Spin-a-choke" Pizza

Easy — Do Ahead

Ingredients:
10 oz. frozen chopped spinach, thawed and drained
14 oz. can artichoke hearts, drained and chopped
½ cup nonfat mayonnaise
1 tsp. crushed garlic
½ cup nonfat Parmesan cheese
2 tbsp. spicy brown mustard
1 Italian bread shell (e.g. Boboli or low-fat store brand)

Directions:
Preheat oven to 350 degrees. Spray cookie sheet or pizza pan with cooking spray. Combine spinach, artichoke hearts, mayonnaise, garlic, Parmesan cheese, and mustard in a medium bowl; mix until completely blended. Spread mixture over pizza shell and bake 20 to 25 minutes until lightly browned. Serve hot or at room temperature.

Serves: 8

Shopping List:
1 Italian bread shell (Boboli or low-fat store brand), 10 oz. package frozen chopped spinach, 14 oz. can artichoke hearts, nonfat mayonnaise, nonfat Parmesan cheese, spicy brown mustard, crushed garlic

Nutrition per serving		Exchanges
calories:	214	1 starch
total fat (13%):	3 g	2 vegetable
carbohydrate:	36 g	½ fat
cholesterol:	0 mg	½ other carbohydrate
dietary fiber:	2 g	
protein:	11 g	carbohydrate choice: 2
sodium:	569 mg	

Artichokes are a good source of magnesium, a mineral that helps control high blood pressure.

Vegetable Quesadillas

Easy

Ingredients:

1 cup chopped onion
1 zucchini, sliced thin
1 yellow squash, sliced thin
1 tsp. minced garlic
4 tomato-basil tortillas

½ cup canned nonfat refried
   beans with chilies
1 cup nonfat shredded
   cheddar cheese
1 cup chunky salsa

Directions:

Spray large nonstick skillet with cooking spray and heat over medium-high heat. Add onion, zucchini, squash, and garlic to skillet; cook, stirring occasionally, until vegetables are tender. Remove skillet from heat. Spread each tortilla with 2 tablespoons beans; divide vegetable mixture among tortillas, placing vegetables on half the tortilla. Sprinkle with cheese; fold top over (side without vegetables). Respray skillet with cooking spray and return to medium heat. Place one or two quesadillas in skillet and cook until bottom is lightly browned. Flip quesadilla and cook on other side until lightly browned and crisp. Serve with salsa.

Serves: 4

Shopping List:

onion, zucchini, yellow squash, canned black beans, low-fat flour tortillas, nonfat shredded Cheddar cheese, chunky salsa (or salsa of choice), minced garlic

Nutrition per serving

calories:	227
total fat (0%):	0 g
carbohydrate:	40 g
cholesterol:	0 mg
dietary fiber:	5 g
protein:	16 g
sodium:	1,052 mg

Exchanges

1 starch
½ very lean meat
5 vegetable

carbohydrate choice: 2½

Onion provides several possible medicinal benefits, from lowering blood cholesterol and blood pressure to reducing the risk of clotting.

BEAUTIFUL BRUNCH, BREADS, AND MUFFINS

BLAST YOUR BRAIN . . .
BANISH BLAHS . . .

BREAK – THE – FAST with . . .

Body boosting
Rejuvenating richness
Energy efficient
Active appetite assailant
Keenly "cultivates koncentration"
Fabulous fuel for fruition of facts
Absolutely axiomatic for analyzing
Sensibly sane for superb skills
Totally terrific for tip-top tonicity!

A body without breakfast is like a plane without wings...a trike with two wheels . . . a car with a half pint of gasoline. You might get off the ground, wobble on wheels, or putter to the nearest pump, but eventually you're bound to CRASH—breakfast is balancing fuel for body and brains!

Breakfast does a body good by . . .

- providing important nutrients you probably won't make up later in the day
- making you feel better, work better, and possibly live longer
- boosting brain function, improving test scores and muscle coordination for athletic performance
- preventing irritable and dragged down feelings
- regulating hunger pangs, boosting metabolism, and reducing sugar cravings
- replenishing blood glucose levels
- making you look and feel a whole heck-of-a-lot better

*According to a report at **www.prevention.com**, "the average breakfast eater gets a huge nutrition head start that breakfast skippers do not seem to make up later." Take time for a morning meal and boost your nutrient intake.*

- Folate   +68%
- Vitamin A   +54%
- Vitamin C   +50%
- Fiber   +40%
- Iron   +40%
- Vitamin E   +38%
- Calcium   +37%

Fill up and **Fuel up** with **Breakfast** Facts:
- According to the USDA Human Nutrition Information Service, there's no evidence that skipping breakfast will help you lose weight. As a matter of fact, studies have shown that "skippers" tend to eat more calorie-dense foods later in the day, missing out on important nutrients and creating a slower, less efficient fat-fighting metabolism than those who breakfast.
- Skipping breakfast may save time, but is it worth the price you pay? Studies show that eating breakfast not only is associated with improved mid-morning energy, attitude, and thinking skills, but also improves memory, concentration and attention. Now what will you do tomorrow morning—rush out the door with makeup or bagel in hand?
- Forget "eat only when you're hungry" as a breakfast rule! It takes time for your body to get used to this new morning fuel since it's not used to working in the morning. Give it a few days . . . it will thank you by providing a burst of energy and wisdom!
- It's not **WHAT** you eat but **WHEN** you eat that makes it breakfast! What do you call leftover pizza, baked potato, turkey sandwich, or cheese crisp in the morning? BREAKFAST!
- Think twice before grabbing that "healthy" muffin or bagel from the local bagel shop or coffee stand. According to the American Institute for Cancer Research, contemporary-size bagels and muffins have quadrupled in size! Old fashioned freezer bagels weighed in at 2 ounces with 140 calories; today's bagel shop bagel equals 4 to 5 slices of bread! Mom's old-fashioned muffins (prior to the days of low-fat living) weighed out at 100 to 130 calories with 3 to 4 grams of fat;

grab a muffin today and you're likely to pick up 400 to 700 calories and 15 to 24 grams of fat! Buyers beware . . . even the low-fat jumbo muffins pack a punch of high-sugar calories!

• Of all the nutritional mistakes you might make, skipping breakfast is the biggest! According to the American Health Foundation, breakfast skippers are more likely to be overweight.

• Americans are eating more nutritious breakfasts than they did thirty years ago, but . . . fewer of them are eating breakfast!

• According to a survey by the Center for Science in the Public Interest, most restaurant chains offer healthy food choices, BUT . . . traditional menu fare is chosen most often.

TOP SELLER: Denny's Original Grand Slam Breakfast . . .

2 pancakes with whipped butter and syrup +
2 eggs +
2 slices bacon +
2 sausage links =
1,070 calories and 62 grams of fat!!!
(Source: USA Today-Health 1996)

• Cereal eaters consume an average of 10% fewer calories than those who select other breakfast foods. They also maintain a better nutritional profile throughout the day with 40% less cholesterol and 20% more of essential vitamins and minerals. Those who start their day with a bowl of cold breakfast cereal tend to consume more fiber and calcium, but less fat, than those who breakfast on other foods. But, watch serving sizes. According to the American Institute for Cancer Research, those crunchy, sugar-coated cereals have increased the morning intake of fat and calories. Why? Because suggested serving sizes are far less than what we pour in our bowls! When was the last time you filled your bowl with ⅓ cup of cereal for a full-meal deal?

Berry Berry Muesli

Easy

Ingredients:
  1 cup nonfat mixed berry yogurt
  1 cup skim milk
  2½ tbsp. brown sugar
  2 cups oatmeal
  2 tbsp. dates
  2 tbsp. Craisins
  1 banana, sliced thin
  cinnamon-sugar (optional)

Directions:
  Combine yogurt, milk, and brown sugar in a medium bowl. Stir in oatmeal, dates, and Craisins. Divide mixture among four cereal bowls and top with sliced banana before serving. Sprinkle with small amount of cinnamon-sugar, if desired.

Serves: 4

Shopping List:
  8 oz. nonfat mixed berry yogurt (or yogurt of choice), 8 oz. skim milk, oatmeal, brown sugar, banana, dates, Craisins, cinnamon-sugar (optional)

Nutrition per serving		Exchanges
calories:	195	½ milk
total fat (5%):	1 g	1 starch
carbohydrate:	43 g	1 fruit
cholesterol:	2 mg	½ other carb
dietary fiber:	4 g	
protein:	7 g	carbohydrate choice: 3
sodium:	74 mg	

Oats are a good source of soluble fiber (beta-glucan) which contributes to lowering LDL (bad) cholesterol.

Berry Wonderful Breakfast Burritos

Average — Do Ahead

Ingredients:
- ½ cup nonfat ricotta cheese
- ½ cup nonfat cream cheese, softened
- ½ cup raspberries
- ½ cup blueberries
- ½ cup strawberries, hulled and sliced
- 1 tbsp. powdered sugar (plus some extra for optional topping)
- 4 low-fat whole-wheat flour tortillas

Directions:

Preheat oven to 350 degrees. Line baking sheet with foil and spray with cooking spray. Combine ricotta and cream cheese in a small bowl; mix until blended smooth and creamy. Combine berries and mix lightly with 1 tablespoon powdered sugar. Divide cheese mixture and spread over tortillas; spoon berry mixture on top. Fold and roll tortillas; place seam side down on baking sheet. Spray lightly with cooking spray. Bake 5 to 8 minutes until cheese is melted and bubbly.

Serves: 4

Shopping List:

low-fat whole wheat flour tortillas, nonfat ricotta cheese, nonfat cream cheese, raspberries, blueberries, strawberries, powdered sugar

Nutrition per serving

calories:	178
total fat (0%):	0 g
carbohydrate:	33 g
cholesterol:	5 mg
dietary fiber:	3 g
protein:	13 g
sodium:	601 mg

Exchanges

1 very lean meat
½ fruit
1 starch
½ other carbohydrate

carbohydrate choice: 2

Blueberries contain anthocyanin, an antioxidant that helps protect skin against cancer and premature aging.

Blueberry Blintzes

Easy — Do Ahead

Ingredients:
⅔ cup nonfat sour cream
1½ tsp. powdered sugar (some extra for topping)
4 to 6 French Style Crepes* (Frieda's or Melissa's)
1 cup blueberries
fruit preserves or blueberry pie filling for topping
(optional)

Directions:
Preheat oven to 400 degrees. Line baking sheet with foil and spray with cooking spray. Combine sour cream and powdered sugar in a small bowl; mix until creamy and smooth. Spread mixture on one side of each crepe. Top with 1 to 2 tablespoons blueberries; roll up jelly-roll style and arrange seam side down on baking sheet. Bake 8-10 minutes until heated through. Serve with additional powdered sugar, preserves or blueberry pie filling.

Serves: 4

Shopping List:
French Style Crepes* (if not available, prepare thin nonfat pancakes from mix), nonfat sour cream, powdered sugar, ½ pint blueberries, fruit preserves or blueberry pie filling

Nutrition per serving
calories:	147
total fat (0%):	0 g
carbohydrate:	34 g
cholesterol:	0 mg
dietary fiber:	3 g
protein:	4 g
sodium:	243 mg

Exchanges
2 other carbohydrates

carbohydrate choice: 2

Skipping breakfast can keep your metabolic rate at 3 to 4% below normal. This can cause a weight gain of 5 to 6 pounds a year!

*French Style Crepes are distributed by Frieda's, Inc. (800-241-1771 or **www.friedas.com**)

*Melissa's Crepes distributed by World Variety Produce, Inc. (800-588-0151 or **www.melissas.com**)

Cinnamon-Apple Cracked Wheat Cereal

Easy

Ingredients:
- 1¼ cups water
- ½ cup cracked wheat
- ¾ tsp. cinnamon
- 1 cup apples, peeled and chopped
- 1½ tbsp. brown sugar

Directions:

Pour water into medium saucepan and bring to a boil over high heat. Add cracked wheat and cinnamon; reduce heat to low and simmer, uncovered, 5 to 7 minutes. Stir in apples; cook 4 to 5 minutes until heated through. Remove from heat; stir in brown sugar; let stand to thicken and serve.

Serves: 2

Shopping List:

cracked wheat, apple, brown sugar, cinnamon

Nutrition per serving

calories:	215
total fat (4%):	1 g
carbohydrate:	50 g
cholesterol:	0 mg
dietary fiber:	4 g
protein:	5 g
sodium:	8 mg

Exchanges

1 starch
1 fruit
1 other carbohydrate

carbohydrate choice: 3

Cinnamon contains cinnamaldehyde, an oil that acts as a stimulant, warming the body and fighting symptoms associated with the flu.

Cinnamon-Apple Puffy Pancakes

Easy — Do Ahead

Ingredients:
½ cup egg substitute
4 egg whites
1 cup skim milk
1 tbsp. sugar
1 cup flour
2 cups canned cinnamon-spiced apple slices

Directions:
Preheat oven to 400 degrees. Combine egg substitute, egg whites, milk, sugar and flour in blender; process until mixture is smooth. Spray large ovenproof skillet with cooking spray and heat over medium-high heat. Pour egg mixture into skillet and cook 1 to 2 minutes until it starts to set on bottom. Place skillet in oven and bake 15 to 20 minutes until pancake puffs and becomes golden brown. Heat apples in microwave on high for 30 to 45 seconds until warmed. Serve over pancake.

Serves: 6

Shopping List:
canned cinnamon-spiced apple slices, egg substitute, eggs, 8 oz. skim milk, flour, sugar

Nutrition per serving

calories:	163
total fat (6%):	1 g
carbohydrate:	32 g
cholesterol:	<1 mg
dietary fiber:	2 g
protein:	8 g
sodium:	87 mg

Exchanges
2 other carbohydrates

carbohydrate choice: 2

Substituting egg whites for whole eggs saves 5 grams of fat and 200 milligrams of cholesterol per egg.

Cinnamon-Spice Oatmeal

Easy

Ingredients:
- 1 cup oatmeal
- 1½ to 1¾ cups skim milk (depending on desired consistency)
- 2 tsp. cinnamon
- 2 tbsp. brown sugar
- ½ cup chopped dates

Directions:
Prepare oatmeal according to package directions with skim milk; stir in cinnamon, brown sugar, and dates.

Serves: 2

Shopping List:
oatmeal, 12 to 16 oz. skim milk, cinnamon, brown sugar, chopped dates

Nutrition per serving

calories:	244
total fat (4%):	1 g
carbohydrate:	51 g
cholesterol:	4 mg
dietary fiber:	4 g
protein:	11 g
sodium:	134 mg

Exchanges

1 milk
1 starch
1 fruit
½ other carbohydrate

carbohydrate choice: 3½

Sulfur-containing foods such as oatmeal have been found to repair and rebuild bone, cartilage, and connective tissue.

Fiber Fabulous Oatmeal

Easy

Ingredients:
    1⅓ cups instant oatmeal
    1⅓ cups skim milk
    ½ cup chopped prunes
    ⅓ cup wheat germ
    3 tbsp. brown sugar

Directions:
    Prepare oatmeal according to package directions (use recommended amount for one or two servings), using skim milk instead of water. If preparing one serving, cut remaining ingredients in thirds. Top with chopped prunes, wheat germ, and brown sugar; mix lightly and serve immediately.

Serves: 3

Shopping List:
    oatmeal, skim milk, prunes, wheat germ, brown sugar

Nutrition per serving		Exchanges
calories:	315	2 starch
total fat (9%):	3 g	1 fruit
carbohydrate:	68 g	½ milk
cholesterol:	2 mg	1 other carbohydrate
dietary fiber:	8 g	
protein:	12 g	carbohydrate choice: 4½
sodium:	72 mg	

Prunes contain both soluble and insoluble fiber contributing to digestive health and reducing blood-cholesterol levels.

Oven-Baked Egg 'n' Potato Casserole

Easy — Do Ahead

Ingredients:

1½ cups egg substitute
4 egg whites
1 cup skim milk
¾ tsp. Mrs. Dash seasoning
1 tsp. onion powder
2 cups nonfat frozen hash brown potatoes
1 cup low-fat turkey ham, chopped
1 cup nonfat shredded Cheddar cheese

Directions:

Preheat oven to 350 degrees. Spray 8-inch baking dish with cooking spray. Combine egg substitute, egg whites, milk, Mrs. Dash seasoning, and onion powder in baking dish; whisk until blended and frothy. Add remaining ingredients and mix lightly. Bake, uncovered, 40 to 50 minutes, until fork inserted in center comes out clean.

Serves: 4

Shopping List:

12 oz. egg substitute, eggs, 8 oz. skim milk, 16 oz. package frozen nonfat shredded hash brown potatoes, low-fat turkey ham (about 8 to 12 oz.), 4 oz. nonfat shredded Cheddar cheese, onion powder, Mrs. Dash seasoning

Nutrition per serving		Exchanges
calories:	251	1½ starch
total fat (4%):	1 g	4 very lean meat
carbohydrate:	24 g	
cholesterol:	25 mg	carbohydrate choice: 1½
dietary fiber:	1 g	
protein:	33 g	
sodium:	512 mg	

Turkey ham contains chromium, which helps your body utilize insulin and reduce the risk of diabetes or low blood sugar.

Overnight French Toast Casserole

Easy — Do Ahead

Ingredients:

½ lb. loaf French bread, cut into ½-inch slices
3 oz. nonfat cream cheese, softened
¾ cup sliced strawberries
3 tbsp. powdered sugar (some extra for topping, optional)
1 cup egg substitute
2 egg whites
⅓ cup skim milk
½ tsp. vanilla extract
butter-flavored cooking spray
syrup or preserves (optional)

Directions:

Spray 9 x 13-inch baking dish with cooking spray. Arrange half the bread slices in a single layer in dish. Combine cream cheese, ½ cup strawberries, and powdered sugar in medium bowl; blend until mixture is smooth and creamy. Spread 2 tablespoons mixture on top of bread slices in baking dish; top with remaining bread to form sandwiches. Combine egg substitute, egg whites, milk, and vanilla in a medium bowl; beat mixture until creamy and frothy. Pour mixture over "sandwiches." Cover with plastic wrap and refrigerate overnight. Preheat oven to 375 degrees. Line baking sheet with foil and spray with butter-flavored cooking spray. Using slotted spoon, transfer sandwiches to baking sheet; discard remaining egg mixture. Bake 12 to 15 minutes; turn sandwiches and bake an additional 10 to 15 minutes, until golden brown. Serve with powdered sugar, syrup, or preserves.

Serves: 4

Shopping List:

3 oz. nonfat cream cheese, ½ lb. loaf French bread, 8 oz. egg substitute, eggs, skim milk, strawberries, powdered sugar, vanilla extract, butter-flavored cooking spray, syrup or preserves (optional)

Nutrition per serving		Exchanges
calories:	241	1½ fruit
total fat (7%):	2 g	1 starch
carbohydrate:	38 g	2 very lean meat
cholesterol:	<.5 mg	
dietary fiber:	2 g	carbohydrate choice: 2½
protein:	16 g	
sodium:	564 mg	

A full meal in one! Carbohydrates, protein, and fruit in a simple-to-prepare breakfast treat!

Whole Wheat Pancakes

Easy — Do Ahead — Freeze

Ingredients:

1⅓ cups flour*
1 cup whole-wheat flour*
1⅓ cup sugar
1⅓ tsp. baking soda
1 tsp. baking powder

1½ tsp. cinnamon
1 cup orange juice
1 cup nonfat vanilla yogurt
½ cup egg substitute

Directions:

Combine flour, whole-wheat flour, sugar, baking soda, baking powder, and cinnamon in a large bowl; mix well. Combine orange juice, yogurt, and egg substitute in a medium bowl; mix until blended smooth. Add yogurt mixture to flour mixture, stirring until ingredients are moistened and blended. Spray large nonstick skillet with cooking spray and heat over medium-high heat. Scoop batter by ¼ to ½ cup into skillet; cook until top of pancake begins to bubble. Flip pancake and cook until browned on both sides. Remove skillet from heat; wrap pancakes in foil to keep warm. Respray skillet with cooking spray and repeat with remaining batter.

Serves: 8

Shopping List:

4 oz. egg substitute, 4 oz. apple butter, 8 oz. maple-flavored syrup, 8 oz. orange juice, 8 oz. nonfat vanilla yogurt, flour, whole-wheat flour, sugar, baking soda, baking powder, cinnamon

Nutrition per serving		Exchanges
calories:	280	4 other carbohydrate
total fat (3%):	1 g	
carbohydrate:	64 g	carbohydrate choice: 4
cholesterol:	1 mg	
dietary fiber:	3 g	
protein:	7 g	
sodium:	234mg	

Orange juice provides instant energy before and after workouts.

*For thicker pancakes, add ¼ to ½ cup additional flour.

Apricot-Ginger Bread

Easy — Do Ahead — Freeze

Ingredients:
1 cup flour
½ cup whole-wheat flour
1¼ tsp. ground ginger
1 tsp. baking powder
¾ tsp. cinnamon
¼ tsp. nutmeg
½ cup cinnamon-flavored applesauce
¼ cup skim milk
¼ cup egg substitute
⅔ cup brown sugar
1½ cups dried chopped apricots

Directions:
Preheat oven to 325 degrees. Spray 9 x 5-inch loaf pan with cooking spray. Combine flour, whole-wheat flour, ginger, baking powder, cinnamon, and nutmeg in a large bowl. Add applesauce, milk, egg substitute and brown sugar; mix until ingredients are moistened. Fold in chopped apricots. Spoon batter into loaf pan; bake 45 to 60 minutes until toothpick inserted in center comes out clean.

Serves: 12

Shopping List:
cinnamon-flavored applesauce, skim milk, egg substitute, flour, whole-wheat flour, brown sugar, ground ginger, cinnamon, nutmeg, baking powder, dried apricots

Nutrition per serving
calories:	153
total fat (0%):	0 g
carbohydrate:	36 g
cholesterol:	0 mg
dietary fiber:	2 g
protein:	3 g
sodium:	43 mg

Exchanges
2 ½ other carbohydrate

carbohydrate choice: 2½

Dried fruits may lose some vitamin C, but they are as nutritious as fresh fruits because they retain iron, potassium, antioxidants, and fiber.

Berry-Orange Muffins

Easy — Do Ahead — Freeze

Ingredients:

½ cup sugar, divided
½ tsp. cinnamon
2½ cups flour
⅓ cup brown sugar
1 tbsp. baking powder
½ cup skim milk
½ cup orange juice

⅓ cup crushed pineapple,
  drained lightly
¼ cup egg substitute
1 tsp. orange peel
1 cup Craisins
butter-flavored cooking
  spray

Directions:

Preheat oven to 325 degrees. Spray muffin pan with cooking spray. Combine ¼ cup sugar and cinnamon in a small bowl and mix well; set aside. Combine flour, ¼ cup sugar, brown sugar, and baking powder in a large mixing bowl; mix until ingredients are blended. Add milk, orange juice, pineapple, egg substitute, and orange peel; add to flour mixture and beat only until ingredients are moistened (do not overmix). Fold in Craisins. Spoon batter into muffin cups (about ¾ full). Bake 18 to 20 minutes until toothpick inserted in center comes out clean. Remove from oven. While muffins are still hot, lightly spray with butter-flavored cooking spray. Immediately sprinkle with reserved cinnamon-sugar mixture. Allow muffins to cool slightly before removing from pan.

Serves: 12

Shopping List:

skim milk, orange juice, egg substitute, canned crushed pineapple, flour, sugar, brown sugar, baking powder, cinnamon, orange peel, Craisins, butter-flavored cooking spray

Nutrition per serving		**Exchanges**
calories:	195	3 other carbohydrates
total fat (0%):	0 g	
carbohydrate:	45 g	carbohydrate choice: 3
cholesterol:	0 mg	
dietary fiber:	1 g	
protein:	4 g	
sodium:	97 mg	

***One glass of freshly squeezed orange juice
can boost absorption of iron from a traditional
American breakfast by 300%.***

Blueberry-Orange Breakfast Rolls

Average — Do Ahead — Freeze

Ingredients:

½ cup sugar
3 tbsp. cornstarch
16½ oz. canned blueberries, drained (reserve juice)
1 cup powdered sugar

3 tbsp. orange juice
1½ lb. frozen bread dough, thawed
butter-flavored cooking spray

Directions:

Line baking sheet with foil and spray with cooking spray. Combine sugar and cornstarch in small saucepan; add reserved blueberry juice and cook over medium heat until mixture thickens. Remove saucepan from heat; add blueberries and stir until lightly mixed. Set aside to cool. Combine powdered sugar and orange juice in small bowl; stir to smooth consistency and set aside. On lightly floured surface, roll bread dough into large rectangle; spray with butter-flavored cooking spray. Starting at long side, roll dough jelly-roll style and pinch edges to seal. Cut into 1½ to 2 inch slices and arrange on baking sheet. Make an indentation in the center of each roll. Spoon 1 tbsp. blueberry filling into each roll. Spray plastic wrap with cooking spray; carefully place wrap (sprayed side down) on dough. Let dough rise until almost double in size (about 35 to 45 minutes). Preheat oven to 375 degrees. Bake blueberry rolls 10 to 15 minutes until lightly browned. Remove from oven and drizzle with orange glaze. Rolls can be frozen and reheated in microwave before serving.

Serves: 3

Shopping List:

1½ lb. frozen bread dough, 16½ oz. can blueberries, sugar, powdered sugar, cornstarch, orange juice, butter-flavored cooking spray

Nutrition per serving

calories:	266
total fat (7%):	2 g
carbohydrate:	59 g
cholesterol:	0 mg
dietary fiber:	2 g
protein:	6 g
sodium:	259 mg

Exchanges

4 other carbohydrates

carbohydrate choice: 4

Blueberries are the second most popular berry in the U.S.

Cheese-Pleasin' Cornbread

Easy — Do Ahead — Freeze

Ingredients:

1 cup yellow cornmeal
1 cup flour
1 tbsp. baking powder
2 tbsp. sugar
¾ cup egg substitute
1 cup nonfat creamer
1 cup nonfat cottage cheese

½ cup nonfat shredded
  Cheddar cheese
¼ cup low-fat shredded
  Cheddar cheese
½ cup canned corn kernels,
  drained
2 tsp. chopped green chilies,
  drained

Directions:

Preheat oven to 400 degrees. Lightly spray square baking dish with cooking spray. In a large bowl, combine cornmeal, flour, baking powder, and sugar; mix well. Combine egg substitute, creamer, and cottage cheese in food processor or blender; process until smooth. Pour into flour mixture and mix until ingredients are moistened. Fold in nonfat and low fat Cheddar cheese, corn, and chilies. Spread batter in baking dish; bake 20 to 30 minutes, until toothpick inserted in center comes out clean. Refrigerate leftover cornbread and reheat before serving.

Serves: 12

Shopping List:

6 oz. egg substitute, 8 oz. nonfat creamer, 8 oz. nonfat cottage cheese, 3 oz. nonfat shredded Cheddar cheese, low-fat shredded Cheddar cheese, canned corn, chopped green chilies, yellow cornmeal, flour, baking powder, sugar

Nutrition per serving		Exchanges
calories:	128	½ very lean meat
total fat (0%):	0 g	1 starch
carbohydrate:	24 g	½ other carbohydrate
cholesterol:	0 mg	
dietary fiber:	1 g	carbohydrate choice: 1½
protein:	6 g	
sodium:	216 mg	

Low-fat cottage cheese, low in calories and fat, contains a balance of phosphorus and calcium. Research has shown that even though phosphorus is an essential mineral, diets that contain more phosphorus than calcium are suspected of encouraging osteoporosis.

"Fruitified" Muffins

Easy — Do Ahead — Freeze

Ingredients:

1¾ cups flour
1 cup oatmeal
¼ cup sugar
½ cup brown sugar
1 tbsp. baking powder
¾ tsp. cinnamon
½ tsp. ground ginger

½ cup egg substitute
½ cup crushed pineapple, drained
1 tsp. vanilla
2 cups shredded carrots
½ cup golden raisins
cinnamon-sugar (optional)

Directions:

Preheat oven to 325 degrees. Spray muffin tin with cooking spray. Combine flour, oatmeal, sugar, brown sugar, baking powder, cinnamon, and ginger in a large mixing bowl; mix well. Add egg substitute, crushed pineapple, and vanilla to flour mixture; mix until ingredients are blended. Fold in carrots and raisins. Spoon batter into muffin cups (about ¾ full) and bake 20 to 25 minutes, until toothpick inserted in center comes out clean. Sprinkle with cinnamon-sugar, if desired.

Serves: 12

Shopping List:

8 oz. packaged shredded carrots, golden raisins, 8 oz. crushed pineapple, egg substitute, flour, oatmeal, sugar, brown sugar, baking powder, cinnamon, ground ginger, vanilla, cinnamon-sugar (optional)

Nutrition per serving		Exchanges
calories:	195	3 other carbohydrates
total fat (5%):	1 g	
carbohydrate:	46 g	carbohydrate choice: 3
cholesterol:	0 mg	
dietary fiber:	2 g	
protein:	4 g	
sodium:	108 mg	

Oats contain saponins that help sweep cholesterol from your body and antioxidants (tocotrienols, ferulic acid and caffeic acid) that help control free radicals, reducing the risk of heart disease and cancer.

"Give 'em a Chance" Millet Muffins

Easy — Do Ahead — Freeze

Ingredients:

1½ cups flour
½ cup whole wheat flour
1 tbsp. baking powder
1 tsp. cinnamon
¼ cup egg substitute
¼ cup applesauce

1 tsp. vanilla extract
⅓ cup orange juice
¼ cup honey
¼ cup brown sugar
¾ cup millet
¾ cup raisins

Directions:

Preheat oven to 325 degrees. Spray muffin tin with cooking spray. Combine flour, whole-wheat flour, baking powder, and cinnamon in a large bowl. Add egg substitute, applesauce, vanilla, orange juice, honey, and brown sugar to flour mixture; mix until ingredients are moistened and blended. Stir in millet and raisins. Fill muffin cups ¾ full and bake 18 to 20 minutes until toothpick inserted in center comes out clean.

Serves: 12

Shopping List:

egg substitute, applesauce, orange juice, flour, whole-wheat flour, brown sugar, honey, millet, raisins, cinnamon, baking powder, vanilla extract

Nutrition per serving

calories:	199
total fat (5%):	1 g
carbohydrate:	44 g
cholesterol:	0 mg
dietary fiber:	3 g
protein:	4 g
sodium:	83 mg

Exchanges

3 other carbohydrate

carbohydrate choice: 3

Millet contains magnesium, essential for regulating heartbeat, helping nerves function, and keeping bones strong.

Jumbo Raisin-Oat Muffins

Easy — Do Ahead — Freeze

Ingredients:

¾ cup brown sugar
¾ cup nonfat vanilla yogurt
½ cup skim milk
¼ cup cinnamon-flavored
  applesauce
1 tsp. vanilla extract
¼ cup egg substitute
1½ cups flour

1 cup yellow cornmeal
½ cup + 2 tbsp. oats,
  divided
1½ tsp. cinnamon
1 tbsp. baking powder
½ tsp. baking soda
½ cup raisins
cinnamon-sugar, for
  topping

Directions:

Preheat oven to 325 degrees. Spray jumbo muffin tin with cooking spray. Combine brown sugar, yogurt, milk, applesauce, vanilla, and egg substitute in a large bowl; mix until blended smooth and creamy. Combine flour, cornmeal, ½ cup oats, cinnamon, baking powder, and baking soda in a ziploc bag; shake until ingredients are well mixed. Gradually pour flour mixture into yogurt mixture, blending after each addition. Mix until all ingredients are moistened. Fold in raisins. Fill muffin cups ¾ full and bake 20 to 25 minutes, until toothpick inserted in center comes out clean. Sprinkle with cinnamon-sugar while warm.

Serves: 6

Shopping List:

6 oz. nonfat vanilla yogurt, skim milk, cinnamon-flavored applesauce, egg substitute, raisins, flour, yellow cornmeal, brown sugar, oats, baking powder, baking soda, cinnamon, vanilla extract, cinnamon-sugar (topping)

Nutrition per serving

calories:	413
total fat (4%):	2 g
carbohydrate:	90 g
cholesterol:	1 mg
dietary fiber:	6 g
protein:	10 g
sodium:	292 mg

Exchanges

6 other carbohydrate

carbohydrate choice: 6

Raisins are a good source of iron, essential for creating hemoglobin in red blood cells, which the body uses to transport oxygen.

Lemon Poppy Seed Muffins

Easy — Do Ahead — Freeze

Ingredients:

1 cup powdered sugar
2 tbsp. + ½ cup skim milk, divided
¾ tsp. lemon extract, divided
2 cups flour
1½ tsp. baking powder
½ cup nonfat yogurt (vanilla or lemon)

¾ cup sugar
2 egg whites
3 tbsp. unsweetened applesauce
1 tbsp. lemon juice
1 tbsp. grated lemon zest
¼ tsp. vanilla extract
1 tbsp. poppy seeds

Directions:

Preheat oven to 325 degrees. Spray muffin tin with cooking spray. Combine powdered sugar, 2 tbsp. skim milk, and ½ tsp. lemon extract in a small bowl; mix until creamy and smooth. Set aside until muffins are cooked and cooled. Combine flour and baking powder in a large mixing bowl; mix well. Combine remaining ingredients in medium bowl; mix until completely blended. Add to flour mixture and mix until ingredients are moistened. Divide batter among muffin cups; bake 20 to 25 minutes until toothpick inserted in center comes out clean. Cool 10 minutes before removing from pan; cool completely. Drizzle with lemon glaze and let stand until glaze hardens.

Serves: 12

Shopping List:

4 oz. nonfat yogurt (vanilla or lemon), skim milk, eggs, unsweetened applesauce, lemon juice, lemon zest, flour, sugar, powdered sugar, baking powder, vanilla extract, lemon extract, poppy seeds

Nutrition per serving

calories:	172
total fat (5%):	1 g
carbohydrate:	39 g
cholesterol:	<.5 mg
dietary fiber:	1 g
protein:	4 g
sodium:	63 mg

Exchanges

2½ other carbohydrates

carbohydrate choice: 2½

Lemons contain limonene, which boosts the immune system and fat metabolization.

Peachy Almond Muffins

Easy — Do Ahead — Freeze

Ingredients:

2 cups flour
¼ cup sugar
½ cup brown sugar
1 tbsp. baking powder
¼ cup egg substitute
⅓ cup peach-flavored applesauce

½ cup skim milk
½ tsp. almond extract
1½ cups chopped peaches
  in juice, drained (reserve
  juice)
1 tbsp. chopped almonds

Directions:

Preheat oven to 325 degrees. Spray muffin tin with cooking spray. Combine flour, sugar, brown sugar, and baking powder in a large mixing bowl. Add egg substitute, applesauce, milk, and almond extract; mix until ingredients are moistened. Fold in peaches and almonds; if batter is too thick, add several drops of reserved peach juice. Spoon batter into muffin cups (about ¾ full) and bake 20 to 25 minutes, until toothpick inserted in center comes out clean.

Serves: 12

Shopping List:

peach-flavored applesauce, egg substitute, skim milk, 15½ oz. can peaches in juice, flour, sugar, brown sugar, baking powder, almond extract, chopped almonds

Nutrition per serving

calories:	163
total fat (6%):	1 g
carbohydrate:	35 g
cholesterol:	0 mg
dietary fiber:	1 g
protein:	4 g
sodium:	99 mg

Exchanges

2 other carbohydrates

carbohydrate choice: 2

Although high in fat, consuming just 1 ounce of nuts four to five times a week has been found to cut heart attack risk by 40 to 50%.

Pineapple-Pumpkin Streusel Muffins

Easy — Do Ahead — Freeze

Ingredients:

⅔ cup canned pumpkin
¾ cup crushed pineapple
1 tsp. vanilla extract
⅓ cup sugar
¾ cup brown sugar, divided
½ cup egg substitute

2½ cups flour, divided
2 tsp. baking powder
1 tsp. baking soda
1 tsp. pumpkin pie spice
1 tsp. cinnamon, divided
1 tsp. dry Butter Buds mix

Directions:

Preheat oven to 325 degrees. Spray muffin tin with cooking spray. Combine pumpkin, pineapple, vanilla, sugar, ½ cup brown sugar, and egg substitute in a large bowl; mix until ingredients are creamy and smooth. Add 2 cups flour, baking powder, baking soda, pumpkin pie spice, and ¾ teaspoon cinnamon; mix until dry ingredients are moistened and blended. Divide batter among 12 muffin cups. Combine remaining flour, brown sugar, and cinnamon in a small bowl; sprinkle with Butter Buds dry mix. Sprinkle several drops of water into flour mixture; crumble with hands. Add just enough water so mixture is crumbly. Sprinkle crumb mixture over muffins. Bake 20 to 25 minutes, until toothpick inserted in center comes out clean.

Serves: 12

Shopping List:

15 oz. can pumpkin, 8 oz. can crushed pineapple, 4 oz. egg substitute, flour, sugar, brown sugar, baking powder, baking soda, pumpkin pie spice, cinnamon, vanilla extract, Butter Buds

Nutrition per serving

calories:	188
total fat (1%):	.3 g
carbohydrate:	43 g
cholesterol:	0 mg
dietary fiber:	1 g
protein:	4 g
sodium:	115 mg

Exchanges

3 other carbohydrates

carbohydrate choice: 3

Pumpkin provides 1,320 international units of vitamin A in ½ cup cooked, mashed pumpkin—this is three and a half times the Recommended Daily Allowance!

Pumpkin Packed Cornbread

Easy — Do Ahead — Freeze

Ingredients:
½ cup canned pumpkin
½ cup nonfat plain yogurt
¼ cup evaporated skim milk
¼ cup brown sugar
¼ cup egg substitute
1 cup cornmeal
1 cup flour
1 tbsp. baking powder
¾ tsp. pumpkin pie spice

Directions:
Preheat oven to 350 degrees. Spray 8- or 9-inch baking dish with cooking spray. Combine pumpkin, yogurt, evaporated milk, brown sugar, and egg substitute in medium bowl; blend until creamy. Add cornmeal, flour, baking powder, and pumpkin pie spice, mixing until ingredients are moistened. Spoon batter into baking dish and bake 20 to 25 minutes, until toothpick inserted in center comes out clean.

Serves: 8

Shopping List:
canned pumpkin, nonfat plain yogurt, evaporated skim milk, egg substitute, cornmeal, flour, brown sugar, baking powder, pumpkin pie spice

Nutrition per serving
calories:	170
total fat (5%):	1 g
carbohydrate:	36 g
cholesterol:	1 mg
dietary fiber:	2 g
protein:	5 g
sodium:	157 mg

Exchanges
2½ other carbohydrate

carbohydrate choice: 2½

Pumpkin is rich in beta-carotene, a powerful antioxidant that reduces the free radical damage that often leads to lung and other cancers. Research shows that eating vegetables rich in beta-carotene more than once a week reduces lung cancer odds by up to 70%.

Tropical Mango Muffins

Easy — Do Ahead — Freeze

Ingredients:

¾ cup + 2 tbsp. sugar, divided
¼ cup + 2 tbsp. brown sugar
1 cup crushed pineapple
½ cup egg substitute
3 cups flour, divided
1 tbsp. baking powder

1 tbsp. grated lime peel
1 cup chopped mangoes
  (fresh or frozen)
1 tbsp. powdered sugar
2 tsp. dry Butter Buds mix
2 tbsp. water

Directions:

Preheat oven to 325 degrees. Lightly spray muffin tin with cooking spray. Combine ¾ cup sugar, ¼ cup brown sugar, pineapple, and egg substitute in a medium mixing bowl and mix well. Gradually add 2½ cups flour and baking powder, stirring well after each addition. Fold in lime peel and mangoes. Divide batter among muffin cups. Combine ½ cup flour, 2 tbsp. sugar, 2 tbsp. brown sugar, powdered sugar, and Butter Buds in a small bowl; mix well. Sprinkle water one tablespoon at a time; mix with fingers until moist and crumbly. Add more water if necessary. Sprinkle topping over muffins and bake 20 to 25 minutes until lightly browned and toothpick inserted in center comes out clean. Let cool 5 minutes before removing muffins from pan. Muffins can be refrigerated or frozen and reheated in microwave.

Serves: 15

Shopping List:

8 oz. can crushed pineapple, 4 oz. egg substitute, flour, sugar, brown sugar, powdered sugar, Butter Buds, baking powder, lime, mangoes

Nutrition per serving		**Exchanges**
calories:	171	1½ other carbohydrate
total fat (0%):	0 g	1 fruit
carbohydrate:	39 g	
cholesterol:	0 mg	carbohydrate choice: 2½
dietary fiber:	1 g	
protein:	4 g	
sodium:	97 mg	

Mangoes are packed with soluble fiber, which helps control appetite and blood-cholesterol levels, and insoluble fiber, which aids digestion. Mangoes are also a powerful source of vitamins A and C.

SENSATIONAL SALAD, SOUP, SANDWICHES, AND WRAPS

◆ ◆ ◆

Top Reasons to Select Simple, Satiating, Sumptuous Soups, Salads, and Sandwiches!

> ### SALADS are . . .
> - natural fat fighters
> - low in calories, low in fat and bursting with vital nutrients
> - an excellent food source for meeting RDA for vegetables and fruits
> - easy to turn into full-course, low-fat meals by adding protein-rich cooked beans, lean poultry, seafood, or nonfat cheese
> - meal extenders—they take longer to munch, crunch, and chomp without added calories or fat
> - a good way to make use of leftovers (barley, rice, potatoes, pasta, poultry, fish, or seafood)

Dress It Up

- **Cruciferous vegetables** that contain cancerfighting nitrogen compounds, vitamin C and folate (*Brussels sprouts, broccoli, cabbage, cauliflower, collard greens, kale, kohlrabi, mustard greens, rutabaga, turnips*)
- Canned **chickpeas**, kidney **beans**, pinto beans, or navy beans for soluble fiber
- Chopped **dried fruit** (*figs, dates, apricots, raisins*) for potassium, vitamin A, and beta-carotene
- Chopped or sliced **fresh fruit** (*apples, nectarines, peaches or grapes*) for fiber, potassium, and vitamin C
- Frozen **peas** or **corn** for calcium, potassium, and vitamin C
- **Tomatoes** for potassium, and vitamins A and C
- **Cooked grains** (*quinoa, rice, couscous*) for protein, potassium, and iron
- **Carrots** and **bell peppers** for fiber and beta-carotene
- **Red onions** for potassium and vitamin C
- **Fresh herbs** (*basil, chervil, chives, dill, marjoram, oregano, parsley, sorrel, tarragon, thyme*)
- **Vinegar** for sharp flavor without fat (*balsamic, cider, champagne, red or white wine, rice, sherry*)
- **Shrimp, crabmeat, turkey,** or **chicken** for low-fat protein plus

"Take it off" Toppers

regular croutons	140 calories/6 grams fat per 2 tbsp. serving
chow mein noodles	30 calories/2 grams fat per 2 tbsp. serving
coconut	35 calories/3 grams fat per 2 tbsp. serving
granola	74 calories/4 grams fat per 2 tbsp. serving
olives	26 calories/2 grams fat per 5 olives
sunflower seeds	104 calories/10 grams fat per 2 tbsp. serving
bacon bits	54 calories/3 grams fat per 2 tbsp. serving
avocado	84 calories/8 grams fat per ¼ avocado
Cheddar cheese	114 calories/10 grams fat per ounce serving
chopped egg	77 calories/6 grams fat per ¼ cup serving
regular salad dressing	140 to150 calories/12 to18 grams of fat per 2 tbsp. serving

---

One more reason to "Dress It Up" and "Take It Off"

2 cups lettuce + all of the "take it off" toppers =
744 calories, 61 whopping grams of fat!!!

That's more fat than a Quarter-pounder with cheese, regular fries, and a chocolate milkshake!

Soup

- is the ultimate comfort, soul-soothing, spirit-lifting food
- can be a nutritious blend of protein, vegetables, and carbohydrates in a single pot
- can be served before, during, after, or as the mainstay of any meal
- is a kitchen time-saver; cook in big batches—freeze for snacks, lunches or quick weeknight meals (For a real time-saver, use frozen vegetables)
- can help you meet the healthful guidelines of the U.S. Department of Agriculture Food Guide Pyramid in just a serving or two each day. Thicken your soups with pureed cooked cauliflower, potatoes, white beans, onions, or rice—you add nutrients, flavor, and density without added calories or fat

- can actually curb your appetite to prevent overeating later in the meal (one study found that eating a bowl of tomato soup before a meal reduced caloric intake later in the meal by 25%)
- is a great way to use up leftover food—toss in cooked rice, pasta, chicken, seafood, or vegetables

---

Sandwiches are . . .

Quick 'n' Simple or No-Prep 'n' Mess Meals

Do Aheads for bag it lunch and munch

Stuffed silly with "good" stuff (lean meat, lean poultry, greens, vegetables, low-fat cheese)

Spread and smeared without added calories and fat (mustard, nonfat mayo or salad dressing)

Fun Facts:

- **2.2 billion** "soup and sandwich" meals are consumed in the United States each year!
- At least ONE sandwich is served in **95% of American households every 14 days!**
- **50% of all sandwiches** are consumed at **lunch.**
- **28% of all sandwiches** are consumed at **dinner.**
- **No Baloney!** Approximately **2.19 billion Oscar Meyer bologna sandwiches** are eaten each year, **6 million each day.** In the second it took for you to read this line, **69 bologna sandwiches were eaten!**
- **What's a sandwich without cheese?** According to a study conducted by the Opinion Research Corporation (ORC), **Americans** eat more than **4.07 billion Kraft Single Cheese Slices** each year, **11.1 million slices** a day and **129 slices** per second!
- According to a study of more than 1,000 American adults (conducted by ORC), the top choices among sandwich eaters are:

  whole: 36%   cut in half: 32%   cut diagonally: 26%
          cut into squares: 3%   other: 3%

Do you live in a sandwich capital? Top 5 cities for sandwich consumption

1. Philadelphia, Pennsylvania
2. Baltimore, Maryland
3. Pittsburgh, Pennsylvania
4. Los Angeles/Long Beach, California
5. Long Island, New York

Asian Chicken Soup with Snow Peas & Noodles

Average — Do Ahead — Freeze

Ingredients:
1½ lb. skinless, boneless chicken tenders, cut into ½-inch cubes
¾ cup chopped celery
5¼ cups nonfat chicken broth
1½ cups water
1½ cups shredded Savoy cabbage
1 cup shredded carrot
1½ cups frozen snow peas, thawed and drained
1 tbsp. low-sodium soy sauce
1 tbsp. dry sherry
1 tsp. sugar
½ tsp. red pepper flakes
¼ cup green onion, sliced thin
4 oz. soba noodles, broken into pieces

Directions:
Spray large soup pot with cooking spray and heat over medium-high heat; add chicken and celery. Cook, stirring frequently, until chicken is cooked through and celery is tender (about 8 to 10 minutes). Add chicken broth, water, cabbage, carrot, snow peas, soy sauce, sherry, sugar and red pepper flakes. Bring to a boil over high heat; reduce heat to low, cover, and simmer 6 to 7 minutes. Add green onion and soba noodles; cook, stirring occasionally until noodles are tender (about 3 to 5 minutes).

Serves: 6

Shopping List:
1½ lb. low-fat chicken tenders, 3 15-oz. cans nonfat chicken broth, low-sodium soy sauce, dry sherry, 4 oz. package soba noodles, ½ lb. Savoy cabbage, celery, packaged shredded carrot (or ½ lb. carrots), 10 oz. package frozen snow peas, green onions, sugar, red pepper flakes

Nutrition per serving		Exchanges
calories:	213	½ starch
total fat (4%):	1 g	3 vegetable
carbohydrate:	23 g	3 very lean meat
cholesterol:	71 mg	
dietary fiber:	2 g	carbohydrate choice: 1½
protein:	28 g	
sodium:	1160 mg	

Most people need about two micrograms a day of vitamin B$_{12}$— you can get a full day's supply from 3 ounces of chicken.

Butternut Squash Soup

Easy — Do Ahead — Freeze

Ingredients:
4 lbs. butternut or acorn squash
2 cups water
28 oz. nonfat chicken or vegetable broth
½ tsp. pepper
1½ cups nonfat croutons (herb-seasoned or zesty garlic)

Directions:
Cut squash in half lengthwise and remove seeds. Preheat oven to 400 degrees. Line baking sheet with foil and spray with cooking spray. Arrange squash halves on baking sheet, cut side down. Bake until skins are browned and squash is tender (about 60 to 75 minutes). Remove from oven and cool 5 minutes. Scoop squash from skins and spoon into large saucepan; mash with potato masher. Add water, broth, and pepper; cook over medium heat, stirring frequently, until soup thickens. Remove from heat, cool completely, and transfer to covered container. Refrigerate overnight. (Soup can be frozen up to 30 days.) Serve soup cold with seasoned croutons.

Serves: 6

Shopping List:
4 lbs. butternut or acorn squash, 28 oz. nonfat broth, nonfat seasoned croutons, pepper

Nutrition per serving		Exchanges
calories:	76	1 starch
total fat (0%):	0 g	
carbohydrate:	19 g	carbohydrate choice: 1
cholesterol:	0 mg	
dietary fiber:	3 g	
protein:	2 g	
sodium:	553 mg	

Butternut squash is considered an all-around protector food; a single serving can meet the RDA for vitamin C, fiber, and carotene.

Chicken-Tortilla Soup

Easy — Do Ahead

Ingredients:
   3 cups nonfat chicken broth
   1 cup water
   ½ lb. skinless, boneless chicken tenders, cubed
   1½ tsp. chili powder
   1⅓ cups canned corn kernels, drained
   2 tbsp. chopped green chilies, drained
   1 cup chunky garden-style salsa
   ½ cup nonfat shredded mozzarella cheese

Directions:
   Combine chicken broth, water, chicken, and chili powder in
   large saucepan; bring to a boil over high heat. Reduce heat
   to low, cover, and simmer 10 to 12 minutes, until chicken is
   cooked through. Stir in corn, chilies, and salsa; heat thoroughly. Just before serving, sprinkle with mozzarella cheese.

Serves: 4

Shopping List:
   24 oz. chicken broth, ½ lb. low-fat chicken tenders, 11 oz. can
   corn kernels, 8 oz. jar chunky garden-style salsa, 2 oz. nonfat shredded mozzarella cheese, green chilies, chili powder

Nutrition per serving		Exchanges
calories:	178	½ starch
total fat (5%):	1 g	2 vegetable
carbohydrate:	18 g	2 very lean meat
cholesterol:	35 mg	
dietary fiber:	4 g	carbohydrate choice: 1
protein:	22 g	
sodium:	1,384 mg	

*Protein is not stored in the body; it must
be replenished throughout the day.
Getting enough protein each day is
a key ingredient for an energized life.*

"Cinna-Melberry" Summer Soup

Easy — Do Ahead

Ingredients:
4 cups cantaloupe cubes
1 cup orange juice
1 tsp. lime juice
¾ tsp. cinnamon
¼ cup fresh blueberries

Directions:
Combine all ingredients except blueberries in food processor or blender; process until smooth and creamy. Pour into bowl, cover, and refrigerate several hours or overnight. Garnish with fresh blueberries before serving.

Serves: 4

Shopping List:
cantaloupe, 8 oz. orange juice, fresh blueberries, lime juice, cinnamon

Nutrition per serving		Exchanges
calories:	90	1½ fruit
total fat (10%):	1 g	
carbohydrate:	22 g	carbohydrate choice: 1½
cholesterol:	0 mg	
dietary fiber:	2 g	
protein:	2 g	
sodium:	16 mg	

Cantaloupe is an excellent source of vitamin A, which helps to protect the body from developing many types of cancer, including cervical, lung and bladder cancer. Vitamin A also helps protect the cardiovascular system from heart attack and lowers the risk of stroke.

SALAD, SOUP SANDWICHES AND WRAPS

Creamy Tomato-Rice Soup

Average — Do Ahead — Freeze

Ingredients:

4 cups canned chopped
    tomatoes, undrained
4 cups water
1½ cups cooked white rice,
    divided
1 cup chopped celery
2 tsp. onion powder

2 tsp. Italian seasoning
1½ tsp. minced garlic
¼ cup tomato paste
1 tbsp. sugar
¼ tsp. black pepper
½ tsp. Mrs. Dash seasoning
1 tbsp. dried parsley

Directions:

Combine tomatoes, water, ½ cup cooked rice, celery, onion powder, Italian seasoning, minced garlic, tomato paste, sugar, pepper and Mrs. Dash seasoning in a large saucepan or soup pot. Bring to a boil over high heat; reduce heat to low, cover, and simmer 30 to 45 minutes. Remove pot from burner, uncover, and let cool 20 to 30 minutes. Transfer soup to food processor or blender and process until smooth (this may need to be done in several batches). Return soup to pan; add remaining rice. Cook soup over medium-high heat until hot. Sprinkle with parsley just before serving.

Serves: 6

Shopping List:

32 oz. canned chopped tomatoes, white rice, 4 oz. tomato paste, celery, onion powder, Italian seasoning, minced garlic, sugar, black pepper, Mrs. Dash seasoning, dried parsley

Nutrition per serving		Exchanges
calories:	120	½ starch
total fat (8%):	1 g	4 vegetable
carbohydrate:	26 g	
cholesterol:	0 mg	carbohydrate choice: 2
dietary fiber:	3 g	
protein:	3 g	
sodium:	273 mg	

Americans obtain more of their vitamins from tomatoes than from any other vegetable.

Manhattan Clam Chowder

Easy — Do Ahead — Freeze

Ingredients:

2 tbsp. nonfat chicken broth
1 cup chopped onion
½ cup chopped carrot
½ cup chopped celery
2½ cups cubed potatoes
3 cups clam juice
28 oz. can diced tomatoes, undrained

2 tsp. dried parsley
1 tsp. Italian seasoning
1 tsp. sugar
½ tsp. garlic powder
1 lb. chopped clams

Directions:

Spray large soup pot or Dutch oven with cooking spray; pour chicken broth into pot and heat over medium-high heat. Add onions, carrots, and celery; cook until vegetables are softened (about 5 minutes). Add potatoes, clam juice, tomatoes, parsley, Italian seasoning, sugar, and garlic powder; bring to a boil over high heat. Reduce heat to medium-low and simmer 20 to 25 minutes until potatoes are tender. Stir in clams; cook over medium heat until heated through.

Serves: 6

Shopping List:

28 oz. can diced tomatoes, 24 oz. clam juice, 16 oz. chopped clams, nonfat chicken broth, carrot, celery, onion, baking potatoes, dried parsley, Italian seasoning, sugar, garlic powder

Nutrition per serving

calories:	156
total fat (6%):	1 g
carbohydrate:	24 g
cholesterol:	26 mg
dietary fiber:	3 g
protein:	13 g
sodium:	539 mg

Exchanges

½ starch
3 vegetable
1 very lean meat

carbohydrate choice: 1½

Americans eat approximately twenty-four pounds of tomatoes per person per year.

Mushroom Barley Soup

Average — Do Ahead — Freeze

Ingredients:
3 cups water
3 cups vegetable broth
1¾ cups chopped onion
1½ tsp. minced garlic
⅔ cup barley
3½ cups chopped mushrooms
2 tsp. dried dill weed

Directions:
Combine water and vegetable broth in a large saucepan; bring to a boil over high heat. Add onion, garlic, and barley to pan; cover, reduce heat to low, and simmer 40 to 45 minutes. Add mushrooms to soup, cover pan, and cook over low heat 15 to 20 minutes. Using a slotted spoon, scoop ¾ of vegetables and barley from pan; place in food processor or blender and process until smooth. Return pureed vegetables to soup; stir in dill. Bring soup to a boil over high heat; serve hot.

Serves: 6

Shopping List:
24 oz. vegetable broth, barley, ¾ lb. mushrooms, 2 onions, minced garlic, dried dill weed

Nutrition per serving		Exchanges
calories:	123	½ starch
total fat (7%):	1 g	3 vegetable
carbohydrate:	24 g	
cholesterol:	0 mg	carbohydrate choice: 1½
dietary fiber:	5 g	
protein:	6 g	
sodium:	398 mg	

Mushrooms are 90% water.

Peach 'n' Berry Summer Soup

Easy — Do Ahead

Ingredients:
2 cups fresh peaches, peeled and sliced
1 ½ tsp. lemon juice
¼ tsp. cinnamon
12 oz. peach nectar
¾ cup nonfat vanilla yogurt, divided
½ cup sliced strawberries

Directions:
Combine peaches, lemon juice, cinnamon, and peach nectar in food processor or blender; process until smooth. Pour into medium bowl; add ½ cup yogurt and stir until mixed. Cover and refrigerate overnight. Serve in bowls with dollop of remaining yogurt and sliced strawberries.

Serves: 4

Shopping List:
2 to 4 peaches, strawberries, 12 oz. peach nectar, lemon juice, 6 oz. nonfat vanilla yogurt, cinnamon

Nutrition per serving		Exchanges
calories:	107	1½ fruit
total fat (0%):	0 g	
carbohydrate:	25 g	carbohydrate choice: 1½
cholesterol:	1 mg	
dietary fiber:	2 g	
protein:	2 g	
sodium:	28 mg	

Fruit juice is rich in vitamin C, which helps to prevent infection, as well as boost iron absorption, the healing of wounds and the formation of collagen.

Sensational Swiss Chard & White Bean Soup

Easy — Do Ahead — Freeze

Ingredients:
1 cup chopped onion (if frozen, thaw and drain)
1 cup chopped celery
1½ cups frozen carrot slices, thawed and drained
2 tsp. garlic powder
2 15-oz. cans white beans, rinsed and drained
2½ cups nonfat chicken broth
1 cup water
12 oz. Swiss chard, stems removed and trimmed
½ cup nonfat Parmesan cheese (optional)

Directions:
Combine all ingredients except Swiss chard and Parmesan cheese in soup pot or Dutch oven. Bring to a boil over high heat; reduce heat to low and simmer, uncovered, 10 to 15 minutes. Stir in Swiss chard; bring to a boil over high heat. Reduce heat to low and simmer 5 to 8 minutes until Swiss chard is tender. Sprinkle soup with Parmesan cheese, if desired.

Serves: 4

Shopping List:
packaged chopped onions (fresh or frozen), celery, 16 oz. frozen carrot slices, 2 15-oz. cans white beans, 22 oz. nonfat chicken broth, 12 oz. Swiss chard, nonfat Parmesan cheese, garlic powder

Nutrition per serving

calories:	338
total fat (3%):	1 g
carbohydrate:	63 g
cholesterol:	0 mg
dietary fiber:	7 g
protein:	22 g
sodium:	1,031 mg

Exchanges
3 starch
3½ vegetable

carbohydrate choice: 4

Swiss chard, a member of the leafy green vegetable family is a good source of folate, which helps the body form new cells.

Shrimp Wonton Soup

Difficult — Do Ahead — Freeze

Ingredients:

½ lb. cooked shrimp,
  chopped fine
1 cup sliced green onion, divided
1 cup shredded carrot, chopped
  fine, divided
1 tbsp. low-sodium soy sauce
⅛ tsp. ground red pepper

8 large wonton wrappers
  (or 16 small)
5 cups oriental broth
5 cups nonfat chicken broth
1 piece fresh gingerroot or
  ½ tsp. ground gingerroot

Directions:

Combine shrimp, ¼ cup green onion, ¼ cup carrot, soy sauce and red pepper in a medium bowl; mix well. To prepare wontons: Place wonton skin on flat surface. Spoon 1 teaspoon (¼ to ½ tsp. if using small wontons) shrimp filling in the center of each wonton skin. Fold lower corner over the filling and tuck the pointed end under the filling. Roll wonton away from you, leaving 1 inch of skin unrolled at the top corner. Use water to moisten the side corner; hold opposite corner and overlap over filling, attaching side corners to each other. Pour oriental broth and chicken broth into soup pot; add ½ cup carrots, ½ cup sliced green onion, and gingerroot. Bring to a boil over high heat; add wontons. Reduce heat to low, cover and simmer 10 to 15 minutes until wontons are soft and vegetables are tender-crisp.

Serves: 6

Shopping List:

wonton wrappers (large or small), ½ lb. cooked shrimp, 40 oz. oriental broth (you can substitute chicken or vegetable broth), 40 oz. nonfat chicken broth, 8 oz. package shredded carrot (or 3 carrots), green onion, fresh (or ground) gingerroot, low-sodium soy sauce, ground red pepper

Nutrition per serving

calories:	131
total fat (7%):	1 g
carbohydrate:	15 g
cholesterol:	111 mg
dietary fiber:	2 g
protein:	14 g
sodium:	1,268 mg

Exchanges

½ starch
2 vegetable
1 very lean meat

carbohydrate choice: 3

Soup can be an excellent low-calorie, low-fat snack; it fills you up fast and provides an array of nutrients.

Snappy Vegetable-Beef Soup

Easy — Do Ahead — Freeze

Ingredients:
12 cups nonfat beef broth
20 oz. frozen sliced or baby carrots
16 oz. sliced mushrooms
2 cups canned kidney beans, drained
3 cups baby spinach leaves
pepper to taste

Directions:
Pour beef broth into large soup pot or Dutch oven. Add carrots and mushrooms; bring to a boil over high heat. Reduce heat to medium and simmer 8 to 10 minutes until carrots and mushrooms are tender. Add beans and spinach leaves; cook over medium heat, about 10 to 15 minutes, until spinach softens. Season with pepper.

Serves: 8

Shopping List:
8 14½-oz. cans nonfat beef broth, 1 lb. mushrooms; 20 oz. frozen sliced or baby carrots, 15½ oz. can kidney beans, 3 cups baby spinach leaves, pepper

Nutrition per serving		Exchanges
calories:	131	1 starch
total fat (14%):	2 g	1½ vegetable
carbohydrate:	20 g	
cholesterol:	0 mg	carbohydrate choice: 1
dietary fiber:	7 g	
protein:	11 g	
sodium:	1,608 mg	

Carrots contain high levels of beta-carotene for protection against sun damage.

3-Step Minestrone Meal

Easy — Do Ahead — Freeze

Ingredients:
  3½ cups nonfat chicken broth
  28 oz. can Italian-style diced tomatoes
  10 oz. frozen green peas
  1 cup uncooked pasta (macaroni, shells, etc.)
  1 lb. fresh spinach leaves, washed and dried
  19 oz. can white beans, rinsed and drained
  nonfat Parmesan cheese (optional)

Directions:
  Combine chicken broth and tomatoes (with juice) in large soup pot or Dutch oven; bring to a boil over high heat. Add peas and pasta; reduce heat to medium and cook 7 to 9 minutes until pasta is tender. Stir in spinach leaves and beans; cook over medium-high heat until spinach leaves wilt and soup is heated through. If soup is too thick, add water or chicken broth and heat through. Sprinkle with Parmesan cheese before serving, if desired.

Serves: 6

Shopping List:
  28 oz. nonfat chicken broth, 28 oz. Italian-style chopped tomatoes, 10 oz. frozen green peas, 8 oz. package pasta, 1 lb. fresh spinach leaves, 19 oz. can white beans (cannelloni), nonfat Parmesan cheese

Nutrition per serving		Exchanges
calories:	244	2 starch
total fat (4%):	1 g	3 vegetable
carbohydrate:	48 g	
cholesterol:	0 mg	carbohydrate choice: 3
dietary fiber:	3 g	
protein:	14 g	
sodium:	928 mg	

Green peas provide vitamin A, folic acid, potassium, protein, and fiber.

Tropical Blend Gazpacho

Easy — Do Ahead

Ingredients:

35 oz. canned crushed tomatoes, undrained

16 oz. canned chopped tomatoes, undrained

1 cup unsweetened pineapple juice

2 cucumbers, cubed

2 cups bell peppers (any color)

4 oz. chopped green chilies

1½ cups diced celery

1½ cups pineapple chunks (fresh or canned)

¾ tsp. garlic powder

¼ tsp. chili powder

¼ tsp. pepper

½ tsp. ground cumin

½ cup chopped cilantro

½ tsp. Tabasco pepper sauce

Directions:

Combine all ingredients in a large mixing bowl; mix well. Cover and refrigerate 3 to 6 hours before serving.

Serves: 6

Shopping List:

35 oz. canned crushed tomatoes, 16 oz. canned chopped tomatoes, 8 oz. unsweetened pineapple juice, 2 cucumbers, 2 bell peppers, fresh cilantro, 4 oz. can chopped green chilies, celery, 15 oz. can pineapple chunks in juice (or use fresh pineapple), garlic powder, chili powder, pepper, ground cumin, Tabasco pepper sauce

Nutrition per serving		Exchanges
calories:	126	3 vegetable
total fat (8%):	1 g	1 fruit
carbohydrate:	29 g	
cholesterol:	0 mg	carbohydrate choice: 2
dietary fiber:	5 g	
protein:	4 g	
sodium:	647 mg	

A five-year study of 48,000 men found that those eating ten servings a week of cooked tomato products had the lowest risk of prostate cancer. Their risk was one-third that of men eating fewer than two servings a week.

Turkey-Rice Soup

Easy — Do Ahead — Freeze

Ingredients:
1 lb. skinless, boneless turkey tenders, cut into ½-inch cubes
1 cup chopped onion
¾ cup chopped celery
3½ cups nonfat chicken broth
1 cup water
½ cup rice (not instant)
1 tsp. dried tarragon

Directions:
Spray soup pot with cooking spray; add turkey, onions, and celery. Cook, stirring frequently, until turkey is lightly browned and vegetables are soft (about 8 to 10 minutes). Add broth, water, rice, and tarragon to pot; bring to a boil over high heat. Reduce heat to low, cover, and simmer 20 to 25 minutes.

Serves: 4

Shopping List:
1 lb. low-fat turkey tenders, 28 oz. nonfat chicken broth, white rice (not instant), 1 onion, celery, dried tarragon

Nutrition per serving		Exchanges
calories:	288	½ starch
total fat (13%):	4 g	3 vegetable
carbohydrate:	24 g	1 lean meat
cholesterol:	79 mg	3 very lean meat
dietary fiber:	1 g	
protein:	36 g	carbohydrate choice: 1½
sodium:	769 mg	

When it comes to optimum energy, WHEN you eat can be as important as WHAT you eat! Eat mini meals six times a day.

Vegetable Barley Chowder

Easy — Do Ahead — Freeze

Ingredients:
6 cups nonfat chicken broth
½ cup pearl barley
2 turnips, cut into ¾-inch chunks
1 cup diced celery
8 oz. package sliced carrots
16 oz. can white beans
1 bunch escarole, rinsed and coarsely chopped
¾ cup chopped green onion
pepper to taste
¼ cup nonfat Parmesan cheese (optional)

Directions:
Combine chicken broth, barley, turnips, celery and carrots in large soup pot; bring to a boil over high heat. Reduce heat to low, cover pot, and simmer 30 to 35 minutes. Add beans (with liquid) to soup; cook over medium heat 10 minutes. Add escarole and green onion; simmer over medium-low heat until wilted. Season with pepper; sprinkle each serving with Parmesan cheese, if desired.

Serves: 6

Shopping List:
48 oz. nonfat chicken broth, pearl barley, 16 oz. can white beans, 2 turnips, celery, 8 oz. package sliced carrot, green onion, 1 bunch escarole, nonfat Parmesan cheese, pepper

Nutrition per serving		Exchanges
calories:	212	2 starch
total fat (4%):	1 g	2½ vegetable
carbohydrate:	42 g	
cholesterol:	0 mg	carbohydrate choice: 3
dietary fiber:	8 g	
protein:	11 g	
sodium:	873 mg	

Barley is a rich source of tocotrienols, a powerful antioxidant that protects against heart disease.

Zesty White Bean Chili

Easy — Do Ahead — Freeze

Ingredients:
>   1½ cups nonfat chicken broth, divided
>   1½ lb. low-fat chicken tenders, cut in 1-inch pieces
>   1½ tsp. onion powder
>   1½ tsp. garlic powder
>   16 oz. can white beans, undrained
>   16 oz. can Mexican-style stewed tomatoes
>   1 tbsp. chili powder
>   ¾ cup low-fat shredded Cheddar cheese

Directions:

Pour ½ cup chicken broth into soup pot or Dutch oven and heat over medium-high heat. Generously sprinkle chicken tenders with onion powder and garlic powder; add to broth and cook, stirring frequently, until chicken is browned and cooked through. Add beans, tomatoes, and chili powder; mix well and bring to a boil over high heat. Reduce heat to medium, cover, and cook 15 to 20 minutes, until thick. Serve with shredded cheese.

Serves: 6

Shopping List:

15 oz. can nonfat chicken broth, 16 oz. can white beans, 1½ lb. low-fat chicken tenders, 16 oz. can Mexican-style stewed tomatoes, 3 oz. low-fat shredded Cheddar cheese, onion powder, garlic powder, chili powder

Nutrition per serving		Exchanges
calories:	252	2 vegetable
total fat (4%):	1 g	4 very lean meat
carbohydrate:	25 g	1 starch
cholesterol:	71 mg	
dietary fiber:	4 g	carbohydrate choice: 1½
protein:	35 g	
sodium:	956 mg	

Beans contain protease inhibitors that interfere with cancer-causing enzymes and prevent the growth of cancer cells.

"Berry" Delicious
Spinach-Chicken Salad

Easy — Do Ahead

Ingredients:
6 cups fresh spinach leaves
2 cups low-fat cooked chicken breast, cubed
1½ cups fresh raspberries, divided
⅓ cup sliced celery
⅓ cup sliced water chestnuts
4 tsp. slivered almonds
1 cup nonfat plain yogurt
1 tbsp. red wine vinegar
2 tsp. sugar

Directions:
Combine spinach, chicken, 1-cup raspberries, celery, water chestnuts, and almonds in a large bowl. In a separate bowl combine remaining raspberries, yogurt, vinegar and sugar; mix until blended and smooth. Divide salad among four plates; drizzle with raspberry dressing and serve.

Serves: 4

Shopping List:
2 bags fresh spinach leaves, 1 lb. low-fat chicken breast or tenders (or cooked chicken strips), 8 oz. nonfat plain yogurt, 1 pint fresh raspberries, celery, sliced water chestnuts, slivered almonds, red wine vinegar, sugar

Nutrition per serving		Exchanges
calories:	158	½ fruit
total fat (11%):	2 g	2 very lean meat
carbohydrate:	18 g	2 vegetable
cholesterol:	36 mg	
dietary fiber:	5 g	carbohydrate choice: 1
protein:	18 g	
sodium:	257 mg	

Raspberries are rich in ellagic acid (a powerful antioxidant that fights cancer), vitamin C (which reduces the risk of heart disease, cancer, infections, and cataracts), and insoluble fiber (which reduces the risk of constipation).

Berry-Rich Chicken Salad

Easy — Do Ahead

SALAD, SOUP SANDWICHES AND WRAPS

Ingredients:
¾ cup raspberry-lemon flavored nonfat yogurt
3 tbsp. nonfat mayonnaise
2 cups fresh raspberries
2 cups low-fat cooked chicken tenders, cubed
½ cup diced green onion
½ cup diced celery
½ cup diced jicama
½ cup diced red bell pepper
16 oz. endive, rinsed and drained
1 tbsp. sliced almonds

Directions:
Combine yogurt and mayonnaise in a medium bowl; add 1½ cups raspberries, cooked chicken, green onion, celery, jicama, and bell pepper to yogurt mixture; mix gently. Cover and refrigerate at least one hour before serving. Arrange endive on plates; top with raspberry-chicken salad. Garnish with remaining raspberries, and sprinkle with almonds.

Serves: 4

Shopping List:
1 pint raspberries, 6 oz. nonfat yogurt (raspberry-lemon or flavor of choice), nonfat mayonnaise, 1 lb. low-fat cooked chicken tenders, green onion, small jicama, celery, red bell pepper, 1 lb. endive, sliced almonds

Nutrition per serving		Exchanges
calories:	199	3 very lean meat
total fat (9%):	2 g	½ fruit
carbohydrate:	20 g	2 vegetable
cholesterol:	71 mg	
dietary fiber:	4 g	carbohydrate choice: 1
protein:	27 g	
sodium:	416 mg	

Raspberries are a great source of vitamin C, an antioxidant that helps fight fatigue and depression.

Bountiful Bean and Corn Salad

Easy — Do Ahead

Ingredients:
4 cups mixed salad greens, torn into bite-size pieces
16 oz. canned black beans, rinsed and drained
15 oz. canned corn kernels, drained
¾ cup red or yellow bell pepper, sliced thin
½ cup red onion, sliced thin
½ cup grape or cherry tomatoes
½ cup nonfat Thousand Island Dressing

Directions:
Combine all ingredients except salad dressing in large bowl; toss with dressing just before serving.

Serves: 4

Shopping List:
1 lb. bag mixed salad greens, 16 oz. can black beans, 15 oz. can corn kernels, red or yellow bell pepper, red onion, grape or cherry tomatoes, nonfat Thousand Island dressing

Nutrition per serving		Exchanges
calories:	246	1½ starch
total fat (4%):	1 g	4 vegetable
carbohydrate:	52 g	1 other carbohydrate
cholesterol:	0 mg	
dietary fiber:	10 g	carbohydrate choice: 3½
protein:	11 g	
sodium:	1,049 mg	

Great for pregnant moms! One cup of beans provides nearly a full day's supply of folate (400 micrograms), which helps prevent birth defects, low birth weight, and premature deliveries.

Cabbage and Cucumber Dill Salad

Easy — Do Ahead

Ingredients:
> 16 oz. package shredded cabbage
> 1 cucumber, peeled and sliced thin
> ½ cup sliced onions
> ½ cup frozen peppers, thawed and drained
> 2 tsp. dried dill weed
> ⅓ cup white vinegar
> ⅓ cup cold water
> ⅓ cup sugar

Directions:
> Combine cabbage, cucumber, onion, and peppers in a large bowl (make sure vegetables are dried); sprinkle with dill. Combine vinegar, water, and sugar in a sealed container; shake to mix until blended. Pour dressing over vegetables; toss until coated. Cover and refrigerate at least 6 hours before serving.

Serves: 4

Shopping List:
> 16 oz. package shredded cabbage (or cabbage mix), cucumber, onion, 10 oz. package frozen peppers, white vinegar, sugar, dried dill weed

Nutrition per serving		Exchanges
calories:	111	3 vegetable
total fat (0%):	0 g	1 other carbohydrate
carbohydrate:	29 g	
cholesterol:	0 mg	carbohydrate choice: 2
dietary fiber:	4 g	
protein:	2 g	
sodium:	24 mg	

Cabbage contains Indole-3 carbinol (I3C) and sulforaphane, making it a potent cancer-fighting food. Indole-3 carbinol acts as an anti-estrogen, taking harmful estrogens from the body that have been linked to breast cancer. Sulforaphane boosts the production of tumor-preventing enzymes.

SALAD, SOUP SANDWICHES AND WRAPS

Citrus Splashed Baby Greens

Easy — Do Ahead

Ingredients:
>   8 cups baby greens, washed and dried
>   ¼ cup chopped red onions
>   ½ cup grape or cherry tomatoes, cut in half
>   1 cup canned mandarin oranges, drained
>   ½ cup nonfat raspberry-vinaigrette dressing

Directions:
>   Combine all ingredients except salad dressing in large bowl; toss with dressing just before serving.

Serves: 4

Shopping List:
>   2 packages baby greens, red onion, grape or cherry tomatoes, 8 oz. can mandarin oranges, nonfat raspberry-vinaigrette dressing

Nutrition per serving

calories:	80
total fat (5%):	.4 g
carbohydrate:	17 g
cholesterol:	0 mg
dietary fiber:	3 g
protein:	2 g
sodium:	328 mg

Exchanges

½ fruit
1 vegetable
½ other carbohydrate

carbohydrate choice: 1

Tomatoes are the number one vegetable that people purchase at least once a week, and are the third most popular vegetable eaten by Americans.

Crunchy Coleslaw

Easy — Do Ahead

SALAD, SOUP SANDWICHES AND WRAPS

Ingredients:
½ cup nonfat mayonnaise
2 tsp. sugar
¾ tsp. cider vinegar
¼ tsp. pepper
2 cups shredded cabbage (red and green)
1 cup broccoli slaw
1 cup shredded carrots
½ cup sliced water chestnuts

Directions:
Combine mayonnaise, sugar, vinegar, and pepper in a small bowl; mix until blended. Toss remaining ingredients in a large bowl; spoon in dressing and toss until mixed. Cover and refrigerate several hours or overnight. For a tropical taste, add pineapple chunks.

Serves: 4

Shopping List:
1 lb. shredded cabbage (red and green), packaged broccoli slaw, 8 oz. shredded carrots, 6 oz. sliced water chestnuts, nonfat mayonnaise, sugar, pepper, cider vinegar

Nutrition per serving		Exchanges
calories:	62	3 vegetable
total fat (0%):	0 g	
carbohydrate:	14 g	carbohydrate choice: 1
cholesterol:	0 mg	
dietary fiber:	2 g	
protein:	1 g	
sodium:	232 mg	

Antioxidants (vitamins C, E, and beta-carotene) play a strong role in protecting your body from chemical reactions that cause heart disease, certain cancers and cataracts.

Enticingly Elegant Fruit Salad

Easy — Do Ahead

Ingredients:
4 kiwifruits, peeled and sliced
1 mango, peeled and diced
½ pineapple, peeled, cored, and diced
2 bananas
1 cup cantaloupe cubes
¼ cup orange juice
2 tbsp. powdered sugar
½ tsp. vanilla extract
⅛ ground ginger
⅛ ground anise
⅛ tsp. ground cloves

Directions:
Combine all the cut-up fruit in a large bowl. Combine orange juice, powdered sugar, vanilla, and spices in a small bowl; mix until completely blended and smooth. Drizzle dressing over fruit and serve immediately.

Serves: 4

Shopping List:
kiwifruits, mango, fresh pineapple, bananas, cantaloupe, orange juice, powdered sugar, vanilla extract, ground ginger, ground anise, ground cloves

Nutrition per serving
calories:	206
total fat (4%):	1 g
carbohydrate:	51 g
cholesterol:	0 mg
dietary fiber:	6 g
protein:	2 g
sodium:	10 mg

Exchanges
2½ fruit
½ other carbohydrate

carbohydrate choice: 3

Kiwifruit is rich in lutein, a carotenoid known to protect eyes from age-related macular degeneration, the leading cause of distorted vision and blindness in the elderly.

Fruit Salad with
Banana-Cream Dressing

Easy — Do Ahead

Ingredients:
- ¾ cup nonfat vanilla yogurt
- 1½ bananas, cut in pieces
- ¾ cup pine-orange-apple juice
- 1 cup cantaloupe cubes
- 1 cup honeydew melon cubes
- 1 cup fresh pineapple chunks
- ¾ cup sliced strawberries
- ½ cup fresh blueberries

Directions:

Combine yogurt, banana, and juice in blender or food processor; process until smooth and creamy. Combine fruit in large mixing bowl; toss with dressing and refrigerate at least 1 hour before serving.

Serves: 4

Shopping List:

cantaloupe, honeydew melon, fresh pineapple, strawberries, blueberries, 6 oz. nonfat vanilla yogurt, bananas, pine-orange-apple juice

Nutrition per serving

calories:	144
total fat (6%):	1 g
carbohydrate:	34 g
cholesterol:	1 mg
dietary fiber:	3 g
protein:	3 g
sodium:	37 mg

Exchanges

2 fruit

carbohydrate choice: 2

Bananas contain magnesium, an important mineral that increases resistance to yeast infections by decreasing inflammation and strengthening immune function.

Jicama, Carrot & Pepper Slaw

Easy — Do Ahead

Ingredients:
   2 cups red and yellow bell pepper, cut into thin strips
   ¾ lb. jicama, peeled and cut into thin strips
   1 cup shredded carrot
   3 tbsp. nonfat mayonnaise
   5 tbsp. lemon juice
   2 tbsp. sugar
   2½ tsp. garlic powder
   2 tsp. minced chipotle chilies
   1½ tsp. chili powder
   pepper to taste

Directions:
   Combine bell peppers, jicama, and carrots in a large bowl; toss until mixed. Combine remaining ingredients except pepper in food processor or blender and process until smooth. Pour dressing over vegetables; toss until coated. Sprinkle with pepper to taste; toss lightly. Cover and refrigerate 3 to 4 hours before serving.

Serves: 4

Shopping List:
   large bell peppers (any color), ¾ lb. jicama, 8 oz. package shredded carrots, nonfat mayonnaise, lemon juice, sugar, garlic powder, chili powder, chipotle chilies, pepper

Nutrition per serving		Exchanges
calories:	61	2 vegetable
total fat (0%):	0 g	½ other carbohydrate
carbohydrate:	18 g	
cholesterol:	0 mg	carbohydrate choice: 1
dietary fiber:	1 g	
protein:	1 g	
sodium:	72 mg	

Store chili powder in your freezer to maintain its levels of beta-carotene.

Marinated Green Bean & Cheese Salad

Easy — Do Ahead

Ingredients:
1 cup frozen whole green beans, cooked tender-crisp
1 cup chopped plum tomatoes
2 tbsp. sliced black olives
1½ tsp. Italian seasoning
¼ cup nonfat Italian dressing
4 oz. nonfat shredded mozzarella cheese

Directions:
Combine green beans, tomatoes, olives, Italian seasoning and salad dressing in a medium bowl; toss until coated. Cover and refrigerate at least 1 hour. Toss salad with shredded cheese just before serving.

Serves: 4

Shopping List:
10 oz. package frozen whole green beans, plum tomatoes, black olives, Italian seasoning, nonfat Italian salad dressing, 4 oz. nonfat shredded mozzarella cheese

Nutrition per serving		Exchanges
calories:	79	1 very lean meat
total fat (11%):	1 g	2 vegetable
carbohydrate:	7 g	
cholesterol:	0 mg	carbohydrate choice: ½
dietary fiber:	1 g	
protein:	10 g	
sodium:	374 mg	

Tomatoes, rich in lycopene, may reduce the risk of heart attack. According to the Mayo Clinic Newsletter, a study of more than 1,300 European men suggested that those consuming the most lycopene from foods had about half the risk of heart attack as men who consumed less.

New "B.L.T." Salad

Easy — Do Ahead

Ingredients:
 4 cups lettuce, torn in bite-size pieces
 2 cups cherry tomatoes, quartered
 1 cup cucumber, peeled and sliced thin
 ½ cup red onion, sliced thin
 4 oz. lox
 1 cup garlic-flavored bagel chips, broken in bite-size pieces
 ½ cup nonfat creamy Italian dressing

Directions:
 Combine all ingredients except dressing in a large salad bowl; pour dressing over salad, toss to mix, and serve.

Serves: 4

Shopping List:
 2 packages torn lettuce, 1 pint cherry tomatoes, cucumber, red onion, 4 oz. lox, garlic-flavored bagel chips, nonfat creamy Italian salad dressing

Nutrition per serving		Exchanges
calories:	109	2 vegetable
fat (17%):	2 g	½ other carbohydrate
carbohydrate:	17 g	½ lean meat
cholesterol:	7 mg	
dietary fiber:	2 g	carbohydrate choice: 1
protein:	8 g	
sodium:	921 mg	

Salmon is rich in B vitamins, responsible for fortifying the body's defenses against stress and depression.

Now THAT'S a FRUIT Salad!

Easy — Do Ahead

Ingredients:
1 cup mango cubes
1 Golden Delicious apple, peeled, cored, and thinly sliced
1 pear, thinly sliced
1 peach, thinly sliced
½ cup red seedless grapes, cut in half
6 dried apricot halves, cut into thin strips
1 tbsp. finely chopped candied ginger
½ cup orange juice
¼ cup apple juice
½ tsp. vanilla extract

Directions:
Combine all the fruit in a large bowl. Combine orange juice, apple juice, and vanilla in a small bowl and mix well; pour over fruit and toss until mixed. Cover and refrigerate 1 to 2 hours before serving. (Do not refrigerate more than 3 hours or fruit will become too soft.)

Serves: 6

Shopping List:
mangoes, Golden Delicious apple, pear, peach, red seedless grapes, dried apricot halves, orange juice, apple juice, candied ginger, vanilla extract

Nutrition per serving		Exchanges
calories:	100	1½ fruit
total fat (9%):	1 g	
carbohydrate:	25 g	carbohydrate choice: 1½
cholesterol:	0 mg	
dietary fiber:	3 g	
protein:	1 g	
sodium:	2 mg	

Pears are a good source of fiber; one medium pear has 16% of the fiber your body needs everyday for good health. Dried apricots are high in vitamin A and a good source of potassium.

Southwestern Bean and Corn Salad

Easy — Do Ahead

Ingredients:
2 cups canned whole green beans, drained
1¾ cups canned garbanzo beans, drained
1¾ cups canned red kidney beans, drained
1½ cups canned whole kernel corn, drained
½ cup chopped red bell pepper
1 onion, thinly sliced and separated into rings
¾ cup nonfat French-style salad dressing*
½ cup nonfat shredded cheddar cheese
8 cups shredded lettuce
8 oz. low-fat baked tortilla chips

Directions:
Combine beans, corn, bell pepper, and onion in a large bowl; toss with salad dressing. Cover bowl and refrigerate at least one hour. Toss with cheese. Serve over shredded lettuce with chips.

Serves: 8

Shopping List:
16 oz. can whole green beans, 15 oz. can garbanzo beans, 15 oz. can kidney beans, 12 oz. can whole kernel corn, nonfat French-style dressing (try nonfat Dorothy Lynch for spicy flavor), 4 oz. nonfat shredded cheddar cheese, 3 8-oz. low-fat baked tortilla chips

Nutrition per serving		Exchanges
calories:	302	2 starches
fat (9%):	3	
carbohydrate:	60 g	6 vegetable
cholesterol:	0 mg	
dietary fiber:	7 g	carbohydrate choice: 4
protein:	13 g	
sodium:	965 mg	

People who consume at least 5 servings of fruits and vegetables a day have a 31% lower risk of stroke.

Spinach-Chicken Salad

Easy — Do Ahead

Ingredients:
1 tbsp. nonfat chicken broth
1½ lb. low-fat chicken tenders, cut in 1-inch pieces
garlic powder to taste
onion powder to taste
pepper to taste
10 oz. packaged baby spinach
1 red onion, sliced into rings
2 grapefruit, peeled, seeded and sectioned
16 oz. can mandarin orange sections, drained
¾ cup nonfat salad dressing of choice

Directions:
Spray large nonstick skillet with cooking spray; add chicken broth and heat over medium-high heat. Sprinkle chicken tenders with garlic powder, onion powder, and pepper (to taste); add to skillet and cook, stirring frequently, 8 to 10 minutes until browned and cooked through. Arrange spinach leaves on large platter; top with sliced onion, grapefruit sections, and mandarin oranges. Drizzle with dressing just before serving.

Serves: 4

Shopping List:
1½ lb. low-fat chicken tenders, red onion, 10 oz. spinach leaves, grapefruit, 16 oz. canned mandarin oranges, 6 oz. nonfat salad dressing of choice, nonfat chicken broth, garlic powder, onion powder, pepper

Nutrition per serving		Exchanges
calories:	202	3 very lean meat
total fat (4%):	1 g	1 vegetable
carbohydrate:	23 g	1 fruit
cholesterol:	71 mg	½ other carbohydrate
dietary fiber:	3 g	
protein:	26 g	carbohydrate choice: 1½
sodium:	590 mg	

Oranges boost your body's ability to absorb iron.

Spinach-Mushroom Salad with Honey-Dijon Dressing

Easy — Do Ahead

Ingredients:
8 cups baby spinach leaves
2 pears, sliced thin
1 red onion, sliced thin
½ lb. sliced mushrooms
½ cup cooked egg whites, chopped
½ cup nonfat honey-Dijon salad dressing

Directions:
Combine all ingredients except salad dressing in a large bowl. Pour dressing into microwave-safe dish and heat on high for 30 to 45 seconds. Pour hot dressing over salad just before serving.

Serves: 4

Shopping List:
2 packages baby spinach leaves, pears, red onion, ½ lb. sliced mushrooms, eggs, nonfat honey-Dijon salad dressing

Nutrition per serving		Exchanges
calories:	152	4 vegetable
total fat (6%):	1 g	1 fruit
carbohydrate:	30 g	
cholesterol:	0 mg	carbohydrate choice: 2
dietary fiber:	6 g	
protein:	9 g	
sodium:	417 mg	

A single pear has a total fiber content of 5 grams; 4 out of the 5 grams are insoluble fiber, which benefits digestive health.

Sugar Sweet Melon Mix

Easy — Do Ahead

SALAD, SOUP, SANDWICHES AND WRAPS

Ingredients:
¼ cup sugar
¼ cup water
½ cantaloupe, cut in cubes or melon balls
1½ cups watermelon, cut in cubes or melon balls
1 cup honeydew melon, cut in cubes or melon balls
1 tbsp. orange juice

Directions:
Combine sugar and water in a small saucepan; bring to a boil over high heat. Reduce heat to low and simmer 1 minute. Pour sugar mixture into glass cup or small bowl and refrigerate at least 1 hour (until completely cooled). Combine cantaloupe, watermelon, and honeydew melon in a large bowl (or scoop out watermelon and use as a serving bowl). Stir orange juice into sugar mixture; drizzle over melon medley before serving.

Serves: 4

Shopping List:
cantaloupe, watermelon, honeydew melon, sugar, orange juice

Nutrition per serving		Exchanges
calories:	94	1 fruit
total fat (0%):	0 g	½ other carbohydrate
carbohydrate:	24 g	
cholesterol:	0 mg	carbohydrate choice: 1½
dietary fiber:	1 g	
protein:	1 g	
sodium:	9 mg	

Cantaloupe is rich in vitamin C and beta-carotene, which are antioxidant compounds that protect against cancer, heart disease, and cataracts.

Sweet and Sassy Slaw

Easy — Do Ahead

Ingredients:
¼ cup cider vinegar
¼ cup nonfat plain yogurt
¼ cup nonfat buttermilk
1½ tbsp. sugar
1½ tbsp. honey
½ tsp. minced garlic
¼ tsp. pepper
16 oz. shredded cabbage (Savoy and red)
½ cup shredded carrot
1 cup peeled and sliced apples
1 cup sliced red bell pepper

Directions:
Combine vinegar, yogurt, buttermilk, sugar, honey, garlic, and pepper in a medium bowl; mix until blended and smooth. Combine remaining ingredients in a large bowl and toss to mix. Pour dressing over cabbage mixture and toss until well coated. Cover and refrigerate at least one hour before serving.

Serves: 4

Shopping List:
16 oz. shredded cabbage (combine Savoy and red), 8 oz. package shredded carrots, apple, red bell pepper, cider vinegar, nonfat plain yogurt, nonfat buttermilk, sugar, honey, minced garlic, pepper

Nutrition per serving		Exchanges
calories:	114	½ fruit
total fat (0%):	0 g	2 vegetable
carbohydrate:	28 g	1 other carbohydrate
cholesterol:	<1 mg	
dietary fiber:	4 g	carbohydrate choice: 2
protein:	3 g	
sodium:	45 mg	

Cabbage, one of the cruciferous vegetables, is rich in Indole-3-carbinol, a phytochemical that may reduce breast and skin cancer tumors and lower bladder cancer risk.

Sweet Potato Salad

Easy — Do Ahead

Ingredients:
½ cup nonfat sour cream
½ cup nonfat mayonnaise
2 tbsp. orange juice
2 tbsp. chopped chives
1 tbsp. curry powder
2⅔ to 3 cups canned sweet potatoes in light syrup,
    drained well
¾ cup chopped celery
pepper to taste

Directions:
In a small bowl, combine sour cream, mayonnaise, orange juice, chives and curry powder; mix well. Cut sweet potatoes into 1-inch cubes; combine with celery in large bowl. Pour dressing over potatoes; sprinkle with pepper and toss until coated. Cover and refrigerate at least 1 hour before serving.

Serves: 6

Shopping List:
2 29-oz. cans cut sweet potatoes in light syrup, celery, 4 oz. nonfat sour cream, 4 oz. nonfat mayonnaise, orange juice, chopped chives, curry powder, pepper

Nutrition per serving		Exchanges
calories:	213	2 starch
total fat (4%):	1 g	1 other carb
carbohydrate:	48 g	
cholesterol:	0 mg	carbohydrate choice: 3
dietary fiber:	5 g	
protein:	5 g	
sodium:	234 mg	

**Sweet potatoes are rich in vitamin A,
an antiwrinkling agent.**

Taco Salad

Easy — Do Ahead

Ingredients:
6 low-fat flour tortillas
14 oz. Gimme Lean meat
  substitute
1¼ oz. taco seasoning mix
water
6 cups shredded lettuce

¾ cup nonfat shredded
  Cheddar cheese
15 oz. can chopped
  tomatoes, drained well
6 tbsp. chopped green onion
1½ cups chunky salsa

Directions:
Preheat oven to 400 degrees. Spray ovenproof bowl with cooking spray; place 1 tortilla over bowl and spray lightly with cooking spray. Bake in oven 3 to 5 minutes until crisp. Remove tortilla and let cool completely at room temperature. Repeat with remaining tortillas. Spray large nonstick skillet with cooking spray; add "meat" to skillet and cook, stirring frequently until browned (about 5 to 7 minutes). Follow directions on taco seasoning packet; add seasonings and water as indicated. Cook according to directions. Arrange 2 cups shredded lettuce in each "tortilla bowl." Top with ½ to ¾ cup "meat" mix; sprinkle with shredded cheese, tomatoes, and green onion. Top with chunky salsa and serve.

Serves: 6

Shopping List:
14 oz. Gimme Lean meat substitute, 1¼ oz. taco seasoning mix, 2 packages shredded lettuce, 3 oz. nonfat shredded Cheddar cheese, 15 oz. can chopped tomatoes, low-fat flour tortillas, 12 oz. chunky salsa, green onion

Nutrition per serving		Exchanges
calories:	259	1 starch
total fat (7%):	2 g	5 vegetable
carbohydrate:	38 g	1 very lean meat
cholesterol:	0 mg	
dietary fiber:	4 g	carbohydrate choice: 2½
protein:	19 g	
sodium:	1,440 mg	

**It takes up to 17 times as much acreage to produce
20 pounds of beef protein as it takes
to produce 356 pounds of soybean protein.**

Thai-Style Broccoli Slaw

Easy — Do Ahead

Ingredients:
2½ cups Rainbow Salad
1 cup peeled and chopped cucumber
¼ cup chopped green onion
3 tbsp. rice wine vinegar
3 tbsp. minced cilantro
1½ tbsp. sugar
⅛ tsp. ground ginger

Directions:
Combine slaw mixture, cucumber, and green onion in a large bowl; mix well. Combine remaining ingredients in Ziploc bag or sealed container; shake until ingredients are blended. Pour over slaw and toss until coated. Cover and refrigerate at least 1 hour before serving; toss slaw and drain excess liquid.

Serves: 4

Shopping List:
16 oz. package Rainbow Salad (package of shredded broccoli, cauliflower, carrot, and red cabbage or substitute broccoli-slaw mixture), cucumber, green onion, cilantro, rice wine vinegar, sugar, ground ginger

Nutrition per serving

calories:	46	
total fat (0%):	0 g	
carbohydrate:	12 g	
cholesterol:	0 mg	
dietary fiber:	2 g	
protein:	1 g	
sodium:	13 mg	

Exchanges
1 vegetable
½ other carbohydrate

carbohydrate choice: 1

Broccoli aids digestion and promotes good bowel health.

Tossin' It Creamy Veggie Salad

Easy — Do Ahead

Ingredients:
8 oz. cooked pasta
1 cup broccoli florets
1 cup cauliflower florets
1 cup sliced carrot
1 cup cherry tomatoes, cut in half
¼ cup nonfat Parmesan cheese
1 cup nonfat Ranch dressing

Directions:
Combine pasta and vegetables in a medium bowl and toss until mixed. Sprinkle with cheese; toss with salad dressing. Cover and refrigerate at least 1 hour before serving.

Serves: 4

Shopping List:
broccoli florets, cauliflower florets, packaged sliced carrots, cherry tomatoes, 8 oz. pasta (rotini, rotelle, macaroni, etc.), 8 oz. nonfat Ranch dressing, nonfat Parmesan cheese

Nutrition per serving		Exchanges
calories:	195	1½ starch
total fat (5%):	1 g	2 vegetable
carbohydrate:	39 g	½ other carbohydrate
cholesterol:	19 mg	
dietary fiber:	4 g	carbohydrate choice: 2½
protein:	7 g	
sodium:	721 mg	

Tomatoes are a powerful source of coumarins and phenolic acids, which have been found to block nitrosamine (a cancer-causing agent) that might otherwise be formed in the body.

Zucchini-Jicama Salad

Easy — Do Ahead

Ingredients:

1 jicama, peeled and grated
1 zucchini, unpeeled and grated
¾ cup shredded carrot
1 cup chopped red onion
3 tbsp. chopped fresh parsley
½ cup nonfat red wine vinaigrette salad dressing

Directions:

Combine all ingredients except salad dressing; toss to mix. Pour dressing over salad just before serving; toss lightly.

Serves: 4

Shopping List:

jicama, zucchini, 8 oz. package shredded carrot, red onion, fresh parsley, nonfat red wine vinaigrette salad dressing

Nutrition per serving

calories:	100
total fat (0%):	0 g
carbohydrate:	33 g
cholesterol:	0 mg
dietary fiber:	2 g
protein:	3 g
sodium:	149 mg

Exchanges

carbohydrate choice: 2

Carrots contain two powerful antioxidants: beta-carotene and alpha-carotene.

Creamy Caesar Salad Splash

Easy — Do Ahead

Ingredients:
1 cup nonfat mayonnaise
⅓ cup skim milk
2 tbsp. cider vinegar
1 tsp. sugar
1 tsp. pepper
1½ tsp. garlic powder
2 tbsp. nonfat Parmesan cheese
1 tsp. Worcestershire sauce

Directions:
Combine ingredients in food processor, blender, or bowl; blend until smooth and creamy. Refrigerate several hours or overnight before serving. Dressing will keep in refrigerator up to 1 month in airtight container.

Serves: 8

Shopping List:
8 oz. nonfat mayonnaise, skim milk, cider vinegar, Worcestershire sauce, nonfat Parmesan cheese, sugar, pepper, garlic powder

SALAD, SOUP, SANDWICHES AND WRAPS

Nutrition per serving		Exchanges
calories:	42	½ other carbohydrate
total fat (0%):	0 g	
carbohydrate:	8 g	carbohydrate choice: ½
cholesterol:	<.5 mg	
dietary fiber:	0 g	
protein:	1 g	
sodium:	233 mg	

Save over 40 grams of fat with low-fat dressing!

Creamy Tarragon Salad Dressing

Easy — Do Ahead

Ingredients:
 ¼ cup nonfat mayonnaise
 ¼ cup nonfat sour cream
 ½ tsp. crushed tarragon leaves
 ⅛ tsp. pepper

Directions:
 Combine all ingredients in a small bowl; mix until blended. Cover and refrigerate several hours before serving over fresh greens.

Serves: 4

Shopping List:
 nonfat mayonnaise, nonfat sour cream, tarragon leaves, pepper

Nutrition per serving		Exchanges
calories:	26	½ other carbohydrate
total fat (0%):	0 g	
carbohydrate:	4 g	carbohydrate choice: ½
cholesterol:	0 mg	
dietary fiber:	6 g	
protein:	1 g	
sodium:	7 mg	

One out of every four American adults has high blood pressure that can be controlled by diet.

Dilly of a Dressing

Easy — Do Ahead

Ingredients:
½ cup nonfat mayonnaise
2 tbsp. Dijon mustard
1 tsp. chopped fresh dill weed
1 tsp. chopped chives
4 tbsp. red wine vinegar
¼ tsp. pepper

Directions:
Combine all ingredients in a bowl and mix until creamy and smooth. Serve over mixed greens, pasta, or potato salad.

Serves: 4

Shopping List:
nonfat mayonnaise, Dijon mustard, red wine vinegar, fresh dill weed, chives, pepper

Nutrition per serving		Exchanges
calories:	54	1 other carbohydrate
total fat (17%):	1 g	
carbohydrate:	12 g	carbohydrate choice: 1
cholesterol:	0 mg	
dietary fiber:	0 g	
protein:	0 g	
sodium:	323 mg	

96.8 million American adults (51% of the population) have high cholesterol levels (over 200) that can be controlled by diet.

Thousand Island Dressing

Easy — Do Ahead

Ingredients:
- 1 cup nonfat mayonnaise
- ⅓ cup skim milk
- 3 tbsp. chili sauce
- 1⅓ tbsp. sweet pickle relish
- 2 tbsp. cider vinegar
- 1 tsp. sugar
- 1 tsp. garlic powder
- 1 tsp. pepper

Directions:

Combine all ingredients in food processor, blender, or bowl; and mix until completely blended. Refrigerate several hours or overnight before serving. Store in airtight container up to 1 month. Great as salad dressing or sandwich spread.

Serves: 8

Shopping List:

8 oz. nonfat mayonnaise, skim milk, chili sauce, sweet pickle relish, cider vinegar, sugar, garlic powder, pepper

Nutrition per serving

calories:	47
total fat (0%):	0 g
carbohydrate:	10 g
cholesterol:	<.5 mg
dietary fiber:	0 g
protein:	1 g
sodium:	312 mg

Exchanges

½ other carbohydrate

carbohydrate choice: ½

The U.S. surgeon general's report on health and nutrition stated that two-thirds of all deaths linked to heart disease, cancer, and associated diseases are diet-related.

Caribbean Chicken Pockets

Easy — Do Ahead

Ingredients:
¼ cup nonfat mayonnaise
¼ cup nonfat plain yogurt
½ cup chopped green chilies
½ tsp. garlic powder
4 pita pockets, cut in half (not all the way through)
¾ lb. skinless, boneless chicken tenders, cooked and
    shredded
½ cup chopped red onion
½ cup peeled and chopped cucumber
1 mango, peeled and chopped
½ cup shredded lettuce

Directions:
Combine mayonnaise, yogurt, chilies, and garlic powder in a small bowl; mix until completely blended. Generously spread mayonnaise mixture on inside of pita pockets. In a medium bowl, combine chicken, red onions, cucumber, and mango; toss until mixed. Divide chicken mixture among pitas; sprinkle with shredded lettuce and serve.

Serves: 4

Shopping List:
¾ lb. low-fat chicken tenders, nonfat mayonnaise, nonfat plain yogurt, red onion, cucumber, shredded lettuce, mango, 4 oz. can chopped green chilies, pita pockets, garlic powder

Nutrition per serving		Exchanges
calories:	248	1 starch
total fat (4%):	1 g	3 vegetable
carbohydrate:	36 g	½ other carbohydrate
cholesterol:	53 mg	2 very lean meat
dietary fiber:	3 g	
protein:	23 g	carbohydrate choice: 2½
sodium:	738 mg	

Mangoes contain 20% more beta-carotene than cantaloupe and 50% more than apricots.

Chicken Caesar Pita Pocket

Easy

Ingredients:
¾ lb. zucchini, cut into strips
¾ lb. yellow squash, cut into strips
1 cup green bell pepper, cut into strips
1 cup red and/or yellow bell pepper, cut into strips
1 lb. low-fat chicken tenders, cut in 1-inch pieces
⅓ cup nonfat Caesar salad dressing
Romaine lettuce
4 whole-wheat pita breads (or pockets), split open
⅓ cup nonfat Parmesan cheese
2 tbsp. chopped fresh parsley

Directions:
Line baking sheet with foil and spray with cooking spray. Preheat broiler. In a Ziploc bag or large bowl, combine zucchini, squash, peppers, chicken and salad dressing; toss until all ingredients are well coated. Spread mixture onto baking sheet; broil 6 to 8 minutes until chicken is completely cooked through and vegetables are lightly browned. Place lettuce leaves in pita bread; fill with chicken-vegetable mixture and sprinkle with Parmesan cheese and parsley.

Serves: 4

Shopping List:
1 lb. low-fat chicken tenders, ¾ lb. zucchini, ¾ lb. yellow squash, green bell pepper, red and/or yellow bell pepper, fresh parsley, Romaine lettuce, nonfat Caesar salad dressing, nonfat Parmesan cheese, whole-wheat pita bread (or pockets)

Nutrition per serving		Exchanges
calories:	287	3 very lean meat
total fat (6%):	2 g	1 starch
carbohydrate:	37 g	2 vegetable
cholesterol:	71 mg	1 other carbohydrate
dietary fiber:	4 g	
protein:	32 g	carbohydrate choice: 2½
sodium:	733 mg	

Parsley contains myristicin and apiol, two compounds found to increase urination (especially helpful during premenstrual bloating). Parsley is also a good source of vitamin C and folate.

Grilled Eggplant Sandwich

Easy

Ingredients:
1 lb. eggplant, cut ¼-inch-thick slices
1 red onion, thinly sliced
pepper to taste
garlic-flavored cooking spray
4 slices sourdough bread slices, toasted
1 cup nonfat pasta sauce with mushrooms or vegetables
½ cup nonfat shredded mozzarella cheese

Directions:
Preheat oven to 450 degrees. Line baking sheet with foil and spray with cooking spray. Place eggplant slices on baking sheet; top with onion slices. Sprinkle pepper over top and spray lightly with garlic-flavored cooking spray. Bake eggplant and onions 7 to 8 minutes until softened. Remove from oven and preheat broiler on high heat. Arrange bread slices on baking sheet; spread each slice with pasta sauce. Top with baked eggplant-onions, pasta sauce, and cheese. Place open-faced sandwiches under broiler and cook 45 to 60 seconds until cheese is melted and lightly browned.

Serves: 4

Shopping List:
8 oz. nonfat pasta sauce with mushrooms or vegetables, 1 lb. eggplant, red onion, nonfat shredded mozzarella cheese, sourdough bread, garlic-flavored cooking spray, pepper

Nutrition per serving		Exchanges
calories:	174	1 starch
total fat (5%):	1 g	3 vegetable
carbohydrate:	30 g	½ very lean meat
cholesterol:	0 mg	
dietary fiber:	1 g	carbohydrate choice: 3
protein:	9 g	
sodium:	591 mg	

**The average U.S. teenager eats over
1,817 pounds of food in a year.**

SALAD, SOUP, SANDWICHES AND WRAPS

No-Cook Chicken-Cheddar Wraps

Easy

Ingredients:
- ⅓ cup nonfat sour cream
- ⅓ cup chunky salsa
- 2 tsp. nonfat mayonnaise
- 1⅓ cups cooked low-fat chicken tenders, cubed
- ⅔ cup nonfat shredded Cheddar cheese
- 2 tbsp. chopped green chilies
- 4 low-fat flour tortillas
- ¾ cup shredded lettuce

Directions:

Combine all ingredients except lettuce and tortillas in a medium bowl; mix until blended. Arrange tortillas on flat surface; sprinkle with shredded lettuce and top with chicken mixture. Roll tortillas and serve with additional salsa and sour cream, if desired.

Serves: 4

Shopping List:

¾ lb. low-fat chicken tenders (or cooked chicken strips), nonfat shredded Cheddar cheese, nonfat sour cream, chunky salsa, nonfat mayonnaise, chopped green chilies, packaged shredded lettuce, low-fat flour tortillas

Nutrition per serving

calories:	280
total fat (3%):	.1 g
carbohydrate:	38 g
cholesterol:	47 mg
dietary fiber:	3 g
protein:	28 g
sodium:	1,012 mg

Exchanges

2 very lean meat
2 starch
2 vegetable

carbohydrate choice: 2½

Vitamin B_{12} deficiency can result in anemia and fatigue; poultry is a good source of vitamin B_{12}.

Open-Faced Vegetarian Grilled Cheese Sandwich

Easy

Ingredients:
8 tsp. Dijon mustard
4 slices sourdough bread
1 cup nonfat shredded Cheddar cheese, divided
½ cup canned artichoke hearts; drained, dried, chopped and divided
1 cup roasted red peppers; drained, chopped, and divided

Directions:
Spray large nonstick skillet with cooking spray; spread 2 teaspoons Dijon mustard on each bread slice. Top with ½ cup cheese, 2 tablespoons artichoke hearts and ½ cup peppers. Cook sandwiches (one or two at a time) in skillet over medium heat until cheese is melted and bread is lightly browned. Remove from skillet and place on foil-lined baking sheet. When all sandwiches are grilled, place under broiler (high heat) until lightly browned on top.

Serves: 4

Shopping List:
4 oz. nonfat shredded Cheddar cheese, 8 oz. can artichoke hearts, 8 oz. jar roasted red peppers, sliced sourdough bread, Dijon mustard

Nutrition per serving

calories:	161
total fat (11%):	2 g
carbohydrate:	24 g
cholesterol:	0 mg
dietary fiber:	1 g
protein:	11 g
sodium:	588 mg

Exchanges

1 starch
2 vegetable
½ very lean meat

carbohydrate choice: 3

When our body becomes infected, we use up essential nutrients like vitamins A, C, and E and minerals like zinc, potassium, chromium, iron and copper. Unless these nutrients are replaced, the stage is set for more serious disorders.

Salsa Chicken Wraps

Easy — Do Ahead

Ingredients:
- 4 low-fat flour tortillas
- 2 cups cooked rice
- 1 cup chunky salsa
- 6 oz. low-fat cooked chicken breast strips
  (Southwestern flavored, if available)
- ½ cup nonfat shredded Cheddar cheese

Directions:

Warm tortillas in microwave or oven. Combine cooked rice, salsa, and chicken strips in medium bowl and mix lightly. Spoon mixture down center of tortilla; sprinkle with cheese. Roll tortilla and serve with additional salsa, if desired.

Serves: 4

Shopping List:

low-fat flour tortillas, 6 oz. low-fat cooked chicken breast strips (southwestern-flavored, if available), 8 oz. chunky salsa, nonfat shredded Cheddar cheese, rice (white, brown, or Mexican-flavored)

Nutrition per serving

calories:	303
total fat (6%):	2 g
carbohydrate:	50 g
cholesterol:	27 mg
dietary fiber:	2 g
protein:	19 g
sodium:	559 mg

Exchanges

1½ very lean meat
2 starch
4 vegetable

carbohydrate choice: 3

Chicken is a symbol of health—high in protein, iron, niacin, and zinc. Stick with skinless, boneless white meat that is significantly lower in fat, calories, cholesterol, and sodium than white or dark meat with skin.

Shredded Barbecue Chicken and Slaw Sandwich

Easy – Do Ahead

Ingredients:

½ cup nonfat mayonnaise
3 tbsp. white vinegar, divided
½ tsp. sugar
¼ tsp. celery seeds
1 tsp. pepper, divided
3½ cups broccoli-slaw mixture
(or Rainbow Salad)

¾ cup barbecue sauce
1 lb. low-fat chicken breasts
or tenders, cooked
and shredded
4 whole-wheat pita
pockets

Directions:

Combine mayonnaise, 2 tablespoons vinegar, sugar, celery seeds, and ½ tsp. pepper in a large bowl; mix until completely blended and smooth. Gradually add slaw mixture, mixing well after each addition until slaw is coated with dressing. Cover and refrigerate 10 to 15 minutes. In a medium saucepan, combine barbecue sauce, shredded chicken, remaining vinegar, and pepper; cover and cook over medium-low heat until heated through (about 10 to 15 minutes). Barbecued chicken mixture can be microwaved on high 3 to 4 minutes until heated through, if preferred. Spoon chicken mixture into pita pocket; top with slaw and serve.

Serves: 6

Shopping List:

1 lb. low-fat cooked chicken tenders, 6 oz. barbecue sauce, nonfat mayonnaise, white vinegar, packaged broccoli-slaw mixture (or Rainbow Salad), whole-wheat pita pockets, sugar, pepper, celery seeds

Nutrition per serving

calories:	198
total fat (5%):	1 g
carbohydrate:	26 g
cholesterol:	47 mg
dietary fiber:	2 g
protein:	20 g
sodium:	734 mg

Exchanges

1 starch
3 vegetable
1½ very lean protein

carbohydrate choice: 2

Chicken is a good source of vitamin E, which may delay heart disease by preventing the oxidation of LDL (bad) cholesterol.

Southwestern Wraps with Black Bean and Corn Salad

Easy — Do Ahead

Ingredients:
16 oz. package shredded lettuce
15 oz. can black beans, rinsed and drained
15 oz. can corn kernels, drained
½ cup chunky salsa
4 Southwestern wraps (or tortillas)

Directions:
In a medium bowl, combine shredded lettuce, beans, corn, and salsa; toss lightly until mixed. Spoon mixture down center of wrap (or tortilla); fold top of tortilla down; fold in sides and roll up. Secure with a toothpick, if needed. Serve with additional salsa, if desired.

Serves: 4

Shopping List:
Southwestern wraps (or low-fat flour tortillas), 16 oz. package shredded lettuce, 15 oz. can black beans, 15 oz. can corn kernels, chunky salsa

Nutrition per serving		Exchanges
calories:	367	3½ starch
total fat (5%):	2 g	4 vegetable
carbohydrate:	75 g	
cholesterol:	0 mg	carbohydrate choice: 5
dietary fiber:	13 g	
protein:	17 g	
sodium:	1,324 mg	

Fiber fights heart disease; breast, colon, and other cancers; artherosclerosis; high cholesterol; high blood pressure; constipation; digestive problems; diabetes; and obesity by carrying the "bad stuff" out of our systems.

Sprouted Turkey Wrap

Easy — Do Ahead

Ingredients:
  4 low-fat whole-wheat or plain tortillas
  ½ cup honey mustard
  12 oz. roasted turkey breast, sliced thin
  1 tomato, sliced thin
  1 cucumber, peeled and sliced thin
  1 cup bean sprouts

Directions:
  Spread each tortilla with 1 tablespoon honey mustard (or to taste). Layer sliced turkey, tomato, and cucumber; top with sprouts. Fold top of tortilla down; fold in sides and roll up. Secure with toothpick. Serve, or cover and refrigerate.

Serves: 4

Shopping List:
  low-fat whole-wheat or plain tortillas, 12 oz. roasted turkey breast, tomato, cucumber, bean sprouts, honey mustard

Nutrition per serving		Exchanges
calories:	339	2 starch
total fat (5%):	2 g	2 vegetable
carbohydrate:	47 g	3 very lean meat
cholesterol:	71 mg	½ other carbohydrate
dietary fiber:	5 g	
protein:	33 g	carbohydrate choice: 3
sodium:	608 mg	

Cucumbers act as a mild diuretic and may contain phytochemicals that can lower blood cholesterol.

Turkey 'n' Cheese Tortilla Wraps

Easy — Do Ahead

Ingredients:
- ¼ cup nonfat mayonnaise
- 1½ tbsp. Dijon mustard
- 4 low-fat flour tortillas
- 12 oz. (nonfat or low-fat) oven-roasted turkey breast
- 4 oz. nonfat Swiss cheese slices
- ½ cup shredded carrot
- ½ cup shredded jicama

SALAD, SOUP, SANDWICHES AND WRAPS

Directions:

Combine mayonnaise and mustard in small cup; mix until blended. Spread one side of each tortilla with mayo-mustard mixture. Divide turkey breast (about 3 to 4 slices each) among tortillas; top with Swiss cheese, shredded carrot, and jicama. Roll tortillas, wrap in plastic wrap, and refrigerate until ready to serve.

Serves: 4

Shopping List:

12 oz. low-fat oven roasted turkey breast, packaged shredded carrots, jicama, low-fat flour tortillas, 4 oz. nonfat Swiss cheese slices, nonfat mayonnaise, Dijon mustard

Nutrition per serving		Exchanges
calories:	343	3 vegetable
total fat (3%):	1 g	2 starch
carbohydrate:	41 g	3 very lean meat
cholesterol:	71 mg	
dietary fiber:	3 g	carbohydrate choice: 3
protein:	37 g	
sodium:	974 mg	

Poultry is a good source of vitamin B$_6$ which is used in amino-acid building and fatty-acid metabolism.

CREATIVE
CHICKEN
AND
TURKEY

◆ ◆ ◆

Why'd the turkey and the chicken cross the road?

To find their way into the meal plans of health-conscious eaters!

According to research released by the National Chicken Council and U.S. Poultry & Egg Association, American consumers are eating eighty-one *pounds of chicken per person per year! At the same time, per capita consumption of turkey has more than doubled in twenty years!*

Why? Convenience, Versatility, *and* Health Value!

These poultry items are low-fat, high-protein food sources that supply easily absorbed iron and zinc, but learn to HANDLE THEM WITH CARE!

- Refrigerate poultry immediately! Never leave it sitting at room temperature!
- Store poultry in well-sealed plastic bag so the juices don't leak onto other foods.
- For safety sake: thaw poultry in the refrigerator. It takes approximately twenty-four hours to thaw a 4-pound chicken in the refrigerator; cut-up poultry will thaw in three to nine hours.
- For quick thawing, use your microwave. Thawing time will vary according to size of poultry.
- ALWAYS wash hands, countertops, cutting boards, and other utensils used to prepare raw poultry before they come in contact with other foods.
- ALWAYS cook poultry well-done, not medium or rare. To check for doneness, pierce poultry with a fork?if juices run clear, not pink, it's done.
- Marinade used to soak raw poultry should NEVER be reused on cooked food.

Apricot Baked Chicken

Easy — Do Ahead — Freeze

Ingredients:
¼ cup apricot preserves, divided
3 tbsp. honey mustard
½ cup cornflake crumbs
2 tbsp. flour
1½ lb. low-fat chicken breasts (boneless, skinless)
½ tsp. garlic powder

Directions:
Preheat oven to 350 degrees. Spray large baking dish with cooking spray. Combine 3 tablespoons preserves, honey mustard, cornflake crumbs, and flour in a small bowl; mix well (mixture will be thick) and set aside. Arrange chicken breasts in single layer in dish; spread chicken on both sides with remaining preserves. Sprinkle with garlic powder. Spread apricot mixture on chicken and bake 20 to 25 minutes until chicken is cooked through. Turn broiler on high heat; broil chicken 45 to 60 seconds until lightly browned and crisp.

Serves: 4

Shopping List:
1½ lb. (boneless, skinless) low-fat chicken breasts, apricot preserves, honey mustard, cornflake crumbs, flour, garlic powder

CREATIVE CHICKEN AND TURKEY

Nutrition per serving		Exchanges
calories:	285	2 other carbohydrates
total fat (3%):	1 g	5 very lean meat
carbohydrate:	30 g	
cholesterol:	106 mg	carbohydrate choice: 2
dietary fiber:	<.5 g	
protein:	36 g	
sodium:	690 mg	

In order to minimize fat intake when eating poultry, select breast and thigh portions (muscle meat) over internal organs; remove skin before cooking or eating.

Barbecued Chicken

Easy — Do Ahead — Freeze

Ingredients:
1 lb. low-fat chicken breasts (boneless, skinless)
garlic powder to taste
onion powder to taste
pepper to taste
½ cup barbecue sauce
2 to 3 drops Tabasco pepper sauce
1 tbsp. Dijon mustard
1 cup chopped green onion

Directions:
Preheat oven to 375 degrees. Line baking sheet with foil and spray with cooking spray. Sprinkle chicken on both sides with garlic powder, onion powder, and pepper. Combine barbecue sauce, Tabasco, Dijon mustard, and green onion in a small bowl; stir until mixed. Spread half the barbecue mixture over chicken; cover pan with foil and bake 15 minutes. Increase heat to 450 degrees; remove cover, brush with remaining barbecue sauce and bake until lightly browned and cooked through (about 10 to 15 minutes).

Serves: 4

Shopping List:
1 lb. low-fat chicken breasts (boneless, skinless), green onion, barbecue sauce, Tabasco pepper sauce, Dijon mustard, garlic powder, onion powder, pepper

Nutrition per serving

calories:	159
total fat (6%):	1 g
carbohydrate:	14 g
cholesterol:	71 mg
dietary fiber:	0 g
protein:	23 g
sodium:	829 mg

Exchanges
1 other carbohydrate
3 very lean meat

carbohydrate choice: 1

Chicken is a good source of protein, iron, niacin, and zinc.

"C.B.C." Burrito Supreme

Easy — Do Ahead

Ingredients:
¾ lb. cooked chicken breast strips
½ cup frozen corn kernels, thawed and drained
½ cup canned black beans, drained
½ cup chopped green chilies, drained
4 low-fat whole-wheat flour tortillas
½ cup cilantro, chopped
½ cup chunky salsa
½ cup nonfat shredded Cheddar cheese

Directions:
Combine cooked chicken strips, corn, beans, and chilies in a microwave-safe dish; mix ingredients and heat on high for 3 to 5 minutes until heated through. Wrap tortillas in paper towels; cook on high in microwave 45 to 60 seconds until softened. Top each tortilla with chicken mixture; sprinkle with cilantro, salsa, and cheese. Roll tortilla and serve.

Serves: 4

Shopping List:
¾ lb. low-fat cooked chicken strips, 10 oz. frozen corn kernels, canned black beans, canned chopped green chilies, low-fat whole-wheat flour tortillas, fresh cilantro, chunky salsa, nonfat shredded Cheddar cheese

Nutrition per serving		Exchanges
calories:	384	1 lean meat
total fat (12%):	5 g	2½ very lean meat
carbohydrate:	48 g	2½ starch
cholesterol:	64 mg	2 vegetable
dietary fiber:	5 g	
protein:	37 g	carbohydrate choice: 3
sodium:	815 mg	

In order to consume the Recommended Daily Allowance for fiber from fast food, you would have to consume over 4,000 calories and 200 grams of fat each day—in a little over one year, the average person would gain over 200 pounds!

"Ch-ch-ch" Enchiladas

Easy — Do Ahead — Freeze

Ingredients:
8 6-inch low-fat corn tortillas
1½ lb. low-fat cooked chicken breast strips, shredded
10 oz. frozen pepper strips, thawed and drained
½ cup low-fat shredded Cheddar cheese
½ cup nonfat shredded Cheddar cheese
4 oz. chopped green chilies
2 cups chunky salsa, divided

Directions:
Preheat oven to 350 degrees. Spray 9 x 13-inch baking dish with cooking spray. Arrange tortillas on flat surface; divide chicken and peppers among tortillas and place in the center. Combine low-fat and nonfat Cheddar cheese in Ziploc bag or bowl; mix well. Top chicken and peppers with 2 tablespoons cheese, 1 to 2 teaspoons chilies and 2 tablespoons salsa (each). Roll tortillas and secure with toothpick. Arrange in baking dish; top with remaining salsa and cheese. Cover with foil and bake 20 minutes. Remove foil and bake 5 minutes until cheese is lightly browned. Serve with low-fat enchilada sauce or salsa.

Serves: 4

Shopping List:
low-fat corn tortillas (6-inch), 1½ lb. low-fat cooked chicken breast strips, 10 oz. frozen pepper strips, 4 oz. can chopped green chilies, nonfat shredded Cheddar cheese, low-fat shredded Cheddar cheese, 16 oz. chunky salsa

Nutrition per serving		Exchanges
calories:	332	2 starch
total fat (11%):	4 g	2 vegetable
carbohydrate:	39 g	3½ very lean meat
cholesterol:	69 mg	
dietary fiber:	5 g	
protein:	35 g	carbohydrate choice: 2½
sodium:	1,711 mg	

Bell peppers are an excellent source of beta-carotene, an antioxidant that delays the effects of aging.

Chicken Fajitas with Cilantro Sauce

Average — Do Ahead — Freeze

Ingredients:

2 tbsp. lime juice
½ tsp. garlic powder
1 to 2 dashes hot pepper sauce
1 lb. low-fat chicken tenders,
   thawed if frozen
½ cup nonfat sour cream
½ cup cilantro leaves

1 onion, sliced thin
10 oz. frozen pepper strips,
   thawed and drained
low-fat flour tortillas
8 oz. package shredded
   lettuce
salsa (optional)

Directions:

Combine lime juice, garlic powder, and pepper sauce in a large Ziploc bag; shake to blend ingredients. Add chicken tenders to bag and toss until well-coated. Refrigerate several hours. Combine sour cream and cilantro leaves in a food processor or blender; process until smooth. Spoon into bowl, cover and refrigerate until ready to serve. Spray large nonstick skillet with cooking spray and heat over medium-high heat. Add chicken (without marinade), sliced onions, and peppers to skillet; cook, stirring frequently, until chicken is browned and cooked through (about 5 to 6 minutes). Wrap tortillas in paper towels; heat in microwave on high heat for 45 to 60 seconds. To assemble fajitas: place a flour tortilla on a plate or flat surface. Sprinkle shredded lettuce down center and top with chicken-vegetable mixture. Spoon sour cream-cilantro sauce on top; fold tortilla around filling and serve with salsa, if desired.

Serves: 4

Shopping List:

1 lb. low-fat chicken breast tenders, 4 oz. nonfat sour cream, 10 oz. package frozen pepper strips, low-fat flour tortillas, onion, 8 oz. package shredded lettuce, fresh cilantro leaves, lime juice, hot pepper sauce, garlic powder, salsa (optional)

Nutrition per serving		**Exchanges**
calories:	277	3 very lean meat
total fat (3%):	1 g	2 starch
carbohydrate:	35 g	1 vegetable
cholesterol:	71 mg	
dietary fiber:	4 g	carbohydrate choice: 2
protein:	31 g	
sodium:	642 mg	

Bell peppers are rich in vitamin A.

Chicken Santa Fe

Easy — Do Ahead

Ingredients:
1 lb. low-fat chicken breasts (boneless, skinless)
extra-spicy Mrs. Dash seasoning to taste
¾ tsp. dried oregano
½ tsp. chili powder
¼ tsp. ground cinnamon
1 cup canned chopped tomatoes, drained
½ cup canned black beans, drained
¼ cup fresh cilantro, chopped
nonfat sour cream (optional)

Directions:
Spray large nonstick skillet with cooking spray and heat over medium-high heat. Generously sprinkle chicken breasts with Mrs. Dash seasoning; cook over medium heat 7 to 8 minutes per side, until center juices run clear when pierced with a fork. Remove skillet from heat; wrap chicken in foil and keep warm. Respray skillet with cooking spray and heat over medium heat. Add dried oregano, chili powder, and cinnamon; cook, stirring constantly, 15 to 30 seconds. Stir in tomatoes and beans; bring to a boil over high heat. Stir in cilantro. Serve over chicken breasts with sour cream on the side, if desired.

Serves: 4

Shopping List:
1 lb. low-fat chicken breasts (boneless, skinless), 15½ oz. can chopped tomatoes, 15½oz. can black beans, fresh cilantro, extra-spicy Mrs. Dash seasoning, dried oregano, chili powder, ground cinnamon, nonfat sour cream (optional)

Nutrition per serving
calories:	143
total fat (6%):	1 g
carbohydrate:	8 g
cholesterol:	71 mg
dietary fiber:	1 g
protein:	26 g
sodium:	490 mg

Exchanges
3 very lean meat
½ vegetable
½ starch

carbohydrate choice: ½

Poultry is rich in three essential B vitamins: niacin, vitamin B_6 and vitamin B_{12}.

Crispy-Coated Southwestern Chicken
Average — Do Ahead — Freeze

Ingredients:

⅓ cup wheat germ
⅔ cup seasoned bread crumbs
2 tsp. chili powder
2 tsp. ground cumin
1 tbsp. dried onion flakes
½ tsp. garlic powder

¼ tsp. cayenne pepper
¼ cup egg substitute
2 tbsp. skim milk
1 lb. low-fat chicken breasts
  (boneless, skinless)
chunky salsa, heated

Directions:

Preheat oven to 400 degrees. Line baking sheet with foil and spray with cooking spray. Combine wheat germ, bread crumbs, chili powder, cumin, onion flakes, garlic powder, and cayenne pepper in a shallow dish; mix well. Combine egg substitute and milk in shallow bowl; mix well. Dip chicken in egg mixture; dredge through crumb mixture until completely coated. Arrange chicken on baking sheet sprinkle with remaining crumb mixture. Bake 20 to 25 minutes until chicken is completely cooked through (juices will run clear when pierced with fork). Pour salsa into microwave-safe bowl; heat on high 30 to 45 minutes until warm and serve with chicken.

Serves: 4

Shopping List:

1 lb. low-fat chicken breasts (boneless, skinless), egg substitute, skim milk, chunky salsa, wheat germ, seasoned bread crumbs, chili powder, ground cumin, dried onion flakes, garlic powder, cayenne pepper

Nutrition per serving		Exchanges
calories:	178	3 very lean meat
total fat (10%):	2 g	½ starch
carbohydrate:	12 g	½ other carbohydrate
cholesterol:	71 mg	
dietary fiber:	2 g	carbohydrate choice: 1
protein:	28 g	
sodium:	352 mg	

Cumin contains curcurmin, a potent anticancer phytochemical, presently being evaluated by the National Cancer Institute as an anticarcinogenic agent.

Dijon Chicken Breasts with Swiss Cheese

Easy — Do Ahead — Freeze

Ingredients:
¼ cup Dijon mustard
2 tbsp. nonfat chicken broth
1 tsp. garlic powder
1 tsp. onion powder
½ tsp. pepper
1 lb. low-fat chicken breasts (boneless, skinless)
4 oz. nonfat (or low-fat) Swiss cheese slices

Directions:
Preheat oven to 375 degrees. Line baking sheet with foil and spray with cooking spray. Combine mustard, chicken broth, garlic powder, onion powder, and pepper in a Ziploc bag; close and shake until ingredients are well mixed. Add chicken to mustard sauce and shake until well coated. Arrange chicken breasts on baking sheet. Bake 20 minutes until golden brown. Top each chicken breast with one slice Swiss cheese; bake 3 to 5 minutes until cheese is melted.

Serves: 4

Shopping List:
1 lb. low-fat chicken breasts (boneless, skinless), 4 oz. nonfat (or low-fat) Swiss cheese slices, Dijon mustard, nonfat chicken broth, garlic powder, onion powder, pepper

Nutrition per serving		Exchanges
calories:	161	4½ very lean meat
total fat (6%):	1 g	
carbohydrate:	4 g	carbohydrate choice: 0
cholesterol:	71 mg	
dietary fiber:	0 g	
protein:	29 g	
sodium:	857 mg	

Making the simple substitution of low-fat dairy products for whole dairy products can save 30 to 40 calories and 4 to 5 grams of fat per ounce.

Fajitas in a Flash

Easy — Do Ahead — Freeze

Ingredients:
¾ lb. low-fat chicken tenders
1½ tsp. extra-spicy Mrs. Dash seasoning
16 oz. frozen peppers and onions
1 envelope fajita seasoning mix
4 low-fat flour tortillas
chunky salsa (optional for topping)
nonfat sour cream (optional for topping)

Directions:
Spray large nonstick skillet or wok with cooking spray; heat over medium-high heat. Generously sprinkle chicken tenders with Mrs. Dash seasoning and add to skillet; cook 5 minutes until chicken is no longer pink. Stir in peppers and onions; cook 2 to 3 minutes until softened. Sprinkle fajita seasoning over top and mix well. Cook 2 to 3 minutes until heated through. Wrap tortillas in paper towel and heat in microwave for 45 to 60 seconds (or wrap in foil and heat in 400 degree oven 3 to 5 minutes). Serve with salsa and sour cream.

Serves: 4

Shopping List:
1 lb. low-fat chicken tenders, 16 oz. package frozen peppers and onions, 1 envelope fajita seasoning mix, low-fat flour tortillas, extra spicy Mrs. Dash seasoning, nonfat sour cream (optional), chunky salsa (optional)

Nutrition per serving		Exchanges
calories:	251	2 very lean meat
total fat (4%):	1 g	1 starch
carbohydrate:	36 g	2 vegetable
cholesterol:	53 mg	½ other carbohydrate
dietary fiber:	4 g	
protein:	22 g	carbohydrate choice: 2
sodium:	1,341 mg	

Boneless, skinless chicken breasts are a good low-fat source of protein and selenium, an antioxidant mineral that is often lacking in our diets.

Finger-Lickin' Chicken Strips

Easy — Do Ahead — Freeze

Ingredients:

¼ cup honey mustard
1 cup nonfat sour cream
1 cup dry-mashed-potato mix
 (garlic-flavored), if available
3 tbsp. nonfat Parmesan cheese
1 tsp. garlic powder

1 tsp. onion powder
1 tsp. paprika
½ tsp. pepper
½ cup egg substitute
1 tbsp. skim milk
1 lb. low-fat chicken tenders

Directions:

Combine honey mustard and sour cream in a small dish; mix until blended. Cover with plastic wrap and refrigerate until ready to serve. Preheat oven to 475 degrees. Line baking sheet(s) with foil and spray with cooking spray. Combine potato mix, Parmesan cheese, garlic powder, onion powder, paprika, and pepper in a shallow dish; mix well. Combine egg substitute and milk in medium bowl and mix with fork until frothy. Dip chicken in egg mixture; dredge in potato mixture until well coated. Place chicken tenders in a single layer on baking sheet; spray lightly with cooking spray. Bake 3 to 4 minutes; turn chicken over, spray top with cooking spray and bake 2 to 3 minutes until golden brown, crispy and cooked through. Serve with honey-mustard sauce (or other condiments of choice).

Serves: 4

Shopping List:

1 lb. low-fat chicken tenders, dry-mashed-potato mix, 8 oz. nonfat sour cream, skim milk, egg substitute, nonfat Parmesan cheese, honey mustard, garlic powder, onion powder, paprika, pepper

Nutrition per serving

calories:	262
total fat (3%):	1 g
carbohydrate:	27 g
cholesterol:	71 mg
dietary fiber:	2 g
protein:	33 g
sodium:	611 mg

Exchanges

4 very lean meat
1 starch
1 other carbohydrate

carbohydrate choice: 2

Chicken is a high-quality source of lean protein that contributes to increased energy levels and improved reaction time.

Grilled Chicken with Fruit 'n' Spicy Salsa

Easy — Do Ahead

Ingredients:
¾ cup chunky home-style applesauce
½ cup chunky salsa
½ tsp. extra-spicy Mrs. Dash seasoning
1 tbsp. lime juice
1 lb. low-fat chicken breasts (skinless, boneless)
garlic powder to taste
onion powder to taste
pepper to taste
2 tbsp. low-sodium teriyaki sauce

Directions:
Combine applesauce, salsa, Mrs. Dash seasoning, and lime juice in a medium bowl; mix well. Cover and refrigerate at least one hour before serving. Spray large nonstick skillet with cooking spray and heat over medium-high heat. Sprinkle chicken breasts with garlic powder, onion powder, and pepper; brush with teriyaki sauce on both sides. Cook chicken 4 to 6 minutes per side until browned and cooked through. Brush with additional sauce while cooking, if desired. Serve with spicy apple salsa.

Serves: 4

Shopping List:
1 lb. low-fat chicken breasts (boneless, skinless), 8 oz. chunky home-style applesauce, chunky salsa, teriyaki sauce, lime juice, garlic powder, onion powder, pepper, extra-spicy Mrs. Dash seasoning

Nutrition per serving		Exchanges
calories:	151	3 very lean meat
total fat (6%):	1 g	½ fruit
carbohydrate:	12 g	½ other carbohydrate
cholesterol:	71 mg	
dietary fiber:	1 g	carbohydrate choice: 1
protein:	24 g	
sodium:	582 mg	

Chicken fights fatigue as an iron-rich food.

Honey Dijon Chicken

Easy — Do Ahead — Freeze

Ingredients:
1 lb. low-fat chicken breasts (boneless, skinless)
2 tsp. garlic powder
½ cup honey Dijon mustard
2 tbsp. nonfat chicken broth
1½ tbsp. mustard seeds

Directions:
Preheat oven to 400 degrees. Line baking sheet with foil and spray with cooking spray. Arrange chicken breasts on baking sheet; sprinkle on both sides with garlic powder. Combine mustard and chicken broth in a small bowl and mix until blended. Generously brush mixture over chicken and sprinkle with mustard seeds. Bake 25 to 30 minutes until chicken is cooked through.

Serves: 4

Shopping List:
1 lb. low-fat chicken breasts (boneless, skinless), honey Dijon mustard, nonfat chicken broth, mustard seeds, garlic powder

Nutrition per serving		Exchanges
calories:	183	3 very lean meat
total fat (10%):	2 g	1 other carbohydrate
carbohydrate:	14 g	
cholesterol:	71 mg	carbohydrate choice: 1
dietary fiber:	0 g	
protein:	24 g	
sodium:	718 mg	

Chicken is power-packed with disease-fighting, energy-boosting vitamins and minerals, most notably three essential B vitamins: niacin (reduces cholesterol and lowers the risk of heart attack); vitamin B$_6$ (maintains immunity and healthy nervous system); and vitamin B$_{12}$ (essential for healthy brain function).

Honey Sweet Chicken Kabobs

Easy — Do Ahead

Ingredients:
¾ cup honey
¾ cup diced red bell peppers
⅓ cup rice vinegar
⅓ cup pineapple juice
¾ tsp. garlic powder
3 to 4 dashes hot pepper sauce
1½ lb. low-fat chicken tenders, cut in chunks
1½ cups pineapple chunks
1 red bell pepper, cut in large pieces

Directions:
Preheat oven to 350 degrees. Line baking sheet(s) with foil and spray with cooking spray. Combine honey, diced peppers, vinegar, pineapple juice, garlic powder, and pepper sauce in a small saucepan; bring to a boil over medium-high heat. Reduce heat to low and cook, stirring frequently, until mixture begins to thicken. Using small to medium bamboo sticks (presoaked in water), alternately place chicken pieces, pineapple, and red pepper. Arrange in single layer on baking sheet. Pour sauce over kabobs and bake 10 to 15 minutes until chicken is no longer pink and sauce is glazed over. These can be prepared ahead and baked just before serving.

Serves: 6

Shopping List:
1 lb. low-fat chicken tenders, 16 oz. can pineapple chunks (or fresh pineapple), 2 red bell peppers, honey, rice vinegar, pineapple juice, hot pepper sauce, garlic powder

Nutrition per serving		Exchanges
calories:	134	1 very lean meat
total fat (0%):	0 g	1 fruit
carbohydrate:	22 g	½ other carbohydrates
cholesterol:	35 mg	
dietary fiber:	.5 g	carbohydrate choice: 1½
protein:	12	
sodium:	139	

Honey may help relieve ulcers by preventing the growth of ulcer-causing bacteria.

Marinated Turkey Roast

Easy — Do Ahead — Freeze

Ingredients:
¾ cup nonfat chicken broth
1 cup water
½ cup low-sodium soy sauce
⅓ cup lemon juice
¾ tsp. ground ginger
1 tsp. garlic powder
½ tsp. pepper
1 ½ lb. whole turkey breast

Directions:
Combine chicken broth, water, soy sauce, lemon juice, ginger, garlic powder and pepper in a Ziploc bag; shake well until ingredients are blended. Remove 1 cup of marinade from bag and set aside. Place turkey breast in bag; turn until coated. Seal and refrigerate overnight. Drain marinade and discard. Preheat oven to 400 degrees. Spray roasting pan with cooking spray; place turkey in pan. Brush with reserved marinade. Bake 10 minutes until lightly browned. Reduce heat to 325 degrees; brush turkey with marinade and bake 35 to 40 minutes until cooked through (when pierced with fork, juices should run clear).

Serves: 4

Shopping List:
1 ½ lb. whole turkey breast, nonfat chicken broth, low-sodium soy sauce, lemon juice, ground ginger, garlic powder, pepper

Nutrition per serving		Exchanges
calories:	259	7 ½ meat
total fat (3%):	1 g	
carbohydrate:	5 g	carbohydrate choice: 0
cholesterol:	141 mg	
dietary fiber:	<.5 g	
protein:	24 g	
sodium:	1,314 mg	

Turkey breast can provide anywhere from 16 to 62% of the daily value for niacin. Poultry also contains vitamin B$_{12}$, essential for healthy brain function.

Raspberry-Glazed Chicken Tenders

Easy — Do Ahead — Freeze

Ingredients:
½ cup seedless red raspberry preserves
2 tsp. minced garlic
3 tbsp. low-sodium soy sauce
3 tbsp. rice vinegar
1½ lb. low-fat chicken tenders
2 tsp. sesame seeds

Directions:
Combine preserves, garlic, pepper, soy sauce, and vinegar in a large Ziploc bag. Seal bag and shake until ingredients are well mixed. Add chicken tenders to bag; toss until coated. Seal bag and refrigerate 2 to 4 hours. Preheat oven to 400 degrees. Line baking sheet with foil and spray with cooking spray. Arrange chicken in single layer on baking sheet; reserve marinade. Bake chicken 12 to 15 minutes. While chicken is cooking, pour marinade into saucepan; bring to a boil over high heat. Cook 8 to 10 minutes until sauce thickens. Brush tenders with sauce; sprinkle with sesame seeds. Bake chicken tenders 12 to 15 minutes longer until cooked through.

Serves: 6

Shopping List:
1½ lb. low-fat chicken tenders, seedless red raspberry preserves, low-sodium soy sauce, rice wine vinegar, minced garlic, sesame seeds

CREATIVE CHICKEN AND TURKEY

Nutrition per serving		Exchanges
calories:	186	3½ very lean meat
total fat (5%):	1 g	1 fruit
carbohydrate:	20 g	
cholesterol:	71 mg	carbohydrate choice: 1
dietary fiber:	<.5 g	
protein:	24 g	
sodium:	540 mg	

***Garlic helps cleanse the blood, prevent clots
and boost the immune system, reducing
the risk of heart disease and stroke.***

Snappy Chicken Stir-Fry

Easy

Ingredients:
1 lb. low-fat chicken tenders
1 tsp. garlic powder
8 oz. frozen pea pods, thawed and drained
10 oz. frozen broccoli, cauliflower, and water chestnut
   mixture, thawed and drained
½ cup stir-fry sauce
2 cups cooked brown rice

Directions:
Spray large nonstick skillet or wok with cooking spray and heat over medium-high heat. Generously sprinkle chicken tenders with garlic powder. Cook 3 to 5 minutes until chicken is no longer pink and is cooked through. Add vegetables and cook 1 to 2 minutes, just until tender-crisp. Add stir-fry sauce and cook until heated through. Toss stir-fry mixture with brown rice and serve.

Serves: 4

Shopping List:
1 lb. low-fat chicken tenders, 8 oz. package frozen pea pods, 10 oz. package frozen broccoli, cauliflower, and water chestnut mixture, stir-fry sauce, brown rice, garlic powder

Nutrition per serving		Exchanges
calories:	297	1½ starch
total fat (6%):	2 g	2 vegetable
carbohydrate:	42 g	3 very lean meat
cholesterol:	71 mg	1 other carbohydrate
dietary fiber:	1 g	
protein:	28 g	carbohydrate choice: 3
sodium:	386 mg	

Broccoli contains lutein and lycopene, antioxidants that may reduce the risk of knee osteoarthritis.

Sweet & Sour Pineapple Chicken

Average

Ingredients:

16 oz. can pineapple tidbits, drain and reserve juice
½ cup ketchup
½ cup water
3 tbsp. low-sodium soy sauce
3 tbsp. cider vinegar
3 tbsp. brown sugar
3 tbsp. cornstarch
¼ tsp. pepper

¼ tsp. ground ginger
2 tbsp. nonfat chicken broth
1 lb. low-fat chicken tenders
¾ cup chopped green onion
12 oz. frozen pepper strips, thawed and drained
6 oz. sliced water chestnuts, drained
cooked rice, white or brown

Directions:

Combine reserved pineapple juice, ketchup, water, soy sauce, vinegar, brown sugar, cornstarch, pepper and ginger in a medium bowl; mix until blended. Spray large nonstick skillet or wok with cooking spray; pour chicken broth into skillet and heat over medium-high heat. Add chicken tenders and green onions to skillet; cook, stirring frequently until lightly browned and cooked through (6 to 7 minutes). Pour pineapple juice mixture into skillet; cook, stirring constantly, over medium heat until sauce becomes bubbly and thick. Stir in pineapple, pepper strips, and water chestnuts; reduce heat to medium-low, cover and cook until heated through. Serve over cooked rice.

Serves: 4

Shopping List:

1 lb. low-fat chicken tenders, 16 oz. can pineapple tidbits, 6 oz. can water chestnuts, 12 oz. package frozen pepper strips, green onion, rice (white or brown), nonfat chicken broth, ketchup, brown sugar, low-sodium soy sauce, cider vinegar, cornstarch, pepper, ground ginger

Nutrition per serving		Exchanges
calories:	339	2 very lean meat
total fat (3%):	1 g	1 fruit
carbohydrate:	59 g	2 starch
cholesterol:	71 mg	1 vegetable
dietary fiber:	2 g	½ other carbohydrate
protein:	26 g	
sodium:	1,016 mg	carbohydrate choice: 4

Peppers are rich in antioxidants and bioflavonoids.

CREATIVE CHICKEN AND TURKEY

Sweet and Spicy Chicken Breasts

Easy — Do Ahead — Freeze

Ingredients:
12 oz. crushed pineapple, undrained
1 tbsp. chopped green onion
1½ tbsp. crushed garlic
⅛ tsp. pepper
1½ tbsp. honey mustard
1 lb. low-fat chicken tenders

Directions:
Combine crushed pineapple, green onion, garlic, pepper, and honey mustard in a Ziploc bag; shake to mix well. Add chicken tenders and toss until coated. Refrigerate 1 hour or overnight. Spray large nonstick skillet with cooking spray and heat over medium-high heat. Remove chicken tenders from bag (reserve marinade) and cook 6 to 8 minutes until browned and cooked through. Pour marinade over chicken; bring to a boil over high heat. Reduce heat to low and simmer 5 minutes. Serve over rice, potatoes or pasta, if desired.

Serves: 4

Shopping List:
1 lb. low-fat chicken tenders, 12 oz. canned crushed pineapple, green onion, crushed garlic, honey mustard, pepper

Nutrition per serving		Exchanges
calories:	167	1 fruit
total fat (5%):	1 g	3 very lean meat
carbohydrate:	16 g	
cholesterol:	71 mg	carbohydrate choice: 1
dietary fiber:	1 g	
protein:	24 g	
sodium:	324 mg	

Pineapple is rich in manganese, a trace mineral essential for certain enzymes to metabolize protein and carbohydrates.

SCRUMPTIOUS SEAFOOD AND FISH

Get Hooked On Fish for Good Health

An excellent source of protein (*a 6-ounce serving provides about 40 grams of protein*) and **low in saturated fat,** a **fish-rich diet** contributes to . . .

- boosting intake of heart-healthy omega-3 fatty acids that help prevent heart disease (especially from such cold-water fish as canned white tuna, salmon, mackerel, sardines, herring, and anchovies)
- decreasing the risk of colon, breast, and other cancers by reducing the body's production of prostaglandins, which encourage tumor growth
- reducing insulin, blood glucose, and triglyceride levels while increasing levels of heart-protective HDL cholesterol
- supporting nerve and brain function (Vitamin B_{12})and boosting immunity (zinc)
- reducing lung inflammation
- promoting larger-birth-weight babies
- reducing calorie and fat intake (as a healthy alternative to other protein-rich foods that are high in saturated fat)

Not at all fishy fish facts:

- For those who have suffered one heart attack, consuming as little as two 3-ounce fish meals per week can reduce the chances of suffering a second fatal heart attack.
- Eating more cold-water fish may help keep arteries from closing after angioplasty (a medical procedure that unclogs blocked blood vessels in the heart).
- British researchers found that men who eat small servings of fish three times a week, while reducing their intake of animal fats, cut the death rate from colon cancer by one-third.
- Eating fish may improve breathing difficulties in those who smoke or live in a smoke-filled household. If you're trying to quit smoking or live with someone who smokes, eating fish is a healthy way to reduce the damage, but it won't stop it!
- Fish oil may contribute to reducing the severity of menstrual cramps and other PMS symptoms.
- Since omega-3 fatty acids are essential for forming healthy nerve cells, eating omega-3-rich fish might stave off depression.

Stop Floundering over Your Favorite Fish Picks

Firm fish Full flavor	Medium-firm Good flavor	Delicate fish Mild flavor	Slim Seafood
swordfish	salmon	flounder	shrimp
monkfish	halibut	orange roughy	scallops
shark	cod	crab	
fresh tuna	catfish	lobster	
halibut	grouper	oysters	
mahi-mahi	haddock	mussels	
	red snapper		

Best cooking methods:
> **broil** (*Cajun Halibut*), **bake** (*Scallops Parmesan*), **grill** (*Tuna with Pineapple-Orange Salsa*), **microwave** (*Seafood Tortilla Wraps*), **poach** (*Salmon*), **stir-fry** (*Tuna*), steam (*fresh or frozen*), or **oven-fry** (*Crunchy Parmesan Fillets*)

DON'T sabotage the sensational value of seafood and fish with deep-fried coatings or by . . .
Smothering,
Saturating, or
Soaking them in butter-rich, oily, or mayo-based sauces!

For Safety's Sake . . .
- DON'T leave fish or seafood out of the refrigerator or freezer.
- DON'T store fish or seafood in the refrigerator for more than 1 to 2 days.
- DON'T reuse any dishes or utensils used to handle raw fish until thoroughly cleaned.
- DON'T marinate fish or seafood at room temperature; keep refrigerated until ready to cook.
- DON'T forget to wash your hands with soapy water before and after handling raw seafood.

SCRUMPTIOUS SEAFOOD AND FISH

Baked Scallops Parmesan

Easy — Do Ahead— Freeze

Ingredients:
½ cup seasoned bread crumbs
garlic powder to taste
¼ cup nonfat Parmesan cheese
1 lb. sea scallops, rinsed and drained
½ cup nonfat plain yogurt

Directions:
Preheat oven to 450 degrees. Line baking sheet with foil and spray with cooking spray. Combine bread crumbs, garlic powder, and Parmesan cheese on paper plate. Dip scallops in yogurt and roll in bread-crumb mixture to coat. Place on baking sheet; spray lightly with cooking spray and bake 10 to 15 minutes until golden brown and cooked through.

Serves: 4

Shopping List:
1 lb. sea scallops, nonfat plain yogurt, seasoned bread crumbs, garlic powder, nonfat Parmesan cheese

Nutrition per serving		Exchanges
calories:	148	½ other carbohydrate
total fat (9%):	2 g	3 very lean meat
carbohydrate:	9 g	
cholesterol:	39 mg	carbohydrate choice: ½
dietary fiber:	0 g	
protein:	23 g	
sodium:	277 mg	

Shellfish contain large amounts of vitamin B_{12}, important for keeping nerves healthy and making red blood cells. Low intake of vitamin B_{12} can lead to memory loss, confusion, slow reflexes, and fatigue.

Cajun Halibut with Mayo-Dijon Sauce

Easy — Do Ahead

Ingredients:

½ cup nonfat mayonnaise
½ cup nonfat sour cream
3 tbsp. sweet pickle relish
2 tsp. Dijon mustard
1 tbsp. paprika
1½ tsp. dried crushed oregano
1½ tsp. dried thyme

1½ tsp. garlic powder
1½ tsp. onion powder
½ tsp. cayenne pepper
1 lb. halibut steaks (thawed
   if frozen)
garlic-flavored cooking
   spray

Directions:

Combine mayonnaise, sour cream, pickle relish, and Dijon mustard in a small bowl; mix well. Cover and refrigerate at least 1 hour before serving. Line baking sheet with foil and spray with cooking spray. Preheat broiler on high heat. Combine paprika, oregano, thyme, garlic powder, onion powder, and cayenne pepper (Cajun spice mix) in a Ziploc bag; shake well until spices are blended. Arrange halibut steaks on baking sheet; spray top of halibut with garlic-flavored cooking spray. Sprinkle with Cajun spice mix. Turn halibut over; spray tops and sprinkle with Cajun spice. Broil halibut 5 to 6 minutes per side (10 to 12 minutes total) until fish flakes easily when tested with fork. Serve with mayo-Dijon sauce.

Serves: 4

Shopping List:

1 lb. halibut steaks, nonfat mayonnaise, nonfat sour cream, sweet pickle relish, Dijon mustard, paprika, dried crushed oregano, dried thyme, garlic powder, onion powder, cayenne pepper, garlic-flavored cooking spray

Nutrition per serving		Exchanges
calories:	199	1 other carbohydrate
total fat (14%):	3 g	1 lean meat
carbohydrate:	14 g	2 very lean meat
cholesterol:	36 mg	
dietary fiber:	0 g	carbohydrate choice: 1
protein:	26 g	
sodium:	423 mg	

Fish provides super heart-healthy benefits:
High in potassium and low in sodium,
fish rates high for helping to keep
blood pressure in a healthy range.

Cajun Shrimp

Easy

Ingredients:
garlic-flavored cooking spray
1 lb. large shrimp, peeled and deveined (tails on)
1 tbsp. Cajun seasoning mix
2 tsp. paprika

Directions:
Spray large nonstick skillet with garlic-flavored cooking spray and heat over medium-high heat. Add shrimp to skillet; lightly spray with cooking spray and sprinkle generously with Cajun seasoning and paprika. Cook, turning frequently, 5 to 6 minutes until shrimp is cooked through and lightly browned. Serve over cooked rice (brown, white, pilaf, wild, etc.).

Serves: 6

Shopping List:
1 lb. large shrimp (tails on), Cajun seasoning, paprika, garlic-flavored cooking spray

Nutrition per serving

calories:	88
total fat (10%):	1 g
carbohydrate:	2 g
cholesterol:	117 mg
dietary fiber:	0 g
protein:	15 g
sodium:	230 mg

Exchanges
2½ very lean meat

carbohydrate choice: 0

Shrimp provides protein and chromium, which prevents cravings by keeping insulin levels stable and boosts the metabolization of fats and carbohydrates.

Crab Cakes with Zip

Easy — Do Ahead

Ingredients:

2 tbsp. prepared horseradish
¾ cup nonfat mayonnaise, divided
1 tbsp. onion powder
1 tbsp. lemon juice
1 tsp. Tabasco pepper sauce
¼ cup egg substitute
1 lb. canned crabmeat, drained

1 cup seasoned bread crumbs
½ tsp. garlic powder
1¼ tbsp. dried parsley
1½ tsp. dry mustard
1 tsp. dried tarragon
¼ tsp. cayenne pepper

Directions:

Combine horseradish, ½ cup mayonnaise, onion powder, lemon juice, and Tabasco sauce in a small bowl and mix well; cover and refrigerate until ready to serve. Combine egg substitute, crabmeat, bread crumbs, ¼ cup mayonnaise, garlic powder, parsley, dry mustard, tarragon, and cayenne pepper in a medium bowl; mix well. Shape mixture into 8 patties. Spray nonstick skillet with cooking spray and heat over medium-high heat. Add crab cakes to skillet (do not overcrowd) and cook 3 to 5 minutes per side. Remove from skillet and wrap in foil to keep warm. Remove skillet from heat and respray with cooking spray. Repeat cooking with remaining crab mixture. Serve with horseradish sauce.

Serves: 4 (2 patties per serving)

Shopping List:

1 lb. canned crabmeat, egg substitute, nonfat mayonnaise, prepared horseradish, Tabasco pepper sauce, lemon juice, seasoned bread crumbs, garlic powder, dried parsley, dry mustard, dried tarragon, cayenne pepper, onion powder

Nutrition per serving		Exchanges
calories:	208	1 lean meat
total fat (13%):	3 g	2 very lean meat
carbohydrate:	19 g	1 starch
cholesterol:	113 mg	
dietary fiber:	<.5 g	carbohydrate choice: 1
protein:	23 g	
sodium:	1,066 mg	

Shellfish is an excellent source of iodine, a difficult-to-obtain trace mineral essential for healthy thyroid function.

SCRUMPTIOUS SEAFOOD AND FISH

Fish in a Flash

Easy — Do Ahead

Ingredients:
1 lb. halibut fillets, or any firm fish
2 tsp. Mrs. Dash seasoning
½ cup lime juice
1 tsp. onion powder
16 oz. can chopped tomatoes, undrained
2 tsp. dried parsley

Directions:
Preheat oven to 350 degrees. Spray shallow baking dish with cooking spray. Place halibut fillets in baking dish; sprinkle generously with Mrs. Dash seasoning. Combine lime juice, onion powder, tomatoes, and parsley in a small bowl; mix well. Pour tomato mixture over fish and bake, uncovered, 15 to 20 minutes, until fish flakes easily with a fork.

Serves: 4

Shopping List:
1 lb. halibut fillets (or any firm fish), 16 oz. can chopped tomatoes, Mrs. Dash seasoning, onion powder, dried parsley, lime juice

Nutrition per serving

calories:	157
total fat (17%):	3 g
carbohydrate:	8 g
cholesterol:	36 mg
dietary fiber:	1 g
protein:	25 g
sodium:	247 mg

Exchanges

2 vegetable
1 lean meat
2 very lean meat

carbohydrate choice: ½

Limes are high in vitamin C, a powerful antioxidant that the body also uses to manufacture collagen.

Grilled Tuna with Pineapple-Orange Salsa

Easy — Do Ahead

Ingredients:
 1 cup pineapple chunks, drained
 ¼ cup orange juice
 1 tbsp. chopped sweet onion (e.g. Vidalia, Walla Walla)
 ½ cup chopped red bell pepper
 24 oz. tuna steaks
 2 tsp. garlic powder
 2 tbsp. low-sodium teriyaki sauce

Directions:
 Combine pineapple, orange juice, onion, and red pepper in a medium bowl and mix well; cover and refrigerate until ready to serve. Sprinkle tuna steaks on both sides with garlic powder. Brush generously with teriyaki sauce. Heat broiler or grill to medium-high heat. Cook (grill or broil) tuna 5 minutes; turn tuna, brush with teriyaki sauce, and cook an additional 5 minutes. Serve with pineapple salsa.

Serves: 4

Shopping List:
 24 oz. tuna steaks, 8 oz. can pineapple chunks, orange juice, sweet onion, red bell pepper, teriyaki sauce, garlic powder

Nutrition per serving		Exchanges
calories:	228	½ fruit
total fat (8%):	2 g	5 very lean meat
carbohydrate:	11 g	½ other carbohydrate
cholesterol:	77 mg	
dietary fiber:	1 g	carbohydrate choice: 1
protein:	41 g	
sodium:	410 mg	

Onions contain dozens of compounds that help reduce cholesterol, thin the blood and prevent hardening of the arteries—all preventive measures against heart disease. The most protective compounds include flavonoids (especially quercetin) and sulfur compounds.

SCRUMPTIOUS
SEAFOOD AND FISH

Halibut with Pineapple Salsa

Easy — Do Ahead

Ingredients:
    2 cups cubed pineapple
    ¼ cup chopped red onion
    2 tbsp. fresh cilantro, chopped
    2 tbsp. lime juice
    ¾ cup chopped red bell pepper
    1 tbsp. chopped green chilies
    1 lb. halibut steaks
    Mrs. Dash seasoning to taste

Directions:
    Combine pineapple, onion, cilantro, lime juice, bell pepper, and green chilies in a small bowl; mix well. Cover and refrigerate at least 1 hour before serving. Preheat oven to 400 degrees. Line baking sheet with foil and spray with cooking spray. Place fish on foil; sprinkle with seasoning and bake 10 to 12 minutes, until fish flakes easily with a fork. Serve halibut with pineapple salsa.

Serves: 4

Shopping List:
    1 lb. halibut steaks, 16 oz. can pineapple chunks in juice, red onion, fresh cilantro, red bell pepper, 4 oz. can chopped green chilies, lime juice, Mrs. Dash seasoning

Nutrition per serving		Exchanges
calories:	174	1 lean meat
total fat (16%):	3 g	2 very lean meat
carbohydrate:	12 g	½ fruit
cholesterol:	36 mg	1 vegetable
dietary fiber:	1 g	
protein:	24 g	carbohydrate choice: 1
sodium:	88 mg	

Pineapple contains bromelain, an important enzyme that helps digestion by breaking down protein.

Lemon Stuffed Sole

Easy — Do Ahead

Ingredients:

2 tsp. nonfat chicken broth
½ cup chopped celery
2 tbsp. chopped onions
2 cups seasoned breadcrumbs
1 tsp. dried dill weed

1 tsp. dried parsley
1 tsp. lemon juice
¼ tsp. lemon pepper
1 lb. sole fillets
¼ cup dry white wine

Directions:

Preheat oven to 350 degrees. Spray 8 x 8-inch baking dish with cooking spray. Spray small nonstick skillet with cooking spray; add chicken broth and heat over medium-high heat. Add celery and onions; cook, stirring frequently, 3 to 5 minutes, until vegetables are softened. In a medium bowl, combine breadcrumbs, celery-and-onion mixture, dill, parsley, lemon juice, and lemon pepper; mix well. Arrange half of the sole fillets in a single layer in baking dish; sprinkle bread-crumb mixture over fillets. Top with remaining fillets. Pour wine over fish, cover with foil, and bake 15 to 20 minutes, until fish flakes easily with a fork.

Serves: 4

Shopping List:

1 lb. sole fillets, celery, onion, seasoned bread crumbs, nonfat chicken broth, dry white wine, dried dill weed, dried parsley, lemon pepper, lemon juice

Nutrition per serving		Exchanges
calories:	167	3 very lean meat
total fat (11%):	2 g	½ starch
carbohydrate:	12 g	½ other carbohydrate
cholesterol:	53 mg	
dietary fiber:	1 g	carbohydrate choice: 1
protein:	21 g	
sodium:	212 mg	

Fish contains lecithin, which some studies have discovered may improve brain function and help counter senility.

SCRUMPTIOUS SEAFOOD AND FISH

Mardi Gras Orange Roughy

Easy

Ingredients:
 1 lb. orange roughy
 1½ tsp. Cajun spice
 1 tbsp. paprika
 lemon pepper to taste

Directions:
 Preheat broiler on high heat. Line baking sheet with foil and spray with cooking spray. Arrange fillets on baking sheet and sprinkle on both sides with Cajun seasoning, paprika, and lemon pepper. Broil 6 to 7 minutes, until browned and fish flakes easily when pierced with a fork.

Serves: 4

Shopping List:
 1 lb. orange roughy, Cajun spice, paprika, lemon pepper

Nutrition per serving		Exchanges
calories:	85	2½ very lean meat
total fat (11%):	1 g	
carbohydrate:	1 g	carbohydrate choice: 0
cholesterol:	23 mg	
dietary fiber:	0 g	
protein:	17 g	
sodium:	73 mg	

Fish not only is one of the leanest protein sources available, but also provides omega-3 fatty acids that contribute to good heart health.

Orange Roughy with Citrus Salsa

Easy — Do Ahead

Ingredients:
 2 cups canned mandarin orange sections, drained,
  cut in thirds
 ¼ cup chopped green onion
 ¼ cup chopped red bell pepper
 1 tbsp. chopped green chilies (mild to hot, depending
  on taste)
 1½ tbsp. fresh cilantro, chopped
 1½ tbsp. lemon juice
 1 tbsp. honey
 1 lb. orange roughy fillets
 garlic-flavored cooking spray
 lemon pepper to taste

Directions:
 Combine mandarin oranges, green onion, bell pepper,
 chilies, cilantro, lemon juice, and honey in a medium bowl;
 mix well. Cover and refrigerate several hours before serving.
 Preheat broiler on high heat. Line baking or broiler sheet
 with foil and spray with cooking spray. Place fish on sheet;
 spray on both sides with garlic-flavored cooking spray and
 sprinkle with lemon pepper. Broil fish 3 to 4 minutes per side,
 until fish flakes easily with a fork. Serve with citrus salsa.

Serves: 4

Shopping List:
 1 lb. orange roughy fillets, 16 oz. can mandarin oranges,
 lemon juice, green onion, fresh cilantro, red bell pepper,
 chopped green chilies, honey, lemon pepper, garlic-flavored
 cooking spray

Nutrition per serving		Exchanges
calories:	143	2 very lean meat
total fat (6%):	1 g	½ fruit
carbohydrate:	16 g	2 vegetable
cholesterol:	23 mg	
dietary fiber:	2 g	carbohydrate choice: 1
protein:	18 g	
sodium:	98 mg	

**Fish provides essential fatty acids and up to
18 vitamins and minerals, including calcium,
zinc and phosphorous.**

SCRUMPTIOUS SEAFOOD AND FISH

Orange Roughy with Tomato-Corn Salsa

Easy — Do Ahead

Ingredients:
¾ cup corn kernels, drained
1½ cups canned chopped tomatoes, drained
2 tbsp. lime juice
2 tbsp. cider vinegar
2 tbsp. fresh cilantro, chopped
2 tbsp. chopped green chilies
pepper to taste
1 lb. orange roughy
lemon pepper to taste

Directions:
Combine all ingredients except fish and lemon pepper in medium bowl; toss until completely mixed. Cover and refrigerate 4 to 6 hours before serving. Preheat broiler on high heat. Line baking sheet with foil and spray with cooking spray. Arrange fish in single layer on baking sheet; lightly spray with cooking spray and sprinkle with lemon pepper. Broil fish 7 to 8 minutes; turn fish after 3 to 4 minutes and cook until fish flakes easily with a fork. Serve with tomato-corn salsa.

Serves: 4

Shopping List:
1 lb. orange roughy, 8 oz. can corn kernels, 15½ oz. can chopped tomatoes, lime juice, cider vinegar, chopped green chilies, fresh cilantro, lemon pepper, pepper

Nutrition per serving		Exchanges
calories:	138	½ starch
total fat (7%):	1 g	1 vegetable
carbohydrate:	15 g	2 very lean meat
cholesterol:	23 mg	
dietary fiber:	3 g	carbohydrate choice: 1
protein:	19 g	
sodium:	472 mg	

Corn lowers cholesterol and boosts energy levels.

Oven-Fried Crunchy Parmesan Fillets

Easy — Do Ahead

Ingredients:
- ¼ cup nonfat plain yogurt
- 2 tbsp. skim milk
- 1 lb. orange roughy fillets
- 1 cup cornflake crumbs
- 2 tsp. garlic powder
- 2 tbsp. nonfat Parmesan cheese
- ½ tsp. ground pepper

Directions:
Preheat oven to 400 degrees. Line baking sheet with foil and spray with cooking spray. Combine yogurt and skim milk in a Ziploc bag and squeeze until blended. Add fish and toss to completely coat fish. Combine cornflake crumbs, garlic powder, Parmesan cheese, and pepper in a medium bowl and mix well; add fish and turn until completely coated with cornflake mixture. Arrange in single layer on baking sheet; spray lightly with cooking spray. Bake uncovered 15 to 20 minutes until fish is lightly browned and flakes easily with a fork. Great with honey mustard!

Serves: 4

Shopping List:
1 lb. orange roughy fillets, nonfat plain yogurt, skim milk, non-fat Parmesan cheese, cornflake crumbs, garlic powder, pepper

Nutrition per serving	
calories:	179
total fat (5%):	1 g
carbohydrate:	19 g
cholesterol:	23 mg
dietary fiber:	0 g
protein:	21 g
sodium:	350 mg

Exchanges
3 very lean meat
1 other carbohydrate

carbohydrate choice: 1

SCRUMPTIOUS SEAFOOD AND FISH

Fish is a good source of vitamins A, D, and B$_2$ (riboflavin), which promote healthy hair and skin.

Poached Salmon

Easy

Ingredients:
1 tbsp. vegetable broth
2 cups mushrooms, quartered
2 tbsp. chopped chives
1 tsp. minced garlic
1 cup dry white wine
12 oz. salmon fillets
1 tsp. dried dill weed
pepper to taste
1 lb. asparagus, cut in pieces

Directions:
Spray large nonstick skillet with cooking spray; add vegetable broth and heat over medium-high heat. Add mushrooms, chives, and minced garlic to skillet; cook, stirring frequently, until tender and golden brown. Add wine and salmon to skillet; sprinkle with dill and pepper. Cover skillet and cook over medium heat 2 to 3 minutes. Add asparagus pieces to skillet, cover, and cook until salmon flakes easily with a fork and asparagus is tender. Transfer salmon to serving platter; pour sauce over top, and arrange asparagus pieces around edges. Serve immediately.

Serves: 4

Shopping List:
12 oz. salmon fillets, 1 lb. asparagus, 1 lb. mushrooms, chopped chives, minced garlic, dried dill weed, pepper, vegetable broth, 8 oz. dry white wine

Nutrition per serving

calories:	178
total fat (15%):	3 g
carbohydrate:	7 g
cholesterol:	44 mg
dietary fiber:	2 g
protein:	21 g
sodium:	67 mg

Exchanges
1 lean meat
2 very lean meat
2 vegetable

carbohydrate choice: ½

Some studies have found that salmon helps counteract the effects of caffeine and alcohol.

Red Snapper with Mango Salsa

Easy — Do Ahead

Ingredients:
3 mangoes, peeled, seeded, and chopped
1 tbsp. minced jalapeno peppers
¾ cup chopped green onion
2 tbsp. fresh cilantro, chopped
2 tbsp. lime juice
1 to 2 dashes hot pepper sauce
1 lb. red snapper fillets
garlic-flavored cooking spray

Directions:
Combine chopped mango, jalapenos, onion, cilantro, lime juice, and hot pepper sauce in a medium bowl; mix well. Cover with plastic wrap and refrigerate 12 to 24 hours. (Salsa will keep up to 5 days in refrigerator.) Heat broiler on high heat. Spray broiler pan with cooking spray. Place fish on rack in broiler pan and spray with garlic-flavored cooking spray. Broil 4 to 6 inches from heat 3 to 5 minutes, until fish is lightly brown and flakes easily with a fork. Serve with mango salsa.

Serves: 4

Shopping List:
1 lb. red snapper fillets, 3 mangoes, green onion, fresh cilantro, chopped jalapeno peppers, lime juice, hot pepper sauce, garlic-flavored cooking spray

Nutrition per serving		Exchanges
calories:	219	3 very lean meat
total fat (8%):	2 g	2 fruit
carbohydrate:	28 g	
cholesterol:	42 mg	carbohydrate choice: 2
dietary fiber:	4 g	
protein:	24 g	
sodium:	107 mg	

Mangoes, rich in beta-carotene, may help slow the aging process, reduce the risk of certain types of cancer, improve lung function, and reduce complications associated with diabetes.

SCRUMPTIOUS SEAFOOD AND FISH

Red Snapper with Summer Squash

Easy — Do Ahead

Ingredients:
- 1 lb. red snapper fillet
- 2 tsp. lemon pepper
- 1 yellow summer squash, sliced thin
- 1 cup shredded carrot
- 1 onion, sliced thin
- 1 tsp. Italian seasoning
- 15½ oz. Italian-style stewed tomatoes, undrained

Directions:

Preheat oven to 350 degrees. Spray baking dish with cooking spray. Arrange fillets in a single layer in dish; sprinkle with lemon pepper. Layer sliced squash, shredded carrot, and sliced onion on top of fish. Sprinkle with Italian seasoning blend and cover with stewed tomatoes. Cover with foil and bake 20 to 25 minutes until fish flakes easily with a fork.

Serves: 4

Shopping List:

1 lb. red snapper fillet, yellow squash, 8 oz. package shredded carrot, onion, 15½ oz. can Italian-style stewed tomatoes, lemon-pepper, Italian seasoning

Nutrition per serving		Exchanges
calories:	162	3 very lean meat
total fat (11%):	2 g	2 vegetable
carbohydrate:	11 g	
cholesterol:	42 mg	carbohydrate choice: 1
dietary fiber:	3 g	
protein:	25 g	
sodium:	228 mg	

Fish is a good source of niacin, a B vitamin that boosts energy metabolism.

Salmon Burger

Easy — Do Ahead

Ingredients:

¾ cup nonfat mayonnaise
1 tsp. onion powder
1 tbsp. orange juice
1½ tsp. low-sodium teriyaki
  sauce
½ tsp. ground ginger
14½ oz. canned salmon,
  drained and picked over

½ cup seasoned bread
  crumbs
¾ tsp. Sante Fe (or South
  west) seasoning blend
1 tsp. garlic powder
¼ tsp. pepper
½ cup egg substitute

Directions:

Preheat oven to 400 degrees. Combine mayonnaise, onion powder, orange juice, teriyaki, and ginger in a small bowl; mix until completely blended. Cover and refrigerate until ready to serve. Combine salmon, breadcrumbs, garlic powder, seasoning blend, pepper, and egg substitute in medium bowl; mix until ingredients hold together. Shape into 4 patties. Spray large nonstick skillet with cooking spray and heat over medium-high heat. Add patties to skillet and cook 5 to 6 minutes per side until lightly browned and crisp. Remove from skillet and keep warm. Repeat with remaining patties and serve with orange-teriyaki-mayo sauce. Salmon burgers can be cooked on the grill (5 to 6 minutes per side), if preferred.

Serves: 4

Shopping List:

14½ oz. canned salmon, egg substitute, nonfat mayonnaise, seasoned bread crumbs, orange juice, low-sodium teriyaki sauce, garlic powder, onion powder, ground ginger, Sante Fe (or Southwest) seasoning blend (e.g., McCormick or Schilling), pepper

Nutrition per serving		Exchanges
calories:	209	2 lean meat
total fat (25%):	6 g	1 very lean meat
carbohydrate:	11 g	1 other carbohydrate
cholesterol:	40 mg	
dietary fiber:	.2 g	carbohydrate choice: 1
protein:	25 g	
sodium:	971 mg	

SCRUMPTIOUS SEAFOOD AND FISH

***Salmon, rich in essential fatty acids,
helps to keep skin moisturized.***

Scallop-Asparagus Stir-Fry

Easy

Ingredients:
¾ lb. scallops
4 oz. oyster mushrooms, sliced
1 tsp. minced garlic
¾ cup nonfat chicken broth
1 tsp. low-sodium soy sauce
1 tbsp. cornstarch
16 oz. frozen asparagus spears, thawed and drained
¼ cup sliced green onion
2 cups cooked brown rice

Directions:
Spray large nonstick skillet or wok with cooking spray and heat over medium-high heat. Add scallops, mushrooms and garlic; cook, stirring frequently, until scallops are cooked through (about 4 to 5 minutes). Combine chicken broth, soy sauce, and cornstarch in a small bowl; mix until completely blended. Stir mixture into skillet with scallops and cook, stirring constantly, until sauce thickens. Add asparagus and green onion; cook 3 to 4 minutes until completely heated through. Serve over cooked brown rice.

Serves: 4

Shopping List:
¾ lb. scallops, 16 oz. frozen asparagus spears, 4 oz. oyster mushrooms, nonfat chicken broth, low-sodium soy sauce, green onion, cornstarch, minced garlic, brown rice

Nutrition per serving		Exchanges
calories:	278	3 very lean meat
total fat (6%):	2 g	1½ starch
carbohydrate:	39 g	2 vegetable
cholesterol:	45 mg	
dietary fiber:	3 g	carbohydrate choice: 3
protein:	27 g	
sodium:	446 mg	

Diet-related cancers account for more than 360,000 deaths in the United States each year.

Scallop Spaghettini

Easy

Ingredients:
8 oz. spaghettini, cooked and drained
2 tbsp. vegetable broth
½ lb. zucchini, cut into ½-inch pieces
½ lb. yellow squash, cut into ½-inch pieces
¾ tsp. garlic powder
1 tsp. red pepper flakes
2 tbsp. lemon juice
1 lb. scallops

Directions:
Cook pasta according to package directions; drain and keep warm. Spray large skillet with cooking spray; add vegetable broth and heat over medium-high heat. Add zucchini, squash, garlic powder, pepper flakes, lemon juice, and scallops. Reduce heat to low, cover, and simmer 6 to 8 minutes until scallops are cooked through. Spoon scallop sauce over pasta; toss lightly and serve.

Serves: 4

Shopping List:
1 lb. scallops, ½ lb. zucchini, ½ lb. yellow squash, 8 oz. spaghettini, vegetable broth, red pepper flakes, lemon juice, garlic powder

Nutrition per serving		Exchanges
calories:	202	1 starch
total fat (9%):	2 g	2 vegetable
carbohydrate:	24 g	2½ very lean meat
cholesterol:	37 mg	
dietary fiber:	2 g	carbohydrate choice: 1½
protein:	23 g	
sodium:	186 mg	

Pasta is an excellent source of complex carbohydrates, providing sustained, slow-released energy.

Scampi with Spinach Noodles

Easy

Ingredients:
1 tbsp. minced garlic
2 tbsp. lemon juice
1½ tsp. Italian seasoning
1 lb. shrimp, uncooked, peeled, and deveined, thawed if frozen
8 oz. spinach fettuccine, cooked and drained
¼ cup nonfat Parmesan cheese

Directions:
Spray nonstick skillet with cooking spray and heat over medium-high heat. Add garlic, lemon juice, and Italian seasoning to skillet; mix well. Add shrimp and cook over medium heat 3 to 4 minutes until shrimp turn pink and are cooked through. Remove from heat and toss with pasta; sprinkle with Parmesan cheese and serve.

Serves: 4

Shopping List:
1 lb. shrimp (uncooked), 8 oz. spinach fettuccine, Italian seasoning, lemon juice, minced garlic, nonfat Parmesan cheese

Nutrition per serving		Exchanges
calories:	314	2 starch
total fat (9%):	4 g	2½ very lean meat
carbohydrate:	35 g	1 lean meat
cholesterol:	237 mg	
dietary fiber:	0 g	carbohydrate choice: 2
protein:	32 g	
sodium:	235 mg	

Garlic contains adenosine, a smooth muscle relaxant, shown to lower high blood pressure.

Seafood & Spinach Fettuccine Alfredo

Easy — Do Ahead

Ingredients:
8 oz. spinach fettuccine, cooked and drained
⅔ cup nonfat ricotta cheese
1 tsp. dried basil
1 tsp. dried chives
2 tsp. sugar
1 tsp. garlic powder
2 tbsp. onion flakes
⅛ tsp. pepper
15½ oz. can chopped tomatoes, undrained
½ lb. cooked shrimp
½ lb. cooked scallops
nonfat Parmesan cheese (optional)

Directions:
Cook pasta according to package directions; drain and keep warm. Spray large nonstick skillet with cooking spray; add cheese, basil, chives, sugar, garlic powder, onion flakes, pepper, and chopped tomatoes to skillet. Bring to a boil over high heat; reduce heat to low and cook, uncovered, 4 to 5 minutes. Add shrimp and scallops; cook 2 to 3 minutes until heated through. Serve sauce over fettuccine; sprinkle with Parmesan cheese, if desired.

Serves: 4

Shopping List:
½ lb. cooked shrimp, ½ lb. cooked scallops, 8 oz. spinach fettuccine, 8 oz. nonfat ricotta cheese, 15½ oz. can chopped tomatoes, dried basil, dried chives, sugar, garlic powder, onion flakes, pepper, nonfat Parmesan cheese (optional)

Nutrition per serving
calories:	256
total fat (7%):	2 g
carbohydrate:	28 g
cholesterol:	143 mg
dietary fiber:	1 g
protein:	33 g
sodium:	586 mg

Exchanges
1 starch
3 vegetable
3 very lean meat

carbohydrate choice: 2

Tomatoes are cancer-fighting power foods, rich in vitamins A and C, and a decent source of fiber.

Seafood Tortilla Wraps

Easy — Do Ahead

Ingredients:

1 cup nonfat sour cream
1½ cups nonfat shredded
   Cheddar cheese
1 tsp. garlic powder
¾ tsp. onion powder
½ tsp. Mrs. Dash seasoning
6½ oz. canned crabmeat, drained

6½ oz. canned baby shrimp,
   chopped
4 low-fat flour tortillas
½ cup chopped green onion
¼ cup low-fat shredded
   Cheddar cheese
salsa (optional)

Directions:

Spray shallow baking dish with cooking spray. Combine sour cream, nonfat cheese, garlic powder, onion powder, Mrs. Dash seasoning, crabmeat and shrimp in a medium bowl; mix until ingredients are blended. Divide seafood mixture among tortillas; sprinkle with green onion. Roll tortillas and arrange seam side down in single layer in shallow baking dish. Sprinkle with low-fat cheese. Microwave on high heat 1 to 1½ minutes until cheese melts, or bake in 325-degree oven 10 to 15 minutes. Serve with nonfat sour cream or salsa, if desired.

Serves: 4

Shopping List:

6½ oz. can crabmeat, 6½ oz. can baby shrimp, 6 oz. nonfat shredded Cheddar cheese, low-fat shredded Cheddar cheese, low-fat flour tortillas, 8 oz. nonfat sour cream, green onion, salsa, garlic powder, onion powder, Mrs. Dash seasoning

Nutrition per serving

calories:	382
total fat (7%):	3 g
carbohydrate:	41 g
cholesterol:	127 mg
dietary fiber:	3 g
protein:	43 g
sodium:	415 mg

Exchanges

1 lean meat
3 very lean meat
2 starch
1 other carbohydrate

carbohydrate choice: 3

According to the National Center for Health Statistics, poor diet contributes to 5 out of the 10 leading causes of death.

Shrimp Fajitas

Easy

Ingredients:
- 1 lb. cooked shrimp
- 2 cups frozen peppers and onions, thawed and drained
- 1 tbsp. lime juice
- ½ tsp. oregano
- ½ tsp. ground cumin
- 2 tsp. crushed garlic
- 1 cup chunky salsa
- 4 low-fat whole-wheat tortillas

Directions:
Spray large skillet with cooking spray and heat over medium heat. Add shrimp, peppers and onions, lime juice, oregano, cumin, and crushed garlic and cook, stirring frequently, about 5 to 6 minutes, until sizzling and heated through. Pour salsa into glass bowl and heat in microwave 45 to 60 seconds until hot. Divide shrimp mixture among tortillas; top with sizzling salsa. Fold tortilla and serve with additional salsa, if desired.

Serves: 4

Shopping List:
1 lb. cooked shrimp, 16 oz. frozen peppers and onions, 8 oz. chunky salsa, low-fat whole-wheat tortillas, lime juice, oregano, ground cumin, minced garlic

Nutrition per serving		Exchanges
calories:	241	1 lean meat
total fat (12%):	4 g	2 very lean meat
carbohydrate:	23 g	1 starch
cholesterol:	175 mg	2 vegetable
dietary fiber:	1 g	
protein:	26 g	carbohydrate choice: 1½
sodium:	485 mg	

Pound for pound, sweet peppers contain twice as much vitamin C as oranges.

Shrimp Quesadillas

Easy

Ingredients:
6 low-fat flour tortillas
1¾ cups nonfat shredded Cheddar cheese
¾ cup chopped tomato
4 oz. can chopped green chilies, drained
¾ lb. frozen cooked shrimp, thawed and drained
salsa

Directions:
Spray large nonstick skillet with cooking spray. Lay tortillas on flat surface; divide cheese, tomatoes, chilies and shrimp among tortillas, placing filling on half the tortilla. Fold other half over filling. Cook one or two quesadillas at a time; cook over medium heat 1 to 2 minutes until bottom is golden brown. Turn tortilla over and cook an additional 1 to 2 minutes until browned. Wrap in foil and keep warm in 300-degree oven or serve immediately. Serve with salsa.

Serves: 6

Shopping List:
low-fat flour tortillas, 7 to 8 oz. nonfat shredded Cheddar cheese, tomato, 4 oz. can chopped green chilies, salsa, ¾ lb. frozen cooked shrimp

Nutrition per serving		Exchanges
calories:	262	1 starch
total fat (3%):	1 g	4 vegetable
carbohydrate:	37 g	2 very lean meat
cholesterol:	87 mg	
dietary fiber:	3 g	carbohydrate choice: 2½
protein:	25 g	
sodium:	935 mg	

Tomatoes contain lycopene, a compound that neutralizes free radicals before they cause damage. Studies have shown that men with high levels of lycopene in their blood are at lower risk for prostate cancer.

So-Simple Salmon Teriyaki

Easy — Do Ahead

Ingredients:
½ cup low-sodium teriyaki sauce
1 lb. salmon fillets
garlic powder

Directions:
Pour teriyaki sauce into Ziploc bag. Sprinkle salmon fillets with garlic powder; place in Ziploc bag, toss until coated, and refrigerate 1 hour. Heat broiler on high heat. Line baking sheet with foil and spray with cooking spray. Remove fish from marinade and arrange on baking sheet. Brush additional sauce on fish and broil 4 to 6 inches from heat for 4 minutes; turn fish, brush with sauce, and broil 4 more minutes, until fish flakes easily with a fork.

Serves: 4

Shopping List:
1 lb. salmon fillets, low-sodium teriyaki sauce, garlic powder

Nutrition per serving

calories:	162
total fat (22%):	4 g
carbohydrate:	6 g
cholesterol:	59 mg
dietary fiber:	0 g
protein:	24 g
sodium:	716 mg

Exchanges

1 lean meat
2 very lean meat
½ other carbohydrate

carbohydrate choice: ½

Salmon is rich in omega-3 fats and other compounds that reduce the risk of heart disease and breast and colon cancers, and reduce inflammation in smokers' lungs.

Spicy Seafood Pasta

Easy — Do Ahead

Ingredients:
- 6 oz. linguine, cooked and drained
- 1 tsp. vegetable broth
- 1 cup diced onions
- 10 oz. can chopped clams, drained
- 2 tsp. minced garlic
- 4 cups nonfat pasta sauce
- 1 tsp. Italian seasoning
- ⅛ tsp. cayenne pepper
- ¾ lb. shrimp, peeled and deveined

Directions:

Cook linguine according to package directions; drain and keep warm. Spray large saucepan with cooking spray; coat with vegetable broth. Add onions to saucepan and cook, stirring frequently, over medium-high heat until tender. Add clams and garlic; cook 1 minute. Add pasta sauce, Italian seasoning, and cayenne pepper; bring to a boil. Reduce heat to medium; add shrimp. Cook until shrimp turn pink and are cooked through. Serve seafood sauce over linguine.

Serves: 4

Shopping List:

6 oz. linguine, 10 oz. can chopped clams, 32 oz. nonfat pasta sauce, ¾ lb. uncooked shrimp, onion (or packaged diced onions), vegetable broth, minced garlic, Italian seasoning, cayenne pepper

Nutrition per serving		Exchanges
calories:	377	3 very lean meat
total fat (7%):	3 g	2 starch
carbohydrate:	54 g	5 vegetable
cholesterol:	175 mg	
dietary fiber:	1 g	carbohydrate choice: 3½
protein:	31 g	
sodium:	865 mg	

Clams are an excellent source of protein. A 4-ounce serving contains fewer than 100 calories and 2 grams of fat. The same serving of meat can contain up to 10 times the fat grams.

Spinach and Salmon Pasta

Average

Ingredients:
 1 lb. salmon fillets
 garlic powder to taste
 1 cup vegetable broth, divided
 1 tbsp. minced garlic
 16 oz. frozen spinach leaves, thawed and drained
 1 lb. angel hair pasta, cooked and drained
 ½ cup nonfat Parmesan cheese

Directions:
 Spray large nonstick skillet with cooking spray; sprinkle salmon fillets with garlic powder. Cook salmon over medium-high heat 5 to 6 minutes per side until fish flakes easily with a fork. Remove from pan; wrap in foil and keep warm. Pour 1 tablespoon vegetable broth into skillet and heat over medium-high heat. Add minced garlic; cook 1 minute. Pour remaining broth into skillet and bring to a boil over high heat. Add spinach leaves; reduce heat to low, cover and simmer 3 to 4 minutes until tender. Slice salmon into bite-size pieces. Combine pasta, sauce, and salmon in large bowl or serving platter; toss lightly to mix. Sprinkle with Parmesan cheese and serve.

Serves: 6

Shopping List:
 1 lb. angel hair pasta, 1 lb. salmon fillets, 16 oz. frozen spinach leaves, vegetable broth, nonfat Parmesan cheese, garlic powder, minced garlic

Nutrition per serving		Exchanges
calories:	437	2 lean meat
total fat (9%):	6 g	3 starch
carbohydrate:	64 g	4 vegetable
cholesterol:	29 mg	
dietary fiber:	4 g	carbohydrate choice: 4
protein:	31 g	
sodium:	310 mg	

Spinach contains significant amounts of riboflavin, vitamin K, and dietary fiber; it also contains folic acid, which helps to prevent neural tube birth defects such as spina bifida.

SCRUMPTIOUS SEAFOOD AND FISH

Teriyaki Snapper

Easy

Ingredients:
1 tbsp. nonfat broth (chicken, oriental, or vegetable)
1 lb. red snapper, cut into 1-inch pieces
1 cup frozen peppers, thawed and drained
16 oz. frozen asparagus spears, thawed and drained,
cut into 1-inch pieces
½ cup teriyaki baste and glaze sauce
2 cups cooked rice (white or brown)

Directions:
Spray large nonstick skillet with cooking spray; add broth and heat over medium-high heat. Add snapper to skillet and cook, stirring frequently, 2 to 3 minutes. Add peppers and asparagus; stir-fry 2 to 3 minutes, until vegetables are tender-crisp and fish flakes easily with a fork. Stir in teriyaki glaze and cook 30 to 45 seconds until heated. Serve over cooked rice.

Serves: 4

Shopping List:
1 lb. red snapper, 10 oz. package frozen peppers, 16 oz. frozen asparagus spears (or cuts), teriyaki baste and glaze sauce (or teriyaki sauce), white or brown rice, nonfat broth (chicken, oriental, or vegetable)

Nutrition per serving		Exchanges
calories:	289	4 very lean meat
total fat (3%):	1 g	1 starch
carbohydrate:	35 g	2 vegetable
cholesterol:	42 mg	½ other carbohydrate
dietary fiber:	2 g	
protein:	31 g	carbohydrate choice: 2
sodium:	1,458 mg	

Fish is a good source of selenium, a mineral that controls the levels of prostaglandins, which in turn reduces the risk of clogged arteries.

Tuna Stir-Fry

Easy

Ingredients:
1 tbsp. vegetable broth
2 cups frozen peppers, thawed and drained
½ tsp. garlic powder
¾ lb. tuna fillet, cut into cubes
1 tbsp. lemon juice
1 lb. fresh spinach, chopped
⅛ tsp. dried red pepper flakes
2 cups cooked rice (white or brown)
¼–½ cup low sodium teriyaki sauce

Directions:
Spray large nonstick skillet with cooking spray; add vegetable broth and heat over medium-high heat. Add peppers to skillet and cook, stirring frequently, 1 to 2 minutes until tender. Add garlic powder, tuna, and lemon juice to skillet; cook over medium heat until tuna is cooked through (5 to 7 minutes). Stir in spinach and cook until spinach softens and wilts; sprinkle with red pepper flakes. Heat teriyaki sauce in microwave-safe bowl; toss tuna mixture with rice and teriyaki. Mix lightly and serve.

Serves: 4

Shopping List:
¾ lb. tuna fillet, 16 oz. frozen pepper strips, 1 lb. fresh spinach, white or brown rice, vegetable broth, low-sodium teriyaki sauce, lemon juice, garlic powder, dried red pepper flakes

Nutrition per serving
calories:	238
total fat (8%):	2 g
carbohydrate:	30 g
cholesterol:	38 mg
dietary fiber:	4 g
protein:	26 g
sodium:	123 mg

Exchanges
3 vegetable
1 starch
2½ very lean meat

carbohydrate choice: 2

Fresh tuna provides adequate amounts of vitamins B (niacin, B_6 and B_{12}) as well as minerals (potassium, phosphorous, copper, selenium, and iodine).

Vegetable-Seafood Casserole

Average — Do Ahead — Freeze

Ingredients:

1 cup nonfat ricotta cheese
2 green onion, chopped fine
2 tbsp. dry sherry
2 tbsp. lemon juice
¼ tsp. garlic powder
¼ tsp. Italian seasoning
8 oz. penne pasta,
  cooked and drained

10 oz. frozen asparagus
  spears, thawed, drained
  and cut into 1-inch pieces
6 oz. canned crabmeat,
  drained
½ cup nonfat Parmesan
  cheese

Directions:

Combine ricotta cheese, onions, sherry, lemon juice, garlic powder, and Italian seasoning in a food processor or blender; process until smooth. Combine cooked pasta, sauce, asparagus, and crabmeat in large skillet or Dutch oven. Cook over medium heat, stirring frequently, until completely heated through. Top each serving with 1 to 2 tablespoons Parmesan cheese.

Serves: ?

Shopping List:

8 oz. nonfat ricotta cheese, 10 oz. frozen asparagus spears, 6 oz. can crabmeat, 8 oz. penne pasta, nonfat Parmesan cheese, green onion, dry sherry, lemon juice, garlic powder, Italian seasoning

Nutrition per serving

calories:	222
total fat (8%):	2 g
carbohydrate:	26 g
cholesterol:	71 mg
dietary fiber:	1 g
protein:	26 g
sodium:	429 mg

Exchanges

1 starch
3 vegetable
2 very lean meat

carbohydrate choice: 2

Pasta is a natural for low-fat cooking; save 248 calories, 32 fat grams by substituting nonfat ricotta cheese for whole cheese.

LUSCIOUS
LEAN
MEATS

◆ ◆ ◆

And Introducing . . .

HEALTHY Lean Meats

Part of a healthy-living Superfood program, Lean Meats are an excellent protein source that, in moderation, provide significant health benefits from building stronger bones to boosting immunity to preventing vitamin and mineral deficiencies.

Lean Meat . . . No longer the enemy, and may even be good for you! According to an article in *Health* Magazine, "a heartening study found that people who ate 6 oz. of lean meat five or more times a week cut their bad cholesterol and raised HDL [good] cholesterol levels. According to the study, they did just as well as those who ate equal amounts of chicken and fish."

EXTRA *READ ALL ABOUT IT!* EXTRA

Ounce for Ounce, Red Meat delivers more protein than any other food source! Protein-rich foods boost energy levels, improve alertness, build and repair muscles, assure proper muscle development, and reduce the risk of iron-deficiency anemia.

But . . . red meat is bad for you . . . right? *WRONG!*

In moderation and cooked properly, lean red meat can be a healthy addition to any diet. It provides . . .

- **44 grams** of **protein** (per 6-ounce serving)
- **iron** (a mineral that helps your body form hemoglobin, which carries oxygen throughout your body and prevents "poop outs")
- **zinc** (an important mineral that helps your immune system fight off infections, colds, and other illnesses)
- **vitamin B$_{12}$** (a vitamin necessary for the prevention of pernicious anemia, a rare blood disorder that causes fatigue, memory loss, and other neurological disorders)

LUSCIOUS LEAN MEATS

- **stearic acid** (a compound responsible for controlling cholesterol levels and keeping arteries clear—some studies have found stearic acid cuts the risk of heart disease by as much as 30%)
- **carnitine** (an essential amino acid used for fat and energy metabolism, also referred to as vitamin BT)

Lean and Meaty words to watch for: *ROUND** (eye round, top round, round tip, bottom round), *LOIN* (top sirloin, top loin, tenderloin), and *CHOICE* (lower in fat than "prime" cuts)

Keeping It Lean 'n' Mean . . .
- Trim all visible fat from meat before cooking.
- Drain ground beef after browning and before adding other ingredients.
- Rely on herbs to perk up the flavor of meat.
- Marinate in low-fat sauces to keep meat tender and moist.
- Take five to cool down before cutting for moist and flavorful meat.
- Cook meat thoroughly to kill harmful bacteria, but . . .
- Don't overcook on the grill. Charred, barbecued meats increase the production of carcinogens.

*All recipes calling for superlean ground beef were prepared using *Laura's Lean Beef,* which is a 4% fat ground round: 1-800-ITS-LEAN or www.laurasleanbeef.com

Baked Pizza Patties

Easy — Do Ahead — Freeze

Ingredients:
 1½ lb. superlean ground beef
 ¾ cup seasoned bread crumbs
 ¼ cup egg substitute
 2 tsp. onion powder
 1 tsp. Italian seasoning
 ⅛ tsp. pepper
 ¾ tsp. garlic powder
 ¾ cup nonfat pasta sauce, divided
 ¾ cup stewed tomatoes, chopped
 6 slices nonfat mozzarella cheese slices

Directions:
Preheat oven to 375 degrees. Line baking sheet with foil and spray with cooking spray. Combine beef, bread crumbs, egg substitute, onion powder, Italian seasoning, pepper, garlic powder, ½ cup pasta sauce, and chopped tomatoes in a medium bowl; mix until blended. Shape mixture into 6 patties and place on baking sheet. Top each patty with one slice cheese; drizzle with remaining pasta sauce. Bake 25 to 30 minutes until patties are cooked through.

Serves: 6

Shopping List:
1½ lb. superlean ground beef, 6 oz. nonfat mozzarella cheese slices, 14½ oz. can stewed tomatoes, 6 oz. nonfat pasta sauce, egg substitute, seasoned bread crumbs, onion powder, Italian seasoning, garlic powder, pepper

Nutrition per serving		Exchanges
calories:	250	2 lean meat
total fat (20%):	5.6 g	2 very lean meat
carbohydrate:	8 g	2 vegetable
cholesterol:	72 mg	
dietary fiber:	0 g	carbohydrate choice: ½
protein:	38 g	
sodium:	465 mg	

Lean meat is a good source of zinc which functions in more than 200 enzymatic reactions; zinc is important for the blending and breakdown of carbohydrates, lipids and proteins, which are essential for tissue growth and repair.

Barbecue Meatloaf

Easy — Do Ahead — Freeze

Ingredients:
> 1½ lb. superlean ground beef
> ½ cup oatmeal
> 1 tsp. garlic powder
> 1 tsp. onion powder
> 2 tsp. Mrs. Dash seasoning
> ½ cup tomato puree
> ¼ cup barbecue sauce

Directions:
> Preheat oven to 350 degrees. Spray 9 x 5 x 3-inch loaf pan with cooking spray. In a medium bowl, combine all ingredients except barbecue sauce; mix well and press into pan. Bake 45 minutes; remove from oven and brush with barbecue sauce. Bake another 15 to 30 minutes until no longer pink and juice is clear.

Serves: 6

Shopping List:
> 1½ lb. superlean ground beef, oatmeal, tomato puree, barbecue sauce, Mrs. Dash seasoning, garlic powder, onion powder

Nutrition per serving		Exchanges
calories:	233	4 very lean meat
total fat (19%):	5 g	1 lean meat
carbohydrate:	9 g	½ other carbohydrate
cholesterol:	95 mg	
dietary fiber:	1 g	carbohydrate choice: ½
protein:	37 g	
sodium:	160 mg	

In moderation, lean meats can provide significant health benefits, from preventing vitamin and mineral deficiencies and boosting immunity to building stronger blood.

Beef 'n' Bean Burritos

Easy — Do Ahead — Freeze

Ingredients:

½ lb. superlean ground beef
1½ tsp. onion powder
½ cup tomato sauce
1 tbsp. chili powder
¾ tsp. ground cumin
½ tsp. garlic powder

¼ tsp. dried oregano
⅛ tsp. ground red pepper
¾ cup nonfat refried beans
4 low-fat flour tortillas
chunky salsa

Directions:

Spray large nonstick skillet with cooking spray; add beef to skillet and sprinkle with onion powder. Cook over medium heat, stirring frequently, until beef is no longer pink (as beef is cooking, break into crumbles). Drain pan if needed. Pour tomato sauce over beef; sprinkle with chili powder, cumin, garlic powder, oregano, and red pepper; mix well and blend with beef mixture. Bring to a boil over high heat; reduce heat to low and simmer 10 minutes. Stir in beans and heat through. Divide mixture among tortillas; fold bottom edge up over filling. Fold in sides, overlapping edges, and serve with salsa.

Serves: 4

Shopping List:

½ lb. superlean ground beef, 6 oz. nonfat refried beans, 4 oz. tomato sauce, low-fat flour tortillas, onion powder, chili powder, ground cumin, garlic powder, dried oregano, ground red pepper, chunky salsa

Nutrition per serving		Exchanges
calories:	248	1 very lean meat
total fat (18%):	5 g	1 lean meat
carbohydrate:	30 g	2 starch
cholesterol:	36 mg	
dietary fiber:	3 g	carbohydrate choice: 2
protein:	20 g	
sodium:	434 mg	

Beef shouldn't be seasoned with any type of salt until it is three-quarters cooked; this helps retain flavor and juiciness.

Beef 'n' Cabbage Casserole

Average — Do Ahead — Freeze

Ingredients:
1½ lb. superlean ground beef
1 tbsp. onion powder
1 tsp. garlic powder
3 cups tomato sauce
3 lb. chopped cabbage
¾ cup white rice
3 cups beef broth

Directions:
Spray large nonstick skillet with cooking spray; add beef and sprinkle with onion and garlic powder. Cook, stirring frequently, over medium heat until beef is browned. Combine beef, tomato sauce, cabbage, and uncooked rice in medium bowl; mix well. Preheat oven to 350 degrees. Spray 9 x 13-inch baking dish with cooking spray; spoon beef mixture into dish and mix lightly. Pour beef broth over top; cover with foil and bake 1 hour. Remove foil and stir; bake, uncovered, an additional 20 to 30 minutes until lightly browned.

Serves: 8

Shopping List:
1½ lb. superlean ground beef, 3 lb. cabbage, 24 oz. tomato sauce, 24 oz. beef broth, white rice, onion powder, garlic powder

Nutrition per serving		Exchanges
calories:	271	½ very lean meat
total fat (17%):	5 g	2 lean meat
carbohydrate:	31 g	1 starch
cholesterol:	54 mg	3 vegetable
dietary fiber:	5 g	
protein:	26 g	carbohydrate choice: ?
sodium:	389 mg	

Dietary cholesterol refers to that which is eaten; the American Heart Association recommends that you eat no more than 300 milligrams of cholesterol each day.

LUSCIOUS LEAN MEATS

Beef 'n' Cheese Party Dip

Easy — Do Ahead

Ingredients:
    1 lb. superlean ground beef
    1 tsp. Mrs. Dash extra-spicy seasoning
    2 cups salsa
    1 cup nonfat sour cream
    2 cups shredded lettuce
    2½ cups nonfat shredded Cheddar cheese

Directions:
    Spray large nonstick skillet with cooking spray; add ground beef and sprinkle with Mrs. Dash seasoning. Cook over medium heat, stirring frequently, until beef is browned. Add salsa and cook until heated through. Press beef-salsa mixture into pie plate or square baking dish. Cover and re-frigerate 2 to 3 hours. Just before serving, spread sour cream over beef; top with shredded lettuce and cheese. Serve cold with baked tortilla chips.

Serves: 6

Shopping List:
    1 lb. superlean ground beef, 16 oz. salsa, 8 oz. nonfat sour cream, packaged shredded lettuce, 10 oz. nonfat shredded Cheddar cheese, Mrs. Dash extra-spicy seasoning

Nutrition per serving		Exchanges	
calories:	269	5 very lean meat	
total fat (17%):	5 g	1 lean meat	
carbohydrate:	10 g	2 vegetable	
cholesterol:	63 mg		
dietary fiber:	1 g	carbohydrate choice: ½	
protein:	41 g		
sodium:	960 mg		

LUSCIOUS LEAN MEATS

According to a Zogby American survey, if Americans were forced to give up one food group forever, 40.5% would give up sweets; 32.9% would give up salty foods; 17.5 % would give up meat and become vegetarians, and 7.6% would cut carbs.

Beef 'n' Ziti Casserole

Difficult — Do Ahead — Freeze

Ingredients:

12 oz. ziti pasta,
  cooked and drained
¾ cup nonfat Parmesan cheese
1 tsp. Italian seasoning
¾ lb. super lean ground
  beef (4% fat)
1 tbsp. onion powder
1 tbsp. garlic powder

3⅓ cups chopped tomatoes,
  drained
1 cup chopped red bell
  pepper
¾ cup nonfat shredded
  mozzarella cheese
⅓ cup seasoned bread
  crumbs

Directions:

Cook ziti according to package directions; drain and return to pot. Add Parmesan cheese and Italian seasoning; toss lightly to coat. Spray large nonstick skillet with cooking spray; add beef, onion powder, and garlic powder. Cook beef, stirring frequently, until browned and crumbled (about 6 to 8 minutes). Remove skillet from heat. Add tomatoes and peppers; mix lightly. Preheat oven to 375 degrees. Spread half the ziti in the baking dish; top with beef mixture, half the mozzarella cheese, remaining pasta and remaining mozzarella. Sprinkle with seasoned breadcrumbs and bake 30 to 35 minutes until bubbly hot and lightly browned on top.

Serves: 6

Shopping List:

red bell pepper, ¾ lb. super lean ground beef, 12 oz. ziti, 3 15-oz. cans chopped tomatoes, nonfat Parmesan cheese, nonfat shredded mozzarella cheese, seasoned bread crumbs, onion powder, garlic powder, Italian seasoning

Nutrition per serving		Exchanges
calories:	527	3½ very lean meat
total fat (9%):	5 g	1 lean meat
carbohydrate:	65 g	2 starch
cholesterol:	48 mg	7 vegetable
dietary fiber:	2 g	
protein:	51 g	carbohydrate
sodium:	998 mg	choice: 4

Lean meat can help alleviate fatigue by stabilizing blood sugar and insulin levels.

Beef Stroganoff with "Egg" Noodles

Average — Do Ahead — Freeze

Ingredients:

1½ lb. superlean ground beef
2 tbsp. onion flakes
½ tsp. garlic powder
¾ tsp. Mrs. Dash seasoning
½ cup sliced mushrooms
1½ cups hot water

4 tsp. beef bouillon granules
3 tbsp. tomato paste
1 cup cold water
3 tbsp. flour
12 oz. yolk-free noodles,
    cooked and drained

Directions:

Spray large nonstick skillet with cooking spray and heat over medium-high heat. Add ground beef, onion flakes, garlic powder, Mrs. Dash seasoning, and mushrooms. Cook, stirring frequently, until beef is browned and mushrooms are soft. Stir in 1½ cups hot water, beef bouillon granules, and tomato paste; bring to a boil over high heat. Combine 1 cup cold water with 3 tablespoons flour; add to beef mixture and mix until blended. Reduce heat to low, cover, and simmer 45 minutes. Serve over cooked yolk-free noodles.

Serves: 6

Shopping List:

1½ lb. superlean ground beef, 2 oz. mushrooms, 12 oz. yolk-free egg noodles, beef bouillon granules, tomato paste, flour, onion flakes, garlic powder, Mrs. Dash seasoning

Nutrition per serving		Exchanges
calories:	407	2 very lean meat
total fat (13%):	6 g	2 lean meat
carbohydrate:	48 g	1½ other carbohydrate
cholesterol:	72 mg	2 starch
dietary fiber:	4 g	2 vegetable
protein:	37 g	
sodium:	289 mg	carbohydrate choice: 3

Beef is significantly leaner than it was twenty years ago but the fat content varies widely. Get familiar with the grades: prime = fattiest; choice = 20% less fat than prime; select = 20% less fat than choice.

Beef Vegetable Soup

Easy — Do Ahead — Freeze

Ingredients:
1½ lb. superlean ground beef
¾ tsp. garlic powder
1 tbsp. onion powder
¾ tsp. Mrs. Dash seasoning
½ cup canned green beans, drained
½ cup canned green peas, drained
½ cup canned carrots, drained
½ cup parsnips, trimmed, peeled, and cubed
½ cup canned corn, drained
4 cups diced tomatoes, undrained
pepper to taste

Directions:
Spray soup pot or large saucepan with cooking spray; add ground beef. Sprinkle beef with garlic powder, onion powder, and Mrs. Dash seasoning; cook over medium heat until beef is browned. Add green beans, peas, carrots, parsnips, corn, and tomatoes; bring to a boil over high heat. Reduce heat to low and simmer 30 to 45 minutes, until heated through. Season with pepper to taste.

Serves: 8

Shopping List:
1 lb. superlean ground beef, parsnip, canned green beans, canned carrot slices, canned peas, canned corn kernels, 32 oz. canned diced tomatoes, garlic powder, onion powder, Mrs. Dash seasoning, pepper

LUSCIOUS LEAN MEATS

Nutrition per serving		Exchanges
calories:	148	½ very lean meat
total fat (18%):	3 g	1 lean meat
carbohydrate:	16 g	3 vegetable
cholesterol:	36 mg	
dietary fiber:	3 g	carbohydrate choice: 1
protein:	16 g	
sodium:	454 mg	

***One-half cup of cooked parsnips has
five times as much vitamin C as the
same amount of cooked carrots.***

Burger 'n' Veggie Pasta

Easy — Do Ahead — Freeze

Ingredients:
1 lb. superlean ground beef
1 tsp. garlic powder
1 tsp. onion powder
½ tsp. Mrs. Dash extra-spicy seasoning
29 oz. can chopped tomatoes
2 tbsp. chopped green chilies, drained
15 oz. can corn kernels, drained
12 oz. spaghettini, cooked and drained

Directions:
Spray large nonstick skillet with cooking spray; add ground beef, garlic powder, onion powder, and Mrs. Dash seasoning to skillet. Cook, stirring frequently until beef is browned and cooked through; drain any liquid from pan. Add tomatoes, chilies and corn to beef; reduce heat to low and cook, stirring occasionally, until heated through (10 to 15 minutes). Serve over cooked spaghettini (or other pasta of choice).

Serves: 6

Shopping List:
1 lb. superlean ground beef, 2 14½-oz. cans chopped tomatoes, 4 oz. can chopped green chilies, 15 oz. can whole corn kernels, 12 oz. spaghettini, garlic powder, onion powder, Mrs. Dash extra-spicy seasoning

Nutrition per serving		Exchanges
calories:	287	1 very lean meat
total fat (16%):	5 g	1 lean meat
carbohydrate:	40 g	1 starch
cholesterol:	48 mg	5 vegetable
dietary fiber:	5 g	
protein:	24 g	carbohydrate choice: ?
sodium:	610 mg	

A government survey found that just 9% of Americans eat the recommended minimum of five servings of fruits and vegetables a day.

Cheeseburger Pasta

Average — Do Ahead — Freeze

Ingredients:

½ lb. superlean ground beef
½ lb. superlean ground turkey
1 tsp. garlic powder
8 oz. spaghetti, cooked and
    drained
1¾ cup Italian-style chopped
    tomatoes, drained

1 oz. onion soup mix
1 cup nonfat sour cream
¾ tsp. Italian seasoning
¾ cup nonfat shredded
    Cheddar cheese
¼ cup low-fat shredded
    Cheddar cheese

Directions:

Preheat oven to 350 degrees. Spray 2-quart casserole with cooking spray. Spray large nonstick skillet with cooking spray; add beef, turkey, and garlic powder. Cook over medium heat until beef and turkey are browned (5 to 8 minutes); drain any liquid from skillet. Combine spaghetti, beef-turkey mixture, tomatoes, onion soup mix, sour cream, and Italian seasoning in casserole. Cover dish with foil and bake 15 to 20 minutes. Combine nonfat and low-fat Cheddar cheese in Ziploc bag or bowl, and mix well. Remove foil from pan, sprinkle with cheese, and bake 12 to 15 minutes until cheese is melted and lightly browned.

Serves: 4

Shopping List:

½ lb. superlean ground beef, ½ lb. superlean ground turkey, 8 oz. spaghetti, 8 oz. nonfat sour cream, 14½oz. can Italian-style chopped tomatoes, onion soup mix, garlic powder, Italian seasoning, nonfat shredded Cheddar cheese, low-fat shredded Cheddar cheese

Nutrition per serving

calories:	363
total fat (10%):	4 g
carbohydrate:	30 g
cholesterol:	85 mg
dietary fiber:	1 g
protein:	47 g
sodium:	1,488 mg

Exchanges

4 very lean meat
1 lean meat
½ other carbohydrate
2 vegetable
1 starch

carbohydrate choice: 2

Several studies have indicated that the equivalent of one half to one clove of garlic per day can lower cholesterol by at least 9%.

Chili Spice Meatballs

Easy — Do Ahead — Freeze

Ingredients:

1¼ cups low-sodium chili sauce, divided
1½ tsp. onion powder, divided
3 tbsp. red wine vinegar
1 tsp. brown sugar
¾ tsp. garlic powder, divided
¼ tsp. dry mustard
¼ tsp. hot pepper sauce
¾ cup bread crumbs
¼ cup egg substitute
½ lb. superlean ground beef
½ lb. superlean ground turkey

Directions:

Preheat oven to 350 degrees. Spray 9 x 13-inch shallow baking dish with cooking spray. In a small saucepan combine 1 cup chili sauce, 1¼ teaspoon onion powder, vinegar, brown sugar, ½ teaspoon garlic powder, dry mustard and hot pepper sauce; cook, stirring frequently, over medium-low heat until heated through. Combine bread crumbs, ¼ cup chili sauce, egg substitute, ¼ teaspoon onion powder and ¼ teaspoon garlic powder in a large bowl; mix well. Add ground beef and turkey; mix ingredients together and shape into 1-inch meatballs. Place in baking dish and bake 15 to 20 minutes until beef is cooked through. Using slotted spoon, transfer meatballs to serving dish. Serve with sauce (hot, cold, or room temperature).

Serves: 8

Shopping List:

½ lb. superlean ground beef, ½ lb. superlean ground turkey, 10 oz. low-sodium chili sauce, bread crumbs, egg substitute, red wine vinegar, brown sugar, dry mustard, onion powder, garlic powder, hot pepper sauce

Nutrition per serving		Exchanges
calories:	137	2 very lean meat
total fat (13%):	2 g	1 other carbohydrate
carbohydrate:	13 g	
cholesterol:	42 mg	carbohydrate choice: 1
dietary fiber:	0 g	
protein:	17 g	
sodium:	162 mg	

Most of the B vitamins (thiamin, B_6, B_{12} and niacin) are concentrated in lean beef and are easily absorbed by the body.

Pepper Steak Stir-Fry

Average

Ingredients:

¼ cup low-sodium soy sauce
¼ cup water
1 tbsp. corn starch
2 to 3 tbsp. beef broth, divided
¾ lb. flank steak, cut into thin strips

2 onions, sliced into rings
10 oz. frozen pepper strips
1 cup cherry tomatoes, cut in half
2 cups cooked rice (white or brown)

Directions:

Combine soy sauce, water, and corn starch in a small bowl; mix well and set aside. Spray large nonstick skillet or wok with cooking spray; pour 1 tablespoon beef broth and heat over medium-high heat. Add beef strips to skillet and cook, stirring frequently, until browned and cooked to taste (do not overcook or meat will be too tough). Remove beef from skillet; respray with cooking spray and add remaining broth to pan. Add onions and peppers to skillet; cook 3 to 4 minutes, stirring frequently, until vegetables are tender-crisp. Return beef to pan; stir in soy sauce mixture and cook, stirring constantly, until mixture becomes thick and bubbly (about 2 to 3 minutes). Add cherry tomatoes halves and heat through. Serve over cooked rice.

Serves: 4

Shopping List:

¾ lb. flank steak, 10 oz. package frozen pepper strips, 2 onions, cherry tomatoes, rice (brown or white), low-sodium soy sauce, corn starch, beef broth

Nutrition per serving		Exchanges
calories:	343	2 lean meat
total fat (16%):	6 g	2 starch
carbohydrate:	45 g	3 vegetable
cholesterol:	53 mg	
dietary fiber:	4 g	carbohydrate choice: 3
protein:	26 g	
sodium:	669 mg	

LUSCIOUS LEAN MEATS

Iron deficiency is the most common nutritional deficiency in the United States. Meat is an important source of iron, a mineral essential for boosting the oxygen-carrying capability of blood.

Salsa Meatballs with Rice

Easy — Do Ahead — Freeze

Ingredients:
   ½ lb. superlean ground beef
   ½ cup seasoned bread crumbs
   ½ cup salsa
   ½ tsp. garlic powder
   2 tsp. beef broth
   2 cups nonfat pasta sauce
   2 cups cooked rice (white or brown)

Directions:
   Combine ground beef, bread crumbs, salsa, and garlic powder in a medium bowl; mix well. Shape into 1½-inch meatballs. Spray large nonstick skillet with cooking spray; add beef broth and heat over medium-high heat. Add meatballs; spray with cooking spray and cook until meatballs are browned on all sides. Stir in pasta sauce. Bring to a boil over high heat. Reduce heat to low, cover, and simmer 15 to 20 minutes until meatballs are cooked through. Serve over cooked rice.

Serves: 4

Shopping List:
   ¾ lb. superlean ground beef, 16 oz. nonfat pasta sauce, rice, beef broth, seasoned bread crumbs, salsa, garlic powder

Nutrition per serving		Exchanges
calories:	320	1 very lean meat
total fat (14%):	5 g	1 lean meat
carbohydrate:	43 g	2½ starch
cholesterol:	54 mg	1 vegetable
dietary fiber:	3 g	
protein:	26 g	carbohydrate choice: 3
sodium:	912 mg	

Placing a small piece of ice inside each meatball before browning will keep them moist.

Southwest-style Sloppy Joes

Easy — Do Ahead — Freeze

Ingredients:
1 lb. superlean ground beef
½ cup chopped green bell pepper
½ tsp. garlic powder
1 tbsp. onion powder
¾ cup barbecue sauce
½ cup corn kernels, drained
¼ cup chopped green chilies, drained
⅛ tsp. Mrs. Dash extra-spicy seasoning
4 pita pockets

Directions:
Spray large nonstick skillet with cooking spray. Add ground beef, bell pepper, garlic powder, and onion powder; cook over medium heat, stirring frequently, until beef is browned and cooked through. Drain any liquid from skillet. Add barbecue sauce, corn, green chilies, and extra-spicy Mrs. Dash seasoning; bring to a boil over high heat. Immediately reduce heat to low, cover and simmer 10 to 15 minutes. Heat pita breads in oven, if desired. Spoon Sloppy Joe mixture into pitas and serve.

Serves: 4

Shopping List:
1 lb. superlean ground beef, 6 oz. barbecue sauce, 6 oz. can corn kernels, 4 oz. can chopped green chilies, green bell pepper, garlic powder, onion powder, Mrs. Dash extra-spicy seasoning, pita pockets

Nutrition per serving		Exchanges
calories:	336	1 very lean meat
total fat (16%):	6 g	2 lean meat
carbohydrate:	34 g	1 other carbohydrate
cholesterol:	72 mg	1 starch
dietary fiber:	2 g	
protein:	32 g	carbohydrate choice: 2
sodium:	820 mg	

LUSCIOUS LEAN MEATS

Americans eat about twenty-five pounds of corn per year from more than 200 varieties. Corn provides vitamins A, B, and C; minerals and potassium, iron, zinc, and magnesium; and fiber.

Spicy Beef

Easy — Do Ahead

Ingredients:

½ cup red wine vinegar
½ tsp. red pepper flakes
¼ cup brown sugar
¾ tsp. garlic powder

½ tsp. cayenne pepper
1 lb. boneless top round
    steak, sliced thin
1 tbsp. beef broth

Directions:

Combine vinegar, pepper flakes, brown sugar, garlic powder, and cayenne pepper in a shallow baking dish. Add steak slices to marinade and turn, coating well. Spray large nonstick skillet or wok with cooking spray; add 1 tablespoon beef broth to skillet and heat over medium-high heat. Remove steak from marinade (save marinade) and place in hot skillet. Cook, stirring frequently, until steak is browned and cooked through (3 to 4 minutes). Serve over cooked pasta or rice.

Serves: 6

Shopping List:

1 lb. boneless top round steak or flank steak, 14½ oz. can beef broth, 4 oz. red wine vinegar, brown sugar, red pepper flakes, garlic powder, cayenne pepper

Nutrition per serving		Exchanges
calories:	180	2 very lean meat
total fat (25%):	5 g	1 lean meat
carbohydrate:	10 g	½ other carb
cholesterol:	63 mg	
dietary fiber:	0 g	carbohydrate choice: ½
protein:	24 g	
sodium:	57 mg	

LUSCIOUS LEAN MEATS

Americans consume an average 75 pounds of beef, 44 pounds of pork, and 40 pounds of chicken per year.

Spinach-Beef Calzone

Average — Do Ahead — Freeze

Ingredients:
½ lb. superlean ground beef
1 tbsp. onion flakes
1 tsp. garlic powder
1½ cups nonfat pasta sauce, divided
10 oz. package frozen chopped spinach, thawed and drained

12 oz. frozen bread dough, thawed
½ cup nonfat shredded mozzarella cheese
¼ cup nonfat Parmesan cheese

Directions:
Lightly spray nonstick skillet with cooking spray and heat over medium heat. Add ground beef, onion flakes, and garlic powder; cook until beef is completely cooked through. Stir in 1 cup pasta sauce and spinach; cook until heated through. Preheat oven to 400 degrees. Line baking sheet with foil and lightly spray with cooking spray. Divide thawed bread dough into 4 equal pieces. Roll each piece into circle or square; spoon beef-spinach mixture onto half of dough. Sprinkle with mozzarella cheese. Fold dough over filling and press with fork to seal. Lightly spray calzone with cooking spray and arrange on baking sheet. Bake 20 to 25 minutes until golden brown and heated through. Heat remaining pasta sauce in microwave for 30 seconds on high heat. Drizzle each calzone with heated pasta sauce and sprinkle with Parmesan cheese, if desired.

Serves: 4

Shopping List:
½ lb. superlean ground beef, 12 oz. frozen bread dough, 16 oz. nonfat pasta sauce, 10 oz. frozen chopped spinach, nonfat shredded mozzarella cheese, nonfat Parmesan cheese, garlic powder, onion flakes

Nutrition per serving		Exchanges
calories:	431	3 starch
total fat (4%):	2 g	3 vegetable
carbohydrate:	62 g	3 very lean meat
cholesterol:	48 mg	
dietary fiber:	4 g	carbohydrate choice: 4
protein:	36 g	
sodium:	669 mg	

Meat contains heme iron, which is up to 15% more absorbable than nonheme iron, the kind found in plant foods.

LUSCIOUS LEAN MEATS

Steak Fajitas

Average — Do Ahead — Freeze

Ingredients:

2 tbsp. beef broth, divided
1½ oz. dry taco seasoning mix
¾ lb. flank steak, cut into strips
1½ cups sliced onion
10 oz. frozen pepper strips, thawed and drained
4 oz. chopped green chilies
4 low-fat flour tortillas

14½ oz. can chopped tomatoes, drained well
¾ cup nonfat shredded Monterey Jack or Cheddar cheese
¾ cup nonfat sour cream
salsa

Directions:

Spray large nonstick skillet with cooking spray; add 1 tablespoon beef broth and heat over medium-high heat. Reserve 1 tablespoon taco seasoning and set aside. Put remaining seasoning in a Ziploc bag; add steak strips and shake until coated. Place steak strips in skillet and cook, stirring frequently, until browned. Remove beef from pan; respray pan and add remaining beef broth. Add onion, peppers, and chilies; sprinkle with remaining taco seasoning and cook 2 to 3 minutes until softened. Return beef to skillet and cook just until heated through. Warm tortillas in oven or microwave. Serve tortillas with beef filling, chopped tomatoes, cheese, sour cream, and salsa.

Serves: 4

Shopping List:

¾ lb. flank steak, 1½ oz. package taco seasoning mix, 10 oz. package frozen pepper strips, 4 oz. can chopped green chilies, nonfat beef broth, 14½oz. can chopped tomatoes, 6 oz. nonfat sour cream, nonfat shredded cheese (Monterey Jack or Cheddar), 2 onions, low-fat flour tortillas, salsa

Nutrition per serving

calories:	423
total fat (13%):	6 g
carbohydrate:	52 g
cholesterol:	54 mg
dietary fiber:	5 g
protein:	36 g
sodium:	2,107 mg

Exchanges

1 very lean meat
2 lean meat
2 starch
5 vegetable

carbohydrate choice: 3½

Lean meat is a good source of zinc, an important mineral that helps your immune system to fight off infections.

Stuffed Peppers

Easy — Do Ahead

Ingredients:

4 red, yellow or green bell peppers
½ lb. superlean ground beef
¼ lb. superlean ground turkey
¾ cup chopped onion
¾ tsp. garlic powder
½ tsp. Mrs. Dash extra-spicy seasoning

1 tbsp. ketchup
1 tsp. Italian seasoning, divided
1 cup cooked brown rice
14½ oz. can Italian-style diced tomatoes, undrained
1 tbsp. tomato paste

Directions:

Preheat oven to 350 degrees. Spray 9 x 13-inch baking dish with cooking spray. Cut bell peppers in half lengthwise; stem and remove seeds. Arrange peppers cut sides up in baking dish. Combine beef, turkey, onion, garlic powder, Mrs. Dash seasoning, ketchup, and ½ teaspoon Italian seasoning in medium bowl; mix well. Divide mixture among bell pepper halves (about ½ cup beef mixture per half pepper). Combine canned tomatoes, tomato paste, and ½ teaspoon Italian seasoning in a small bowl; mix well. Spoon sauce over peppers; cover dish with foil and bake 40 to 45 minutes. Remove foil and bake 5 to 10 minutes until bubbly hot and cooked through.

Serves: 4

Shopping List:

4 red, yellow, or green bell peppers; onion; ½ lb. superlean ground beef; ¼ lb. superlean ground turkey; brown rice; ketchup; tomato paste; 14½ oz. can Italian-style diced tomatoes; garlic powder; Mrs. Dash extra-spicy seasoning; Italian seasoning

LUSCIOUS LEAN MEATS

Nutrition per serving

calories:	230
total fat (16%):	4 g
carbohydrate:	25 g
cholesterol:	60 mg
dietary fiber:	2 g
protein:	25 g
sodium:	497 mg

Exchanges

1 very lean meat
1 lean meat
½ starch
4 vegetable

carbohydrate choice: 1½

When a steak is labeled "lean" it cannot have more than 10% fat; "superlean" contains no more than 5% fat. On the other hand, "lean" or "superlean" ground beef can have as much as 22% fat.

Tamale Pie

Easy — Do Ahead

Ingredients:

½ lb. superlean ground beef
½ cup chopped onion
½ cup chopped green bell pepper
⅛ tsp. garlic powder
15 oz. can tomato sauce
16 oz. can kidney beans
¾ cup corn kernels, drained

1½ tsp. chili powder
½ tsp. ground cumin
⅛ tsp. cayenne pepper
4 low-fat corn tortillas
¾ cup nonfat shredded
  Cheddar cheese

Directions:

Preheat oven to 350 degrees. Spray large nonstick skillet with cooking spray; add beef, onions, bell pepper, and garlic powder to skillet and mix lightly. Cook over medium heat, stirring frequently, until beef is browned and cooked through. Drain liquid from skillet and remove from burner. Add tomato sauce, beans, corn, chili powder, cumin, and cayenne pepper to skillet and mix well. Preheat oven to 350 degrees. Spray 1 ½-quart casserole with cooking spray. Spread one-quarter beef mixture over bottom of casserole; top with corn tortilla or tortillas to cover. Repeat process, ending with beef and bean mixture on top. Sprinkle cheese over top and bake 40 to 45 minutes until bubbly and hot.

Serves: 4

Shopping List:

½ lb. superlean ground beef, onion, green bell pepper, low-fat corn tortillas, nonfat shredded Cheddar cheese, 15 oz. can tomato sauce, 16 oz. can kidney beans, 8 oz. can corn kernels, garlic powder, chili powder, ground cumin, cayenne pepper

Nutrition per serving		Exchanges
calories:	363	2 very lean meat
total fat (12%):	5 g	1 lean meat
carbohydrate:	50 g	2 starch
cholesterol:	36 mg	3 vegetable
dietary fiber:	11 g	
protein:	32 g	carbohydrate choice: 3
sodium:	1,363 mg	

Beware: When beef or hamburger is labeled "75% lean" it still has a 24% fat content by weight.

Vermicelli with Spicy Meatballs

Easy — Do Ahead — Freeze

Ingredients:
1 lb. superlean ground beef (4% fat)
¼ cup seasoned bread crumbs
¼ cup mild salsa
1 tbsp. minced garlic
16 oz. nonfat pasta sauce
8 oz. vermicelli, cooked and drained

Directions:
Combine beef, bread crumbs, salsa, and garlic in a medium bowl and mix well. Shape into 1½-inch meatballs. Spray large nonstick skillet with cooking spray and heat over medium-high heat. Add meatballs; spray with cooking spray and cook until meatballs are well browned on all sides. Pour in pasta sauce; bring to a boil over high heat. Reduce heat to low, cover, and simmer 15 to 20 minutes until meatballs are completely cooked through. Place hot vermicelli on platter and top with meatball sauce. Serve immediately.

Serves: 4

Shopping List:
1 lb. superlean ground beef, 16 oz. nonfat pasta sauce, 8 oz. vermicelli pasta, seasoned bread crumbs, mild salsa, minced garlic

Nutrition per serving		Exchanges
calories:	324	2 lean meat
total fat (14%):	5 g	2 very lean meat
carbohydrate:	26 g	1 starch
cholesterol:	95 mg	2 vegetable
dietary fiber:	6 g	
protein:	40 g	carbohydrate choice: 1½
sodium:	511 mg	

LUSCIOUS LEAN MEATS

A recent study conducted by researchers at Johns Hopkins University, the University of Minnesota, and the Chicago Center for Clinical Research found that a heart-healthy diet that contains six ounces of lean red meat five or more days a week may actually lower cholesterol enough to reduce the risk of heart disease by 10%.

Zesty Beef 'n' Bean Chili

Easy — Do Ahead — Freeze

Ingredients:
1 lb. superlean ground beef
1 cup chopped onion
½ tsp. garlic powder
¼ tsp. pepper
⅓ cup tomato paste
10 ½ oz. can tomato sauce
15½oz. can kidney beans
1 tbsp. chili powder
½ tsp. oregano

Directions:
Spray large saucepan or Dutch oven with cooking spray. Add beef, onion, and garlic powder to pan; cook, stirring frequently, until beef is browned and cooked through. Add pepper, tomato paste, tomato sauce, beans, chili powder, and oregano to beef mixture and bring to a boil over high heat. Reduce heat to low and simmer, uncovered 20 to 25 minutes.

Serves: 4

Shopping List:
1 lb. superlean ground beef, onion, 10½ oz. can tomato sauce, 6 oz. can tomato paste, 15½ oz. can kidney beans, garlic powder, pepper, chili powder, oregano

Nutrition per serving		Exchanges
calories:	327	1½ very lean meat
total fat (17%):	6 g	2 lean meat
carbohydrate:	33 g	1 starch
cholesterol:	72 mg	3 vegetable
dietary fiber:	9 g	
protein:	36 g	carbohydrate choice: 2
sodium:	896 mg	

Beef provides amino acids that have a very high absorption and utilization rate—90%.

SENSATIONAL SOY

♦ ♦ ♦

SO, SO, SO SOY!

So what's all the fuss about? As a single food source, SOY FOODS supply generous amounts of essential nutrients, anticancer compounds, vitamins (especially B vitamins), fatty acids, soluble fiber, folic acid, potassium, iron, calcium, and zinc. SOY FOODS are the only "complete" vegetable protein that supplies all eight amino acids without cholesterol. WHEW—now that's something worth eating!

The American Heart Association, along with the **U.S. Food and Drug Administration** (FDA), is encouraging everyone to add soy protein to their low-fat, low-cholesterol diet in the effort to lower the risk of heart disease. The American Heart Association has found a connection between high soy diets (consuming 50 to 60 grams per day) and lower LDL, or bad, cholesterol levels; soy products alone won't complete the healthy living puzzle. It is essential to combine increased soy intake with nutritious meal plans and regular exercise.

What you probably already know:
- Soy products come from soybeans.
- Soy foods include tofu, soy milk, fresh green soybeans (edamame), soy nuts, and fermented foods such as tempeh and miso.
- Soy is an excellent source of:
  - dietary fiber
  - protein
  - vitamin B_6
- Soy is a healthy (low cholesterol, low saturated fat) alternative to meat.
- Soy may help fight cancer.
- Soy foods prevent or improve other health conditions including high cholesterol levels, heart disease, diabetes, high blood pressure, gallstones, kidney disease, and osteoporosis.

- Soy foods contain isoflavones that may help women combat the effects of menopause (including hot flashes and bone loss).
- Soy products are on the rise; they are no longer confined to the shelves of health food stores.
- Soy foods are economically practical, sensible, simple substitutions for a healthy alternative diet.
- Soy foods are virtually tasteless, but . . .

Did you know . . .
- Soy foods easily assume the flavor of the food (e.g., soy sauce, teriyaki sauce, chili, etc.) with which they are combined?
- The United States produces almost half of the world's soybeans, but . . .
- The Japanese consume more soybeans and soy products (more than ten times that of Americans) than any other single population on Earth?
- Japanese have a longer life expectancy than any other population on Earth?
- Japanese women are affected by breast cancer only one-quarter as much as American women?
- Japanese are affected by colon cancer one-third the incidence of that among Americans?
- When Japanese give up their soy-based diet, the incidence of cancer increases?
- The American Heart Association, along with the U.S. Food and Drug Administration is encouraging e veryone to add soy protein to their diet?
- The report on the phytochemical profile of soy foods shows they provide levels of phytochemicals that cannot be consumed in reasonable amounts from other foods?
- The FDA recently issued a ruling allowing the information regarding the health benefits of soy protein to be printed on the packaging of any soy food products containing at least 6.25 grams of protein?

So what's the simplest way to make sensible soy substitutions in the daily meal plan?

- Pour soy milk over breakfast cereal instead of dairy milk.
- Drink one glass of soy milk each day (try vanilla- or chocolate-flavored milk; stick with the nonfat variety.)
- Substitute soy milk for dairy milk in baked goods.
- Substitute soy flour in baked recipes for 15 to 20% of the total flour amount (do not substitute total amounts of flour as soy flour does not contain gluten and products will not bake properly).
- Replace eggs in baking recipes by substituting one tablespoon soy flour + 2 tablespoons water for each egg.
- Substitute ½ cup tofu per egg used in baked recipes.
- Add tofu to scrambled eggs.
- Carry soy nuts with you for a tote 'n' go snack. Watch what you eat—these nuts are still high in calories and fat!
- Sprinkle salads with flavored soy nuts.
- Serve fresh or frozen soybeans (simply boiled or steamed) as the perfect accompaniment to any meal.
- Substitute tofu for mayonnaise or sour cream (partial or whole portions) in your favorite dips, dressings, or sauces.
- Blend tofu into fruit smoothies.
- Substitute soy protein "crumbles" to your favorite taco, lasagna, chili, or other recipes that are usually meat-based.
- Use texturized soy protein (TSP) in tacos, meat loaf, chili, spaghetti sauce, etc., in place of meat. To rehydrate TSP, combine each cup of TSP with ½ cup boiling water.
- Add cubed firm tofu to soups and stir-fries.
- Partially substitute silken tofu for strained yogurt or cream cheese in dips, sauces, or baked recipes.

Merely adding soy foods will not guarantee a life free of disease. The American Heart Association recommends that consumers:

- combine their soy intake with a nutritious diet, consisting of fish, lean meats, poultry, whole grains, low-fat dairy products, fruits, and vegetables.
- continue to limit their intake of saturated fat and cholesterol.
- replace foods that are high in saturated fat and cholesterol with soy foods, rather than simply adding soy to their diet.

The bottom line . . .
Incorporating soy foods into your diet is a sensible and simple solution toward a lifetime of health.

"This is a stew with potent properties as an antioxidant and with phytosterols that compete against the hormone-related cancers; it's a hormone-deflecting, tumor-suppressing, blood-thinning, virus-fighting, cholesterol-lowering warrior."

(Source: Stephanie Beling, M.D., *Power Foods*)

SO YOU SAY YOU WANT TO SUBSTITUTE SOY? IT'S SO, SO, SO SOYFULLY EASY!

Substitute	For	Save		
		Calories	*Fat*	*Cholesterol*
½ cup textured vegetable protein (beef-flavor)	3 oz. lean ground beef	99	14 g	71 mg
½ cup textured vegetable protein (chicken-flavor)	3 oz. chicken breast w/o skin	58	3 g	77 mg
¼ cup mashed tofu light	1 egg	53	4.5 g	213 mg
1 cup nonfat soy milk	1 cup skim milk	—	—	—

SENSATIONAL SOY

Artichoke-Spinach Spread

Average — Do Ahead

Ingredients:

4 whole-wheat pita breads
garlic-flavored cooking spray
1½ tsp. garlic powder, divided
10 ½ oz. tofu light
1 tbsp. lemon juice
¾ tsp. onion powder
¾ tsp. Mrs. Dash seasoning

10 oz. frozen chopped
  spinach, thawed, drained,
  and dried
1 cup artichoke hearts,
  drained, chopped fine
¼ cup chopped green onion
½ cup nonfat Parmesan
  cheese

Directions:

Preheat oven to 400 degrees. Line baking sheet(s) with foil and spray with cooking spray. Cut each pita into 8 equal pieces; arrange in single layer on baking sheet. Spray pitas with garlic-flavored cooking spray and sprinkle with 1 teaspoon garlic powder. Bake 4 to 5 minutes; remove from oven. Combine tofu, lemon juice, ½ teaspoon garlic powder, onion powder, and Mrs. Dash seasoning in food processor or blender; process until smooth. Scrape tofu mixture into medium bowl; add spinach, artichoke hearts, and onion. Mix until ingredients are blended. Spoon spinach mixture on top of pita chips; sprinkle with Parmesan cheese. Turn broiler on high heat. Broil pitas just until cheese is lightly browned.

Serves: 8

Shopping List:

10½ oz. tofu light, 10 oz. package frozen chopped spinach, 14 oz. can artichoke hearts, nonfat Parmesan cheese, whole-wheat pita breads, green onion, lemon juice, garlic powder, onion powder, Mrs. Dash seasoning, garlic-flavored cooking spray

Nutrition per serving		**Exchanges**
calories:	107	1 starch
total fat (8%):	1 g	1 vegetable
carbohydrate:	18 g	
cholesterol:	0 mg	carbohydrate choice: 1
dietary fiber:	1 g	
protein:	7 g	
sodium:	232 mg	

Artichokes contain silymarin, a flavonoid that may provide protection against skin cancer.

SENSATIONAL SOY

Breaded Tofu Snackers

Easy — Do Ahead — Freeze

Ingredients:
- ¾ cup cornflake crumbs
- ¼ cup nonfat Parmesan cheese
- 1 tsp. garlic powder
- 1 tsp. onion powder
- ¾ tsp. Mrs. Dash seasoning
- ½ cup egg substitute
- 1 lb. tofu light, cut into sticks or cubes

Directions:
Preheat oven to 375 degrees. Line baking sheet with foil and spray with cooking spray. Combine cornflake crumbs, Parmesan cheese, garlic powder, onion powder, and Mrs. Dash seasoning in shallow baking dish and mix well; pour egg substitute into small bowl and whisk lightly. Dip tofu sticks into egg substitute; roll in cornflake mixture and coat well. Arrange on baking sheet; spray lightly with cooking spray and bake 30 to 40 minutes until lightly browned and crisp. Serve with ketchup, salsa, or honey mustard.

Serves: 4

Shopping List:
1 lb. tofu light, cornflake crumbs, nonfat Parmesan cheese, egg substitute, garlic powder, onion powder, Mrs. Dash seasoning

Nutrition per serving		Exchanges
calories:	139	1 starch
total fat (6%):	1 g	2 very lean meat
carbohydrate:	17 g	
cholesterol:	0 mg	carbohydrate choice: 1
dietary fiber:	0 g	
protein:	14 g	
sodium:	353 mg	

One-half cup of tofu (the equivalent of one adult serving) provides 18 grams of soy protein. Consuming an average of 47 grams of soy protein per day has been associated with significant reductions in total blood cholesterol, LDL, and triglyceride levels.

Mini Rice Cakes with Tofu-Cheese Spread

Easy — Do Ahead

Ingredients:
¼ cup nonfat ricotta cheese
¼ cup tofu light
2 cups shredded carrot
¼ cup chopped cucumbers
¾ cup chopped red bell pepper
3 tbsp. chopped green onion
½ tsp. garlic powder
2 tsp. dried parsley
¼ tsp. dried thyme
1 tbsp. lemon juice
12 mini rice cakes (flavor of choice)
chopped chives (optional)

Directions:
Combine ricotta cheese and tofu in food processor or blender. Process until creamy and smooth. Spoon mixture into medium bowl; add remaining ingredients except rice cakes and mix until all ingredients are blended. Cover and refrigerate at least 1 hour before serving. Spread on flavored rice cakes; garnish with chopped chives, if desired.

Serves: 4

Shopping List:
2 oz. nonfat ricotta cheese, 2 oz. tofu light, 8 oz. package shredded carrots, cucumber, red bell pepper, green onions, mini rice cakes, garlic powder, dried parsley, dried thyme, lemon juice, chives (optional)

Nutrition per serving		Exchanges
calories:	84	½ starch
total fat (11%):	1 g	2 vegetable
carbohydrate:	16 g	
cholesterol:	3 mg	carbohydrate choice: 1
dietary fiber:	2 g	
protein:	5 g	
sodium:	72 mg	

Tofu has a high protein content and is easily digested, especially for those with sensitive stomachs.

Spinach-Tofu Snackers

Easy — Do Ahead

Ingredients:
10½ oz. tofu light
1 tbsp. lemon juice
½ tsp. garlic powder
¾ tsp. onion powder
½ tsp. dried tarragon
¼ tsp. pepper
10 oz. frozen chopped spinach, thawed and drained
½ cup shredded carrot
½ cup shredded zucchini

Directions:
Combine tofu and lemon juice in blender or food processor; process until smooth. Add garlic powder, onion powder, tarragon, and pepper; process until blended. Spoon tofu mixture into bowl; add spinach, carrot and zucchini. Mix well. Serve on toasted French bread slices, low-fat crackers, or pita crisps.

Serves: 8

Shopping List:
10½ oz. tofu light, 10 oz. frozen chopped spinach, packaged shredded carrots, zucchini, lemon juice, garlic powder, onion powder, dried tarragon, pepper

Nutrition per serving

calories:	32
total fat (0%):	0 g
carbohydrate:	4 g
cholesterol:	0 mg
dietary fiber:	1 g
protein:	4 g
sodium:	62 mg

Exchanges
½ meat
1 vegetable

carbohydrate choice: 0

Soy helps reduce cholesterol levels, as well as prevent heart disease and diabetes.

SENSATIONAL SOY

Mexican Bean and Salsa Dip

Easy — Do Ahead

Ingredients:
  ½ cup soybeans, rinsed and drained
  1½ cups canned black beans, rinsed and drained
  1½ tsp. lemon juice
  2 tbsp. canned chopped tomatoes
  ¾ tsp. onion powder
  2 tbsp. chopped green chilies
  1 tsp. chili powder
  ½ tsp. ground cumin
  ½ tsp. garlic powder
  ¾ cup chunky salsa
  ½ cup nonfat Cheddar soy cheese, grated

Directions:
  Combine soybeans, black beans, lemon juice, tomatoes, onion powder, chilies, chili powder, cumin, and garlic powder in a food processor or blender; process until smooth. Spread bean mixture in shallow baking dish (glass); top with salsa and sprinkle with shredded cheese. Microwave on high 45 to 60 seconds or bake in 350 degree oven (5 to 10 minutes) until cheese is melted. Serve with low-fat baked tortilla chips.

Serves: 8

Shopping List:
  soybeans, 15 oz. can black beans, canned chopped tomatoes (or 1 small tomato), 4 oz. can chopped green chilies, nonfat Cheddar soy cheese, chunky salsa, lemon juice, onion powder, chili powder, ground cumin, garlic powder

Nutrition per serving		Exchanges
calories:	76	1 starch
total fat (12%):	1 g	
carbohydrate:	11 g	carbohydrate choice: 1
cholesterol:	2 mg	
dietary fiber:	2 g	
protein:	5 g	
sodium:	334 mg	

Soy foods are packed with powerful antioxidants that interfere with free radical damage (for cancer prevention).

Date Bran Muffins

Easy — Do Ahead — Freeze

Ingredients:

1½ cups bran cereal
½ cup chopped dates
½ cup boiling water
¼ cup egg substitute
¾ cup nonfat vanilla soy milk
½ cup cinnamon applesauce

¼ cup corn syrup
½ cup all-purpose flour
¼ cup whole-wheat flour
¼ cup soybean flour
½ cup brown sugar
2 tsp. baking powder

Directions:

Preheat oven to 325 degrees. Spray muffin tin with cooking spray. Combine cereal and dates in large mixing bowl; pour boiling water over top and stir until mixed. Set aside to cool. In a separate bowl, combine egg substitute, soy milk, applesauce, and corn syrup; gradually add remaining ingredients, mixing well after each addition. Stir in cereal mixture and mix until all ingredients are moistened. Fill muffin cups three-quarters full and bake 25 to 30 minutes, until toothpick inserted in center comes out clean.

Serves: 12

Shopping List:

bran cereal, chopped dates, all-purpose flour, whole-wheat flour, soybean flour, brown sugar, baking powder, cinnamon applesauce, nonfat vanilla soy milk, corn syrup, egg substitute

Nutrition per serving		Exchanges
calories:	133	2 other carbohydrate
total fat (7%):	1 g	
carbohydrate:	31 g	carbohydrate choice: 2
cholesterol:	0 mg	
dietary fiber:	4 g	
protein:	4 g	
sodium:	128 mg	

Although dried fruits lose vitamin C when dried, they do retain most of their minerals and are especially rich in beta-carotene. A date cluster can weigh up to 25 pounds, supplying 250% more potassium than an orange and 64% more than a banana ounce for ounce.

SENSATIONAL SOY

Honey of a Pumpkin Bread

Easy — Do Ahead — Freeze

Ingredients:

¼ cup sugar
½ cup honey
¼ cup crushed pineapple
1 egg white
¼ cup egg substitute
¾ tsp. vanilla
1 cup canned pumpkin

½ cup all-purpose flour
½ cup whole-wheat flour
½ cup soybean flour
1 tbsp. baking powder
2 tsp. cinnamon
¾ tsp. pumpkin pie spice
½ cup Craisins
cinnamon-sugar, for topping

Directions:

Preheat oven to 325 degrees. Spray 9 x 5-inch loaf pan with cooking spray. Combine sugar, honey, crushed pineapple, egg white, egg substitute, and vanilla in a large mixing bowl; mix until blended smooth. Stir in pumpkin and mix well. Add flours, baking powder, cinnamon, and pumpkin pie spice to pumpkin mixture; stir until ingredients are moistened and blended. Fold in Craisins. Spoon batter into loaf pan; sprinkle with cinnamon-sugar and bake 1 hour, until toothpick inserted in center comes out clean. Let bread cool 10 minutes before removing from pan; cool completely before slicing.

Serves: 12

Shopping List:

16 oz. can pumpkin, 8 oz. can crushed pineapple, egg substitute, eggs, whole-wheat flour, all-purpose flour, soybean flour, sugar, honey, vanilla, baking powder, cinnamon, pumpkin pie spice, Craisins (or other dried fruit)

Nutrition per serving		Exchanges
calories:	139	2 other carbohydrates
total fat (0%):	0 g	
carbohydrate:	32 g	carbohydrate choice: 2
cholesterol:	0 mg	
dietary fiber:	2 g	
protein:	4 g	
sodium:	90 mg	

Honey contains antioxidants that contribute to the prevention of cellular damage as the result of aging.

Lemon-Berry Muffins

Easy — Do Ahead — Freeze

Ingredients:

¾ cup all-purpose flour
¾ cup whole-wheat flour
½ cup soy bean flour
2 tsp. baking powder
¼ cup sugar
¼ cup brown sugar
¼ cup egg substitute

1 cup nonfat vanilla soy milk
½ tsp. lemon extract
½ tsp. vanilla
2 tbsp. unsweetened
   applesauce
1 cup blueberries (fresh or
   frozen)
1 tbsp. powdered sugar

Directions:

Preheat oven to 325 degrees. Spray muffin tin with cooking spray. Combine flours, baking powder, sugar, and brown sugar in a medium bowl. Add egg substitute, soy milk, lemon extract, vanilla, and applesauce to flour mixture; stir until ingredients are moistened and blended. Pour in blueberries; sprinkle with powdered sugar and fold into batter. Divide batter among 12 muffin cups; bake 20 to 25 minutes until toothpick inserted in center comes out clean.

Serves: 12

Shopping List:

8 oz. nonfat vanilla soy milk, all-purpose flour, whole-wheat flour, soybean flour, sugar, brown sugar, powdered sugar, egg substitute, unsweetened applesauce, fresh or frozen blueberries, baking powder, lemon extract, vanilla extract

Nutrition per serving

calories:	106
total fat (0%):	0 g
carbohydrate:	23 g
cholesterol:	0 mg
dietary fiber:	1 g
protein:	3 g
sodium:	67 mg

Exchanges

1½ other carbohydrate

carbohydrate choice: 1½

SENSATIONAL SOY

Soy is rich in phytoestrogen (genistein and daidzein) that may block the negative effects of natural estrogens or supplement them when they're running low.

Ranchero Breakfast Burrito

Easy

Ingredients:
  1 lb. tofu light
  2 tsp. onion powder
  1 tsp. garlic powder
  1 tsp. Mrs. Dash seasoning
  ¼ tsp. pepper
  1 tsp. parsley flakes
  ½ cup chunky salsa
  4 low-fat flour tortillas

Directions:
  Spray nonstick skillet with cooking spray and heat over medium heat. Crumble tofu into skillet; sprinkle generously with onion powder, garlic powder, Mrs. Dash seasoning, pepper, and parsley. Cook, stirring frequently, until heated through. Remove from heat. Pour salsa into microwave-safe dish; heat 30 to 45 seconds. Add salsa to tofu and mix lightly. Spoon into center of tortillas; roll, fold, wrap, and serve.

Serves: 4

Shopping List:
  1 lb. tofu light, chunky salsa, low-fat flour tortillas, onion powder, garlic powder, Mrs. Dash seasoning, pepper, parsley flakes

Nutrition per serving		Exchanges
calories:	171	1 starch
total fat (5%):	1 g	1 vegetable
carbohydrate:	28 g	½ other carbohydrate
cholesterol:	0 mg	
dietary fiber:	2 g	carbohydrate choice: 2
protein:	13 g	
sodium:	586 mg	

Parsley helps hay fever sufferers by slowing down the body's secretion of histamine, the chemical that sets off allergy symptoms.

Strawberry Oatmeal Pancakes

Easy — Do Ahead — Freeze

Ingredients:

1¼ cups oatmeal
2 cups nonfat vanilla soy milk
¼ cup egg substitute
1½ tbsp. brown sugar
¾ cup all-purpose flour
¾ cup whole-wheat flour

1 tbsp. baking powder
1 cup sliced strawberries
Butter Buds, optional
light syrup or preserves
  (optional)

Directions:

Combine oatmeal, soy milk, egg substitute, and brown sugar in a medium bowl and mix lightly; let stand 10 minutes. Gradually add flours and baking powder to oat mixture. Fold in sliced strawberries. Spray large nonstick skillet with cooking spray and heat over medium-high heat. Pour ½ cup batter per pancake into skillet; cook until bubbles form on top. Flip pancake and cook until golden brown. Remove skillet from heat; respray with cooking spray. Add pancake batter and return to heat; repeat process with remaining batter. Sprinkle with Butter Buds and serve with lite syrup or heated preserves, if desired.

Serves: 6

Shopping List:

16 oz. nonfat vanilla soy milk, oatmeal, egg substitute, all-purpose flour, whole-wheat flour, brown sugar, baking powder, strawberries, Butter Buds (optional), lite syrup or preserves (optional)

Nutrition per serving

calories:	214
total fat (13%):	3 g
carbohydrate:	42 g
cholesterol:	0 mg
dietary fiber:	5 g
protein:	9 g
sodium:	194 mg

Exchanges

2 starch
½ fruit
½ other carbohydrate

carbohydrate choice: 3

SENSATIONAL SOY

James W. Anderson, M.D., a professor at the University of Kentucky College of Medicine, discovered that the high-fiber diets he developed for his diabetic patients not only brought down insulin requirements but also lowered their blood cholesterol levels.

Unsinfully Soyful Banana Bread

Easy — Do Ahead — Freeze

Ingredients:

¾ cup all-purpose flour
¾ cup whole-wheat flour
½ cup soybean flour
1 tsp. cinnamon
2 tsp. baking powder
¼ cup sugar
½ cup brown sugar

½ cup crushed pineapple
¼ cup egg substitute
1 tsp. vanilla
1 cup mashed bananas
¼ cup nonfat vanilla soy
   milk
½ cup raisins

Directions:

Preheat oven to 325 degrees. Spray 9 x 5-inch loaf pan with cooking spray. In a large mixing bowl, combine flours, cinnamon, baking powder, sugar, and brown sugar; mix well. Add pineapple, egg substitute, vanilla, bananas, milk, and raisins. Mix until all ingredients are moistened; do not overmix. Pour batter into loaf pan; bake 45 to 60 minutes, until toothpick inserted in center comes out clean. Cool in pan 10 minutes; remove and let cool before slicing.

Serves: 12

Shopping List:

2 to 3 bananas, canned crushed pineapple, raisins, nonfat vanilla soy milk, egg substitute, all-purpose flour, whole-wheat flour, soybean flour, sugar, brown sugar, cinnamon, baking powder, vanilla extract

Nutrition per serving		Exchanges
calories:	161	2 other carbohydrate
total fat (6%):	1 g	
carbohydrate:	36 g	carbohydrate choice: 2
cholesterol:	0 mg	
dietary fiber:	2 g	
protein:	5 g	
sodium:	67 mg	

Although no one knows exactly how much soy you need each day to gain health benefits, it seems that even just one serving a day might be sufficient.
One serving of soy equals:
½ cup soybeans, 4 oz. tofu, or 8 oz. soy milk.

Color-Me-Soy Slaw

Easy — Do Ahead

Ingredients:
5¼ oz. tofu light
2 tbsp. frozen apple juice concentrate, undiluted
1 tbsp. honey
1 tbsp. lemon juice
¼ tsp. cinnamon
2 cups shredded cabbage
½ cup seedless grapes
½pear, cored and chopped
1 apple, cored and chopped
½ cup canned pineapple tidbits, drained

Directions:
Combine tofu, apple juice concentrate, honey, lemon juice, and cinnamon in a food processor or blender; process until smooth. Combine cabbage, grapes, pear, apple, and pineapple in a medium bowl and mix well; pour dressing over cabbage mixture and toss until ingredients are coated. Cover with plastic wrap and refrigerate several hours before serving.

Serves: 4

Shopping List:
5¼ oz. tofu light, pear, apple, ¼ lb. seedless grapes, 6 oz. can pineapple tidbits, shredded cabbage mix, frozen apple juice concentrate, honey, lemon juice, cinnamon

Nutrition per serving		Exchanges
calories:	106	½ fruit
total fat (8%):	1 g	2 vegetable
carbohydrate:	24 g	½ other carbohydrate
cholesterol:	0 mg	
dietary fiber:	3 g	carbohydrate choice: 1½
protein:	4 g	
sodium:	39 mg	

SENSATIONAL SOY

Research studies show that eating a half head of cabbage each day may help prevent certain types of cancer. Cabbage contains the chemical indole, which has been proven to prevent breast cancer. Eating cabbage once a week may reduce the risk of colon cancer by 60%.

Cabbage Slaw with Spicy Soy-Pepper Dressing

Easy — Do Ahead

Ingredients:
1 cup chopped bell pepper (any color)
½ package (10½ oz.) tofu light
2 tbsp. herb-flavored vinegar
½ tsp. caraway seeds
1 tbsp. Dijon mustard
pepper to taste
16 oz. shredded cabbage

Directions:
Combine all ingredients except cabbage in food processor or blender; process until smooth. Toss cabbage with dressing; cover and refrigerate several hours or overnight before serving.

Serves: 4

Shopping List:
10½ oz. tofu light, 16 oz. package shredded cabbage, bell pepper (any color), herb-flavored vinegar, Dijon mustard, caraway seeds, pepper

Nutrition per serving		Exchanges
calories:	56	1 vegetable
total fat (16%):	1 g	½ other carbohydrate
carbohydrate:	11 g	½ very lean meat
cholesterol:	0 mg	
dietary fiber:	3 g	carbohydrate choice: 1
protein:	4 g	
sodium:	99 mg	

Soy foods provide the protective benefits of estrogen without raising cancer risks.

SENSATIONAL SOY

Southwestern Soy Salad

Easy — Do Ahead

Ingredients:
½ cup canned soybeans
1 cup canned black beans, drained
½ cup canned corn kernels, drained
½ cup chopped red bell pepper
½ cup chopped tomatoes
¼ cup sliced green onion
¼ cup sliced red onion
½ tsp. garlic powder
½ cup nonfat Italian salad dressing
⅓ tsp. chili powder
2 tsp. lemon juice
2 tsp. fresh cilantro, chopped

Directions:
Combine soybeans, black beans, corn, bell pepper, tomatoes, green onion, red onion, and garlic powder in a large bowl. Combine salad dressing, chili powder, lemon juice, and cilantro in a sealed container; shake until ingredients are blended. Pour dressing over bean mixture; toss lightly. Cover bean salad and refrigerate at least 6 hours before serving.

Serves: 6

Shopping List:
canned soybeans, canned black beans, 8 oz. can corn kernels, nonfat Italian salad dressing, red pepper, tomato, green onion, red onion, cilantro, lemon juice, garlic powder, chili powder

Nutrition per serving		Exchanges
calories:	93	2 vegetable
total fat (10%):	1 g	½ starch
carbohydrate:	17 g	
cholesterol:	0 mg	carbohydrate choice: 1
dietary fiber:	2 g	
protein:	5 g	
sodium:	316 mg	

Tofu is high in protein, low in calories and sodium, and a good source of calcium and iron.

SENSATIONAL SOY

Creamed Corn Chowder

Easy — Do Ahead

Ingredients:
    3 cups cubed potatoes
    1 tbsp. onion powder
    2 cups water
    1 tsp. chicken bouillon granules
    ⅛ tsp. pepper
    14½ oz. can cream-style corn
    1 cup nonfat soy milk
    8 oz. can corn kernels, drained

Directions:
    Combine potatoes, onion powder, water, bouillon, and pepper in a medium saucepan; bring to a boil over high heat. Reduce heat to low and simmer 8 to 10 minutes until potatoes are tender. Remove pan from heat; stir in cream-style corn. Pour 2 cups soup mixture into food processor or blender and process just until blended. Pour mixture back into saucepan; add milk and corn kernels and cook until heated through.

Serves: 4

Shopping List:
    1 lb. potatoes, 14½ oz. can cream-style corn, 8 oz. can corn kernels, 8 oz. nonfat soy milk, chicken bouillon granules, onion powder, pepper

Nutrition per serving

		Exchanges
calories:	253	3 starch
total fat (4%):	1 g	1 other carbohydrate
carbohydrate:	57 g	
cholesterol:	0 mg	carbohydrate choice: 4
dietary fiber:	7 g	
protein:	7 g	
sodium:	535 mg	

Although 82% of Americans believe a poor diet can increase their risk of cancer, only 17% are willing to change their diet to reduce the risk.

Vegetable-Soy Soup

Easy — Do Ahead — Freeze

Ingredients:
½ cup soy beans
½ cup canned white beans
1¾ cups water
2 cups vegetable broth
¼ tsp. garlic powder
1 tsp. onion powder
2 tsp. dried thyme
2 tsp. dried basil
1 tbsp. dried parsley
1 cup frozen baby carrots
¾ cup frozen green peas
1 cup chopped tomatoes
½ cup chopped celery

Directions:
Combine all ingredients in a large soup pot or Dutch oven; bring to a boil over high heat. Reduce heat to low and simmer 30 to 45 minutes until vegetables are tender.

Serves: 4

Shopping List:
soybeans, 15 oz. can white beans, 16 oz. vegetable broth, 10 oz. frozen baby carrots, 10 oz. frozen green peas, 14½ oz. can chopped tomatoes, celery, garlic powder, onion powder, dried thyme, dried basil, dried parsley

Nutrition per serving

calories:	249
total fat (4%):	1 g
carbohydrate:	80 g
cholesterol:	0 mg
dietary fiber:	8 g
protein:	13 g
sodium:	519 mg

Exchanges

2½ starch
7 vegetable

carbohydrate choice: 5

SENSATIONAL SOY

According to the National Cancer Society, only 9% of all Americans eat enough fruits and vegetables.

Mashed Eggplant & Tofu Casserole
Difficult — Do Ahead

Ingredients:

1½ lb. eggplant,
cooked and mashed
2 tsp. vegetable broth
1 cup chopped onion
¾ cup chopped red bell pepper
1 tsp. minced garlic
5 oz. tofu light, squeezed dry

½ cup nonfat shredded
mozzarella cheese
¼ cup nonfat Parmesan
cheese, divided
1½ cups seasoned bread
crumbs, divided
1½ tsp. Italian seasoning
½ tsp. red pepper flakes

Directions:

Preheat oven to 350 degrees. Spray 1⅓ quart baking dish with cooking spray. Spray nonstick skillet with cooking spray; add vegetable broth to skillet and heat over medium-high heat. Add onions, bell peppers, and minced garlic to skillet; cook, stirring frequently, 10 to 12 minutes, until vegetables are softened. Add vegetable mixture to eggplant mix. Stir in tofu, mozzarella cheese, 2 tablespoons Parmesan cheese, 1¼ cups seasoned breadcrumbs, Italian seasoning, and red pepper flakes; mix well. Spoon mixture into baking dish; sprinkle with remaining breadcrumbs and Parmesan cheese. Bake casserole 30 to 40 minutes until lightly browned and bubbly hot.

Serves: 4

Shopping List:

1 lb. eggplant, onion, red bell pepper, 5 oz. tofu light, nonfat shredded mozzarella cheese, nonfat Parmesan cheese, seasoned bread crumbs, vegetable broth, Italian seasoning, minced garlic, red pepper flakes

Nutrition per serving		Exchanges
calories:	260	1 starch
total fat (10%):	3 g	6 vegetable
carbohydrate:	44 g	1 very lean meat
cholesterol:	0 mg	
dietary fiber:	2 g	carbohydrate choice: 3
protein:	16 g	
sodium:	470 mg	

Eggplant and zucchini are members of a new category of foods called "fruit-vegetables."

Meatless Meat Sauce

Easy — Do Ahead — Freeze

Ingredients:
28 oz. can stewed tomatoes
½ cup shredded carrot
1 tbsp. onion powder
1 tsp. dried Italian seasoning
1 lb. Smart Ground meatless crumbles
pepper to taste

Directions:
Combine tomatoes, carrot, onion powder, and Italian seasoning in a medium saucepan; bring to a boil over high heat. Reduce heat to low and simmer 5 to 8 minutes until carrots are softened. Add meatless crumbles; bring to a boil over high heat. Reduce heat to low and simmer 10 to 15 minutes until heated through. Season with pepper to taste.

Serves: 4

Shopping List:
1 lb. Smart Ground meatless crumbles, 28 oz. can stewed tomatoes, packaged shredded carrot, onion powder, Italian seasoning, pepper

Nutrition per serving

calories:	186
total fat (0%):	0 g
carbohydrate:	24 g
cholesterol:	0 mg
dietary fiber:	6 g
protein:	23 g
sodium:	1,046 mg

Exchanges
2 very lean meat
5 vegetable

carbohydrate choice: 1½

Soy helps fight breast prostate, colon, and endometrial cancer.

SENSATIONAL SOY

Super-Soy Stirfry

Average

Ingredients:

1 tbsp. low-sodium soy sauce
1½ tsp. rice vinegar
8 oz. tofu light, cut in bite-size pieces
2 tsp. vegetable broth
¼ tsp. garlic powder
⅛ tsp. ground ginger
1 onion, sliced thin
1 cup cauliflower florets

1 cup broccoli florets
1 cup red bell pepper, sliced
½ cup sliced water chestnuts
¾ cup pea pods
½ cup low-sodium teriyaki sauce
1½ tsp. corn starch
1½ tsp. cold water
2 cups cooked brown rice

Directions:

Spray large nonstick skillet with cooking spray and heat over medium-high heat. Combine soy sauce and rice vinegar in a medium bowl; add tofu and toss until well coated. Pour mixture into skillet and cook, stirring frequently, until tofu starts to brown. Remove from pan and set aside. Respray skillet; add vegetable broth and heat over medium-high heat. Sprinkle garlic powder and ginger over broth; add vegetables and cook, stirring constantly, 3 to 4 minutes until tender-crisp. Pour teriyaki sauce over vegetables; cover pan and steam 2 to 3 minutes. Combine corn starch and cold water in a small cup; mix until blended. Remove cover from pan, increase heat to high and add corn starch mixture. Stir until sauce becomes thick and bubbly. Stir in tofu and cook until heated through. Serve over brown rice.

Serves: 4

Shopping List:

8 oz. tofu light, ½ lb. broccoli florets, ½ lb. cauliflower florets, onion, red bell pepper, 6 oz. can water chestnuts, ¾ lb. pea pods, low-sodium soy sauce, low-sodium teriyaki sauce, rice vinegar, vegetable broth, corn starch, brown rice, garlic powder, ground ginger

Nutrition per serving		Exchanges
calories:	222	1 starch
total fat (4%):	1 g	3 vegetable
carbohydrate:	42 g	1 other carbohydrate
cholesterol:	0 mg	
dietary fiber:	3 g	carbohydrate choice: 3
protein:	11 g	
sodium:	1,597 mg	

A half cup Edamame (soybeans) equals 22 grams of protein.

Vegetarian Sloppy Joes

Easy — Do Ahead

Ingredients:

14 oz. Gimme Lean meat substitute
1½ tbsp. onion flakes
1 tsp. minced garlic
1 cup chopped zucchini
1 cup chopped yellow squash
1 cup sliced mushrooms
¾ cup chopped red bell pepper

1¾ cups chopped tomatoes, undrained
½ cup barbecue sauce
1 tsp. Italian seasoning
½ tsp. Mrs. Dash seasoning
6 whole-wheat pita pockets (or other low fat bread of choice)

Directions:

Spray large nonstick skillet with cooking spray. Add meat substitute, onion flakes, and garlic to skillet; cook, stirring frequently, until "meat" is crumbled and browned (about 5 to 7 minutes). Add zucchini, squash, mushrooms, and bell pepper; cover and cook over medium heat until vegetables are tender. Add tomatoes, barbecue sauce, and seasonings; cook over medium heat until most of the liquid has evaporated and mixture is heated through. Serve Sloppy Joes on pita bread, sourdough bread, rolls, or other low-fat bread of choice.

Serves: 6

Shopping List:

14 oz. Gimme Lean meat substitute, 2 zucchini, 2 yellow squash, ¼ lb. mushrooms, red bell pepper, 14½ oz. can chopped tomatoes, barbecue sauce, onion flakes, minced garlic, Italian seasoning, Mrs. Dash seasoning, whole-wheat pita pockets, or other low fat bread of choice

Nutrition per serving

calories:	249
total fat (4%):	1 g
carbohydrate:	44 g
cholesterol:	0 mg
dietary fiber:	3 g
protein:	16 g
sodium:	1,000 mg

Exchanges

2 starch
2 vegetable
½ other carbohydrate
1 very lean meat

carbohydrate choice: 3

SENSATIONAL SOY

Zucchini and yellow squash, members of the summer squash family, are low in calories and a good source of vitamin A.

Veggie-Rich Chili

Easy — Do Ahead — Freeze

Ingredients:
28 oz. can crushed tomatoes
3 cups water
1½ tsp. garlic powder
1 tbsp. onion powder
1¼ cups frozen corn kernels, thawed and drained
1¼ cup frozen carrots, thawed, drained and cut in half
1½ cups frozen pepper strips, thawed and drained
½ cup chopped green chilies, drained
8 oz. tofu light, chopped fine
1½ tbsp. chili powder
1½ tsp. Italian seasoning
15 oz. can kidney beans, rinsed and drained
15 oz. soy beans

Directions:
Combine all the ingredients except soybeans and kidney beans in a large soup pot or Dutch oven; bring to a boil over high heat. Reduce heat and simmer 30 to 45 minutes until vegetables are tender. Add beans and continue cooking 10 to 15 minutes, until heated through. Great topping for baked potatoes!

Serves: 8

Shopping List:
28 oz. can crushed tomatoes, 8 oz. tofu light, 15 oz. can kidney beans, 15 oz. soybeans, 4 oz. can chopped green chilies, 10 oz. frozen corn kernels, 10 oz. frozen baby carrots, 10 oz. frozen pepper strips, garlic powder, onion powder, chili powder, Italian seasoning

Nutrition per serving		Exchanges
calories:	199	1 starch
total fat (18%):	4 g	3 vegetable
carbohydrate:	32 g	1 very lean meat
cholesterol:	0 mg	
dietary fiber:	6 g	carbohydrate choice: 2
protein:	14 g	
sodium:	579 mg	

Tofu is high in protein and B vitamins. It is rather bland when eaten alone, but it takes on the flavor of any food with which it's combined .

Orzo Pilaf

Easy

Ingredients:
5¼ oz. tofu light
¼ cup vegetable broth
⅛ tsp. pepper
¼ tsp. garlic powder
¼ tsp. Italian seasoning
¾ tsp. onion powder
2 cups cooked orzo

Directions:
Combine tofu, vegetable broth, pepper, garlic powder, Italian seasoning and onion powder in a food processor or blender and process until smooth. Pour sauce over cooked orzo and mix well. Spray large nonstick skillet with cooking spray; add pasta mixture and cook, stirring frequently, 10 to 12 minutes until lightly browned. Serve immediately.

Serves: 4

Shopping List:
5¼ oz. tofu light, orzo, vegetable broth, pepper, garlic powder, Italian seasoning, onion powder

Nutrition per serving		Exchanges
calories:	198	2 starch
total fat (5%):	1 g	1 very lean meat
carbohydrate:	35 g	
cholesterol:	0 mg	carbohydrate choice: 2
dietary fiber:	2 g	
protein:	11 g	
sodium:	78 mg	

Read labels on tofu products; they can vary significantly in nutritional content.

SENSATIONAL SOY

Sweet and Sassy Baked Beans

Easy — Do Ahead — Freeze

Ingredients:
　　2 cups cooked beans, Great Northern or navy beans
　　1 cup soybeans
　　1 tbsp. onion powder
　　½ tsp. garlic powder
　　2 cups tomato sauce
　　¼ cup + 2 tbsp. brown sugar
　　1 tbsp. cider vinegar
　　1 tsp. mustard
　　½ tsp. ginger
　　½ tsp. cinnamon
　　¼ tsp. allspice

Directions:
　　Preheat oven to 350 degrees. Spray 1½-quart casserole with cooking spray. Combine all ingredients in casserole and mix well. Cover with foil and bake 1 hour; remove foil and bake 30 to 45 minutes.

Serves: 6

Shopping List:
　　1 lb. Great Northern or navy beans, 8 oz. soybeans, 16 oz. tomato sauce, brown sugar, cider vinegar, mustard, ginger, cinnamon, allspice, onion powder, garlic powder

Nutrition per serving		Exchanges
calories:	207	2 starch
total fat (9%):	2 g	½ other carbohydrate
carbohydrate:	40 g	
cholesterol:	0 mg	carbohydrate choice: 2½
dietary fiber:	1 g	
protein:	10 g	
sodium:	511 mg	

Soybeans are the only vegetable natural food to contain all the essential amino acids the body needs to synthesize protein.

Banana-Oatmeal Raisin Cookies

Easy — Do Ahead — Freeze

Ingredients:

¼ cup egg substitute
1 egg white
¾ cup brown sugar
½ cup sugar
2 tsp. vanilla
2 tbsp. corn syrup
½ cup nonfat vanilla soy milk
2 cups mashed bananas

1½ cups all-purpose flour
1 cup whole wheat flour
½ cup soybean flour
1 tsp. cinnamon
2 tsp. baking powder
1½ cups oatmeal
¾ cup raisins

Directions:

Combine egg substitute, egg white, brown sugar, sugar, vanilla, corn syrup, soy milk, and bananas in a large mixing bowl; blend with electric mixer until creamy and smooth. Gradually add flours, cinnamon, and baking powder, blending after each addition. Fold in oatmeal and raisins. Wrap dough in plastic wrap and refrigerate 1 to 3 hours. Preheat oven to 350 degrees. Line baking sheet with foil and spray with cooking spray. Drop dough by tablespoonfuls about 1½inch apart on baking sheet. Bake 12 to 15 minutes until edges are lightly browned. Cool cookies 1 to 2 minutes before removing from baking sheet.

Serves: 24

Shopping List:

2 bananas, 4 oz. nonfat vanilla soy milk, oatmeal (instant or old-fashioned), soybean flour, all-purpose flour, whole-wheat flour, sugar, brown sugar, baking powder, cinnamon, corn syrup, vanilla, egg substitute, whole eggs, raisins

Nutrition per serving

calories:	132
total fat (0%):	0 g
carbohydrate:	29 g
cholesterol:	0 mg
dietary fiber:	1 g
protein:	4 g
sodium:	40 mg

Exchanges

2 other carbohydrate

carbohydrate choice: 2

SENSATIONAL SOY

Oatmeal is associated with regulating blood levels, lowering cholesterol levels, and removing toxins.

Chocolate Chip Cake

Easy — Do Ahead — Freeze

Ingredients:
½ cup applesauce
½ cup mashed bananas
¼ cup nonfat vanilla soy milk
¼ cup egg substitute
1 tsp. vanilla
½ cup sugar
½ cup brown sugar
½ cup wholewheat flour
½ cup all-purpose flour
¼ cup soybean flour
2 tsp. baking powder
½ tsp. baking soda
¼ cup miniature chocolate chips

Directions:
Preheat oven to 350 degrees. Spray 9-inch baking dish with cooking spray. Combine applesauce, mashed bananas, milk, egg substitute, vanilla, sugar, and brown sugar in a large mixing bowl; blend with electric mixer until creamy and smooth. Add flours, baking powder, and baking soda; mix until ingredients are moistened and blended. Fold in chocolate chips. Pour batter into baking dish and bake 30 to 35 minutes, until toothpick inserted in center comes out clean.

Serves: 8

Shopping List:
1 banana, 4 oz. applesauce, nonfat vanilla soy milk, egg substitute, whole wheat flour, all-purpose flour, soybean flour, sugar, brown sugar, baking powder, baking soda, vanilla, miniature chocolate chips

Nutrition per serving		Exchanges
calories:	216	3 other carbohydrate
total fat (8%):	2 g	
carbohydrate:	47 g	carbohydrate choice: 3
cholesterol:	0 mg	
dietary fiber:	1 g	
protein:	4 g	
sodium:	150 mg	

Why add soy products? They're good for you and easy to substitute into a normal diet.

Chocolate Pudding

Easy — Do Ahead

Ingredients:

5⅛ ounce chocolate instant pudding and pie filling

2¼ cups nonfat vanilla soy milk

Directions:

Prepare pudding according to package directions, substituting nonfat vanilla soy milk for dairy milk.

Serves: 6

Shopping List:

5⅛ oz. chocolate instant pudding and pie filling, 18 oz. nonfat vanilla soy milk

Nutrition per serving

calories:	116
total fat (0%):	0 g
carbohydrate:	23 g
cholesterol:	0 mg
dietary fiber:	0 g
protein:	2 g
sodium:	366 mg

Exchanges

1½ other carbohydrate

carbohydrate choice: 1½

Soyfoods contain isoflavones, a group of flavonoids that help fight coronary heart disease.

Cinnamon-Raisin Gingerbread

Easy — Do Ahead — Freeze

Ingredients:

½ cup brown sugar
⅓ cup corn syrup
½ cup nonfat vanilla soy milk,
  warmed
⅓ cup canned crushed pineapple
2 tsp. ground ginger
¼ cup egg substitute
⅔ cup all-purpose flour
½ cup whole-wheat flour

⅓ cup soybean flour
1 tsp. cinnamon
½ tsp. nutmeg
1 tsp. baking soda
½ tsp. baking powder
½ cup raisins
1 cup nonfat Cool Whip,
  thawed (optional)

Directions:

Preheat oven to 350 degrees. Spray 8-inch-square baking dish with cooking spray. Combine brown sugar, corn syrup, soy milk, pineapple, ginger, and egg substitute in a large bowl; mix with electric mixer or spoon until creamy and smooth. Gradually add flours, cinnamon, nutmeg, baking soda, and baking powder, mixing well after each addition. Mix until dry ingredients are moistened and blended. Fold in raisins. Spread batter in baking dish and bake 30 to 40 minutes until toothpick inserted in center comes out clean. Serve warm with dollop of Cool Whip, if desired.

Serves: 8

Shopping List:

4 oz. nonfat vanilla soy milk, egg substitute, 6 oz. can crushed pineapple, raisins, all-purpose flour, whole-wheat flour, soybean flour, brown sugar, ground ginger, cinnamon, nutmeg, baking soda, baking powder, corn syrup, nonfat Cool Whip (optional)

Nutrition per serving

calories:	214
total fat (0%):	0 g
carbohydrate:	49 g
cholesterol:	0 mg
dietary fiber:	2 g
protein:	4 g
sodium:	154 mg

Exchanges

3 other carbohydrate

carbohydrate choice: 3

Raisins are a good source of boron, which may help bones utilize calcium more efficiently.

Tofu Pumpkin Pudding

Easy — Do Ahead

Ingredients:
16 oz. tofu light, soft
15 oz. pumpkin puree
½ cup sugar
¼ cup brown sugar
1½ tsp. pumpkin pie spice
½ tsp. cinnamon
nonfat Cool Whip, thawed

Directions:
Spray pie pan with cooking spray. Combine all ingredients in medium bowl and mix until blended smooth. Pour into pan and bake 45 to 60 minutes until toothpick inserted in center comes out clean. Serve with Cool Whip.

Serves: 6

Shopping List:
16 oz. tofu light (soft), 15 oz. can pumpkin puree, sugar, brown sugar, pumpkin pie spice, cinnamon, nonfat Cool Whip dessert topping

Nutrition per serving

calories:	178
total fat (10%):	2 g
carbohydrate:	35 g
cholesterol:	0 mg
dietary fiber:	1 g
protein:	7 g
sodium:	62 mg

Exchanges
2 other carbohydrates

carbohydrate choice: 2

Pumpkin, a member of the winter squash family, contributes to heart health as well as fighting cancers of the stomach, esophagus, lung, bladder, larynx, and prostate.

SENSATIONAL SOY

"Fantabulous" Smoothie

Easy

Ingredients:
¾ cup frozen raspberries
¾ cup frozen peaches
½ cup frozen tropical fruit mix
1 kiwi fruit, peeled and sliced
1 cup nonfat yogurt
1 cup pineapple juice
1 cup vanilla soy milk

Directions:
Combine all ingredients in blender and process until smooth and creamy.

Serves: 2

Shopping List:
frozen raspberries, frozen peaches, frozen tropical fruit mix, kiwi fruit, 8 oz. nonfat yogurt (vanilla, raspberry-lemon, strawberry-kiwi, or flavor of choice), 8 oz. pineapple juice, 8 oz. nonfat vanilla soy milk

Nutrition per serving		**Exchanges**
calories:	241	2 fruit
total fat (11%):	3 g	1 other carbohydrate
carbohydrate:	48 g	
cholesterol:	3 mg	carbohydrate choice: 3
dietary fiber:	5 g	
protein:	9 g	
sodium:	88 mg	

Soy increases bone density in postmenopausal women.

"S.O.S." Smoothie

Easy

Ingredients:
8 oz. tofu light
1 cup frozen strawberries
1 banana
1 cup nonfat vanilla soy milk
1 cup strawberry-orange juice
3 tbsp. honey

Directions:
Combine all ingredients in blender and process until creamy and smooth.

Serves: 2

Shopping List:
8 oz. tofu light, frozen strawberries, banana, 8 oz. nonfat vanilla soy milk, 8 oz. strawberry-orange juice, honey

Nutrition per serving

		Exchanges
calories:	342	1 medium fat meat
total fat (6%):	6 g	2 fruit
carbohydrate:	63 g	2 other carbohydrate
cholesterol:	0 mg	
dietary fiber:	3 g	carbohydrate choice: 4
protein:	14 g	
sodium:	101 mg	

Strawberries are a good source of fiber, vitamin C, and ellagic acid, which may prevent cataracts, cancer, and constipation.

SENSATIONAL SOY

Soyfully Sensational Shake

Easy

Ingredients:
8 oz. tofu light
2 cups nonfat vanilla soy milk
⅔ cup frozen juice concentrate
1 cup frozen mixed berries
1 banana
½ cup frozen peaches

Directions:
Combine all ingredients in blender; process until creamy and smooth. If you desire a "slushier" texture, add several ice cubes; process until creamy and serve.

Serves: 2

Shopping List:
8 oz. tofu light, 16 oz. nonfat vanilla soy milk, 6 oz. frozen juice concentrate (any flavor), frozen mixed berries, frozen peaches, banana

Nutrition per serving		Exchanges
calories:	372	1 lean meat
total fat (10%):	4 g	4 fruit
carbohydrate:	75 g	1 other carbohydrate
cholesterol:	0 mg	
dietary fiber:	4 g	carbohydrate choice: 5
protein:	13 g	
sodium:	131 mg	

Tofu is high in protein, low in calories and sodium, and a good source of calcium and iron.

PERFECT PASTA, POTATOES, AND RICE

◆ ◆ ◆

Hunger-Appeasing, Low-Fat, Complex Carbohydrates

providing **sustained and slow-released Energy, Natural mood-boosting chemicals,** *and powerful* **Nutrients!**

Convenient, Inexpensive, Long-lasting, Easy-to-cook, and Versatile

POTATOES, PASTA, RICE
can keep you **GOING . . . AND GOING . . . AND GOING . . .**

Preserve their goodness!

Don't *smear, smother, or souse with fat-laden sauces or spreads that sabotage all the health benefits provided in these powerful **SuperFoods!***

The most and least you need to know . . .

- Potatoes, pasta, and rice have unfairly fallen to the ranks of bad rap food myths. Dispel such rumors: It's not what's in 'em, but what you put on 'em that reduces their health value. Think clean and lean!

- A medium-size baked potato with skin packs an incredible amount of potassium (*maintains water balance in the body*) 609 mg!

- Potatoes' high potassium power can help your body absorb more calcium, reducing the risk for osteoporosis.

- Potatoes are an excellent source of vitamin B_6 (pyridoxine), responsible for preparing protein so that it can be efficiently used as a source of energy.

- Potatoes fill you up without filling you out (as long as you keep them "clean"), contributing to healthy weight maintenance.

- Potatoes boost levels of serotonin, the feel-good brain chemical that also keeps a lid on appetite.

- Cut your cooking time by almost half—boil potatoes for 15 minutes; drain, dry, and bake until tender.

- Prevent pasta from sticking *without* adding oil; use 5 quarts of water per pound of pasta, stir regularly, add sauce immediately after draining, and/or spritz drained noodles with cooking spray and toss lightly.

- Rinse pasta only if you're serving it cold or cooking it into another dish, such as lasagna or baked casserole.
- Fresh is not always best! Dried pasta wins hands down for convenience, versatility, and long life!
- How to measure pasta for perfect portions: 2 oz. dry pasta per serving!
- There are more than 600 varieties of pasta worldwide— good chance you'll discover one to suit your tastes!

Mix and match

Thin sauces that coat each strand	Rich, creamy, hearty meat sauces	Chunky sauces or casseroles	Soup, stew or salads
angel hair	fettuccine	rotini	orzo
vermicelli	long fusilli	farfalle	ditalini
thin spaghetti	spaghetti	penne	tubetti
capellini	linguine	rigatoni	pastina
		shells	
		ziti	

- Rice, the world's third leading grain, is the staple food for half the world!
- Rice is attributed with preventing such chronic diseases as heart disease, high blood pressure, diabetes, and certain cancers.
- Rice is an excellent food source for stabilizing blood-sugar levels; it provides steady levels of energy, assists with diabetes control, and can help prevent excessive weight gain.
- Rice is an important source of Vitamin B_1 (thiamine), a coenzyme that contributes to protein metabolism, fat synthesis, and nervous system functions.
- Rice is considered a safe staple food, especially for those with wheat allergies or celiac disease; it is gluten-free and hypoallergenic.
- Rice, combined with beans or vegetables, can serve as a complete protein source.
- Did you know . . . wild rice is not rice at all! It is actually the seed of an aquatic freshwater grass, found predominately in the Great Lakes region of North America. Packed with nutrition, wild rice is a rich source of protein, B vitamins, and essential minerals.

Cheesy Mashed Potatoes

Easy — Do Ahead

Ingredients:
1½ lb. red potatoes, unpeeled, cut into quarters
2 tbsp. nonfat cream cheese, softened
1 tbsp. nonfat chicken broth
2 tbsp. skim milk
¾ tsp. garlic powder
¾ tsp. ground pepper
Butter Buds dry mix to taste
1 tbsp. chopped chives

Directions:
Place potatoes in a large pot; cover with cold water and bring to a boil over high heat. Reduce heat to medium; cover and cook 20 to 30 minutes, until potatoes are tender and easily pierced with a fork. Drain potatoes well. Spray pot with cooking spray; return potatoes to pot (off heat). Add cream cheese, chicken broth, milk, garlic powder, and pepper; using potato masher (do not use food processor, blender, or electric mixer), mash potatoes to desired consistency. Transfer to serving bowl and sprinkle with Butter Buds and chopped chives.

Serves:4

Shopping List:
1½ lb. red potatoes, nonfat cream cheese, skim milk, nonfat chicken broth, chives, Butter Buds dry mix, garlic powder, pepper

Nutrition per serving
calories:	160
total fat (0%):	0 g
carbohydrate:	36 g
cholesterol:	.1 mg
dietary fiber:	3 g
protein:	4 g
sodium:	61 mg

Exchanges
2 starch
½ other carbohydrate

carbohydrate choice: 2½

According to the USDA, Americans eat enough potatoes to cover a four-lane highway encircling the Earth six times!

"Double Up" Sweet Potatoes

Easy — Do Ahead

Ingredients:

1½ lb. sweet potatoes, unpeeled
½ cup golden raisins
3 tbsp. brown sugar
½ tsp. cinnamon
1 cup canned crushed pineapple, drained

Directions:

Preheat oven to 400 degrees. Pierce potatoes with a fork; bake 1 hour, until tender. Remove potatoes from oven and cool at room temperature 10 to 15 minutes. Cut potatoes in half lengthwise; carefully scoop pulp from potatoes (leaving skin intact) and place in medium bowl. Mash potato pulp; add remaining ingredients and mix until blended. Scoop potato mixture back into shells. Bake 10 to 15 minutes until heated through.

Serves:6

Shopping List:

3 medium sweet potatoes, 8 oz. can crushed pineapple, golden raisins, brown sugar, cinnamon

Nutrition per serving		Exchanges
calories:	209	2 fruit
total fat (0%):	0 g	½ other carbohydrate
carbohydrate:	52 g	1 starch
cholesterol:	0 mg	
dietary fiber:	4 g	carbohydrate choice: 3½
protein:	3 g	
sodium:	16 mg	

Sweet potatoes are packed with antioxidants (vitamins C and E and beta-carotene), which help prevent cancer and heart disease.

Home Fries

Easy — Do Ahead

Ingredients:

20 oz. package Simply Potatoes diced with onions
1 cup chopped red bell pepper
¾ cup chopped onions
2 tsp. nonfat chicken broth
1½ tsp. Mrs. Dash seasoning
1 tsp. pepper
½ tsp. garlic powder

Directions:

Preheat oven to 425 degrees. Spray 8- or 9-inch baking dish with cooking spray. Combine all ingredients in baking dish and bake, stirring occasionally, 35 to 40 minutes, until potatoes are tender and golden brown.

Serves:4

Shopping List:

20 oz. package Simply Potatoes diced with onions, red bell pepper, onion (or packaged chopped onion), nonfat chicken broth, Mrs. Dash seasoning, pepper, garlic powder

Nutrition per serving		Exchanges
calories:	216	2 starch
fat (0%):	0 g	3 vegetable
carbohydrate:	50 g	
cholesterol:	0 mg	carbohydrate choice: 3
dietary fiber:	1 g	
protein:	5 g	
sodium:	21 mg	

Potatoes are rich in vitamin C, a powerful antioxidant that boosts immunity and protects the body from invading viruses.

Mashed Potatoes with Grilled Onions

Average — Do Ahead

Ingredients:
¼ cup nonfat chicken broth
4 sweet onions, sliced thin
6 baking potatoes, peeled and cubed
½ cup skim milk
¼ tsp. pepper
¾ tsp. Mrs. Dash seasoning

Directions:
Spray large nonstick skillet with cooking spray; add chicken broth and heat over medium-high heat. Add onions and cook, stirring frequently, until onions are golden brown and soft. While onions are cooking, place potatoes in large saucepan. Pour in enough water to cover potatoes and bring to a boil over high heat. Reduce heat to low, cover, and simmer 8 to 10 minutes until potatoes are tender. Drain well. Spray saucepan with cooking spray; return potatoes to pan and mash with fork or potato masher. Add milk, pepper, and seasoning; mash until smooth and creamy. Remove 2 to 3 tablespoons onions from pan; add remaining onions to potato mixture and mix well. Cook over medium heat until heated through. Top with reserved onions and serve.

Serves:6

Shopping List:
6 baking potatoes, 4 sweet onions (Vidalia or Walla Walla), 4 oz. skim milk, nonfat chicken broth, Mrs. Dash seasoning, pepper

Nutrition per serving		Exchanges
calories:	194	2 starch
total fat (0%):	0 g	2 vegetable
carbohydrate:	44 g	
cholesterol:	0 mg	carbohydrate choice: 3
dietary fiber:	5 g	
protein:	5 g	
sodium:	54 mg	

***Onions have potent antioxidants. They contain calcium, magnesium, phosphorus, sulfur, potassium, sodium, iron, and vitamins A, B, and C.
To avoid tears when cutting up onions, store them in the refrigerator for several hours.***

Orange and Gold Gratin Potatoes

Average — Do Ahead

Ingredients:
 1 lb. sweet potatoes, peeled and sliced thin
 1 lb. baking potatoes, peeled and sliced thin
 ¼ cup reconstituted Butter Buds (liquid form)
 ½ tsp. garlic powder
 ¼ tsp. pepper
 1 cup nonfat herb or garlic-seasoned croutons, crushed
 ⅓ cup chopped green onion

Directions:
 Preheat oven to 350 degrees. Spray 11 x 7-inch baking dish with cooking spray. Combine sweet and baking potato slices and just enough water to cover in a large saucepan; bring to a boil and cook for 1 minute, just until softened. Drain potatoes and place in a large bowl. Combine reconstituted Butter Buds with garlic powder and pepper; mix until blended. Drizzle potatoes with 2 tablespoons butter mixture and toss lightly until coated. Arrange potatoes in baking dish, overlapping as needed. Combine crushed croutons, remaining butter mixture, and green onion in medium bowl; sprinkle over potatoes and bake 25 to 20 minutes until lightly browned and crisp.

Serves:4

Shopping List:
 1 lb. sweet potatoes, 1 lb. baking potatoes, nonfat croutons (herb or garlic-seasoned), green onion, Butter Buds, garlic powder, pepper

Nutrition per serving		**Exchanges**
calories:	245	2 starch
total fat (0%):	0 g	2 other carbohydrate
carbohydrate:	57 g	
cholesterol:	0 mg	carbohydrate choice: 4
dietary fiber:	6 g	
protein:	5 g	
sodium:	50 mg	

The average American consumes 120 pounds of potatoes each year; unfortunately, most of those consumed are in the form of high-calorie, fat-saturated French fries and potato chips.

Perfectly Potatoes Pie Crust

Easy — Do Ahead

Ingredients:

3½ to 4 cups Simply Potatoes shredded nonfat
   hash brown potatoes
butter-flavored cooking spray
pepper to taste
Mrs. Dash seasoning to taste

Directions:

Preheat oven to 425 degrees. Spray pie plate with cooking spray. Press shredded potatoes into pie plate to form a crust; mold potatoes until firmly packed. Lightly spray potatoes with butter-flavored cooking spray and sprinkle with pepper and seasoning, as desired. Bake 25 to 20 minutes until golden brown and crisp. If using for quiche, bake 15 to 20 minutes until lightly browned. Potatoes will continue cooking with additional quiche ingredients.

Serves: 6

Shopping List:

20 oz. Simply Potatoes shredded nonfat hash brown potatoes, butter-flavored cooking spray, pepper, Mrs. Dash seasoning

Nutrition per serving		Exchanges
calories:	84	1 starch
total fat (0%):	0 g	
carbohydrate:	19 g	carbohydrate choice: 1
cholesterol:	0 mg	
dietary fiber:	2 g	
protein:	2 g	
sodium:	33 mg	

According to Seeds of Change: Food Histories, the United States exports 8 million cubic tons of processed potatoes to Asia as "American" (not "French") fries.

PERFECT PASTA, POTATOES, AND RICE

Rosemary-Garlic New Potatoes

Easy — Do Ahead — Freeze

Ingredients:
1 lb. new red potatoes, cut in half
3 tbsp. nonfat chicken broth
1 tbsp. lemon juice
1 tsp. minced garlic
1 tbsp. fresh rosemary, chopped

Directions:
Preheat oven to 400 degrees. Spray shallow baking dish with cooking spray. Place potatoes in large saucepan; cover with water and simmer over medium heat 8 to 10 minutes, just until tender. Drain potatoes and return to low heat; cook until potatoes are dried (2 to 3 minutes). Add chicken broth, lemon juice, garlic, and rosemary to pan; cook over medium heat until potatoes are coated. Place potato mixture in baking dish; bake 15 minutes. Turn potatoes and bake an additional 15 to 20 minutes until golden brown and tender.

Serves: 4

Shopping List:
1 lb. new red potatoes, nonfat chicken broth, lemon juice, minced garlic, fresh rosemary

Nutrition per serving		Exchanges
calories:	110	1½ starch
total fat (0%):	0 g	
carbohydrate:	25 g	carbohydrate choice: 1½
cholesterol:	0 mg	
dietary fiber:	3 g	
protein:	3 g	
sodium:	42 mg	

Rosemary contains high amounts of geraniol, a protease inhibitor that may block natural carcinogens from forming tumors.

Stuffed Potatoes

Easy — Do Ahead

Ingredients:
3 large baking potatoes
½ cup nonfat plain yogurt
½ cup nonfat ricotta cheese
3 tbsp. nonfat Parmesan cheese
¾ tsp. garlic powder
3 tbsp. chopped chives
1½ cups nonfat shredded mozzarella cheese

Directions:
Preheat oven to 400 degrees. Scrub potatoes clean and pierce them several times with a fork. Bake 1 hour in oven; let cool 10 to 15 minutes (until easy enough to handle). Cut potatoes in half lengthwise; scoop out pulp (leaving skin intact) and place in medium bowl. Mash potato pulp with fork; add yogurt, ricotta cheese, Parmesan cheese, and garlic powder; mix until ingredients are light and fluffy (use electric mixer, if possible). Stir in chives. Scoop potato mixture into shells; sprinkle with mozzarella cheese. Place potatoes under broiler and cook (watching closely) until lightly browned.

Serves: 6

Shopping List:
3 baking potatoes, 4 oz. nonfat plain yogurt, 4 oz. nonfat ricotta cheese, nonfat Parmesan cheese, 6 oz. nonfat shredded mozzarella cheese, chives, garlic powder

Nutrition per serving		Exchanges
calories:	189	2 starch
total fat (0%):	0 g	1 very lean meat
carbohydrate:	29 g	
cholesterol:	4 mg	carbohydrate choice: 2
dietary fiber:	3 g	
protein:	17 g	
sodium:	286 mg	

Potatoes are considered the "almost perfect" food, rich in vitamins, minerals, and complex carbohydrates.

Sweet Potato 'n' Nana Souffle

Easy — Do Ahead

Ingredients:
  2 cups canned sweet potatoes, mashed
  1 cup mashed bananas
  3 tbsp. brown sugar
  ½ tsp. cinnamon
  ½ cup nonfat sour cream
  ½ cup egg substitute

Directions:
  Preheat oven to 350 degrees. Spray 1-quart casserole with cooking spray. Combine all ingredients in a large bowl; beat with electric mixer until light and fluffy. Bake 20 to 25 minutes until lightly browned and puffy.

Serves: 4

Shopping List:
  29 oz. can sweet potatoes, 3 bananas, egg substitute, nonfat sour cream, brown sugar, cinnamon

Nutrition per serving		Exchanges
calories:	229	1½ starch
total fat (4%):	1 g	1 fruit
carbohydrate:	53 g	1 other carbohydrate
cholesterol:	0 mg	
dietary fiber:	4 g	carbohydrate choice: 3½
protein:	5 g	
sodium:	90 mg	

Sweet potatoes are a good source of vitamin C; a 4-ounce serving provides 28 milligrams, nearly half the Recommended Daily Allowance.

Thyme-Roasted Potatoes

Easy — Do Ahead — Freeze

Ingredients:
garlic-flavored cooking spray
2 tbsp. nonfat chicken broth
1 tsp. dried thyme
1½ tsp. paprika
1½ tsp. garlic powder
1 lb. red potatoes, cut in half lengthwise

Directions:
Preheat oven to 475 degrees. Spray shallow baking dish or roasting pan with garlic-flavored cooking spray. Combine chicken broth, thyme, paprika, and garlic powder in a medium bowl. Dip cut side of potato into broth and seasonings; place potatoes cut side up in baking dish. Sprinkle remaining mixture over potatoes. Bake 35 to 45 minutes until potatoes are roasted golden brown and tender.

Serves: 4

Shopping List:
1 lb. red potatoes, nonfat chicken broth, dried thyme, garlic powder, paprika, garlic-flavored cooking spray

Nutrition per serving

calories:	110
total fat (0%):	0 g
carbohydrate:	25 g
cholesterol:	0 mg
dietary fiber:	3 g
protein:	3 g
sodium:	31 mg

Exchanges

1½ starch

carbohydrate choice: 1½

Potato skins contain antioxidants and protease inhibitors, important for preventing and fighting cancer. Protease inhibitors block the activation of viruses and carcinogens in the intestines.

PERFECT PASTA, POTATOES, AND RICE

Baked Spinach Linguine

Easy — Do Ahead — Freeze

Ingredients:
8 oz. linguine, cooked and drained
½ cup nonfat shredded mozzarella cheese
¼ cup low-fat shredded mozzarella cheese
1 cup nonfat sour cream
16 oz. frozen chopped spinach, thawed and drained
⅓ cup egg substitute
¾ tsp. Italian seasoning
1 tsp. crushed garlic
2 cups nonfat pasta sauce
2 tbsp. nonfat Parmesan cheese

Directions:
Cook pasta according to package directions; drain. Preheat oven to 350 degrees. Spray 1½-quart baking dish with cooking spray. Combine nonfat and low-fat mozzarella cheese, sour cream, spinach, egg substitute, Italian seasoning, and garlic in a medium bowl; mix until blended. Stir in cooked pasta. Spoon pasta mixture into baking dish and cover with pasta sauce. Bake 20 to 25 minutes; sprinkle with Parmesan cheese and bake 5 to 10 minutes until bubbly and heated through.

Serves: 4

Shopping List:
8 oz. linguine, 16 oz. package frozen chopped spinach, 16 oz. jar nonfat pasta sauce, 8 oz. nonfat sour cream, nonfat shredded mozzarella cheese, low-fat shredded mozzarella cheese, nonfat Parmesan cheese, egg substitute, crushed garlic, Italian seasoning

Nutrition per serving
calories:	244
total fat (7%):	2 g
carbohydrate:	34 g
cholesterol:	19 mg
dietary fiber:	3 g
protein:	21 g
sodium:	668 mg

Exchanges
2 very lean meat
1 starch
4 vegetable

carbohydrate choice: 2

Spinach contains large amounts of lutein and beta-carotene, important for maintaining good eye health.

Barley with Curry, Carrots & Almonds

Easy — Do Ahead

Ingredients:
- 1½ cups nonfat chicken broth
- ½ cup water
- ⅔ cup quick-cooking barley
- ¾ cup chopped carrot
- 2 tsp. onion powder
- 1 tsp. curry powder
- 1 tbsp. sliced almonds, toasted

Directions:
Combine chicken broth, water, barley, carrot, onion powder, and curry in medium saucepan; bring to a boil over high heat. Reduce heat to low, cover, and simmer 12 to 15 minutes until barley is tender. Remove lid and cook 3 to 5 minutes; stir in toasted almonds and serve.

Serves: 4

Shopping List:
14½ oz. can nonfat chicken broth, quick-cooking barley, 2 carrots, sliced almonds, onion powder, curry powder

Nutrition per serving

calories:	153
total fat (6%):	1 g
carbohydrate:	29 g
cholesterol:	0 mg
dietary fiber:	6 g
protein:	6 g
sodium:	361 mg

Exchanges

1½ starch
1 vegetable

carbohydrate choice: 2

***One-half cup of cooked barley provides
15 grams of complex carbohydrates,
a good source of constant energy.***

Caesar's Garden Pasta

Easy

Ingredients:
12 oz. linguine
1 cup frozen peas, thawed and drained
¾ cup frozen sliced carrots, thawed and drained
1 cup frozen pepper strips, thawed and drained
1 cup sliced mushrooms
14 oz. can chopped tomatoes, undrained
12 oz. nonfat Caesar salad dressing
pepper
nonfat Parmesan cheese

Directions:
Cook linguine according to package directions. Add peas, carrots, peppers, and mushrooms during last 2 to 3 minutes of cooking; drain in colander. Return pasta and vegetables to saucepan, but keep off burner. Add chopped tomatoes and salad dressing. Return pan to medium heat and cook until heated through. Sprinkle with pepper and Parmesan cheese and serve.

Serves: 6

Shopping List:
12 oz. linguine, 10 oz. package frozen peas, 10 oz. package frozen carrot slices, 10 oz. package frozen pepper strips, ½ lb. sliced mushrooms, 14 oz. can chopped tomatoes, 12 oz. bottle nonfat Caesar salad dressing, nonfat Parmesan cheese, pepper

Nutrition per serving		Exchanges
calories:	309	2½ starch
total fat (3%):	1 g	3 vegetable
carbohydrate:	64 g	½ other carbohydrate
cholesterol:	0 mg	
dietary fiber:	2 g	carbohydrate choice: 4
protein:	9 g	
sodium:	712 mg	

Pasta is a heart-healthy food, low in fat and sodium, and rich in minerals (manganese, iron, phosphorus, copper, magnesium, and zinc).

Capers and Penne Pasta

Easy — Do Ahead

Ingredients:

8 oz. penne pasta, cooked
and drained
2 tbsp. nonfat chicken broth
½ cup chopped onion
1 oz. chopped capers

1½ tsp. chopped garlic
3 cups canned chopped
tomatoes, undrained
¾ tsp. Italian seasoning
nonfat Parmesan cheese

Directions:

Cook pasta according to package directions; drain and keep warm. Pour chicken broth into nonstick skillet and heat over medium-high heat. Add onion; cook until softened, about 2 to 3 minutes. Add capers and garlic; cook 1 minute. Add tomatoes (with juice) and Italian seasoning; bring to a boil over high heat. Reduce heat to medium and boil sauce 5 to 6 minutes. Toss penne with sauce; sprinkle with Parmesan cheese, if desired.

Serves: 4

Shopping List:

8 oz. penne pasta, 2 14½-oz. cans ready-cut tomatoes, onion (or packaged chopped onions), capers, chopped garlic, nonfat chicken broth, Italian seasoning, nonfat Parmesan cheese

Nutrition per serving		Exchanges
calories:	481	5 starch
total fat (7%):	4 g	3 vegetable
carbohydrate:	94 g	
cholesterol:	98 mg	carbohydrate choice: 6
dietary fiber:	4 g	
protein:	19 g	
sodium:	980 mg	

According to the American Institute for Cancer Research Newsletter (Spring 1996), organosulfides are the sulfur compounds that give allium vegetables (onion, garlic, shallots, leeks, chives) their pungent taste and smell. "Organosulfides seem to concentrate in the liver and influence how our bodies process toxic chemicals, including carcinogens in our environment. The suspicion is that organosulfides keep our bodies from using toxic chemicals to make dangerous products helping them make harmless ones instead."

PERFECT PASTA, POTATOES, AND RICE

Egg Noodles in Parmesan Cream Sauce

Easy — Do Ahead

Ingredients:

6 oz. yolk-free egg noodles, cooked and drained
1 cup nonfat sour cream
⅓ cup nonfat Parmesan cheese, divided
1 tbsp. fresh chives, chopped
¾ tsp. garlic powder
1 tbsp. reconstituted Butter Buds (liquid form)

Directions:

Cook noodles according to package directions; drain well and place in large serving bowl. Combine sour cream, 3 tablespoons Parmesan cheese, chives, and garlic powder in a small bowl; mix until ingredients are completely blended. Drizzle Butter Buds over noodles; mix lightly. Stir in sour cream mixture until blended; top with remaining Parmesan cheese and serve.

Serves: 4

Shopping List:

6 oz. yolk-free egg noodles, 8 oz. nonfat sour cream, nonfat Parmesan cheese, fresh chives, garlic powder, Butter Buds

Nutrition per serving

calories:	170
total fat (0%):	0 g
carbohydrate:	28 g
cholesterol:	0 mg
dietary fiber:	2 g
protein:	11 g
sodium:	969 mg

Exchanges

1½ starch
½ other carbohydrate

carbohydrate choice: 2

According to the American Institute for Cancer Research Newsletter (1999), a diet high in total fat possibly increases the risk of lung, colorectal, breast and prostate cancers and is linked to a higher risk of heart disease and stroke. One serving of "regular" Egg Noodles in Parmesan Cream Sauce contains 357 calories, 20 grams fat (50%), and 78 milligrams cholesterol. Count your savings with low-fat substitutions.

Ginger-Sweet Chicken and Pasta

Easy

Ingredients:
2 cups cooked pasta (rotelle, rotini, or shells)
1 lb. low-fat chicken tenders, cut into ½-inch pieces
1½ tsp. garlic powder
16 oz. frozen stir-fry vegetable mixture
1½ cups sweet and sour sauce
¾ tsp. ground ginger

Directions:
Cook pasta according to package directions; drain and keep warm. Spray large nonstick skillet with cooking spray and heat over medium-high heat. Add chicken tenders and sprinkle generously with garlic powder; cook 2 to 3 minutes over medium-high heat, stirring frequently, until chicken is brown. Add vegetable mixture, sauce, and ginger; bring to a boil. Reduce heat to low, cover, and simmer over low heat 3 to 4 minutes until chicken is no longer pink and vegetables are tender-crisp. If sauce gets too thick, add a little water. Toss with pasta and serve.

Serves: 4

Shopping List:
8 oz. pasta (rotelle, rotini, or shells), 1 lb. low-fat chicken tenders, 16 oz. package stir-fry vegetable mix, 12 oz. bottle sweet and sour sauce, garlic powder, ground ginger

Nutrition per serving

calories:	252
total fat (4%):	1 g
carbohydrate:	32 g
cholesterol:	71 mg
dietary fiber:	4 g
protein:	32 g
sodium:	416 mg

Exchanges

3 very lean meat
½ starch
3 vegetable
½ other carbohydrate

carbohydrate choice: 2

Ginger has been recognized as a highly potent healing food, relieving conditions such as motion sickness, digestive problems, migraine headaches, arthritis, high cholesterol, and dangerous blood clots.

Mediterranean Penne Pasta with Shrimp

Easy

Ingredients:
8 oz. penne or ziti pasta, cooked and drained
1 lb. frozen (uncooked) shrimp, thawed and drained
10 oz. frozen chopped spinach, thawed and drained
½ cup nonfat sour cream
½ cup nonfat plain yogurt
⅓ cup reduced-fat crumbled feta cheese
¾ tsp. Italian seasoning
¾ tsp. garlic powder

Directions:
Cook pasta according to package directions; add shrimp and spinach during last 2 to 3 minutes of cooking time. Cook until shrimp turn pink and spinach is wilted; drain well and place in large serving bowl. Combine remaining ingredients in small bowl and mix until blended; pour sauce over pasta, toss lightly, and serve.

Serves: 4

Shopping List:
8 oz. penne or ziti pasta, 1 lb. frozen (uncooked) shrimp, 10 oz. frozen chopped spinach, 4 oz. nonfat sour cream, 4 oz. nonfat plain yogurt, 4 oz. reduced-fat crumbled feta cheese, Italian seasoning, garlic powder

Nutrition per serving

calories:	284
total fat (16%):	5 g
carbohydrate:	26 g
cholesterol:	184 mg
dietary fiber:	2 g
protein:	33 g
sodium:	378 mg

Exchanges
1 starch
1 vegetable
1 lean meat
2 very lean meat
½ other carbohydrate

carbohydrate choice: 2

Shrimp is an excellent source of calcium, providing 6 milligrams in a ¼ cup serving.

Mint Orzo

Easy — Do Ahead

Ingredients:
- 1 tbsp. nonfat chicken broth
- 1 leek, cut in half lengthwise and sliced thin
- 1 cup orzo, cooked and drained
- ¼ cup fresh mint, chopped
- 1 tbsp. lemon juice
- 1 tsp. lemon zest
- ¼ tsp. lemon pepper

Directions:
Spray large nonstick skillet with cooking spray; add 1 tablespoon chicken broth and heat over medium-high heat. Add sliced leeks and cook 5 to 6 minutes, until tender. Add cooked orzo, fresh mint, lemon juice, lemon zest, and lemon pepper. Cook until heated through.

Serves: 4

Shopping List:
8 oz. orzo, leek, mint, lemon, lemon pepper

Nutrition per serving		Exchanges
calories:	116	1½ starch
total fat (8%):	1 g	
carbohydrate:	25 g	carbohydrate choice: 1½
cholesterol:	0 mg	
dietary fiber:	0 g	
protein:	4 g	
sodium:	20 mg	

Nonalcoholic red wine contains as many polyphenols (block blood clots and atherosclerosis) as the "real thing ."

Mushroom Kasha with "Ties"

Average

Ingredients:

2¼ cups nonfat chicken broth, divided
1 cup kasha, uncooked
1 cup farfalle pasta, cooked and drained

2 cups onion, sliced thin
1 tsp. minced garlic
12 oz. shiitake mushrooms
1 tbsp. lemon juice
1½ tsp. Italian seasoning

Directions:

Pour 2 cups chicken broth into saucepan and bring to a boil over high heat. Add kasha, cover, reduce heat to low, and simmer 8 to 10 minutes, until tender. Spoon kasha into baking dish; fluff with fork and gently fold in cooked pasta. Set aside; cover to keep warm. Spray nonstick skillet with cooking spray and heat over medium-high heat. Add onion slices and cook, stirring frequently, until softened. Add garlic, mushrooms, lemon juice, and Italian seasoning. Cook over medium heat 5 to 6 minutes, until mushrooms soften. Add remaining chicken broth; slightly increase heat and cook, stirring frequently, about 2 minutes, until completely heated through. Spoon mixture over kasha and pasta; serve immediately.

Serves: 4

Shopping List:

farfalle pasta (also called bowtie pasta), kasha, 20 oz. nonfat chicken broth, 2 onions, minced garlic, 12 oz. shiitake mushrooms, lemon juice, Italian seasoning

Nutrition per serving		Exchanges
calories:	545	5 starch
carbohydrate:	112 g	3 vegetable
cholesterol:	0 mg	1 other carbohydrate
dietary fiber:	6 g	
protein:	19 g	carbohydrate choice: 7
sodium:	440 mg	

Shiitake mushrooms are renowned for their therapeutic qualities. Research studies have found that these mushrooms may stimulate the immune system, lower blood cholesterol, improve circulation, and block some of the bad effects of saturated fats.

Mushroom Medley Pasta

Average — Do Ahead

Ingredients:

¾ cup bowtie or farfalle pasta, cooked and drained
3 tbsp. nonfat chicken broth
1 cup sliced crimini mushrooms
1 cup sliced shiitake mushrooms
1 cup sliced button mushrooms
1 tbsp. minced garlic
¼ tsp. crushed red pepper
1¾ cups canned Italian-style crushed tomatoes
1 tbsp. tomato paste
¼ cup nonfat Parmesan cheese

Directions:

Prepare pasta according to package directions; drain well and keep warm. Spray large nonstick skillet with cooking spray; add chicken broth and heat over medium-high heat. Add mushrooms, garlic, and red pepper to skillet; cook, stirring frequently, until mushrooms are tender (about 1 minute). Add crushed tomatoes and tomato paste and mix well. Bring to a boil over high heat; immediately reduce heat to low and simmer 5 to 10 minutes. Serve sauce over cooked pasta or toss before serving. Sprinkle with Parmesan cheese.

Serves: 4

Shopping List:

¼ lb. crimini mushrooms, ¼ lb. shiitake mushrooms, ¼ lb. button mushrooms, 15½ oz. can Italian-style crushed tomatoes, bowtie or farfalle pasta, nonfat chicken broth, tomato paste, nonfat Parmesan cheese, minced garlic, crushed red pepper

Nutrition per serving

calories:	138
total fat (6%):	1 g
carbohydrate:	28 g
cholesterol:	0 mg
dietary fiber:	1 g
protein:	7 g
sodium:	513 mg

Exchanges

1 starch
3 vegetable

carbohydrate choice: 2

Mushrooms are a great way to add texture and flavor to meatless dishes. Studies from China and Japan, where mushrooms are a dietary staple, indicate that shiitake mushrooms can lower cholesterol and stimulate the immune system.

PERFECT PASTA, POTATOES, AND RICE

Orzo with Green Chilies and Cheese

Easy — Do Ahead

Ingredients:
1 cup orzo, cooked and drained
4 oz. chopped green chilies
1 cup nonfat sour cream
¾ cup nonfat shredded mozzarella cheese
¼ cup low-fat shredded mozzarella cheese

Directions:
Preheat oven to 450 degrees. Spray shallow baking dish with cooking spray. Cook orzo according to package directions; drain and set aside. Combine chilies and sour cream in a medium bowl; add orzo and nonfat and low-fat mozzarella cheese. Toss until ingredients are well mixed. Spoon orzo mixture into baking dish; bake 10 to 15 minutes until bubbly and hot.

Serves: 4

Shopping List:
orzo pasta, 4 oz. can chopped green chilies, 8 oz. nonfat sour cream, nonfat shredded mozzarella cheese, low-fat shredded mozzarella cheese

Nutrition per serving		Exchanges
calories:	131	1 starch
fat (7%):	1 g	1 very lean meat
carbohydrate:	17 g	1 vegetable
cholesterol:	0 mg	
dietary fiber:	0 g	carbohydrate choice: 1
protein:	11 g	
sodium:	374 mg	

Chilies can aid in digestion by accelerating the flow of gastric juices; they are also a good source of vitamins A and C.

Pasta with Broccoli Cream Sauce

Average

Ingredients:

6 oz. rotini pasta, cooked and drained

2 tbsp. + ⅔ cup nonfat chicken broth, divided

1 tsp. garlic powder

1 tsp. curry powder

3 cups broccoli florets

2 cups cauliflower florets

1 cup chopped red bell pepper

1 cup nonfat sour cream

2 tbsp. + 2 tsp. flour

2 tsp. prepared mustard

¼ cup nonfat Parmesan cheese, optional

Directions:

Cook pasta according to package directions; drain and keep warm. Spray large nonstick skillet with cooking spray; add 2 tablespoons chicken broth and heat over medium-high heat. Sprinkle garlic powder and curry powder over broth and mix lightly. Stir in broccoli, cauliflower, and bell pepper. Cook, stirring constantly, 5 to 6 minutes until vegetables are tender-crisp. Remove skillet from heat. Combine sour cream, ⅔ cup chicken broth, flour, and mustard in a medium saucepan; stir in vegetable mixture. Cook, stirring constantly, until sauce is thick and bubbly. Add pasta; toss until coated and heated through. Serve with Parmesan cheese, if desired.

Serves: 4

Shopping List:

6 oz. rotini pasta (you can substitute rotelle, gemelli, or shells), nonfat chicken broth, 8 oz. nonfat sour cream, mustard, 1½ lb. broccoli florets, 1 lb. cauliflower florets, 1 red bell pepper, nonfat Parmesan cheese, flour, garlic powder, curry powder

Nutrition per serving		**Exchanges**
calories:	277	1 starch
total fat (3%):	1 g	3 vegetable
carbohydrate:	50 g	1 other carbohydrate
cholesterol:	0 mg	
dietary fiber:	1 g	carbohydrate choice: 3
protein:	16 g	
sodium:	302 mg	

Green peas provide vitamin A, folic acid, potassium, protein, and fiber.

Ratatouille Pasta with Pizazz

Easy — Do Ahead

Ingredients:
12 oz. whole-wheat spaghetti, cooked and drained
1½ cups peeled and cubed eggplant
1½ cups cubed zucchini
½ cup chopped onion
16 oz. Italian-style stewed tomatoes, undrained
1¾ cup nonfat pasta sauce
1½ tsp. garlic powder
¾ tsp. crushed red pepper
nonfat Parmesan cheese (optional)

Directions:
Cook spaghetti according to package directions; drain well and keep warm. Spray large nonstick skillet with cooking spray and heat over medium-high heat. Add eggplant, zucchini, and onion to skillet; cook 3 to 4 minutes, stirring frequently, until vegetables are softened. Add tomatoes, pasta sauce, garlic powder, and red pepper. Bring to a boil over high heat; reduce heat to low and simmer, uncovered, 10 to 15 minutes, until vegetables are tender and sauce is heated through. Serve over cooked pasta; sprinkle with Parmesan cheese, if desired.

Serves: 6

Shopping List:
12 oz. whole-wheat spaghetti, 12 oz. nonfat pasta sauce, 16 oz. can Italian-style stewed tomatoes, 1 lb. eggplant, 2 to 3 zucchinis, onion (or packaged chopped onion), garlic powder, crushed red pepper, nonfat Parmesan cheese (optional)

Nutrition per serving		Exchanges
calories:	260	1½ starch
total fat (3%):	1 g	6 vegetable
carbohydrate:	53	
cholesterol:	0 mg	carbohydrate choice: 3½
dietary fiber:	2 g	
protein:	9 g	
sodium:	486 mg	

Studies show that whole grains can help protect your heart by lowering blood cholesterol and blood pressure, controlling blood sugar, and lowering blood triglycerides.

Rotini with Broccoli and Cheese
Easy — Do Ahead

Ingredients:
2 cups rotini, cooked and drained
2 cups skim milk
2 tbsp. cornstarch
20 oz. frozen chopped broccoli
1 cup nonfat shredded Cheddar cheese
4 oz. nonfat Parmesan cheese
2 to 3 drops Tabasco pepper sauce
2 tsp. Worcestershire sauce
pepper to taste

Directions:
Cook pasta according to package directions; drain and keep warm. Spray medium saucepan with cooking spray; add milk and cornstarch to pan. Cook, stirring constantly, over medium-low heat until milk begins to thicken. Stir in broccoli, Cheddar and Parmesan cheese; cook, stirring constantly, until cheese melts and sauce thickens. Remove pan from heat; stir in Tabasco sauce, Worcestershire sauce, and pepper. Add rotini to cheese sauce and toss until coated.

Serves: 4

Shopping List:
12 oz. rotini pasta, 2 10-oz. packages frozen chopped broccoli, 1 pint skim milk, 4 oz. nonfat shredded Cheddar cheese, 4 oz. nonfat Parmesan cheese, cornstarch, Worcestershire sauce, Tabasco pepper sauce, pepper

Nutrition per serving		Exchanges
calories:	320	1 starch
total fat (3%):	1 g	3 vegetable
carbohydrate:	50 g	1 milk
cholesterol:	2 mg	2 very lean meat
dietary fiber:	0 g	
protein:	30 g	carbohydrate choice: 3
sodium:	638 mg	

***Broccoli is the number one anticancer vegetable,
rich in beta-carotene, vitamin C, and calcium.***

PERFECT PASTA, POTATOES, AND RICE

Shrimp and Artichoke Fusilli

Easy — Do Ahead

Ingredients:

8 oz. fusilli pasta, cooked and drained
2 tbsp. dry sherry
⅓ cup + 2 tbsp. nonfat chicken broth, divided
16 oz. can stewed tomatoes, undrained
15 oz. can artichoke hearts, drained
2 tsp. Italian seasoning
⅛ tsp. crushed red pepper flakes
½ tsp. garlic powder
1 tbsp. onion powder
1 lb. medium shrimp, peeled and deveined
nonfat Parmesan cheese (optional)

Directions:

Cook fusilli according to package directions; remove from heat but do not drain. Spray large nonstick skillet with cooking spray; add sherry and ⅓ cup chicken broth. Cook over medium heat 1 to 2 minutes. Add tomatoes, artichoke hearts, Italian seasoning, red pepper flakes, garlic powder, onion powder, remaining chicken broth, and shrimp; cook over medium heat until shrimp turn pink and sauce is heated through. Drain fusilli; toss with sauce and serve with Parmesan cheese, if desired.

Serves: 6

Shopping List:

1 lb. medium shrimp, 8 oz. fusilli, 16 oz. can stewed tomatoes, 15 oz. can artichoke hearts, nonfat chicken broth, dry sherry, garlic powder, onion powder, Italian seasoning, red pepper flakes, nonfat Parmesan cheese (optional)

Nutrition per serving		Exchanges
calories:	202	1 starch
total fat (9%):	2 g	2½ vegetable
carbohydrate:	26 g	2 very lean meat
cholesterol:	117 mg	
dietary fiber:	1 g	carbohydrate choice: 2
protein:	21 g	
sodium:	434 mg	

Complex carbohydrates (pasta, rice, grains, breads, cereal, legumes, vegetables) allow glucose to be released into your blood more slowly than simple carbohydrates. This helps to regulate blood-sugar levels, especially in those with hyperglycemia, hypoglycemia, or diabetes mellitus.

Spinach-Cheese Lasagna Rolls

Average — Do Ahead — Freeze

Ingredients:

6 oz. lasagna noodles, cooked and drained
¼ cup egg substitute
1½ cups nonfat ricotta cheese
½ cup low-fat ricotta cheese
⅓ cup + 2 tbsp. nonfat Parmesan cheese, divided

10 oz. frozen chopped spinach, thawed, drained, and dried
1½ cups nonfat pasta sauce
¾ cup nonfat shredded mozzarella cheese

Directions:

Preheat oven to 350 degrees. Spray 12 x 2-inch baking dish with cooking spray. Cook lasagna noodles according to package directions; drain and set aside. Combine egg substitute, nonfat and low-fat ricotta cheese, and ⅓ cup Parmesan cheese in medium bowl; mix well. Stir in spinach. Spoon a thin layer of pasta sauce to cover bottom of baking dish. Place ¼ cup spinach mixture on each noodle; roll lasagna around mixture and place seam side down in baking dish. Repeat with remaining noodles and broccoli mixture. Pour remaining pasta sauce over top; sprinkle with mozzarella and 2 tablespoons Parmesan cheese. Cover baking dish with foil and bake 35 to 40 minutes until hot and bubbly. Remove cover and bake 5 minutes until cheese is lightly browned.

Serves: 4

Shopping List:

6 oz. lasagna noodles, 10 oz. frozen chopped spinach, 12 oz. pasta sauce, 12 oz. nonfat ricotta cheese, 4 oz. low fat ricotta cheese, nonfat Parmesan cheese, nonfat shredded mozzarella cheese, egg substitute

Nutrition per serving		Exchanges
calories:	365	2 starch
total fat (2%):	1 g	4½ vegetable
carbohydrate:	51 g	3 very lean meat
cholesterol:	20 mg	
dietary fiber:	2 g	carbohydrate choice: 3½
protein:	38 g	
sodium:	819 mg	

Eating pasta without protein may leave you feeling sluggish one to two hours later due to changes in blood sugar levels. Lasagna (with or without meat) is packed with cheese-powered protein.

PERFECT PASTA, POTATOES, AND RICE

Spinach Fettuccine Turkey Strips

Easy

Ingredients:

12 oz. spinach fettuccine, cooked and drained
1 tbsp. nonfat chicken broth
1 lb. skinless, boneless turkey breast, cut in strips
2 tsp. garlic powder
1 tsp. Italian seasoning
2 cups nonfat pasta sauce
nonfat Parmesan cheese (optional)

Directions:

Cook pasta according to package directions; drain and keep warm. Spray nonstick skillet with cooking spray; pour chicken broth into skillet and heat over medium-high heat. Sprinkle turkey strips with garlic powder and Italian seasoning; add to skillet. Cook, stirring frequently, 4 to 6 minutes until lightly browned and cooked through. Reduce heat to medium; pour in pasta sauce and cook until heated through (about 3 to 5 minutes). Serve over spinach pasta and sprinkle with Parmesan cheese, if desired.

Serves: 4

Shopping List:

1 lb. skinless, boneless turkey breast (or tenders), 15-16 oz. nonfat pasta sauce, 12 oz. spinach fettuccine, nonfat chicken broth, garlic powder, Italian seasoning, nonfat Parmesan cheese (optional)

Nutrition per serving

calories:	474
total fat (8%):	4 g
carbohydrate:	60 g
cholesterol:	187 mg
dietary fiber:	1 g
protein:	47 g
sodium:	417 mg

Exchanges

1 lean meat
3 very lean meat
3 starch
3 vegetable

carbohydrate choice: 4

A 3-ounce serving of white meat turkey breast provides 1 to 2 milligrams of iron, 8% of the recommended daily allowance for women.

Spinach Linguine Alfredo

Easy — Do Ahead

Ingredients:
12 oz. linguine, cooked and drained
10 oz. frozen chopped spinach, thawed and drained
1¼ cups nonfat cream cheese, softened
½ cup skim milk
1 tbsp. red wine vinegar
1 tsp. chicken bouillon granules
¾ tsp. Italian seasoning
1 tsp. garlic powder
½ cup nonfat Parmesan cheese, divided

Directions:
Cook pasta according to package directions; drain and keep warm. Combine spinach, cream cheese, milk, vinegar, bouillon granules, Italian seasoning, garlic powder, and 2 tablespoons Parmesan cheese in food processor or blender; process until smooth. Spray medium saucepan with cooking spray; spoon spinach mixture into saucepan and cook over medium heat, stirring frequently, until completely heated through (about 4 to 6 minutes). Toss with pasta; top with remaining Parmesan cheese and serve immediately.

Serves: 4

Shopping List:
12 oz. linguine, 10 oz. frozen chopped spinach, 12 oz. nonfat cream cheese, skim milk, nonfat Parmesan cheese, red wine vinegar, chicken bouillon granules, garlic powder, Italian seasoning

Nutrition per serving		Exchanges
calories:	245	1½ starch
total fat (4%):	1 g	2 vegetable
carbohydrate:	39 g	½ other carbohydrate
cholesterol:	1 mg	
dietary fiber:	3 g	carbohydrate choice: 2½
protein:	22 g	
sodium:	888 mg	

Frozen spinach retains all the vitamins and minerals, keeping it just as nutritious as fresh spinach.

Spinach Orzo

Easy — Do Ahead

Ingredients:
4 cups nonfat broth (chicken or vegetable)
2 cups orzo
16 oz. frozen chopped spinach, thawed and drained
1 tsp. Italian seasoning
¾ cup nonfat Parmesan cheese

Directions:
Spray saucepan with cooking spray. Combine broth, orzo, spinach, and Italian seasoning in saucepan; bring to a boil over high heat. Reduce heat to low, cover, and simmer over low heat 20 minutes until liquid is absorbed. Sprinkle with cheese and cook until heated through.

Serves: 4

Shopping List:
32 oz. nonfat broth (chicken or vegetable), orzo pasta, 16 oz. frozen chopped spinach, nonfat Parmesan cheese, Italian seasoning

Nutrition per serving		Exchanges
calories:	446	5 starch
total fat (4%):	2 g	2 vegetable
carbohydrate:	82 g	
cholesterol:	0 mg	carbohydrate choice: 5½
dietary fiber:	6 g	
protein:	25 g	
sodium:	1,132 mg	

Spinach is a good source of folate, which functions as a coenzyme, important for making new cells in the body.

"Squashly" Mostaccioli

Easy — Do Ahead — Freeze

Ingredients:

3 cups mostaccioli, cooked and drained
27½ oz. jar nonfat pasta sauce
1½ cups nonfat shredded mozzarella cheese
1½ cups sliced mushrooms
1½ cups sliced yellow squash
1½ cups sliced zucchini
1½ cups cubed eggplant
½ cup low-fat shredded mozzarella cheese
¼ cup nonfat Parmesan cheese

Directions:

Preheat oven to 375 degrees. Spray 9 x 13-inch baking dish with cooking spray. Combine mostaccioli, pasta sauce, nonfat mozzarella, mushrooms, squash, zucchini, and eggplant in a large bowl; mix until ingredients are well blended. Spoon into baking dish; top with low-fat mozzarella and Parmesan cheese. Bake 20 to 25 minutes until bubbly and lightly browned on top.

Serves: 6

Shopping List:

12 oz. mostaccioli, 27½-oz. jar nonfat pasta sauce, low-fat shredded mozzarella cheese, 6 oz. nonfat shredded mozzarella cheese, nonfat Parmesan cheese, 8 to 12 oz. package sliced mushrooms, 2 yellow squash, 2 zucchini, 1 lb. eggplant

Nutrition per serving

calories:	251
total fat (7%):	2 g
carbohydrate:	36 g
cholesterol:	0 mg
dietary fiber:	2 g
protein:	19 g
sodium:	681 mg

Exchanges

1 very lean meat
1 starch
5 vegetable

carbohydrate choice: 2½

Eggplant is a good source of potassium, which helps prevent constipation and insomnia.

Tarragon Chicken Pasta

Easy — Do Ahead

Ingredients:

2 cups cooked pasta
2 cups sliced mushrooms
1 cup broccoli florets
1 cup cauliflower florets
1 cup skim milk
1 tbsp. cornstarch
½ tsp. dried tarragon
½ tsp. garlic powder

2 cups fresh spinach,
  shredded
2 cups low-fat chicken
  tenders, cooked and cubed
½ cup nonfat Swiss
  cheese, shredded
nonfat Parmesan
  cheese (optional)

Directions:

Cook pasta according to package directions; add mushrooms, broccoli, and cauliflower during the last 5 to 6 minutes of cooking. Combine milk, cornstarch, tarragon, and garlic powder in a medium saucepan. Cook over medium heat, stirring constantly, until mixture comes to a boil and thickens. Stir in spinach, chicken, and Swiss cheese; cook, stirring frequently, until spinach wilts and cheese melts. Pour sauce over pasta; toss lightly and serve with Parmesan cheese, if desired.

Serves: 4

Shopping List:

8 oz. pasta (mostaccioli, rigatoni, or ziti), 1 lb. sliced mushrooms, ¾ lb. broccoli florets, ¾ lb. cauliflower florets, 8 oz. skim milk, 16 oz. package fresh spinach, ¾ lb. low-fat chicken tenders, nonfat Swiss cheese, cornstarch, dried tarragon, garlic powder, nonfat Parmesan cheese (optional)

Nutrition per serving		Exchanges
calories:	270	1 starch
total fat (3%):	1 g	3 vegetable
carbohydrate:	29 g	3½ very lean meat
cholesterol:	71 mg	
dietary fiber:	3 g	carbohydrate choice: 2
protein:	33 g	
sodium:	447 mg	

Cauliflower is a powerful cancer-fighting food, containing phytonutrients, sulforophane, and indole-3-carbinol.

Vegetable Couscous

Easy — Do Ahead

Ingredients:

1¾ cups V8 juice
1 tbsp. curry powder
1 tsp. garlic powder
1 tsp. ground coriander
½ tsp. ground ginger
½ tsp. ground cumin
½ tsp. cayenne pepper
¾ cup water
1 cup couscous, uncooked

1 cup frozen carrot slices,
   thawed and drained
10 oz. frozen broccoli
   florets, thawed and
   drained
1 cup frozen pepper strips,
   thawed and drained
½ cup golden raisins

Directions:

Combine V8 juice, curry powder, garlic powder, coriander, ginger, cumin, and cayenne pepper in a Ziploc bag; shake until ingredients are blended. Pour ¾ cup juice mixture and ¾ cup water in a medium saucepan; bring to a boil over high heat. Stir in couscous; remove from heat, cover and let stand until all liquid is absorbed (about 8 minutes). Pour remaining juice into medium saucepan and bring to a boil over high heat; add carrots, broccoli and peppers. Cook over medium-high heat 2 to 3 minutes until vegetables are tender. Stir in raisins. Spoon couscous onto center of platter; surround with spiced vegetable mixture.

Serves: 4

Shopping List:

14 oz. V8 juice, couscous, 10 oz. package frozen carrot slices, 10 oz. frozen broccoli florets, 10 oz. frozen pepper strips, golden raisins, curry powder, garlic powder, ground coriander, ground ginger, ground cumin, cayenne pepper

Nutrition per serving

calories:	301
total fat (3%):	1 g
carbohydrate:	66 g
cholesterol:	0 mg
dietary fiber:	13 g
protein:	11 g
sodium:	433 mg

Exchanges

2½ fruit
3 vegetable
1 starch

carbohydrate choice: 4½

Couscous, a low-fat carbohydrate, provides adequate amounts of fiber, B vitamins, and iron.

Apple-Raisin Rice

Easy — Do Ahead

Ingredients:
- 2 tbsp. vegetable broth
- 1 cup shredded carrot
- 1 cup sliced green onion
- 2 cups chopped apples (unpeeled)
- 3 cups cooked brown rice
- ½ cup raisins

Directions:

Spray large nonstick skillet with cooking spray; add vegetable broth and heat over medium-high heat. Add carrot, green onion, and apples to skillet; cook, stirring frequently, until carrots and apples are tender. Stir in rice and raisins; cook, stirring frequently, 2 to 3 minutes until completely heated through.

Serves: 6

Shopping List:

brown rice, vegetable broth, raisins, shredded carrot (or 2 carrots), green onions, 2 apples

Nutrition per serving		**Exchanges**
calories:	244	2 starch
total fat (4%):	1 g	3 vegetable
carbohydrate:	48 g	
cholesterol:	0 mg	carbohydrate choice: 3
dietary fiber:	3 g	
protein:	14 g	
sodium:	928 mg	

*Even though carbohydrates are relatively low in calories, overeating **ANYTHING** will put on pounds, especially when laden with butter, oil, or cream sauce.*

PERFECT PASTA, POTATOES, AND RICE

Asian Rice Pilaf

Easy

Ingredients:
1¾ cup oriental broth*
2 tsp. onion powder
¼ tsp. garlic powder
1½ cups brown rice
1 tbsp. low-sodium soy sauce
¼ tsp. red pepper flakes
½ cup sliced green onion

Directions:
Combine broth, onion powder, garlic powder, rice, soy sauce, and red pepper flakes in medium saucepan; bring to a boil over high heat. Reduce heat to low, cover, and simmer 15 minutes, until rice is tender and liquid is absorbed. Stir in green onion; cover and let stand 5 minutes. Fluff with fork and serve.

Serves: 6

Shopping List:
14½ oz. can oriental broth (*you can substitute chicken, vegetable, or beef broth), brown rice, low-sodium soy sauce, red pepper flakes, green onions, garlic powder, onion powder

Nutrition per serving
calories:	181
total fat (10%):	2 g
carbohydrate:	37 g
cholesterol:	0 mg
dietary fiber:	3 g
protein:	5 g
sodium:	333 mg

Exchanges
2 starch

carbohydrate choice: 2

Brown rice has only its husk removed during milling; this process keeps the bran (the storehouse of fiber, vitamins, minerals, and phytochemicals) intact.

Bulgur-Brown Rice Pilaf with Green Beans and Cheese

Easy — Do Ahead

Ingredients:
1½ cups vegetable broth
½ cup instant brown rice
½ cup bulgur
10 oz. frozen green beans
½ cup nonfat shredded Cheddar cheese
2 tsp. sliced almonds, toasted

Directions:
Combine vegetable broth, rice, bulgur and green beans in large saucepan; bring to a boil over high heat. Reduce heat to low, cover, and simmer 15 to 18 minutes until rice and bulgur are tender. Sprinkle cheese over rice mixture and toss lightly; add toasted almonds and serve.

Serves: 4

Shopping List:
14½ oz. can vegetable broth, instant brown rice, bulgur, 10 oz. frozen cut green beans, 2 oz. nonfat shredded Cheddar cheese, sliced almonds

Nutrition per serving		Exchanges
calories:	255	2½ starch
total fat (11%):	3 g	2 vegetable
carbohydrate:	47 g	
cholesterol:	0 mg	carbohydrate choice: 3
dietary fiber:	8 g	
protein:	13 g	
sodium:	494 mg	

Whole grains, such as brown rice and bulgur, provide a good supply of vitamin B_6, chromium, selenium, and magnesium; these nutrients are critical for energy production.

Cheesy Lentil and Brown Rice Casserole

Easy — Do Ahead

Ingredients:
¾ cup dried lentils, sorted and rinsed
½ cup brown rice, uncooked
3 cups nonfat broth (chicken or vegetable)
¾ cup nonfat shredded Cheddar cheese
¼ cup low-fat shredded Cheddar cheese

Directions:
Preheat oven to 375 degrees. Lightly spray 2-quart casserole dish with cooking spray. Combine lentils, rice, broth, and nonfat cheese in baking dish; toss lightly until mixed. Cover with foil and bake 45 to 60 minutes, until rice is tender; top with low-fat cheese and bake 5 minutes, until cheese is melted.

Serves: 6

Shopping List:
dried lentils, brown rice, 24 oz. nonfat broth (chicken or vegetable), low-fat shredded Cheddar cheese, nonfat shredded Cheddar cheese

Nutrition per serving		Exchanges
calories:	173	1 very lean meat
total fat (5%):	1 g	2 starch
carbohydrate:	27 g	
cholesterol:	2 mg	carbohydrate choice: 2
dietary fiber:	1 g	
protein:	13 g	
sodium:	629 mg	

**Lentils are a low-fat, high-protein
alternative to meat.**

Double "A" Rice

Easy — Do Ahead

Ingredients:
3 cups instant rice, uncooked
2 16-oz. cans stewed tomatoes, undrained
2 14-oz. cans artichoke hearts, undrained
10 oz. package frozen asparagus spears, thawed and
    drained,
    cut in 1-inch pieces

Directions:
Combine all ingredients in a large saucepan or skillet. Bring to a boil over high heat; reduce heat to low, cover, and simmer 8 to 10 minutes until rice is tender and liquid is absorbed.

Serves: 6

Shopping List:
instant rice, 2 16-oz. cans stewed tomatoes, 2 14-oz. cans artichoke hearts, 10 oz. frozen asparagus spears or cuts

Nutrition per serving		Exchanges
calories:	362	2½ starch
total fat (2%):	1 g	7 vegetable
carbohydrate:	80 g	
cholesterol:	0 mg	carbohydrate choice: 5
dietary fiber:	8 g	
protein:	13 g	
sodium:	519 mg	

Artichoke hearts contain silymarin, a powerful antioxidant that may prevent certain types of cancer. They are an excellent source of fiber and magnesium, loaded with folate, and a good source of vitamin C.

Hot Carriba Beans and Rice

Average — Do Ahead

Ingredients:

⅔ cup instant white rice (uncooked)
⅓ cup + 1 tbsp. nonfat chicken broth
⅓ cup water
1 cup chopped onion
½ cup chopped celery
½ cup chopped green bell pepper
1½ tsp. minced garlic

1 cup canned chopped tomatoes, drained
¼ tsp. ground cumin
¼ tsp. crushed red pepper
15 oz. can black beans, rinsed and drained
¼ cup fresh cilantro, chopped
½ cup nonfat Parmesan cheese

Directions:

Cook rice according to package directions (microwave or stove-top) using ⅓ cup chicken broth and ⅓ cup water. Set aside and keep warm. Spray large nonstick skillet with cooking spray; add 1 tablespoon chicken broth and heat over medium-high heat. Add onion, celery, bell pepper, and garlic to skillet; cook, stirring frequently, until vegetables are tender (5 to 6 minutes). Add tomatoes, cumin, and red pepper; cook, stirring frequently, 2 to 3 minutes. Stir in cooked rice, beans, and cilantro; cook over medium heat until heated through. Sprinkle with Parmesan cheese before serving.

Serves: 4

Shopping List:

instant white rice, nonfat chicken broth, 14½ oz. can chopped tomatoes, 15 oz. can black beans, onion, celery, green bell pepper, minced garlic, fresh cilantro, nonfat Parmesan cheese, crushed red pepper, ground cumin

Nutrition per serving		Exchanges
calories:	174	1 starch
total fat (5%):	1 g	4 vegetable
carbohydrate:	31 g	
cholesterol:	0 mg	carbohydrate choice: 2
dietary fiber:	5 g	
protein:	12 g	
sodium:	689 mg	

When carbohydrates and protein are eaten together, protein is used more efficiently as a source of energy.

PERFECT PASTA, POTATOES, AND RICE

Lemon Rice

Easy

Ingredients:
- 1 cup rice, white or brown
- ¼ tsp. garlic powder
- 1 tsp. lemon peel
- 2 cups nonfat chicken broth
- ⅛ tsp. pepper
- 2 tsp. dried parsley

Directions:

Combine rice, garlic powder, lemon peel, broth, and pepper in a medium saucepan; bring to a boil over high heat. Reduce heat to low, cover, and simmer 15 to 20 minutes until rice is tender and liquid is absorbed. Stir in parsley and serve.

Serves: 6

Shopping List:

rice (white or brown), 16 oz. nonfat chicken broth, garlic powder, dried parsley, pepper, lemon peel

Nutrition per serving		**Exchanges**
calories:	121	1½ starch
total fat (7%):	1 g	
carbohydrate:	24 g	carbohydrate choice: 1½
cholesterol:	0 mg	
dietary fiber:	2 g	
protein:	3 g	
sodium:	263 mg	

Energy metabolism is the process that converts food into fuel; for efficient energy metabolism, include a wide assortment of nutrients.

Mushroom Risotto

Easy

Ingredients:

1½ cups nonfat beef broth
½ cup water
¼ lb. sliced mushrooms
½ tsp. garlic powder
½ tsp. Italian seasoning
2 cups instant rice
¾ cup nonfat Parmesan cheese

Directions:

Combine beef broth, water, mushrooms, garlic powder, and Italian seasoning in a medium saucepan; bring to a boil over high heat. Add rice and Parmesan cheese; cover, remove from heat, and let stand 5 minutes. Fluff with fork and serve.

Serves: 4

Shopping List:

14½-oz. can beef broth, ¼ lb. sliced mushrooms, instant rice, nonfat Parmesan cheese, garlic powder, Italian seasoning

Nutrition per serving

calories:	138
total fat (2%):	.3 g
carbohydrate:	26 g
cholesterol:	0 mg
dietary fiber:	1 g
protein:	8 g
sodium:	532 mg

Exchanges

1 starch
3 vegetable

carbohydrate choice: 2

*According to the **American Institute for Cancer Research Newsletter** (1999), "strong evidence shows that a shift toward a plant-based diet rich in a variety of vegetables, fruits, whole grains and beans and away from a diet of high-fat animal and processed foods, will help you achieve a longer and healthier life."*

PERFECT PASTA, POTATOES, AND RICE

Orzo with Wheat Berries and Mushrooms
Average — Do Ahead

Ingredients:
3 cups water
¾ cup wheat berries
1½ cups orzo
1 tbsp. + ½ cup vegetable broth, divided
2 cups sliced mushrooms (button or shiitake)
1 cup carrot slices

1¾ cup canned Italian-style chopped tomatoes, undrained
1 cup tomato sauce
½ tsp. instant broth and seasoning (chicken, vegetable, or beef)
½ tsp. crushed fennel seeds
⅛ tsp. red pepper

Directions:
Pour water into large saucepan or Dutch oven; bring to a boil over high heat. Add wheat berries; reduce heat to low, cover, and simmer 45 to 60 minutes. Add orzo to pan and cook, uncovered, 10 to 15 minutes until pasta and wheat berries are tender. Drain liquid; cover pan and set aside to keep warm. Spray medium saucepan with cooking spray; add 1-tablespoon vegetable broth and heat over medium-high heat. Add mushrooms and carrots; cook, stirring frequently, until vegetables are tender-crisp. Stir in tomatoes, tomato sauce, ½ cup vegetable broth, instant broth granules, fennel seeds, and red pepper; bring to a boil over high heat. Reduce heat to low and cook, uncovered, 20 to 25 minutes until completely heated through. Spoon orzo mixture into large serving bowl; top with sauce and serve.

Serves: 4

Shopping List:
wheat berries, orzo, ½ lb. mushrooms, 2 carrots, 14½ oz. can Italian-style chopped tomatoes, 8 oz. tomato sauce, 14½ oz. can vegetable broth, instant broth and seasoning granules (chicken, vegetable, or beef), fennel seeds, red pepper

Nutrition per serving
calories:	353
total fat (6%):	2 g
carbohydrate:	73 g
cholesterol:	0 mg
dietary fiber:	4 g
protein:	14 g
sodium:	782 mg

Exchanges
2 4 starch
2 vegetable

carbohydrate choice: 5

Mushrooms are a source of mood-soothing B vitamins.

Paella

Easy — Do Ahead — Freeze

Ingredients:
3 cups chopped onion
2½ tbsp. minced garlic
1½ cups basmati rice, uncooked
14 oz. can artichoke hearts, drained
3 cups nonfat broth (chicken or vegetable)
10 oz. frozen broccoli cuts, thawed and drained
10 oz. frozen pea pods, thawed and drained
1½ cups frozen pepper strips, thawed and drained
1½ lb. cooked shrimp

Directions:
Spray a large nonstick skillet with cooking spray and heat over medium-high heat. Add onion and garlic to skillet and cook, stirring frequently, 5 to 6 minutes, until onions are soft. Add rice, artichoke hearts and broth; heat to boiling over high heat. Reduce heat to low, cover, and simmer 10 to 15 minutes. Stir in broccoli, pea pods, peppers, and shrimp; cover skillet and cook 5 to 10 minutes until liquid is absorbed and paella is heated through.

Serves: 6

Shopping List:
3 onions (or 16 oz. package chopped onion), basmati rice, 14 oz. can artichoke hearts, 10 oz. package frozen broccoli cuts, 10 oz. package frozen pea pods, 16 oz. frozen pepper strips, 1½ lb. cooked shrimp, 24 oz. nonfat broth (chicken or vegetable), minced garlic

Nutrition per serving

calories:	360
total fat (5%):	2 g
carbohydrate:	59 g
cholesterol:	174 mg
dietary fiber:	6 g
protein:	28 g
sodium:	430 mg

Exchanges
2 very lean meat
2 starch
6 vegetable

carbohydrate choice: 4

Onions contain compounds that help lower cholesterol, thin the blood, and prevent hardening of the arteries, all of which contribute to the prevention of heart disease.

PERFECT PASTA, POTATOES, AND RICE

Red and Green Rice Veracruz

Easy — Do Ahead

Ingredients:
2 tsp. nonfat chicken broth
1½ cups instant brown rice
1 cup chopped onion
2 tsp. crushed garlic
2 14-oz. cans tomatoes and green chilies, undrained
1¾ cup tomato sauce
1 tsp. chopped green chilies

Directions:
Spray nonstick skillet with cooking spray; pour chicken broth into skillet and heat over medium-high heat. Add rice, onion, and garlic to skillet; cook, stirring frequently, until rice is golden brown. Stir in remaining ingredients. Reduce heat to low, cover, and simmer 12 to 15 minutes until rice is tender.

Serves: 4

Shopping List:
2 14-oz. cans tomatoes with green chilies, 16 oz. can tomato sauce, instant brown rice, nonfat chicken broth, chopped green chilies, onion (or packaged chopped onion), crushed garlic

Nutrition per serving
calories:	154
total fat (4%):	1 g
carbohydrate:	55 g
cholesterol:	0 mg
dietary fiber:	4 g
protein:	5 g
sodium:	1265 mg

Exchanges
1 starch
3 vegetable

carbohydrate choice: 2

According to the Women.com website (June 2000), only one in five women who were trying to lose weight was doing it the right way: by both cutting calories and increasing exercise.

Rice Cakes

Easy — Do Ahead

Ingredients:
¾ cup brown rice, uncooked
¾ cup nonfat broth (chicken or vegetable)
¾ cup chopped chives
½ cup chopped mushrooms

Directions:
Cook rice according to package directions substituting chicken broth for water (if more liquid is needed, add water). Stir in chopped chives and mushrooms. Cover and let stand 10 minutes. Divide mixture and shape into muffin cups. Serve rice balls as the perfect accompaniment to any fish, chicken, or soup. (If adding to soup, shape rice balls and place in hot soup just before serving.

Serves: 4

Shopping List:
brown rice, nonfat broth (chicken or vegetable), chives, ¼ lb. mushrooms

Nutrition per serving

calories:	134	
total fat (7%):	1.1 g	
carbohydrate:	28 g	
cholesterol:	0 mg	
dietary fiber:	2 g	
protein:	3 g	
sodium:	172 mg	

Exchanges

1½ starch
1 vegetable

carbohydrate choice: 2

Brown rice contains selenium, a trace mineral found to decrease anxiety and depression.

Risotto Primavera

Average — Do Ahead

Ingredients:

1 cup frozen asparagus cuts, thawed and drained
½ cup frozen pea pods, thawed and drained
½ cup canned sliced water chestnuts
1 cup Arborio rice
3½ cups nonfat broth (chicken or vegetable), divided
1 tbsp. onion powder
½ tsp. garlic powder

Directions:

Spray large nonstick skillet with cooking spray and heat over medium-high heat. Add asparagus, pea pods, and water chestnuts to skillet; cook, stirring frequently, until vegetables are tender-crisp (about 3 to 4 minutes). Remove from skillet and keep warm. Remove skillet from burner and respray with cooking spray; return to heat and add rice to skillet. Cook, stirring constantly, 1 minute. Gradually stir in ¾ cup broth, stirring until the liquid is absorbed. Add remaining broth, stirring frequently and cook until most of the broth is absorbed. Stir in vegetables, onion powder, and garlic powder; cook 3 to 4 minutes until heated through.

Serves: 4

Shopping List:

10 oz. package frozen asparagus cuts, 10 oz. package frozen pea pods, 6 oz. can sliced water chestnuts, Arborio rice, 28 oz. nonfat broth (chicken or vegetable), onion powder, garlic powder

Nutrition per serving		Exchanges
calories:	221	2 starch
total fat (8%):	2 g	3 vegetable
carbohydrate:	45 g	
cholesterol:	0 mg	carbohydrate choice: 3
dietary fiber:	4 g	
protein:	6 g	
sodium:	796 mg	

Asparagus is an excellent source of folate, a B vitamin essential for helping cells regenerate.

Shiitake Mushrooms and Brown Rice

Easy — Do Ahead

Ingredients:
- 2 tbsp. vegetable broth
- 1 cup sliced shiitake mushrooms
- 1 cup asparagus pieces, cut 1-inch thick
- ¼ tsp. garlic powder
- 3 cups cooked brown rice
- ¼ cup sliced green onion
- ¼ tsp. lemon pepper

Directions:
Spray large nonstick skillet or wok with cooking spray; add vegetable broth and heat over medium-high heat. Add mushrooms, asparagus, and garlic powder; cook, stirring frequently, until vegetables are tender-crisp (about 1 to 2 minutes). Add cooked rice, green onion, and lemon pepper; stir until ingredients are mixed. Cook over medium heat until thoroughly heated. Great with chicken or fish.

Serves: 6

Shopping List:
¼ lb. shiitake mushrooms, ¼ lb. asparagus, green onion, brown rice, vegetable broth, garlic powder, lemon pepper

Nutrition per serving		Exchanges
calories:	131	1 starch
total fat (7%):	1 g	2½ vegetable
carbohydrate:	28 g	
cholesterol:	0 mg	carbohydrate choice: 2
dietary fiber:	0 g	
protein:	4 g	
sodium:	20 mg	

One-half cup of cooked brown rice contains 43 milligrams of magnesium, nearly four times the amount found in cooked white rice.

PERFECT PASTA, POTATOES, AND RICE

Spanish-Style Couscous
Easy

Ingredients:
1 cup nonfat chicken broth
2 tsp. onion powder
½ tsp. garlic powder
½ tsp. ground cumin
¾ cup frozen green peas, thawed and drained
¾ cup canned Mexican-style chopped tomatoes
2 tsp. dried cilantro
¾ cup quick-cooking couscous

Directions:
Combine broth, onion powder, garlic powder, cumin, peas, tomatoes, and cilantro in medium saucepan; bring to a boil over high heat. Stir in couscous; remove pan from heat, cover, and let stand 5 minutes. Fluff with fork before serving.

Serves: 6

Shopping List:
8 oz. nonfat chicken broth, 14½ oz. can Mexican-style chopped tomatoes, 10 oz. frozen green peas, couscous, onion powder, garlic powder, cumin, dried cilantro

Nutrition per serving		Exchanges
calories:	118	1 starch
total fat (0%):	0 g	2 vegetable
carbohydrate:	23 g	
cholesterol:	0 mg	carbohydrate choice: 1½
dietary fiber:	4 g	
protein:	5 g	
sodium:	271 mg	

Carbohydrates are 100% pure energy; they metabolize quickly and provide a quick boost in blood-sugar levels.

Vegetable Risotto

Easy — Do Ahead

Ingredients:
3½ cups nonfat vegetable broth, divided
½ cup chopped onion
1 cup shredded carrot
1 cup Arborio rice
1½ cups frozen broccoli florets, thawed and drained
1½ cups frozen cauliflower florets, thawed and drained
¼ cup nonfat Parmesan cheese

Directions:
Spray nonstick skillet with cooking spray. Pour 1 tablespoon vegetable broth into skillet and heat over medium-high heat. Add chopped onion and shredded carrot; cook, stirring frequently, for 1 minute. Add rice; cook until rice turns golden brown. Add remaining broth and cook, uncovered, over medium heat until liquid is absorbed and rice is tender. Add broccoli and cauliflower to rice mixture; cook until heated through. Sprinkle with Parmesan cheese and toss lightly before serving.

Serves: 4

Shopping List:
28 oz. nonfat vegetable broth, packaged chopped onion (or 1 onion), packaged shredded carrot, Arborio rice, 16 oz. frozen broccoli florets, 16 oz. frozen cauliflower florets, nonfat Parmesan cheese

Nutrition per serving		Exchanges
calories:	228	2½ starch
total fat (3%):	1 g	1 vegetable
carbohydrate:	48 g	
cholesterol:	0 mg	carbohydrate choice: 3
dietary fiber:	3 g	
protein:	8 g	
sodium:	860 mg	

Carrots are rich in beta-carotene, which contributes to reducing the risk of heart disease, cancer, and macular degeneration (the leading cause of vision loss in older adults).

Wild Rice Stuffing

Easy — Do Ahead

Ingredients:
3¾ cups nonfat chicken broth, divided
½ lb. sliced mushrooms
½ cup wild rice
½ tsp. garlic powder
1 tsp. dried rosemary
¼ cup brown rice
½ cup red bell pepper, cut into strips

Directions:
Pour 2 tablespoons broth into large saucepan and heat over medium-high heat. Add mushrooms and cook 7 to 10 minutes until lightly browned. Stir in wild rice; drizzle with 2 tablespoons of broth. Cook 5 minutes. Add remaining broth, garlic powder, and rosemary to pan and bring to a boil over high heat. Reduce heat to low, cover, and simmer 15 minutes. Add brown rice and pepper strips; cover and cook over low heat 30 to 35 minutes, until rice is tender.

Serves: 4

Shopping List:
wild rice, brown rice, 30 oz. nonfat chicken broth, ½ lb. sliced mushrooms, red bell pepper, garlic powder, dried rosemary

Nutrition per serving		Exchanges
calories:	143	1½ starch
total fat (6%):	1 g	1 vegetable
carbohydrate:	29 g	
cholesterol:	0 mg	carbohydrate choice: 2
dietary fiber:	.2 g	
protein:	5 g	
sodium:	847 mg	

Rosemary has been found to enhance memory and help combat mild depression, headaches, and migraines.

VIGOROUS
VEGETABLES

VEGETABLES FOR VIM, VIGOR, AND VORACIOUS APPETITES

Eat your way to health with "practically perfect" foods! Low-fat, cholesterol-free, nutrient-rich vegetables are packed with essential vitamins, minerals, complex carbohydrates, and fiber that add color, texture, and a multitude of flavors to any meal!

According to the *American Institute for Cancer Research Newsletter* (Fall 1999), eating more vegetables and fruits may be THE MOST IMPORTANT nutritional change you can make. The 1997 AICR report, "Food, Nutrition, and the Prevention of Cancer: A Global Perspective," shows that "if the only change people made to their lives was to eat five or more servings of fruits and vegetables each day, worldwide cancer rates would drop by 20%. That works out to 2 million more lives untouched by cancer this year alone."

- AICR suggests that eating at least 5 servings of **vegetables** and fruits, rich in naturally occurring antioxidants and phytochemicals, each day may prevent up to 20% of cancer cases.

- Most **vegetables**, low in calories and fat, fill you up without filling you out. Eat more for less!

- Increasing your intake of **vegetables** and fruits while cutting back on meat and high-fat dairy may help you limit your intake of heart-damaging saturated fat and cholesterol. Vegetables, rich in antioxidants and other phytochemicals, may prevent fatty deposits from forming in blood vessels.

- **Vegetables** and fruits are rich in soluble fiber, helping to lower blood cholesterol.

- **Vegetables** and fruits provide folate, a vitamin that helps lower blood levels of homocysteine, another risk factor for heart disease.

- Rich in potassium and magnesium, **vegetables** can be credited with lowering blood pressure.

- According to the AICR, recent studies suggest that diets high in **vegetables** and fruits may decrease the risk of stroke by up to 25%.

- Lower the risk of cataracts and macular degeneration (two of the most common causes of adult blindness) by consuming **vegetables** rich in vitamin C and certain carotenoids.

Vegetables and fruits are high-fiber foods, which reduce the risk of diverticulosis. Diverticulosis, a disease marked by inflamed and painful pouches in the intestinal wall, occurs in one-third of individuals over the age of fifty and two-thirds of those over the age of eighty. A high-fiber diet is the best defense against this disease.

Eating **vegetables** and fruits helps stabilize blood-sugar levels; rich in complex carbohydrates and fiber, the sugar is absorbed much slower into the blood stream than the "sugar rush" you might receive from other foods.

Vegetables, rich in minerals (calcium, magnesium, and potassium), may help relieve and prevent symptoms of menstrual cramps and PMS. Calcium and magnesium act as natural tranquilizers while potassium relieves symptoms of premenstrual bloating by reducing fluid retention. The high mineral content of **vegetables** protects against the development of anemia, osteoporosis, and excessive menstrual bleeding.

Treat your **vegetables** with T.L.C. to preserve nutrients, flavors, and "healthy" integrity!

- Microwave or steam to preserve colors, flavors, and nutrients.
- Plain and simple goes a long way. Flavor with seasonings, spices, or low-fat broths; don't bury the "good stuff" in butter-, cream-, or cheese-laden sauces.
- Splash on flavor with lemon juice, fresh herbs, or flavored vinegars without adding calories and fat.
- Toss fresh or frozen vegetables into cooking water when preparing pasta.
- Keep a bowl of cut-up veggies in the fridge—the first thing you see may be the best snack you'll grab!
- Add spinach, broccoli, bell pepper, tomatoes, onion, sprouts, etc. to pizza, sandwiches, and omelets.

Don't let winter months keep you out in the cold! The American Institute for Cancer Research "urges the public to maintain consumption of vegetables and fruits throughout the winter months by integrating frozen and canned fruits and vegetables into the diet." Whether fresh, canned, or frozen, vegetables are "powerful tools that make the everyday fight against cancer faster, easier, and more flavorful." (Source: http://www.aicr.org)

Au Gratin Carrots and Potatoes

Easy — Do Ahead

Ingredients:
2 lb. gold potatoes, peeled and sliced thin
2½ tsp. Mrs. Dash seasoning, divided
1 cup chopped onion, divided
2 cups carrot slices
1¼ cups nonfat broth (chicken or vegetable)
¼ cup nonfat Parmesan cheese

Directions:
Preheat oven to 400 degrees. Spray shallow 2½- to 3-quart casserole with cooking spray. Arrange half the potato slices in the bottom of casserole (overlapping as needed). Sprinkle with 1 teaspoon Mrs. Dash seasoning and ½ cup chopped onion. Top with sliced carrots; sprinkle with 1 teaspoon seasoning and remaining onion. Top with remaining potato slices; sprinkle with seasoning. Pour broth over vegetables; cover and bake 25 to 20 minutes until vegetables are tender. Uncover, sprinkle with Parmesan cheese, and bake an additional 20 to 25 minutes until tender and golden brown.

Serves: 6

Shopping List:
2 lb. gold potatoes, onion (or packaged chopped onion), 12 oz. package carrot slices, 14½ oz. can nonfat broth (vegetable or chicken), nonfat Parmesan cheese, Mrs. Dash seasoning

Nutrition per serving		Exchanges
calories:	180	1½ starch
total fat (0%):	0 g	3 vegetable
carbohydrate:	40 g	
cholesterol:	0 mg	carbohydrate choice: 2½
dietary fiber:	6 g	
protein:	5 g	
sodium:	255 mg	

Women who eat at least 5 carrots a week are 70% less likely to suffer a stroke than those who eat carrots once a month.

Braised Vegetables

Easy — Do Ahead — Freeze

Ingredients:

1½ tbsp. + 1½ cups nonfat broth (chicken or vegetable), divided
½ lb. potatoes, cut in large chunks
½ lb. sweet potatoes, cut in large chunks
½ lb. small mushrooms
9 oz. frozen artichoke hearts
10 oz. frozen baby carrots
2 tsp. garlic powder
1 tsp. dried dill
pepper to taste

Directions:

Spray large saucepan or Dutch oven with cooking spray; pour 1½ tablespoons broth into pan and heat over medium-high heat. Add all of the potatoes and mushrooms; cook, stirring frequently, until vegetables are lightly browned. Pour remaining broth into pan; add frozen artichokes, frozen carrots, and garlic powder. Reduce heat to low, cover pan, and cook 30 to 35 minutes until potatoes are tender. Add more broth as needed to keep vegetables moist. Sprinkle vegetable medley with dill and pepper. Serve over rice, couscous, orzo or other pasta, if desired.

Serves: 6

Shopping List:

15½ oz. can nonfat broth (chicken or vegetable), ½ lb. potatoes, ½ lb. sweet potatoes, ½ lb. small mushrooms, 10 oz. package frozen baby carrots, 9 oz. package frozen artichoke hearts, garlic powder, dried dill weed, pepper

Nutrition per serving

calories:	127
total fat (0%):	0 g
carbohydrate:	29 g
cholesterol:	0 mg
dietary fiber:	4 g
protein:	4 g
sodium:	301 mg

Exchanges

1 starch
2½ vegetable

carbohydrate choice: 2

Sweet potatoes are rich in vitamin A, a potential protectant reducing the risk of lung cancer. One cup of sweet potatoes provides more than 43,000 international units of vitamin A, eight times the Recommended Daily Allowance.

Broccoli Au Gratin

Easy — Do Ahead — Freeze

Ingredients:
16 oz. frozen broccoli cuts, thawed and drained
⅔ cup evaporated skim milk
2 tbsp. lemon juice
¼ cup egg substitute
¾ cup nonfat Parmesan cheese

Directions:
Preheat oven to 375 degrees. Spray 9-inch pie plate or quiche dish with cooking spray. Arrange broccoli cuts in dish. Combine milk, lemon juice, and egg substitute in a medium bowl; mix until ingredients are completely blended. Pour mixture over broccoli; sprinkle with cheese. Bake 30 to 35 minutes until bubbly and lightly browned.

Serves: 4

Shopping List:
16 oz. package frozen broccoli cuts, evaporated skim milk, lemon juice, egg substitute, nonfat Parmesan cheese

Nutrition per serving		Exchanges
calories:	118	2 vegetable
total fat (0%):	0 g	½ milk
carbohydrate:	18 g	½ very lean meat
cholesterol:	2 mg	
dietary fiber:	4 g	carbohydrate choice: 1
protein:	14 g	
sodium:	231 mg	

One serving of broccoli contains 200% of the vitamin C you need for the day.

Broccoli Spears with Dijon Cream Sauce

Easy

Ingredients:
2 10-oz. frozen broccoli spears, cooked and drained
1½ cups skim milk
3 tbsp. flour
⅛ tsp. pepper
2 tbsp. nonfat sour cream
2 tsp. dried dill weed
1 tbsp. Dijon mustard
nonfat Parmesan cheese (optional)

Directions:
Cook broccoli according to package directions; keep warm. Spray large saucepan with cooking spray. Combine milk, flour, and pepper in pan; whisk until blended. Cook over medium heat, stirring frequently, until sauce begins to boil and thickens (2 to 3 minutes). Whisk in sour cream, dill and mustard; cook over medium heat until heated through. Arrange broccoli on serving platter; drizzle with Dijon sauce and sprinkle with Parmesan cheese, if desired.

Serves: 4

Shopping List:
2 10-oz. packages frozen broccoli spears, 12 oz. skim milk, nonfat sour cream, Dijon mustard, nonfat Parmesan cheese (optional), flour, pepper, dried dill weed

Nutrition per serving

calories:	111
total fat (8%):	1 g
carbohydrate:	20 g
cholesterol:	2 mg
dietary fiber:	6 g
protein:	9 g
sodium:	144 mg

Exchanges

1 vegetable
½ milk
½ other carbohydrate

carbohydrate choice: 1

Broccoli's superpowers include its rich supply of folate, essential for normal tissue growth, as well as a protection against cancer, heart disease, and birth defects.

Creamed Corn with Chilies

Easy

Ingredients:

3 tbsp. nonfat chicken broth
2 tbsp. chopped green bell pepper
2 tbsp. chopped onion
16 oz. whole kernel corn, drained
2 tbsp. chopped green chilies
3 oz. nonfat cream cheese, cubed
⅓ cup skim milk
½ tsp. pepper
¾ tsp. no-salt seasoning

Directions:

Spray large saucepan with cooking spray; add chicken broth to pan and heat over medium-high heat. Cook bell pepper and onion in broth, stirring frequently, until vegetables are tender (about 3 to 4 minutes). Add remaining ingredients to saucepan and cook, stirring constantly, until cheese is melted and corn is heated through.

Serves: 4

Shopping List:

16 oz. can whole kernel corn, 3 oz. nonfat cream cheese, skim milk, chopped green chilies, nonfat chicken broth, green bell pepper, onion, pepper, no-salt seasoning

Nutrition per serving		Exchanges
calories:	118	1 starch
total fat (7%):	1 g	2 vegetable
carbohydrate:	25 g	
cholesterol:	<.5 mg	carbohydrate choice: 1½
dietary fiber:	5 g	
protein:	6 g	
sodium:	539 mg	

***Corn is a respectable source of iron and zinc,
a good source of potassium and very low in sodium
(28 milligrams per cup).***

Creamed Spinach with Onions

Easy

Ingredients:
1 tsp. nonfat chicken broth
1 cup sliced onion
1 lb. fresh spinach, cut into bite-size pieces
1 tbsp. flour
1 cup evaporated skim milk
1 tbsp. nonfat Parmesan cheese
½ tsp. garlic powder

Directions:
Spray large nonstick skillet with cooking spray; add broth and heat over medium-high heat. Add onion to skillet; reduce heat to low and cook, stirring frequently, 5 to 7 minutes until onion is softened. Add spinach; cook, stirring frequently, until spinach wilts (3 to 4 minutes). Sprinkle flour into skillet and stir with spinach; gradually add milk, stirring constantly, and cook until sauce thickens (2 to 3 minutes). Sprinkle spinach with Parmesan cheese and garlic powder; toss lightly and serve.

Serves: 4

Shopping List:
1 lb. fresh spinach, onion, 8 oz. evaporated skim milk, nonfat chicken broth, flour, nonfat Parmesan cheese, garlic powder

Nutrition per serving		Exchanges
calories:	102	2 vegetable
total fat (9%):	1 g	½ milk
carbohydrate:	17 g	
cholesterol:	3 mg	carbohydrate choice: 1
dietary fiber:	4 g	
protein:	9 g	
sodium:	175 mg	

Spinach is an excellent source of iron, a mineral your body needs to produce red blood cells and transport oxygen. One-half cup of spinach provides 3 milligrams of iron, 20% of the RDA for women and 30% of the RDA for men.

Crustless Spinach Quiche

Easy — Do Ahead — Freeze

Ingredients:
- ½ cup egg substitute
- 4 egg whites
- 15 oz. nonfat ricotta cheese
- ¾ cup skim milk
- 1½ tsp. onion powder
- ¼ tsp. pepper
- 3 tbsp. cornstarch
- 1 cup nonfat Parmesan cheese, divided
- 2 10-oz. frozen chopped spinach, thawed and drained

Directions:

Preheat oven to 350 degrees. Spray 9-inch pie plate with cooking spray. Combine egg substitute, egg whites, ricotta cheese, milk, onion powder, pepper, cornstarch, and ¾ cup Parmesan cheese in a large bowl; using whisk or fork, blend ingredients until frothy. Fold in spinach. Spoon mixture into pie plate; sprinkle with remaining Parmesan cheese and bake 35 to 40 minutes until toothpick inserted in center comes out clean.

Serves: 6

Shopping List:

2 10-oz. packages frozen chopped spinach, 15 oz. nonfat ricotta cheese, skim milk, 4 oz. nonfat Parmesan cheese, egg substitute, eggs, cornstarch, onion powder, pepper

Nutrition per serving		Exchanges
calories:	166	2 very lean meat
total fat (0%):	0 g	4 vegetable
carbohydrate:	20 g	
cholesterol:	12 mg	carbohydrate choice: 1
dietary fiber:	2 g	
protein:	24 g	
sodium:	418 mg	

Spinach is a good source of calcium, magnesium, and potassium, which help relieve and prevent the symptoms of PMS and menstrual cramps. Calcium and magnesium act as natural tranquilizers, reducing menstrual pain, discomfort, and irritability.

Eggplant-Zucchini Cheese Bake

Average — Do Ahead — Freeze

Ingredients:

2 tbsp. nonfat chicken broth
2 cups frozen pepper strips,
  thawed and drained
1 lb. eggplant, cut into
  ¾-inch pieces
2 zucchini, cut into
  ¼-inch pieces

4 tsp. sugar, divided
¼ cup water
16 oz. lasagna noodles,
  cooked and drained
4 cups nonfat pasta sauce
4 cups nonfat shredded
  mozzarella cheese

Directions:

Preheat oven to 375 degrees. Spray 9 x 13-inch baking dish with cooking spray. Spray large nonstick skillet with cooking spray; add chicken broth and heat over medium-high heat. Add peppers, eggplant, zucchini, 2 tsp. sugar and water to skillet; bring to a boil over high heat. Reduce heat to low, cover, and simmer 15 minutes, until vegetables are tender. Remove cover and cook until liquid evaporates. Arrange one-fourth lasagna noodles on bottom of dish; spread with ⅓ vegetable mixture. Top with 1 cup pasta sauce and sprinkle with 1 cup cheese. Repeat layers ending with cheese. Bake, uncovered, 40 to 45 minutes until hot, bubbly and lightly browned.

Serves: 10

Shopping List:

16 oz. lasagna noodles, 1 lb. eggplant, 2 zucchini, 16 oz. frozen pepper strips, 1 lb. nonfat shredded mozzarella cheese, 32 oz. nonfat pasta sauce, sugar, nonfat chicken broth

Nutrition per serving		Exchanges
calories:	289	1 very lean meat
total fat (6%):	2 g	5 vegetable
carbohydrate:	41 g	1½ starch
cholesterol:	39 mg	
dietary fiber:	1 g	carbohydrate choice: 3
protein:	22 g	
sodium:	641 mg	

Researchers are still discovering favorite foods that hold promise for a longer and healthier life.

Fruitful Stuffing

Easy — Do Ahead

Ingredients:
2½ cup nonfat chicken broth, divided
2 tsp. minced garlic
1 cup chopped celery
1 cup chopped onion
14 oz. Croutettes (bread cubes)
1 Granny Smith apple, cubed (with or without skin)
⅓ cup dried apricot halves, chopped
⅓ cup dried prunes, chopped

Directions:
Pour ½ cup chicken broth into large saucepan or Dutch oven and heat over medium-high heat. Add garlic, celery, and onion; cook, stirring frequently, until vegetables are softened. Add remaining chicken broth, bread cubes, apple, apricots, and prunes; mix until ingredients are moistened. Remove pan from heat. Preheat oven to 350 degrees. Spray 9 x 13-inch baking dish with cooking spray. Place stuffing in dish and bake 45 to 60 minutes until lightly browned.

Serves: 8

Shopping List:
14 oz. Croutettes (or other bread cube stuffing), 20 oz. nonfat chicken broth, celery, Granny Smith apple, onion (or packaged chopped onion), dried apricot halves, dried prunes, minced garlic

Nutrition per serving

calories:	236
total fat (8%):	2 g
carbohydrate:	49 g
cholesterol:	0 mg
dietary fiber:	2 g
protein:	7 g
sodium:	956 mg

Exchanges
2 starch
1 fruit

carbohydrate choice: 3

Apples are high in soluble fiber, vitamin C, and pectin, which help reduce and stabilize cholesterol levels.

Garlic-Roasted Cauliflower and Brussels Sprouts

Easy — Do Ahead — Freeze

Ingredients:
  garlic-flavored cooking spray
  2 cups fresh cauliflower florets
  1 cup fresh Brussels sprouts, cut in half lengthwise
  1½ tsp. crushed garlic
  ¼ tsp. dried rosemary
  ¼ tsp. pepper

Directions:
  Preheat oven to 450 degrees. Spray large baking sheet with garlic-flavored cooking spray. Arrange cauliflower and Brussels sprouts in a single layer on baking sheet; spray with cooking spray and sprinkle with garlic, rosemary, and pepper. Bake 15 to 20 minutes until vegetables are lightly browned and tender. Serve hot or at room temperature.

Serves: 4

Shopping List:
  1 lb. cauliflower, ½ lb. Brussels sprouts, crushed garlic, dried rosemary, pepper, garlic-flavored cooking spray

Nutrition per serving		Exchanges
calories:	29	1 vegetable
total fat (0%):	0 g	
carbohydrate:	6g	carbohydrate choice: 1
cholesterol:	0 mg	
dietary fiber:	3 g	
protein:	2 g	
sodium:	16 mg	

Brussels sprouts, miniature members of the cabbage family, are full of phytonutrients (sulforaphane and indole-3-carbinol) that may protect against cancer.

Gimme Greens Casserole

Easy — Do Ahead

Ingredients:
  1 cup nonfat ricotta cheese
  1 cup nonfat cottage cheese
  ½ cup egg substitute
  1 tsp. garlic powder
  ¼ tsp. pepper
  ¾ cup nonfat Parmesan cheese, divided
  10 oz. frozen chopped spinach, thawed and drained
  10 oz. frozen chopped broccoli, thawed and drained

Directions:
  Preheat oven to 375 degrees. Spray 9-inch pie plate with cooking spray. Combine ricotta cheese, cottage cheese, egg substitute, garlic powder, pepper, and ½ cup Parmesan cheese in a large bowl; mix well. Fold in spinach and broccoli. Spoon mixture into baking dish; top with remaining Parmesan cheese and bake 25 to 20 minutes, until toothpick inserted in center comes out clean and edges are lightly browned.

Serves: 6

Shopping List:
  10 oz. package frozen chopped spinach, 10 oz. package frozen chopped broccoli, 8 oz. nonfat ricotta cheese, 8 oz. nonfat cottage cheese, 4 oz. egg substitute, nonfat Parmesan cheese, garlic powder, pepper

Nutrition per serving

calories:	101
total fat (0%):	0 g
carbohydrate:	12 g
cholesterol:	8 mg
dietary fiber:	1 g
protein:	16 g
sodium:	278 mg

Exchanges

1½ very lean meat
2½ vegetable

carbohydrate choice: 1

Broccoli not only contain indole-3-carbinol and sulforaphane (powerful cancer-fighting compounds), it is also a good source of beta-carotene, vitamin C, and calcium.

Green Beans Parmesan

Easy — Do Ahead

Ingredients:

2½ cups nonfat vegetable broth
1 lb. fresh green beans, trimmed
½ cup nonfat Parmesan cheese
pepper to taste

Directions:

Bring vegetable broth to a boil over high heat; add green beans and cook 5 to 7 minutes until beans are tender-crisp. (Beans can be microwaved on high 5 to 7 minutes until tender-crisp.) Using a slotted spoon, transfer green beans from broth (discard broth) into serving bowl; sprinkle with Parmesan cheese and pepper. Toss beans lightly and serve.

Serves: 4

Shopping List:

1 lb. fresh green beans, 20 oz. nonfat vegetable broth, nonfat Parmesan cheese, pepper

Nutrition per serving		Exchanges
calories:	75	3 vegetable
total fat (0%):	0 g	
carbohydrate:	14 g	carbohydrate choice: 1
cholesterol:	0 mg	
dietary fiber:	2 g	
protein:	6 g	
sodium:	356 mg	

Green beans are a good source of the antioxidant vitamins beta-carotene and C, and are a good source of fiber.

Honey-Coated Baby Carrots

Easy

Ingredients:
16 oz. fresh baby carrots
1½ tbsp. honey
1½ tsp. reconstituted Butter Buds (liquid form)
¼ tsp. ground allspice

Directions:
Bring medium saucepan of water to a boil over high heat. Add carrots; reduce heat to low, cover, and simmer 8 to 10 minutes until tender-crisp (do not overcook). Combine honey, Butter Buds, and allspice in a small cup; drizzle over carrots and serve.

Serves: 4

Shopping List:
16 oz. package baby carrots, honey, Butter Buds, ground allspice

Nutrition per serving		Exchanges
calories:	74	2 vegetable
total fat (0%):	0 g	½ other carbohydrate
carbohydrate:	18 g	
cholesterol:	0 mg	carbohydrate choice: 1
dietary fiber:	4 g	
protein:	1 g	
sodium:	40 mg	

A one-half cup serving of cooked carrots contains 12 milligrams of beta-carotene, almost twice the amount needed to receive health benefits.

Lemon-Pepper Butternut Squash

Easy — Do Ahead

Ingredients:
1½ lb. butternut squash, peeled and seeded
¼ cup reconstituted Butter Buds (liquid form)
½ tsp. marjoram
1 tsp. lemon juice
½ tsp. pepper
1 tbsp. minced shallots

Directions:
Preheat oven to 425 degrees. Slice butternut squash into ½-inch-thick slices. Combine reconstituted Butter Buds, marjoram, lemon juice, pepper, and shallots in a large Ziploc bag; shake until ingredients are blended. Add squash slices to bag and toss until completely coated. Line baking sheet with foil and spray with cooking spray. Arrange squash slices on baking sheet; pour sauce over top. Bake 35 to 45 minutes, turning several times, until squash is lightly browned.

Serves: 6

Shopping List:
1½ lb. butternut squash, shallots, Butter Buds, marjoram, pepper, lemon juice

Nutrition per serving		Exchanges
calories:	43	2 vegetable
total fat (0%):	0 g	
carbohydrate:	11 g	carbohydrate choice: 1
cholesterol:	0 mg	
dietary fiber:	0 g	
protein:	1 g	
sodium:	4 mg	

Butternut squash provides vitamins A and C, potassium, and fiber. Foods rich in fiber contribute to a reduction in the risk for colon cancer.

Old-Fashioned Bean Casserole

Easy — Do Ahead

Ingredients:

2 tbsp. nonfat chicken broth
1 cup chopped onion
1 tsp. minced garlic
2 tsp. chili powder
4 cups canned kidney beans, rinsed and drained
28 oz. Mexican-style stewed tomatoes, drained and
    chopped
¼ tsp. pepper
¼ cup nonfat shredded Cheddar cheese
¼ cup low-fat shredded Cheddar cheese

Directions:

Preheat oven to 350 degrees. Spray 2-quart casserole with cooking spray. Spray large nonstick skillet with cooking spray; add chicken broth and heat over medium-high heat. Add onion and garlic; cook until softened. Stir in chili powder, beans, tomatoes, and pepper. Cook 1 to 3 minutes until heated. Spread half the bean mixture into casserole; top with nonfat cheese. Repeat with remaining ingredients, ending with low-fat cheese. Bake 25 to 20 minutes until cooked through and browned on top.

Serves: 6

Shopping List:

2 15-oz. cans kidney beans, 28 oz. can Mexican-style stewed tomatoes, onion (or packaged chopped onion), nonfat shredded Cheddar cheese, low-fat shredded Cheddar cheese, nonfat chicken broth, minced garlic, chili powder, pepper

Nutrition per serving		Exchanges
calories:	202	½ very lean meat
total fat (4%):	1 g	1½ starch
carbohydrate:	36 g	3 vegetable
cholesterol:	1 mg	
dietary fiber:	10 g	carbohydrate choice: 2½
protein:	14 g	
sodium:	1,225 mg	

*Beans can lower cholesterol in just about anyone,
but the higher your cholesterol,
the better they work.*

Oriental Almond Green Beans

Easy

Ingredients:
1 lb. fresh green beans, stems removed
2½ tbsp. sherry
1¼ tbsp. low-sodium soy sauce
½ tsp. minced garlic
¼ tsp. ground ginger
⅛ tsp. crushed red pepper flakes
½ cup frozen pepper strips, thawed and drained
1 tbsp. toasted almonds

Directions:
Bring a large pot of water to a boil; add beans and cook until tender, 7 to 8 minutes. Drain beans and return to pot. Combine sherry, soy sauce, garlic, ginger, red pepper, and pepper strips in a small pan or microwavable dish. Cook over medium heat until heated through. Pour sauce over green beans and toss until beans are well coated. Arrange on serving platter and sprinkle with toasted almonds.

Serves: 4

Shopping List:
1 lb. fresh green beans, 10 oz. package frozen pepper strips, sherry, low-sodium soy sauce, minced garlic, ground ginger, crushed red pepper flakes, toasted almonds

Nutrition per serving		Exchanges
calories:	71	3 vegetable
total fat (13%):	1 g	
carbohydrate:	12 g	carbohydrate choice: 1
cholesterol:	0 mg	
dietary fiber:	3 g	
protein:	3 g	
sodium:	179 mg	

***Green beans are a good source of fiber,
aiding elimination and promoting
a healthy digestive system.***

Oven-Fried Artichokes

Easy — Do Ahead — Freeze

Ingredients:

½ cup egg substitute
¼ cup skim milk
1 cup cornflake crumbs
½ cup nonfat Parmesan cheese
1 tbsp. garlic powder
1½ tsp. onion powder
3 13¾-oz. cans artichoke hearts, drained and dried

Directions:

Preheat oven to 400 degrees. Line baking sheet with foil and spray with cooking spray. Combine egg substitute and milk in a small bowl; combine cornflake crumbs, Parmesan cheese, garlic powder, and onion powder in a shallow dish and mix well. Dip artichoke hearts in egg mixture; roll in cornflake crumbs and place on baking sheet. Bake 10 to 15 minutes until golden brown and crisp. Great with Garlic Aioli (see appetizers).

Serves: 6

Shopping List:

3 13¾-oz. cans artichoke hearts, cornflake crumbs, nonfat Parmesan cheese, skim milk, 4 oz. egg substitute, garlic powder, onion powder

Nutrition per serving		Exchanges
calories:	167	3 vegetable
total fat (5%):	1 g	1 very lean meat
carbohydrate:	33 g	1 other carbohydrate
cholesterol:	0 mg	
dietary fiber:	0 g	carbohydrate choice: 2
protein:	12 g	
sodium:	397 mg	

Artichokes contain a little bit of a lot of good things: calcium, iron, phosphorous, niacin, vitamin C, potassium, and magnesium.

Portabellos Parmigiana

Easy — Do Ahead

Ingredients:
  1 cup seasoned bread crumbs
  1 tsp. garlic powder
  ¾ cup nonfat Parmesan cheese, divided
  4 large portabello mushroom caps
  1 cup nonfat pasta sauce
  ¾ cup nonfat shredded mozzarella cheese
  ¼ cup low-fat shredded mozzarella cheese

Directions:
  Preheat oven to 400 degrees. Line baking sheet with foil and spray with cooking spray. Combine bread crumbs, garlic powder, and ¼ cup Parmesan cheese on a paper plate; mix well. Lightly spray mushroom caps with cooking spray; roll in bread-crumb mixture until well coated. Bake mushrooms 10 minutes; remove from oven and cover with pasta sauce. Combine nonfat and low-fat mozzarella cheese in a bowl or Ziploc bag; mix well. Sprinkle mozzarella and remaining Parmesan cheese over top; bake 5 to 10 minutes until cheese is melted and lightly browned.

Serves: 4

Shopping List:
  4 portabello mushroom (caps if available), seasoned bread crumbs, 8 oz. nonfat pasta sauce, nonfat Parmesan cheese, nonfat shredded mozzarella cheese, low-fat mozzarella cheese, garlic powder

Nutrition per serving		Exchanges
calories:	155	½ starch
total fat (6%):	1 g	2 vegetable
carbohydrate:	17 g	2 very lean meat
cholesterol:	0 mg	
dietary fiber:	1 g	carbohydrate choice: 1
protein:	17 g	
sodium:	556 mg	

Mushrooms inhibit tumor growth and boost the immune system.

Roasted Carrots and Leeks

Easy — Do Ahead

Ingredients:
 4 oz. frozen baby carrots, thawed and drained
 1 small bunch leeks, washed and cut into 3-inch pieces
 butter-flavored cooking spray
 ½ tsp. dried thyme
 ⅛ tsp. pepper

Directions:
 Preheat oven to 350 degrees. Spray roasting pan with cooking spray. Arrange baby carrots and leeks in pan; spray with butter-flavored spray. Sprinkle vegetables with thyme and pepper. Roast 10 to 15 minutes (turn once or twice while baking) until vegetables become tender and golden brown.

Serves: 4

Shopping List:
 4 oz. frozen baby carrots, 1 small bunch leeks, dried thyme, pepper, butter-flavored cooking spray

Nutrition per serving

calories:	30
total fat (0%):	0 g
carbohydrate:	7 g
cholesterol:	0 mg
dietary fiber:	2 g
protein:	1 g
sodium:	23 mg

Exchanges
1 vegetable

carbohydrate choice: 1

Leeks contain phytochemicals such as allicin and diallyl disulfide; these phytochemicals block or suppress cancer-causing agents, boost immunity and prevent infection.

Sesame Spinach

Easy

Ingredients:
2 tbsp. sugar
1 tbsp. low-sodium soy sauce
garlic-flavored cooking spray
2 tsp. sesame seeds
20 oz. fresh spinach, stems discarded, washed and lightly
dried

Directions:
Combine sugar and soy sauce in a small bowl; set aside. Spray large nonstick skillet with garlic-flavored cooking spray and heat over medium-high heat. Add sesame seeds and cook, stirring constantly, until just lightly toasted. Remove from skillet; respray skillet with cooking spray (off burner). Add spinach and cook 3 to 5 minutes until wilted. Drain spinach; transfer to serving bowl. Toss spinach with soy mixture; sprinkle with sesame seeds and toss until mixed.

Serves: 4

Shopping List:
20 oz. fresh spinach (prepackaged), low-sodium soy sauce, sugar, sesame seeds, garlic-flavored cooking spray

Nutrition per serving

calories:	64
total fat (14%):	1 g
carbohydrate:	11 g
cholesterol:	0 mg
dietary fiber:	4 g
protein:	5 g
sodium:	244 mg

Exchanges

2 vegetable
½ other carbohydrate

carbohydrate choice: 1

People who eat spinach, collard greens, and other dark green leafy vegetables 5 or 6 times a week have about a 43% lower risk for macular degeneration than those who eat it once a month.

Spaghetti Squash with Vegetable Medley

Average — Do Ahead

Ingredients:

4 lb. spaghetti squash
1 tbsp. vegetable broth
1 tsp. minced garlic
½ cup shredded carrot
1 zucchini, unpeeled and
  julienne-sliced
¼ cup water

¼ cup low-sodium soy sauce
1 cup frozen pepper strips,
  thawed and drained
1 tsp. dried basil
¼ tsp. red pepper flakes
¼ cup nonfat Parmesan
  cheese, divided

Directions:

Place spaghetti squash in large pot or Dutch oven; cover with water and bring to a boil over high heat. Reduce heat to low and simmer 25 to 20 minutes, until skin pierces easily with a fork. Drain squash and cool. Cut squash in half lengthwise; remove and discard seeds. Pull strands out of shell and place in large bowl. Spray large nonstick skillet or wok with cooking spray; pour vegetable broth into skillet and heat over medium-high heat. Add garlic, carrot, zucchini, water, and soy sauce to skillet; mix lightly. Stir in spaghetti squash. Stir-fry over medium-high heat 4 to 5 minutes, until carrot and zucchini are tender-crisp. Add pepper strips, basil, red pepper, and 2 tablespoons Parmesan cheese; cook 2 to 3 minutes until heated through. Spoon mixture onto serving platter; top with remaining Parmesan cheese and serve.

Serves: 4

Shopping List:

4 lb. spaghetti squash, packaged shredded carrot, 1 zucchini, 10 oz. frozen pepper strips, nonfat vegetable broth, low-sodium soy sauce, nonfat Parmesan cheese, minced garlic, dried basil, red pepper flakes

Nutrition per serving		Exchanges
calories:	147	6 vegetable
total fat (6%):	1 g	
carbohydrate:	30 g	carbohydrate choice: 2
cholesterol:	0 mg	
dietary fiber:	6 g	
protein:	6 g	
sodium:	671 mg	

Spaghetti squash is a nutritious and low-calorie vegetable version of pasta.

Steam-It Summer Squash

Easy — Do Ahead

Ingredients:
½ cup nonfat chicken broth
1 lb. yellow squash, cut into ½-inch chunks
1 lb. zucchini, cut into ½-inch chunks
½ cup chopped green onion
pepper to taste
Mrs. Dash seasoning to taste
1 tsp. dry Butter Buds

Directions:
Pour chicken broth into skillet and bring to a boil over high heat. Add squash and zucchini, cover and simmer over medium heat 3 to 4 minutes, until cooked through. Add green onion and cook, stirring frequently, over high heat until liquid evaporates. Using a slotted spoon, transfer squash mixture to serving platter. Sprinkle with pepper, Mrs. Dash seasoning, and Butter Buds; toss until mixed.

Serves: 4

Shopping List:
1 lb. yellow squash, 1 lb. zucchini, green onion, nonfat chicken broth, Mrs. Dash seasoning, Butter Buds, pepper

Nutrition per serving		Exchanges
calories:	43	2 vegetable
total fat (20%):	1 g	
carbohydrate:	9 g	carbohydrate choice: ½
cholesterol:	0 mg	
dietary fiber:	3 g	
protein:	3 g	
sodium:	103 mg	

Yellow squash and zucchini are low in sodium and fat, good food sources for controlling blood pressure and weight.

Sweet and Sour Red Onions

Easy — Do Ahead

Ingredients:
1 tsp. nonfat broth (chicken or vegetable)
2 red onions, cut into quarters
2 tbsp. frozen pineapple juice concentrate
1 tbsp. wine vinegar
pepper to taste

Directions:
Spray nonstick skillet with cooking spray; pour broth into skillet and heat over medium-high heat. Add onion and cook, stirring frequently (separate pieces), until onion begins to soften. Stir in remaining ingredients; reduce heat to low and simmer 12 to 15 minutes until onion is tender. Great as baked potato topping!

Serves: 4

Shopping List:
2 red onions, frozen pineapple juice concentrate, nonfat broth (chicken or vegetable), wine vinegar, pepper

Nutrition per serving		Exchanges
calories:	45	1 vegetable
total fat (0%):	0 g	½ other carbohydrate
carbohydrate:	11 g	
cholesterol:	0 mg	carbohydrate choice: 1
dietary fiber:	1 g	
protein:	1 g	
sodium:	5 mg	

Onions contain quercetin, a phytochemical that helps keep airways from becoming congested.

Sweet and Spicy Carrots

Easy

Ingredients:
16 oz. frozen baby carrots
½ cup apricot preserves
1 tsp. ground ginger
1 tbsp. reconstituted Butter Buds (liquid form)

Directions:
Cook carrots according to package directions (boil or microwave). Combine remaining ingredients in a small saucepan or microwavable dish. Heat over medium heat until preserves are melted. Serve over carrots.

Serves: 4

Shopping List:
16 oz. package frozen baby carrots, apricot preserves, ground ginger, Butter Buds

Nutrition per serving		Exchanges
calories:	154	2 vegetable
total fat (0%):	0 g	2 other carbohydrate
carbohydrate:	38 g	
cholesterol:	0 mg	carbohydrate choice: 2½
dietary fiber:	5 g	
protein:	1g	
sodium:	71 mg	

Carrots are the richest source of beta-carotene, which converts to vitamin A in the body. A lack of vitamin A is associated with poor night vision.

Sweet Potato "Fried" Cakes

Easy — Do Ahead — Freeze

Ingredients:
1½ lb. sweet potatoes, shredded
½ lb. potatoes, shredded
2 tsp. onion powder
⅓ cup flour
¼ cup egg substitute
¾ tsp. ground ginger
¼ tsp. cinnamon
¼ tsp. pepper

Directions:
Line baking sheet with foil and spray with cooking spray. Combine all ingredients in a large bowl and mix until ingredients are moistened and hold together. Spray large nonstick skillet with cooking spray and heat over medium-high heat. For each pancake, drop 1 tablespoon mixture into hot pan; flatten with back of spoon or spatula. Cook 2 minutes; turn, flatten, and cook 1 to 2 minutes until golden brown. Remove pan from heat. Place pancakes on baking sheet. Respray pan with cooking spray and return to heat. Repeat process with remaining sweet potato mixture. Keep "pancakes" warm in oven (about 300 degrees).

Serves: 6

Shopping List:
1½ lb. sweet potatoes, ½ lb. potatoes, egg substitute, flour, onion powder, ground ginger, cinnamon, pepper

Nutrition per serving		**Exchanges**
calories:	182	2½ starch
total fat (0%):	0 g	
carbohydrate:	41 g	carbohydrate choice: 2½
cholesterol:	0 mg	
dietary fiber:	4 g	
protein:	4 g	
sodium:	27 mg	

Potatoes are a great source of energy—one medium potato has almost three times more potassium than one medium orange.

Vegetable Stir-Fry

Easy

Ingredients:
3 to 6 tbsp. nonfat vegetable broth, divided
1 cup chopped green onion
1 sweet potato, peeled and sliced thin
1 green bell pepper, cut into strips
½ cup shredded carrot
1 zucchini, thinly sliced
3 cups cooked brown rice
1 cup sliced mushrooms
½ cup sliced water chestnuts, cut in half
½ cup honey
½ cup low-sodium soy sauce

Directions:
Spray large nonstick skillet with cooking spray. Pour 3 tablespoons vegetable broth into skillet and heat over medium-high heat. Add green onions, sweet potato, bell pepper, carrots, and zucchini to skillet; cook, stirring frequently 2 to 3 minutes until tender. Add cooked rice, mushrooms and water chestnuts; cook, stirring frequently, 3 to 4 minutes until heated through. If necessary, add remaining chicken broth to keep vegetables moist. Combine honey and soy sauce in a small cup; drizzle over vegetables, mix, and serve.

Serves: 6

Shopping List:
1 sweet potato, 1 green bell pepper, green onion, packaged shredded carrot, 1 zucchini, 8 oz. package sliced mushrooms, 6 oz. can sliced water chestnuts, brown rice, nonfat vegetable broth, honey, low-sodium soy sauce

Nutrition per serving		Exchanges
calories:	204	1½ starch
total fat (4%):	1 g	3 vegetable
carbohydrate:	46 g	½ other carbohydrate
cholesterol:	0 mg	
dietary fiber:	2 g	carbohydrate choice: 3
protein:	4 g	
sodium:	441 mg	

Brown rice is a key player in heart-protection plans. It's high fiber content protects against breast and colon cancer.

Veggie Pancakes

Easy — Do Ahead — Freeze

Ingredients:
10 oz. shredded carrots
10 oz. frozen chopped spinach, thawed, drained and
    squeezed dry
12 oz. package shredded potatoes
1 tbsp. onion powder
½ cup flour
½ cup egg substitute
¼ tsp. pepper

Directions:
Line baking sheets with foil and spray with cooking spray.
Combine all ingredients in a large bowl and mix well until
moistened. Spray nonstick skillet with cooking spray and
heat over medium-high heat. Drop 1 heaping tablespoon
vegetable mixture into hot skillet; flatten with the back of
spoon or spatula. Cook 2 minutes per side; turn and cook,
pressing down, until crispy brown. Remove skillet from
heat; place pancakes on baking sheet and place in warm
oven (about 300 degrees). Respray skillet (off heat) and repeat procedure with remaining "pancake" batter. Serve with
applesauce or nonfat sour cream.

Serves: 6

Shopping List:
10 oz. package shredded carrots, 10 oz. package frozen
chopped spinach, 12 oz. package shredded potatoes (e.g.,
Simply Potatoes), egg substitute, flour, onion powder, pepper

Nutrition per serving		Exchanges
calories:	110	1 starch
total fat (0%):	0 g	2 vegetable
carbohydrate:	24 g	
cholesterol:	0 mg	carbohydrate choice: 1½
dietary fiber:	4 g	
protein:	5 g	
sodium:	73 mg	

***Spinach provides at least 20% of the Daily Value of
folate per serving. Folate, a B vitamin,
is linked to the prevention of birth defects
(spina bifida), heart attacks, stroke,
and colorectal cancer.***

ONE-DISH
MEALS

Beef-a-Roni

Easy — Do Ahead — Freeze

Ingredients:

¾ lb. superlean ground beef
1½ tsp. Mrs. Dash seasoning
2 tbsp. onion flakes
8 oz. rotini macaroni, uncooked
28 oz. canned Mexican-style
   chopped tomatoes
1 cup chopped green bell pepper
½ cup water

1 tsp. chili powder
1 tsp. dried oregano
1 tsp. sugar
½ tsp. pepper
¾ cup nonfat shredded
   Cheddar cheese
¼ cup low-fat shredded
   Cheddar cheese

Directions:

Spray large nonstick skillet with cooking spray and heat over medium-high heat. Add beef to skillet; sprinkle with Mrs. Dash seasoning and onion flakes. Cook, stirring frequently to crumble beef; cook until browned. Drain skillet. Stir in uncooked pasta, tomatoes, green pepper, water, chili powder, oregano, sugar, and pepper; bring to a boil over high heat. Reduce heat to low, cover, and simmer 20 to 25 minutes, until pasta is tender. Sprinkle cheese over pasta mixture; cover and heat until cheese is melted.

Serves: 4

Shopping List:

½ lb. superlean ground beef (4% fat), 8 oz. rotini macaroni, 28 oz. can Mexican-style chopped tomatoes, green bell pepper, nonfat shredded Cheddar cheese, low-fat shredded Cheddar cheese, Mrs. Dash seasoning, onion flakes, chili powder, dried oregano, sugar, pepper

Nutrition per serving

calories:	450
total fat (10%):	5 g
carbohydrate:	56 g
cholesterol:	73 mg
dietary fiber:	1 g
protein:	44 g
sodium:	1,194 mg

Exchanges

1 lean meat
3 very lean meat
3 starch
2½ vegetable

carbohydrate choice: 4

Lean meats provide lots of high-quality protein, as well as iron, B vitamins, phosphorous, and zinc.

Beef 'n' Ziti Casserole

Difficult — Do Ahead — Freeze

ONE DISH MEALS

Ingredients:

12 oz. ziti pasta,
  cooked and drained
¾ cup nonfat Parmesan
  cheese
1 tsp. Italian seasoning
¾ lb. super lean ground
  beef (4% fat)
1 tbsp. onion powder

1 tbsp. garlic powder
3⅓ cups chopped tomatoes,
  drained
1 cup chopped red bell pepper
¾ cup nonfat shredded
  mozzarella cheese
⅓ cup seasoned bread
  crumbs

Directions:

Cook ziti according to package directions; drain and return to pot. Add Parmesan cheese and Italian seasoning; toss lightly to coat. Spray large nonstick skillet with cooking spray; add beef, onion powder, and garlic powder. Cook beef, stirring frequently, until browned and crumbled (about 6 to 8 minutes). Remove skillet from heat. Add tomatoes and peppers; mix lightly. Preheat oven to 375 degrees. Spread half the ziti in the baking dish; top with beef mixture, half the mozzarella cheese, remaining pasta and remaining mozzarella. Sprinkle with seasoned breadcrumbs and bake 30 to 35 minutes until bubbly hot and lightly browned on top.

Serves: 6

Shopping List:

red bell pepper, ¾ lb. super lean ground beef, 12 oz. ziti, 3 15-oz. cans chopped tomatoes, nonfat Parmesan cheese, nonfat shredded mozzarella cheese, seasoned bread crumbs, onion powder, garlic powder, Italian seasoning

Nutrition per serving

calories:	527
total fat (9%):	5 g
carbohydrate:	65 g
cholesterol:	48 mg
dietary fiber:	2 g
protein:	51 g
sodium:	998 mg

Exchanges

3½ very lean meat
1 lean meat
2 starch
7 vegetable

carbohydrate choice: 4

Lean meat can help alleviate fatigue by stabilizing blood sugar and insulin levels.

Chicken, Broccoli, and Noodle Casserole

Average — Do Ahead — Freeze

Ingredients:

6 oz. yolk-free egg noodles
1 tbsp. nonfat chicken broth
¼ cup chopped onion
¼ cup chopped red bell pepper
10 oz. frozen chopped broccoli, thawed and drained
1 lb. low-fat chicken tenders, cooked and cubed

4 oz. sliced mushrooms
1 cup nonfat shredded cheese (mozzarella or Swiss)
1 cup low-fat shredded cheese (mozzarella or Swiss)
1 cup nonfat sour cream
¾ cup evaporated skim milk
½ cup egg substitute

Directions:

Preheat oven to 350 degrees. Spray 12 x 8-inch baking dish with cooking spray. Prepare noodles according to package directions; drain and set aside. Spray large skillet with cooking spray; pour chicken broth into skillet and heat over medium-high heat. Add onion and bell pepper; cook, stirring frequently, until onion is tender. Add broccoli, chicken, mushrooms, and noodles; mix well. Remove from heat. Combine cheeses, sour cream, evaporated milk, and egg substitute in medium bowl; mix until blended smooth. Pour cheese mixture into skillet and mix with noodles. Spoon mixture into baking dish; cover with foil and bake 30 to 35 minutes until bubbly and heated through.

Serves: 6

Shopping List:

6 oz. yolk-free egg noodles, 1 lb. low-fat chicken tenders, 10 oz. frozen chopped broccoli, 8 oz. nonfat sour cream, 6 oz. evaporated skim milk, 4 oz. nonfat shredded cheese (mozzarella or Swiss), 4 oz. low-fat shredded cheese (mozzarella or Swiss), egg substitute, 1 onion (or packaged chopped onion), red bell pepper, 4 oz. sliced mushrooms, nonfat chicken broth

Nutrition per serving

calories:	321
total fat (6%):	2 g
carbohydrate:	32 g
cholesterol:	54 mg
dietary fiber:	2 g
protein:	41 g
sodium:	477 mg

Exchanges

1 starch
3 vegetable
4½ very lean meat

carbohydrate choice: 2

According to a poll by the Epcot Center, broccoli (and cauliflower) ranked first for "favorite" veggie.

Chicken Chowder

Easy — Do Ahead — Freeze

Ingredients:

2 tbsp. + 2 cups nonfat chicken broth, divided
2 cups chopped onion
½ cup chopped celery
14 oz. canned chopped tomatoes, undrained
12 oz. frozen sliced carrot
⅓ cup dry white wine

16 oz. package cubed potatoes
½ tsp. garlic powder
½ tsp. thyme
2 to 3 drops Tabasco sauce
1 lb. low-fat chicken tenders, cut into 1-inch pieces
pepper to taste

ONE DISH MEALS

Directions:

Spray large saucepan with cooking spray; add 2 tablespoons chicken broth and heat over medium-high heat. Add onion and celery; cook, stirring frequently, 1 minute. Cover pan; reduce heat to medium-low and simmer 4 to 5 minutes until vegetables are softened. Add tomatoes (with juice), carrot, wine, and remaining broth. Cover pan and cook over medium-low heat 10 to 12 minutes. Add potato chunks, garlic powder, thyme, and Tabasco sauce; cover and simmer 20 to 25 minutes until potatoes are tender. Add chicken and cook 7 to 8 minutes until chicken is cooked through. Season with pepper.

Serves: 4

Shopping List:

1 lb. low-fat chicken tenders, 12 oz. package frozen sliced carrot, 16 oz. package cubed potatoes (refrigerator section), 2 onions (or packaged chopped onion), celery, 14 oz. can chopped tomatoes, 18 oz. nonfat chicken broth, dry white wine, garlic powder, thyme, Tabasco pepper sauce, pepper

Nutrition per serving		Exchanges
calories:	301	2 starch
total fat (3%):	1 g	3 vegetable
carbohydrate:	43 g	2 very lean meat
cholesterol:	71 mg	
dietary fiber:	8 g	carbohydrate choice: 3
protein:	28 g	
sodium:	1194 mg	

Potatoes, the world's number 1 vegetable crop, are rich in chlorogenic acid, potassium, and vitamin C.

Chicken-Lentil Casserole with Sun-Dried Tomatoes

Easy — Do Ahead — Freeze

Ingredients:

3¼ cups nonfat chicken broth
¾ cup lentils, uncooked
¾ cup chopped onion
½ cup brown rice, uncooked
1½ tsp. Italian seasoning
1 tsp. crushed garlic
¾ cup nonfat shredded Swiss (or mozzarella) cheese

2 cups cooked chicken breast strips, diced
¾ cup sun-dried tomatoes (not in oil)
nonfat Parmesan cheese

Directions:

Preheat oven to 350 degrees. Spray 1½- to 2-quart casserole with cooking spray. Combine chicken broth, lentils, onion, rice, Italian seasoning, crushed garlic, Swiss cheese, and chicken in baking dish. Stir until ingredients are well mixed. Cover with lid or heavy-duty foil and bake 1½ to 2 hours, until rice and lentils are tender; stir every 30 minutes. Remove from oven. Gently fold in dried tomatoes; sprinkle with Parmesan cheese. Bake 5 to 8 minutes until cheese is melted.

Serves: 6

Shopping List:

26 oz. nonfat chicken broth, cooked chicken breast strips, sun-dried tomatoes (not packed in oil), lentils, brown rice, onion (or packaged chopped onions), nonfat cheese (Swiss or mozzarella), nonfat Parmesan cheese, Italian seasoning, crushed garlic

Nutrition per serving

calories:	264
total fat (11%):	2 g
carbohydrate:	31 g
cholesterol:	47 mg
dietary fiber:	2 g
protein:	29 g
sodium:	720 mg

Exchanges

1½ starch
3 vegetable
3 very lean meat

carbohydrate choice: 2

Brown rice is the most nutritious rice, containing abundant amounts of fiber, complex carbohydrates, and essential B vitamins.

Chicken-Lentil Stew

Easy — Do Ahead

Ingredients:

2 tbsp. + 6 cups nonfat chicken broth, divided
1 cup chopped onion
1 cup lentils
16 oz. package cubed potatoes
1 lb. low-fat chicken tenders, cubed

4 oz. sliced water chestnuts
1 cup chopped green onion
1 tbsp. rice vinegar
1 tbsp. low-sodium soy sauce
½ to 1 tsp. cayenne pepper, divided
dried parsley

Directions:

Spray large pot or Dutch oven with cooking spray; add 2 tablespoons chicken broth and heat over medium-high heat. Add onion and cook, stirring frequently, 2 to 3 minutes until tender. Add remaining broth, lentils, and potatoes; bring to a boil over high heat. Reduce heat to low, cover, and simmer 45 to 50 minutes until lentils are tender. Add chicken, water chestnuts, green onion, vinegar, soy sauce, and ½ teaspoon cayenne pepper. Cover pot and cook over medium-low heat until chicken is cooked through (about 7 to 10 minutes). Sprinkle stew with parsley and cayenne pepper to taste. Stir until heated through.

Serves: 6

Shopping List:

1 lb. low-fat chicken tenders, 1 onion (or packaged chopped onion), green onion, 16 oz. package cubed potatoes (Simply Potatoes), 48 to 50 oz. nonfat chicken broth, 4 oz. can sliced water chestnuts, lentils, rice vinegar, low-sodium soy sauce, cayenne pepper, dried parsley

Nutrition per serving

calories:	278
total fat (3%):	1 g
carbohydrate:	41 g
cholesterol:	47 mg
dietary fiber:	3 g
protein:	27 g
sodium:	1,193 mg

Exchanges

2 very lean meat
2 starch
2½ vegetable

carbohydrate choice: 3

Lentils, virtually fat-free, are an excellent protein alternative to meat. One cup cooked lentils provides 16 grams protein while 3 ounces (about ⅓ cup) lean ground beef provides 15 grams of protein.

Chicken Ratatouille

Easy — Do Ahead — Freeze

Ingredients:
2 tbsp. nonfat chicken broth
16 oz. frozen pepper strips, thawed and drained
1 cup frozen chopped onion, thawed and drained
1½ tsp. garlic powder
1 lb. eggplant, unpeeled and cut into ¾-inch pieces
28 oz. Italian-style stewed tomatoes
1 tsp. Italian seasoning
1 zucchini, cut into ¾-inch strips
1 yellow squash, cut into ¾-inch strips
¾ lb. low-fat chicken tenders, cooked and cubed

Directions:
Pour chicken broth into large saucepan and heat over medium-high heat. Add peppers, onion, garlic powder, eggplant, tomatoes, and Italian seasoning to pan; cover and cook over low heat 25 to 20 minutes, until vegetables are tender. Add zucchini and squash to pan; cook over medium-low heat until tender (about 10 minutes). Stir in cooked chicken; cook until heated through (5 to 8 minutes).

Serves: 4

Shopping List:
1 lb. eggplant, 1 zucchini, 1 yellow squash, 16 oz. package frozen pepper strips, 10 oz. package frozen chopped onion, 28 oz. can Italian-style stewed tomatoes, ¾ lb. low-fat chicken tenders, nonfat chicken broth, Italian seasoning, garlic powder

Nutrition per serving		Exchanges
calories:	195	6 vegetable
total fat (5%):	1 g	1½ very lean meat
carbohydrate:	28 g	
cholesterol:	53 mg	carbohydrate choice: 2
dietary fiber:	4 g	
protein:	22 g	
sodium:	1,008 mg	

Zucchini and yellow squash, members of the "summer squash" group, serve as a decent source of fiber while low in calories.

Chicken Skillet Dinner

Easy — Do Ahead — Freeze

Ingredients:
1 lb. low-fat chicken breasts (boneless, skinless)
½ tsp. garlic powder
½ tsp. onion powder
½ tsp. dried rosemary
1 cup nonfat chicken broth
10 oz. frozen baby carrots
1 cup frozen green peas

Directions:
Spray large nonstick skillet with cooking spray and heat over medium-high heat. Sprinkle chicken breasts with garlic powder, onion powder, and rosemary on both sides. Cook 4 to 5 minutes per side until browned. Add chicken broth, carrots and peas. Bring to a boil over high heat. Cover and reduce heat to low; simmer 15 to 20 minutes, until chicken and vegetables are cooked through.

Serves: 4

Shopping List:
1 lb. low-fat chicken breasts (boneless, skinless), 8 oz. non-fat chicken broth, 10 oz. frozen baby carrots, 10 oz. frozen baby peas, garlic powder, onion powder, dried rosemary

Nutrition per serving

calories:	152
total fat (6%):	1 g
carbohydrate:	11 g
cholesterol:	71 mg
dietary fiber:	3 g
protein:	25 g
sodium:	525 mg

Exchanges
2 very lean meat
2 vegetable
½ starch

carbohydrate choice: 1

Light chicken meat (without skin) is a good source of niacin; niacin helps your body use carbohydrates and fat efficiently, maintain a healthy intestinal tract, and keep skin healthy.

Chili Spiced Bean and Veggie Wraps

Easy — Do Ahead

Ingredients:

1 cup frozen broccoli cuts
1 cup frozen pepper strips
1 cup frozen chopped onion
15 oz. can black beans, rinsed and drained
1 tbsp. chili powder
½ tsp. garlic powder
½ cup nonfat sour cream
6 low-fat flour tortillas
½ cup nonfat shredded Cheddar cheese

Directions:

Spray large nonstick with cooking spray and heat over medium-high heat. Add broccoli, peppers, and onion; cook, stirring frequently, until vegetables are tender (3 to 4 minutes). Reduce heat to medium low. Add beans, chili powder, and garlic powder to vegetables; cook 2 to 4 minutes until completely heated through. Remove from heat; immediately stir in sour cream and mix until blended. Wrap tortillas in paper towels; warm in microwave oven on High for 10 to 15 seconds. Divide bean mixture among tortillas; sprinkle with shredded cheese. Fold in sides of tortillas; roll tightly and secure with toothpick. Serve with salsa and sour cream, if desired.

Serves: 6

Shopping List:

10 oz. package frozen broccoli cuts, 10 oz. package frozen pepper strips, frozen chopped onion, 15 oz. can black beans, nonfat shredded Cheddar cheese, 4 oz. nonfat sour cream, low-fat flour tortillas, chili powder, garlic powder

Nutrition per serving		Exchanges
calories:	290	1 very lean meat
total fat (3%):	1 g	2½ starch
carbohydrate:	53 g	3 vegetable
cholesterol:	0 mg	
dietary fiber:	7 g	carbohydrate choice: 3½
protein:	17 g	
sodium:	907 mg	

Beans are rich in folate; folate deficiency can result in anemia, infections, confusion and weakness.

Cream Chicken and Wild Rice Soup

Average — Do Ahead

Ingredients:

2 cups nonfat chicken broth, divided
½ cup chopped onion
1 cup chopped celery
½ cup flour
½ tsp. pepper
2 cups cooked wild rice

2 cups low-fat chicken tenders, cooked and cut in 1-inch pieces
1 cup nonfat sour cream
2 cups skim milk
2 tbsp. chopped green onions

ONE DISH MEALS

Directions:

Spray large saucepan or Dutch oven with cooking spray; add 1½ teaspoons chicken broth and heat over medium-high heat. Add onion and celery; cook, stirring frequently, until vegetables are slightly softened (about 4 to 6 minutes). Reduce heat to medium; gradually stir in flour and pepper. Add remaining chicken broth and cook, stirring constantly, until mixture comes to a boil and thickens. Boil 1 minute, stirring constantly. Stir in cooked rice, chicken, sour cream, and milk; cook over medium heat, stirring constantly, until soup is thick and creamy (if you want a thinner consistency, add more milk or chicken broth). Garnish with green onions before serving.

Serves: 4

Shopping List:

16 oz. nonfat chicken broth, onion (or prepackaged chopped onions), celery, green onions, ¾ lb. low-fat chicken tenders (uncooked or cooked), wild rice, 8 oz. nonfat sour cream, 16 oz. skim milk, flour, pepper

Nutrition per serving

calories:	320
total fat (3%):	1 g
carbohydrate:	39 g
cholesterol:	72 mg
dietary fiber:	2 g
protein:	36 g
sodium:	796 mg

Exchanges

½ milk
3½ very lean meat
2 starch

carbohydrate choice: 2½

Wild rice contains twice as much protein as white rice and is high in B complex vitamins.

Crustless Chicken-Vegetable Quiche

Easy — Do Ahead — Freeze

Ingredients:

2 tbsp. cornflake crumbs
3 tbsp. flour
1 tsp. dried basil
¼ tsp. garlic powder
⅛ tsp. pepper
1 cup skim milk
1 tbsp. Dijon mustard
½ cup egg substitute
2 cups low-fat chicken tenders, cooked and cubed
1 cup frozen chopped broccoli, thawed and drained
1 cup frozen cauliflower, chopped, thawed, and drained
¼ cup nonfat shredded Cheddar cheese
¼ cup low-fat shredded Cheddar cheese

Directions:

Preheat oven to 350 degrees. Spray 9-inch pie plate with cooking spray. Sprinkle cornflake crumbs over bottom of pie plate. Combine flour, basil, garlic powder, and pepper in a large bowl; stir in milk, mustard, egg substitute, chicken, broccoli, cauliflower and nonfat cheese. Spoon mixture into pie plate; sprinkle with low-fat cheese and bake 40 to 45 minutes until toothpick inserted in center comes out clean.

Serves: 4

Shopping List:

10 oz. package frozen chopped broccoli, 10 oz. package frozen cauliflower florets, 8 oz. skim milk, nonfat shredded Cheddar cheese, low-fat shredded Cheddar cheese, ¾ lb. low-fat chicken tenders, 4 oz. egg substitute, cornflake crumbs, flour, Dijon mustard, dried basil, garlic powder, pepper

Nutrition per serving		Exchanges
calories:	221	3 vegetable
total fat (8%):	2 g	4 very lean meat
carbohydrate:	17 g	
cholesterol:	71 mg	carbohydrate choice: 1
dietary fiber:	3 g	
protein:	34 g	
sodium:	637 mg	

Cauliflower is a good source of cancer-fighting glucosinolates (phytochemicals).

Full O' Beans Pizza
Easy — Do Ahead

Ingredients:
16 oz. Italian bread shell
16 oz. nonfat refried beans
4 oz. chopped green chilies
1 tbsp. onion flakes
1 cup Mexican-style chopped tomatoes, drained
1½ cups frozen pepper strips, thawed and drained
1 cup nonfat shredded mozzarella cheese
½ cup low-fat shredded mozzarella cheese

Directions:
Preheat oven to 425 degrees. Place bread shell on baking sheet or pizza pan. Spread crust with refried beans; top with chilies and onion and mix lightly. Arrange chopped tomatoes and peppers on pizza; sprinkle with mozzarella cheese. Bake 7 to 10 minutes until cheese is melted and lightly browned.

Serves: 4

Shopping List:
16 oz. package Italian bread shell, 16 oz. can nonfat refried beans, 4 oz. can chopped green chilies, 14½ oz. can Mexican-style chopped tomatoes, 12 oz. package frozen pepper strips, 4 oz. nonfat shredded mozzarella cheese, low-fat shredded mozzarella cheese, onion flakes

Nutrition per serving		Exchanges
calories:	414	3 starch
total fat (9%):	4 g	4 vegetable
carbohydrate:	64 g	1 lean meat
cholesterol:	.4 mg	½ very lean meat
dietary fiber:	6 g	
protein:	27	carbohydrate choice: 4
sodium:	1,449 mg	

Chili peppers contain mucokinetic (mucus-moving) agents that release watery fluids, thinning out and moving secretions from the lungs away from air passages

Garlic Shrimp with Mushrooms

Easy

Ingredients:
2 tsp. white wine or nonfat vegetable broth
1 lb. shrimp, peeled and deveined (thawed if frozen)
1 tbsp. minced garlic
3 cups sliced mushrooms
1 cup green onion, cut into 1-inch pieces
¼ cup nonfat vegetable broth
2 cups cooked rice

Directions:
Spray nonstick skillet with cooking spray; add 2 teaspoons wine or vegetable broth and heat over medium-high heat. Add shrimp and garlic to skillet and cook 1 to 2 minutes. Add mushrooms, green onion, and vegetable broth; cook, stirring frequently, until shrimp are no longer pink and vegetables are heated through. Serve over cooked rice.

Serves: 4

Shopping List:
1 lb. shrimp (peeled and deveined), 1½ lb. sliced mushrooms, green onion, nonfat vegetable broth, white wine (optional), minced garlic, rice

Nutrition per serving		Exchanges
calories:	240	1 starch
total fat (8%):	2 g	3 vegetable
carbohydrate:	32 g	2 very lean meat
cholesterol:	174 mg	
dietary fiber:	2 g	carbohydrate choice: 2
protein:	23 g	
sodium:	279 mg	

Shrimp provides calcium, which contributes to strong bones and teeth, muscle contraction and relaxation, blood clotting, nerve function and lower blood pressure.

Hawaiian Ham and Pineapple Pizza

Easy — Do Ahead

ONE DISH MEALS

Ingredients:
16 oz. Italian bread shell
1 cup + 2 tbsp. tomato sauce
½ tsp. garlic powder
2 cups low-fat honey ham, cubed or sliced
8 oz. canned pineapple tidbits, well drained
¾ cup green bell pepper, cut into strips
1 cup nonfat shredded mozzarella cheese
½ cup low-fat shredded mozzarella cheese

Directions:
Preheat oven to 400 degrees. Spray pizza pan or baking sheet with cooking spray. Place bread shell on pan; spread top of shell with tomato sauce. Sprinkle garlic powder over sauce. Top with ham, pineapple, green pepper, nonfat and low fat cheese. Bake 10 to 12 minutes until cheese is melted and pizza is hot.

Serves: 6

Shopping List:
16 oz. Italian bread shell (e.g., Boboli), 10 oz. tomato sauce, ½ to ¾ lb. low-fat honey ham, 8 oz. can pineapple tidbits, 1 green bell pepper, 4 oz. nonfat shredded mozzarella cheese, low-fat shredded mozzarella cheese, garlic powder

Nutrition per serving		Exchanges
calories:	263	1 starch
fat (10%):	3 g	½ fruit
carbohydrate:	36 g	3 vegetable
cholesterol:	11 mg	1 lean meat
dietary fiber:	2 g	1 very lean meat
protein:	19 g	
sodium:	891 mg	carbohydrate choice: 2½

Pineapple is a rich source of vitamin C and manganese. One cup of pineapple chunks provides over 2 milligrams of manganese, more than 100% of the Recommended Daily Allowance.

Hearty Chicken and Bean Stew

Easy — Do Ahead — Freeze

Ingredients:

3½ cups nonfat chicken broth, divided
2 tsp. chopped fresh garlic
2 onions, quartered
10 oz. frozen baby carrots, thawed and drained
4 cups low-fat chicken tenders, cooked and cubed
1 fennel bulb, sliced lengthwise
16 oz. white beans, drained, divided
2 cups water

Directions:

Pour 2 tablespoons broth into large saucepan or Dutch oven; heat over medium-high heat. Add garlic, onion, and carrots; cook 5 minutes, until tender. Add chicken, fennel, 1 cup beans, remaining broth, and water; bring to a boil over high heat. Reduce heat to low and simmer, uncovered 20 to 25 minutes until vegetables are tender. Place remaining beans in food processor or blender; puree. Add pureed beans to stew and cook over low heat until thick and heated through.

Serves: 6

Shopping List:

28 oz. nonfat chicken broth, 10 oz. package frozen baby carrots, ¾ to 1 lb. low-fat chicken tenders, 16 oz. white beans, fennel bulb, 2 onions, fresh garlic

Nutrition per serving		Exchanges
calories:	217	3 vegetable
total fat (4%):	1 g	2 very lean meat
carbohydrate:	25 g	1 starch
cholesterol:	58 mg	
dietary fiber:	2 g	carbohydrate choice: 2
protein:	27 g	
sodium:	775 mg	

Fennel provides phytoestrogens, preventing breast cancer and relieving menstrual cramping.

Maple Glazed Chicken and More

Easy

Ingredients:
1½ lb. low-fat chicken breasts (boneless, skinless)
garlic powder to taste
pepper to taste
½ cup maple-flavored syrup
3 tbsp. Dijon mustard
1 tsp. sage
20 oz. packaged potato cubes
16 oz. frozen baby carrots
1 cup frozen green beans

Directions:
Preheat oven to 350 degrees. Spray 9 x 13-inch baking dish with cooking spray. Arrange chicken breasts in baking dish; sprinkle generously with garlic powder and pepper. Combine syrup, mustard, and sage in a small cup; mix well. Spoon mixture over chicken; bake 10 to 15 minutes. Add potatoes, carrots, and green beans to baking dish; spoon sauce over vegetables and cook 15 to 20 minutes until vegetables are tender and chicken is cooked through. Baste with syrup mixture several times while baking.

Serves: 6

Shopping List:
1½ lb. low-fat chicken breast (boneless, skinless), 20 oz. package potato cubes (e.g., Simply Potatoes), 16 oz. package frozen baby carrots, 10 oz. package frozen green beans, maple-flavored syrup, Dijon mustard, sage, garlic powder, pepper

Nutrition per serving		Exchanges
calories:	303	2½ very lean meat
total fat (3%):	1 g	3 vegetable
carbohydrate:	49 g	1 starch
cholesterol:	71 mg	1 other carbohydrate
dietary fiber:	4 g	
protein:	27 g	carbohydrate choice: 3
sodium:	320 mg	

A recent Harvard study found that eating one carrot a day cuts the risk of stroke by 68%.

Mexican Pita Pizzas

Easy

Ingredients:
>   6 whole pita breads
>   15 oz. canned Mexican-style stewed tomatoes, drained
>   2 cups chopped cooked chicken (skinless, boneless)
>   4 oz. chopped green chilies
>   1 cup nonfat shredded Cheddar cheese
>   ½ cup low-fat shredded Mexican, taco-seasoned, or
>   Cheddar cheese

Directions:
>   Preheat oven to 350 degrees. Line baking sheet with foil and spray with cooking spray. Arrange pita breads in a single layer on baking sheet. Spread with stewed tomatoes; top with chicken, chilies, nonfat and low fat cheese. Bake 8 to 10 minutes until cheese is melted and pizzas are hot.

Serves: 6

Shopping List:
>   pita bread (or pockets); 15 oz. can Mexican-style stewed tomatoes; skinless, boneless chicken breast or tenders (cooked or raw); 4 oz. chopped green chilies; 4 oz. fat-free shredded Cheddar cheese; 2 oz. low-fat shredded Mexican, taco-seasoned, or Cheddar cheese

Nutrition per serving		Exchanges
calories:	241	2½ very lean meat
total fat (7%):	2 g	3 vegetable
carbohydrate:	28 g	1 starch
cholesterol:	49 mg	
dietary fiber:	1 g	carbohydrate choice: 2
protein:	28 g	
sodium:	1,149 mg	

***Low in fat and calories, high in protein
and carbohydrates, pitas are a good choice
for sandwiches, pizzas, breakfast
scrambles, and more.***

Pineapple-Chicken Pizza
Easy — Do Ahead

Ingredients:
1 low-fat pizza crust*
½ cup tomato sauce
1 tsp. Italian seasoning
1½ cups nonfat shredded mozzarella cheese, divided
½ lb. skinless, boneless chicken breast tenders,
    cooked and cubed
1½ cups canned pineapple chunks in juice, drained
3 tbsp. chopped green onion

Directions:
Preheat oven to 425 degrees. Line baking sheet with foil or
spray pizza pan with cooking spray. Prepare crust according
to package directions. Spread crust with tomato sauce;
sprinkle with Italian seasoning and ½ cup mozzarella
cheese. Arrange chicken, pineapple, and green onion on
crust. Top with remaining mozzarella cheese. Bake pizza 15
to 20 minutes until crust and cheese are lightly browned.

Serves: 6

Shopping List:
low fat pizza crust (*Ragu Pizza Crust mix, low-fat Italian
bread shell, low-fat flour tortilla, or French bread); 6 oz.
tomato sauce; 16 oz. can pineapple chunks in juice; ½ lb.
low fat chicken tenders; green onion; Italian seasoning

Nutrition per serving		Exchanges
calories:	276	3 very lean meat
total fat (3%):	1 g	1 vegetable
carbohydrate:	37 g	1 starch
cholesterol:	28 mg	1 fruit
dietary fiber:	2 g	
protein:	27 g	carbohydrate choice: 2½
sodium:	754 mg	

*Arthritis may get its start as a vitamin deficiency. Some
studies show that cartilage cannot grow without
adequate levels of pantothenic acid. Without the
production of new cartilage to replace damaged or
worn spots in your joints, deterioration occurs,
possibly leading to osteoarthritis.*

Polenta with Meatless Chili

Easy — Do Ahead

Ingredients:
1½ tbsp. nonfat vegetable broth
1½ lb. chopped mushrooms
4 oz. chopped green chilies, drained
2 tbsp. ground cumin
3 tbsp. chili powder
16 oz. canned black beans, drained
16 oz. canned red kidney beans, drained
½ cup nonfat pasta sauce
1 cup instant polenta, cooked
½ cup nonfat shredded Cheddar cheese

Directions:
Pour vegetable broth into medium-size saucepan and heat over medium-high heat. Add mushrooms to pan; reduce heat to low, cover, and simmer 8 to 10 minutes until mushrooms are tender. Add chilies, cumin, chili powder, black beans, kidney beans, and pasta sauce to pan; cover and cook over low heat 40 to 45 minutes. Serve chili over cooked polenta; sprinkle with cheese, if desired.

Serves: 4

Shopping List:
16 oz. can black beans, 16 oz. can red kidney beans, 4 oz. chopped green chilies, instant polenta, 1½ lb. mushrooms, nonfat pasta sauce, nonfat shredded Cheddar cheese, vegetable broth, ground cumin, chili powder

Nutrition per serving		Exchanges
calories:	417	4 starch
total fat (6%):	3 g	4 vegetable
carbohydrate:	79 g	
cholesterol:	0 mg	carbohydrate choice: 5
dietary fiber:	13 g	
protein:	25 g	
sodium:	1,436 mg	

Black beans are a good source of fiber, protein, iron, and folic acid. One cup black beans contains 7 grams of fiber; 15 grams of protein; 20% of the Recommended Daily Allowance for iron; and 64% of the Recommended Daily Allowance for folic acid.

Rainbow Angel Hair Pasta

Easy — Do Ahead

Ingredients:

8 oz. angel hair pasta, cooked and drained
½ cup nonfat broth (chicken or vegetable)
1 cup chopped red bell pepper
½ cup chopped zucchini
½ cup chopped yellow squash
1 cup sliced mushrooms
¼ cup chopped green onion
1 tsp. Italian seasoning
¾ tsp. garlic powder
¼ tsp. pepper
1 cup canned chopped tomatoes, drained
¼ cup nonfat Parmesan cheese

Directions:

Cook pasta according to package directions; drain and keep warm. Pour broth into large saucepan; bring to a boil over medium-high heat. Add peppers, zucchini, squash, mushrooms, green onion, Italian seasoning, garlic powder, and pepper; cook over medium heat until vegetables are tender (about 4 to 5 minutes). Stir in tomatoes and cook 1 to 2 minutes until heated through. Spoon vegetable sauce over angel hair pasta and sprinkle with cheese.

Serves: 4

Shopping List:

8 oz. angel hair pasta, red bell pepper, zucchini, yellow squash, sliced mushrooms, green onion, 8 oz. can chopped tomatoes, nonfat broth (chicken or vegetable), nonfat Parmesan cheese, Italian seasoning, garlic powder, pepper

Nutrition per serving		Exchanges
calories:	259	2 starch
total fat (3%):	1 g	4½ vegetable
carbohydrate:	51 g	
cholesterol:	0 mg	carbohydrate choice: 3½
dietary fiber:	4 g	
protein:	11 g	
sodium:	257 mg	

Mushrooms contain cancer-fighting folic acid. Just 5 mushrooms supply 12% of the Recommended Daily Allowance for a mere 25 calories.

Seafood Creole

Easy — Do Ahead

ONE DISH MEALS

Ingredients:

¾ cup nonfat chicken broth
1½ cups frozen green beans, thawed and drained
1 cup frozen pepper strips, thawed and drained
1½ cups frozen carrot slices, thawed and drained
2 tsp. minced garlic
¾ lb. halibut, cubed
28 oz. can Creole-seasoned stewed tomatoes
1 lb. cooked shrimp (thawed if frozen)
cooked rice (optional)

Directions:

Combine all ingredients except shrimp in large saucepan; bring to a boil over high heat. Reduce heat to medium, cover, and cook 20 minutes. Add shrimp and cook until heated through. Serve over rice, if desired.

Serves: 6

Shopping List:

1 lb. cooked shrimp, ¾ lb. halibut, 16 oz. package frozen green beans, 10 oz. package frozen pepper strips, 16 oz. package frozen carrot slices, 28 oz. can Creole-style stewed tomatoes (if not available, use regular or other-flavored stewed tomatoes), nonfat chicken broth, minced garlic

Nutrition per serving		Exchanges
calories:	206	3 vegetable
total fat (13%):	3 g	1 lean meat
carbohydrate:	16 g	2 very lean meat
cholesterol:	135 mg	
dietary fiber:	3 g	carbohydrate choice: 1
protein:	29 g	
sodium:	556 mg	

Tomatoes contain the superstrength antioxidant lycopene, found to inhibit the growth of breast, lung, endometrial, and prostate cancer cells. They also contain coumaric acid and chlorogenic acid, two compounds that block the effects of nitrosamines (cancer-causing compounds).

Seafood-Rice Chowder

Easy — Do Ahead

ONE DISH MEALS

Ingredients:
7 oz. canned salmon, drained
7 oz. canned tuna in water, drained
10 oz. corn kernels, frozen or canned
28 oz. can stewed tomatoes
16 oz. clam juice
½ cup long-grain white rice
¾ tsp. garlic powder
¼ tsp. onion powder
2 to 3 drops Tabasco pepper sauce
¼ tsp. pepper

Directions:
Combine all ingredients except Tabasco and pepper in a medium saucepan; bring to a boil over high heat. Reduce heat to low, cover and simmer until rice is tender (20 to 25 minutes). Season with Tabasco and pepper.

Serves: 4

Shopping List:
7 oz. can salmon, 7 oz. can tuna in water, 10 oz. frozen or canned corn kernels, 28 oz. can stewed tomatoes, 16 oz. jar clam juice, long-grain white rice, garlic powder, onion powder, pepper, Tabasco pepper sauce

Nutrition per serving		Exchanges
calories:	328	1 lean meat
total fat (11%):	4 g	1½ very lean meat
carbohydrate:	46 g	2 starch
cholesterol:	36 mg	3 vegetable
dietary fiber:	5 g	
protein:	30 g	carbohydrate choice: 3
sodium:	1,151 mg	

Salmon is an excellent source of omega-3 fatty acids, which lower triglyceride levels, increase HDL (good cholesterol levels), prevent blood clots, and improve blood pressure.

Seafood Stew

Easy — Do Ahead

Ingredients:

2 tbsp. + ½ cup nonfat chicken broth
1 cup frozen chopped onion, thawed and drained
1 cup frozen pepper strips, thawed and drained
8 oz. sliced mushrooms
8 oz. clam juice
28 oz. can Italian-style stewed tomatoes
16 oz. package cubed potatoes
1⅓ tbsp. dried basil
½ lb. monkfish fillets, cut into 1-inch pieces
½ lb. scallops
pepper to taste

Directions:

Spray large saucepan or Dutch oven with cooking spray. Pour 2 tablespoons chicken broth into pan and heat over medium-high heat. Add onion and peppers to pan; cook 1 to 2 minutes until tender. Add sliced mushrooms, clam juice, remaining chicken broth, stewed tomatoes, potatoes, and basil to pan. Cover and cook over low heat until potatoes are tender (10 to 15 minutes). Add monkfish and scallops to pan; season with pepper. Cook 3 to 5 minutes until seafood is cooked through.

Serves: 4

Shopping List:

½ lb. monkfish fillets, ½ lb. scallops, 10 oz. frozen chopped onion, 10 oz. package frozen pepper strips, 8 oz. sliced mushrooms, 16 oz. package cubed potatoes, 8 oz. jar clam juice, 28 oz. can Italian-style stewed tomatoes, nonfat chicken broth, dried basil, pepper

Nutrition per serving		Exchanges
calories:	274	1½ starch
total fat (5%):	2 g	4 vegetable
carbohydrate:	43 g	2 very lean meat
cholesterol:	33 mg	
dietary fiber:	5 g	carbohydrate choice: 3
protein:	24 g	
sodium:	1,010 mg	

Potatoes are rich in potassium and magnesium, minerals that help reduce blood pressure.

Shrimp and Veggie Salad

Easy — Do Ahead

Ingredients:

½ cup nonfat mayonnaise
½ cup nonfat yogurt
¼ cup chopped green onion
1½ tbsp. cider vinegar
1½ tsp. Dijon mustard
pepper to taste
10 cups romaine lettuce, torn into bite-size pieces
8 oz. package mesclun (or baby greens)
16 oz. package vegetable medley (broccoli, cauliflower, carrot)
1 cucumber, peeled and diced
½ cup chopped red onion
2 cups grape tomatoes, cut in half
1 lb. cooked shrimp
1 cup roasted red peppers, drained
1 cup nonfat shredded Cheddar cheese

Directions:

Combine mayonnaise, yogurt, green onion, vinegar, Dijon mustard, and pepper in food processor or blender; process until creamy and smooth. Cover and refrigerate until ready to serve. Combine remaining ingredients in a large mixing bowl; drizzle with dressing and toss until mixed and coated. Substitute cooked scallops or chicken strips for shrimp, if desired.

Serves: 6

Shopping List:

4 oz. nonfat mayonnaise, 4 oz. nonfat sour cream, 4 oz. nonfat shredded Cheddar cheese, 3 packages Romaine lettuce in bite-size pieces, 8 oz. package mesclun (or baby greens), green onion, 16 oz. package vegetable medley (not frozen), cucumber, red onion, 1 pint grape (or cherry) tomatoes, roasted red peppers, 1 lb. cooked shrimp, cider vinegar, Dijon mustard, pepper

Nutrition per serving		Exchanges
calories:	212	3 very lean meat
total fat (8%):	2 g	3 vegetable
carbohydrate:	22 g	½ other carbohydrate
cholesterol:	148 mg	
dietary fiber:	5 g	carbohydrate choice: 1½
protein:	27 g	
sodium:	694 mg	

Broccoli's cancer-fighting power includes beta-carotene, indoles, and isothiocyanates.

Skillet-Fried Chicken with Tomatoes and Cheese

Easy

ONE DISH MEALS

Ingredients:

¼ cup flour
¼ tsp. pepper
1 lb. low-fat chicken breasts
   (boneless, skinless)
2 tbsp. nonfat chicken broth
28 oz. can chopped tomatoes,
   drained

½ tsp. crushed tarragon
1½ tsp. garlic powder
4 oz. nonfat Swiss
   cheese slices
cooked rice, couscous,
   or pasta (optional)

Directions:

Spray large nonstick skillet with cooking spray. Combine flour and pepper in a Ziploc bag; add chicken breasts and toss until coated. Pour chicken broth into skillet and heat over medium-high heat; add chicken to skillet and cook over medium heat until chicken is cooked through (about 4 to 5 minutes per side). Remove chicken from skillet and keep warm. Add tomatoes, tarragon, and garlic powder to skillet; cook over low heat until heated through. Return chicken to skillet; place one slice cheese on each chicken breast. Cover pan and cook over low heat until cheese melts. Serve with cooked rice, couscous, or pasta.

Serves: 4

Shopping List:

1 lb. low-fat chicken breasts (boneless, skinless), 28 oz. can chopped tomatoes, 4 oz. nonfat Swiss cheese slices, nonfat chicken broth, flour, crushed tarragon, garlic powder, pepper, rice, couscous, or pasta (optional)

Nutrition per serving

calories:	226
total fat (4%):	1 g
carbohydrate:	21 g
cholesterol:	71 mg
dietary fiber:	2 g
protein:	30 g
sodium:	1,001 mg

Exchanges

3 very lean meat
5 vegetable

carbohydrate choice: 1½

According to the Mayo Clinic Health Letter (September 1998), tomatoes contain a lot of nutrients, including the vitamins C and B complex and the minerals iron and potassium.

Vegetarian Burger Pizza

Easy — Do Ahead

Ingredients:
1 low-fat pizza crust*
¾ cup nonfat pasta sauce
1 tsp. Italian seasoning
1½ cups nonfat shredded mozzarella cheese, divided
3 nonfat veggie burgers, thawed
2 tbsp. nonfat Parmesan cheese

Directions:
Preheat oven to 425 degrees. Line baking sheet with foil or spray pizza pan with cooking spray. Prepare crust according to package directions. Spread crust with pasta sauce; sprinkle with Italian seasoning and ½ cup mozzarella cheese. Break up veggie burgers and arrange on pizza crust. Top with Parmesan cheese and remaining mozzarella cheese. Bake pizza 15 to 20 minutes until crust and cheese are lightly browned.

Serves: 6

Shopping List:
low-fat pizza crust (*Ragu Pizza Quick Crust mix, low-fat Italian bread shell, low-fat flour tortilla, French bread, etc.), frozen nonfat vegetable burgers, 6 oz. nonfat shredded mozzarella cheese, nonfat Parmesan cheese; 6 oz. nonfat pasta sauce, Italian seasoning

Nutrition per serving

calories:	220
total fat (4%):	1 g
carbohydrate:	29 g
cholesterol:	0 mg
dietary fiber:	2 g
protein:	20 g
sodium:	1,001 mg

Exchanges
1 starch
1 other carbohydrate

carbohydrate choice: 2

The average American who lives to the age of seventy-two eats 72,135 meals or 35.5 tons of food in a lifetime.

Very Veggie Calzones

Average — Do Ahead — Freeze

Ingredients:

16 oz. frozen bread dough, thawed
flour
1 cup sliced mushrooms
½ cup shredded zucchini
½ cup shredded carrot
½ cup chopped red bell pepper
¼ cup sliced green onion
¾ tsp. garlic powder

¾ tsp. Italian seasoning
1 cup nonfat shredded mozzarella cheese, divided
½ cup low-fat shredded mozzarella cheese, divided
1 egg white
1 tsp. water

Directions:

Preheat oven to 425 degrees. Line baking sheet with foil and spray with cooking spray. Tear off 6 equal pieces of bread dough. Roll each piece on a lightly floured surface into a square. Combine mushrooms, zucchini, carrot, red pepper, green onion, garlic powder, and Italian seasoning in a medium bowl; toss to mix. Sprinkle 3 tablespoons nonfat cheese and 1 tablespoon low-fat cheese on each square, leaving a ½-inch edge. Divide vegetable mixture evenly among calzones. Fold dough over and seal with fork. Combine egg white and water in a small cup; brush on calzones. Cut 2 to 3 slits on top of each calzone and bake 12 to 15 minutes until golden brown.

Serves: 6

Shopping List:

16 oz. frozen bread dough, 4 oz. nonfat shredded mozzarella cheese, low-fat shredded mozzarella cheese, 4 oz. sliced mushrooms, 1 zucchini, packaged shredded carrot, 1 red bell pepper, green onion, eggs, flour, garlic powder, Italian seasoning

Nutrition per serving

calories:	291
total fat (9%):	3 g
carbohydrate:	47 g
cholesterol:	0 mg
dietary fiber:	3 g
protein:	18 g
sodium:	454 mg

Exchanges

1 very lean meat
3½ vegetable
2 starch

carbohydrate choice: 3

According to the USDA Agriculture Research Service, red bell pepper is one of the best vegetable sources of phytochemicals.

Virtually Vegetarian Quiche

Average — Do Ahead

Ingredients:

4 slices sourdough bread,
  cut ¼-inch thick
garlic-flavored cooking spray
1 cup nonfat shredded Cheddar
  cheese
1½ cups frozen broccoli florets,
  thawed and drained
1½ cups frozen cauliflower
  florets, thawed and drained
½ tsp. tarragon

1 tsp. dried parsley
1 tsp. chopped chives
1 tsp. garlic powder
¼ cup low-fat shredded
  Cheddar cheese
6 egg whites
1 cup egg substitute
1 cup evaporated skim milk
pepper to taste

Directions:

Preheat oven to 350 degrees. Spray 10-inch deep dish pie plate with cooking spray. Arrange bread slices on bottom of dish; tear or cut any slices to cover dish. Sprinkle with ½ cup nonfat Cheddar cheese. Arrange broccoli and cauliflower on top of cheese. Sprinkle with tarragon, parsley, chives, garlic powder, and remaining cheese. Combine egg whites, egg substitute, and milk in a medium bowl; whisk until blended and frothy. Season with pepper to taste. Pour egg mixture into baking dish; bake 30 to 40 minutes, until eggs are set. Remove from oven and cool at room temperature 5 to 10 minutes before slicing.

Serves: 6

Shopping List:

whole eggs, 8 oz. egg substitute, 8 oz. evaporated skim milk, frozen broccoli florets, frozen cauliflower florets, 4 oz. nonfat shredded Cheddar cheese, 2 oz. low-fat shredded Cheddar cheese, ½ lb. sourdough bread, tarragon, dried parsley, chopped chives, garlic powder, garlic-flavored cooking spray

Nutrition per serving		Exchanges
calories:	192	½ starch
total fat (5%):	1 g	3 vegetable
carbohydrate:	24 g	2 very lean meat
cholesterol:	2 mg	
dietary fiber:	3 g	carbohydrate choice: 1½
protein:	21 g	
sodium:	539 mg	

Calcium intake lowers heart disease risk by about a third. Nonfat dairy products are the most effective.

Wild Mushroom Pizza

Easy — Do Ahead — Freeze

Ingredients:
  1 low-fat pizza crust*
  ¾ cup nonfat pasta sauce
  1 tsp. garlic powder
  2 cups morel mushrooms, sliced
  2 cups shiitake mushrooms, sliced
  2 cups oyster mushrooms, sliced
  ¾ cup chopped onion
  1½ cups nonfat shredded mozzarella cheese
  ½ cup nonfat Parmesan cheese

Directions:
  Preheat oven to 425 degrees. Line baking sheet with foil or spray pizza pan with cooking spray. Prepare crust according to package directions. Spread crust with pasta sauce; sprinkle with garlic powder. Arrange mushrooms on pizza crust; sprinkle with chopped onion. Top with mozzarella and Parmesan cheese. Bake pizza 15 to 20 minutes, until crust and cheese are lightly browned.

Serves: 6

Shopping List:
  low-fat pizza crust (*Ragu Pizza Quick Crust mix, low-fat Italian bread shell, low-fat flour tortilla, French bread, etc.), 6 oz. nonfat pasta sauce, ½ lb. morel mushrooms, ½ lb. shiitake mushrooms, ½ lb. oyster mushrooms, onion, 6 oz. nonfat shredded mozzarella cheese, nonfat Parmesan cheese, garlic powder

Nutrition per serving

calories:	241
total fat (4%):	1 g
carbohydrate:	36 g
cholesterol:	0 mg
dietary fiber:	2 g
protein:	20 g
sodium:	652 mg

Exchanges

2 very lean meat
3 vegetable
1 starch

carbohydrate choice: 2

Researchers at the Arizona Cancer Center found that people who had high amounts of the trace mineral selenium had significantly fewer cancers.

ENERGY-
BOOSTING
RECIPES

Eating for Energy

Food tastes good. Food fills you up. Food satisfies your cravings. But, more important . . . Food Is YOUR Fuel, your best source of nutrients to optimize health and performance. Make the best choices now for the best body today and tomorrow!

Energy (fuel) begets **Energy** (endurance, power, strength)!

Couch potatoes and **marathoners** alike need the same nutrients
—**carbohydrates, proteins, vitamins,
minerals, fiber, water,** and **fat**—
but more "active lifestyles" require more fuel input
for optimal energy output!

Boost energy, build energy sources by including essential macro-nutrients in your daily meal plan with . . .

M(oderation) V(ariety) *and* W(hole foods).

- **55 to 60% carbohydrates** (as prime energy source): fruits, vegetables, legumes, oat bran, whole grains, and whole-wheat products including breads, crackers, rice cakes, bagels, cereals, brown rice, pasta, barley, couscous, wheat germ
- **10 to 15% protein** (plays a minor role in energy production, but is essential for overall balanced nutrition and health by helping to build and repair muscles and tissues; fights disease and illness; and produce hormones): fish, poultry, lean meats, tofu, beans, egg whites, low-fat dairy products
- **<30% fat** (provides stored energy, supports and protects vital organs, and helps circulate, store, and absorb fat-soluble vitamins, but high-fat diets can increase the risk of heart disease and certain cancers): select monounsaturated and polyunsaturated fat sources (olive, peanut, canola, corn, sunflower, safflower, soybean oils and avocados) over saturated fats (animal fat sources, coconut and palm oils) and trans-fatty acids (hydrogenated foods)

- **WATER!!! Calorie-free, fat-free, cost-free super-packed ENERGY source!** Drink one quart (4 cups) of caffeine-free, nonalcoholic fluid for every 1,000 calories of food you eat (based on healthy weight). Drink 2 cups of water before exercising and 4 to 6 ounces every 15 to 20 minutes while exercising.

DON'T D.E.P.L.E.T.E. your valuable energy!

Don't skip meals!

Eat Breakfast! Of all the nutritional mistakes you might make, skipping breakfast is the biggest!

Plan for energy slumps with snack attacks!

Listen to your body!

Eat mini-meals throughout the day to keep your body properly fueled.

Time it right—stay fueled throughout the day to avoid late-night binges.

Eat BEFORE you get too hungry (avoid refrigerator raids and fast food frenzies)!

Banana-Berry-Orange Blast

Easy — Do Ahead

Ingredients:
- ½ cup nonfat banana-strawberry yogurt
- ¼ cup nonfat cream cheese, softened
- 1 tbsp. honey
- ½ tsp. cinnamon
- 1 banana, sliced
- 1 cup mandarin orange sections, drained well
- ½ cup frozen raspberries, thawed and drained
- ½ cup frozen blueberries, thawed and drained
- ½ cup frozen strawberries, thawed and drained
- 1 cup Grape Nuts cereal
- 4 tsp. sliced almonds

Directions:

Combine yogurt, cream cheese, honey, and cinnamon in a small bowl; mix until blended creamy and smooth. Cover with plastic wrap and refrigerate at least 1 hour. In each of four parfait glasses, layer ½ sliced banana, ½ cup mandarin oranges, 2 tablespoons raspberries, 2 tablespoons blueberries, 2 tablespoons strawberries, ½ cup cereal and 1 teaspoon almonds with a layer of cheese mixture in the center and on top.

Serves: 4

Shopping List:

4 oz. nonfat banana-strawberry yogurt, 2 oz. nonfat cream cheese, banana, 10 oz. can mandarin orange sections, frozen raspberries, frozen blueberries, frozen strawberries, Grape Nuts cereal, sliced almonds, honey, cinnamon

Nutrition per serving		Exchanges
calories:	290	3 fruit
total fat (6%):	2 g	1 starch
carbohydrate:	66 g	½ other carbohydrate
cholesterol:	1 mg	
dietary fiber:	7 g	carbohydrate choice: 4½
protein:	8 g	
sodium:	318 mg	

Bananas and oranges are good sources of pectin, which is being studied as a significant factor in helping the body increase HDL (good) cholesterol levels (good cholesterol).

Cheese "Egg'ls"

Average — Do Ahead

Ingredients:
1 cup egg substitute
8 egg whites
3 tbsp. skim milk
pepper to taste
4 English muffins, cut in half
butter-flavored cooking spray
4 nonfat cheese slices (American, Cheddar, or Swiss)

Directions:
Spray shallow baking dish with cooking spray. Combine egg substitute, egg whites, skim milk, and pepper in baking dish; whisk until frothy. Cover with plastic wrap and microwave on high 10 to 12 minutes until cooked through. Remove and let stand 5 minutes before cutting eggs into four equal pieces. Spray cut side of English muffins with butter-flavored cooking spray; toast lightly. Preheat broiler on high heat. Line baking sheet with foil and spray with cooking spray; arrange 4 muffin halves on baking sheet. Top each muffin with egg and sliced cheese; place under broiler 45 to 60 seconds, until cheese is just melted. Top with remaining muffin halves and serve.

Serves: 4

Shopping List:
English muffins, 8 oz. egg substitute, whole eggs, skim milk, 4 oz. nonfat cheese slices, pepper, butter-flavored cooking spray

Nutrition per serving		Exchanges
calories:	241	2½ very lean meat
total fat (4%):	1 g	2 starch
carbohydrate:	30 g	
cholesterol:	0 mg	carbohydrate choice: 2
dietary fiber:	1 g	
protein:	25 g	
sodium:	834 mg	

Microwaving is a form of steaming, an excellent way to preserve nutrients. Studies have shown that microwaving conserves more B vitamins and vitamin C than other cooking methods.

Oats of Energy Muffins

Easy — Do Ahead — Freeze

Ingredients:

1 cup nonfat vanilla yogurt
½ cup skim milk
1 cup rolled oats
½ cup wheat germ
¼ cup crushed pineapple, drained
¼ cup sugar
¾ cup brown sugar
¼ cup egg substitute

1 cup whole-wheat flour
2 tsp. baking powder
¾ tsp. cinnamon
1 cup shredded zucchini,
    squeezed dry
½ cup raisins
cinnamon-sugar (optional)

Directions:

Preheat oven to 325 degrees. Spray muffin tin with cooking spray. Combine yogurt, skim milk, and oats in a medium bowl; cover with plastic wrap and set aside for 20 to 30 minutes until oats soften. Combine remaining ingredients (except cinnamon-sugar) in a large bowl and mix well; add oat mixture and mix until ingredients are blended. Fill muffin cups three-quarters full and bake 25 to 20 minutes until toothpick inserted in center comes out clean. Sprinkle with cinnamon-sugar while hot, if desired.

Serves: 12

Shopping List:

8 oz. nonfat vanilla yogurt, 4 oz. skim milk, egg substitute, 8 oz. can crushed pineapple, raisins, ½ lb. zucchini, rolled oats, wheat germ, whole-wheat flour, brown sugar, baking powder, cinnamon, sugar (or cinnamon-sugar mix)

Nutrition per serving

calories:	148
total fat (6%):	1 g
carbohydrate:	31 g
cholesterol:	1 mg
dietary fiber:	3 g
protein:	5 g
sodium:	84 mg

Exchanges

2 other carbohydrate

carbohydrate choice: 2

Wheat germ can turn rancid very rapidly; be sure to purchase it in vacuum-packed containers, store opened containers in refrigerator, and use by date specified on the label.

Sweet and Smooth Banana Mango Treat

Easy

Ingredients:

2½ cups mangoes, peeled and chopped
1 banana
½ cup nonfat yogurt (vanilla or banana)
2 tsp. honey
½ tsp. vanilla
3 ice cubes
1½ tbsp. wheat germ

Directions:

Combine all ingredients except wheat germ in blender; process until smooth and creamy. Spoon mixture into bowls and sprinkle with wheat germ. Serve immediately.

Serves: 4

Shopping List:

3 mangoes, banana, 4 oz. nonfat yogurt (vanilla or banana), honey, vanilla, wheat germ

Nutrition per serving		Exchanges
calories:	143	½ other carbohydrate
total fat (6%):	1 g	1½ fruit
carbohydrate:	35 g	
cholesterol:	1 mg	carbohydrate choice: 2
dietary fiber:	4 g	
protein:	3 g	
sodium:	21 mg	

Choose "treats" with nutritional value—foods that have empty calories offer few nutrients.

Yogurt 'n' Fruit Morning Madness

Easy

Ingredients:
1⅓ cups nonfat yogurt (vanilla, banana, or strawberry)
¾ cup nonfat cottage cheese
3 tbsp. brown sugar
2 tsp. vanilla
1½ cups sliced strawberries
1 cup seedless grapes (red or green)
2 bananas, cut into large chunks
¾ cup low-fat granola
¼ cup chopped dates

Directions:
Combine yogurt, cottage cheese, brown sugar, and vanilla in a food processor or blender and process until creamy and smooth. Combine strawberries, grapes, and bananas in a medium bowl and toss lightly. Spoon yogurt mixture over top; sprinkle with granola and dates. Serve immediately.

Serves: 4

Shopping List:
10 oz. nonfat yogurt (vanilla, banana, or strawberry), 6 oz. nonfat cottage cheese, 1½ pints strawberries, ½ lb. seedless grapes, 2 bananas, chopped dates, brown sugar, vanilla, low-fat granola

Nutrition per serving		Exchanges
calories:	278	½ milk
total fat (3%):	1 g	2 fruit
carbohydrate:	61 g	1 starch
cholesterol:	2 mg	½ other carbohydrate
dietary fiber:	4 g	
protein:	11 g	carbohydrate choice: 2½
sodium:	354 mg	

Grape skins contain a high concentration of resveratrol, which may block the formation of coronary artery plaque, as well as inhibit the formation and growth of tumor.

"Honeyplum" Shake

Easy

Ingredients:
3 whole plums, pitted
1 cup nonfat vanilla yogurt
2 tbsp. honey
2 tbsp. wheat germ
3 to 5 ice cubes

Directions:
Combine all ingredients in blender; process until smooth and creamy.

Serves: 2

Shopping List:
3 plums, 4 oz. nonfat vanilla yogurt, honey, wheat germ

Nutrition per serving

calories:	168
total fat (5%):	1 g
carbohydrate:	37 g
cholesterol:	1 mg
dietary fiber:	3 g
protein:	4 g
sodium:	37 mg

Exchanges

1½ other choice
1 fruit

carbohydrate choice: 2½

***Eating 2 to 3 tablespoons of wheat germ
each day can help get rid of pimples.***

Orange-Berry Smoothie

Easy

Ingredients:
3 cups frozen mixed berries
1 cup nonfat mixed berry yogurt (or flavor of choice)
½ cup frozen orange juice concentrate (or flavor of choice)
2 tbsp. wheat germ
1 tbsp. honey

Directions:
Combine all ingredients in blender; process until smooth and creamy.

Serves: 2

Shopping List:
12 to 16 oz. package frozen mixed berries, 8 oz. nonfat yogurt (flavor of choice), 6 oz. frozen juice concentrate (flavor of choice), wheat germ, honey

Nutrition per serving		Exchanges
calories:	239	2½ fruit
total fat (8%):	2 g	½ milk
carbohydrate:	52 g	½ other carbohydrate
cholesterol:	3 mg	
dietary fiber:	10 g	carbohydrate choice: 3½
protein:	8 g	
sodium:	76 mg	

Wheat germ is a good source of B vitamins, vitamin E, and protein.

PostWorkout Power Shake

Easy

Ingredients:
- ¾ cup frozen strawberries
- ½ cup frozen rhubarb
- ¾ cup frozen peaches
- 1 cup nonfat yogurt (flavor of choice)
- 2 tbsp. honey
- 1 cup skim milk
- 1 cup orange juice
- 2 tbsp. protein powder

Directions:
Combine all ingredients in blender; process until smooth and creamy.

Serves: 2

Shopping List:
10 oz. frozen strawberries, 10 oz. frozen rhubarb, 10 oz. frozen peaches, 8 oz. nonfat yogurt (flavor of choice), 8 oz. skim milk, 8 oz. orange juice, honey, protein powder

Nutrition per serving		Exchanges
calories:	359	1 milk
total fat (3%):	1 g	3 fruit
carbohydrate:	76 g	1 other carbohydrate
cholesterol:	6 mg	
dietary fiber:	9 g	carbohydrate choice: 5
protein:	16 g	
sodium:	148 mg	

Rhubarb is a great source of insoluble fiber, which speeds waste through the intestines and helps lower the risk of colon cancer.

Protein Power-Pack in a Cup

Easy

Ingredients:
　1 cup frozen strawberries
　1 cup frozen tropical fruit mix
　1 cup nonfat strawberry-banana yogurt
　4 tbsp. protein powder
　2 tbsp. sugar
　1 cup skim milk
　1 cup strawberry-orange juice

Directions:
　Combine all ingredients in blender and process until creamy and smooth.

Serves: 2

Shopping List:
　10 oz. package frozen strawberries, 10 oz. package frozen tropical fruit, 8 oz. nonfat strawberry-banana yogurt (or flavor of choice), 8 oz. skim milk, 8 oz. strawberry-orange juice, sugar, protein powder

Nutrition per serving		Exchanges
calories:	308	1 milk
total fat (3%):	1 g	2 fruit
carbohydrate:	56 g	1 other carbohydrate
cholesterol:	7 mg	
dietary fiber:	4 g	carbohydrate choice: 4
protein:	22 g	
sodium:	157 mg	

Berries are a good source of ellagic acid, fiber, and vitamin C, which reduce the risk of cancer of the stomach and esophagus.

Quick Pick-Me-Up Carrot-Apple Salad

Easy — Do Ahead

Ingredients:
3 cups shredded carrot
1 cup grated apples
½ cup nonfat yogurt (plain, vanilla, or pineapple)
½ cup canned crushed pineapple, lightly drained
½ cup raisins

Directions:
Combine all ingredients in a medium bowl; toss until blended and coated. Cover and refrigerate at least one hour before serving.

Serves: 6

Shopping List:
12 oz. shredded carrot, 1 apple, 6 oz. nonfat yogurt (plain, vanilla, or pineapple), canned crushed pineapple, raisins

Nutrition per serving	
calories:	78
total fat (0):	0g
carbohydrate:	19 g
cholesterol:	1 mg
dietary fiber:	3 g
protein:	2 g
sodium:	38 mg

Exchanges
1 vegetable
1 fruit

carbohydrate choice: 1

***Healthy snacking increases energy,
boosts metabolism, and provides
a good usable source of nutrients.***

Super Slaw

Easy — Do Ahead

Ingredients:
⅓ cup nonfat mayonnaise
⅓ cup nonfat sour cream
3 tbsp. cider vinegar
1 tbsp. lemon pepper
3 cups skinless, boneless chicken tenders, cooked and
    cubed
4 cups shredded cabbage
4 cups canned pineapple tidbits, drained
3 cups cubed cantaloupe
1 cup red seedless grapes, halved

Directions:
Combine mayonnaise, sour cream, cider vinegar, and lemon pepper in a small bowl; mix until ingredients are blended. Combine remaining ingredients in large bowl; toss with dressing and coat well. Cover and refrigerate at least 1 hour before serving.

Serves: 6

Shopping List:
nonfat mayonnaise, nonfat sour cream, cider vinegar, lemon pepper, 1½ lb. low-fat chicken tenders, 16 oz. shredded cabbage, 2 16-oz. cans pineapple tidbits, ½ lb. seedless grapes, 1½ lb. cantaloupe

Nutrition per serving

calories:	281
total fat (13%):	4 g
carbohydrate:	43 g
cholesterol:	53 mg
dietary fiber:	4 g
protein:	22 g
sodium:	394 mg

Exchanges
½ other carbohydrate
2 fruit
1 vegetable
1 lean meat
1 very lean meat

carbohydrate choice: 3

***Increase iron absorption by eating
more vitamin C–rich foods.***

Brown Rice Teriyaki Chicken Bowl

Easy — Do Ahead — Freeze

Ingredients:
2 cups cooked brown rice
¾ lb. cooked chicken strips, cut into chunks
2 cups frozen stir-fry vegetables, thawed and drained
½ cup low-sodium teriyaki sauce

Directions:
Combine all ingredients in medium bowl. Cook in microwave 3 to 4 minutes until heated through.*

Serves: 4

Shopping List:
brown rice, 6 oz. nonfat pasta sauce, egg substitute, nonfat shredded Cheddar cheese, nonfat Parmesan cheese, 5 oz. nonfat shredded mozzarella cheese, low-fat shredded mozzarella cheese, red bell pepper, ½ lb. cauliflower florets, ½ lb. broccoli florets, 1 oz. mushrooms, garlic powder

Nutrition per serving		Exchanges
calories:	249	1 starch
total fat (4%):	1 g	3 vegetable
carbohydrate:	34 g	2½ very lean meat
cholesterol:	42 mg	
dietary fiber:	3 g	carbohydrate choice: 2
protein:	26 g	
sodium:	1238 mg	

Doctors and researchers agree that loading your plate with fruits, vegetables, beans, and whole grains (plus trimming fat) can significantly cut a woman's risk of heart disease.

* Recipe can be prepared in individual servings (½ cup brown rice + 3 oz. chicken strips + ½ cup vegetables + 2 tbsp. teriyaki sauce—heat 1 to 2 minutes in microwave)

Chicken-Potato Packet Meal

Easy — Do Ahead — Freeze

Ingredients:
½ cup barbecue sauce, divided
1 lb. skinless, boneless chicken breasts
1 tsp. Mrs. Dash extra-spicy seasoning
1 tsp. garlic powder
¼ tsp. pepper
2 cups frozen pepper strips, thawed and drained
16 oz. Simply Potatoes, sliced thin
1 onion, sliced thin

Directions:
Preheat oven to 350 degrees. Tear four foil pieces (approximately 16 x 16) and spray on one side with cooking spray. Place spray side up on flat surface; spoon 1 tablespoon barbecue sauce onto foil and spread lightly. Top with chicken breast; season with Mrs. Dash, garlic powder, and pepper. Divide peppers, potatoes, and onion among chicken breasts; top with remaining barbecue sauce. Fold foil and seal edges. Bake 35 to 45 minutes until chicken is cooked through.

Serves: 4

Shopping List:
1 lb. skinless, boneless chicken breasts; 4 oz. barbecue sauce; 16 oz. package frozen pepper strips; 16 oz. package Simply Potatoes (sliced); onion; garlic powder; Mrs. Dash extra-spicy seasoning; pepper

Nutrition per serving		Exchanges
calories:	278	½ other carbohydrate
total fat (3%):	1 g	2 starch
carbohydrate:	42 g	2 vegetable
cholesterol:	71 mg	2 very lean meat
dietary fiber:	4 g	
protein:	26 g	carbohydrate choice: 3
sodium:	729 mg	

Did you know . . . protein was named after the Greek word proteios *(which means of prime importance) more than 150 years ago?*

Crispy Chicken Bites

Easy — Do Ahead — Freeze

Ingredients:

¼ cup egg substitute
¼ cup skim milk
¾ cup cornflake crumbs
½ cup reduced-fat wheat
   crackers, crushed
¾ tsp. garlic powder
¾ tsp. onion powder

¼ tsp. pepper
1 lb. skinless, boneless
   chicken tenders, cut into
   1-inch pieces
sweet and sour sauce,
   barbecue sauce, ketchup
   or honey-mustard

ENERGY BOOSTING RECIPES

Directions:

Preheat oven to 400 degrees. Line baking sheet with foil and spray with cooking spray. Combine egg substitute and milk in medium bowl; whisk to blend. Combine cornflake crumbs, crushed crackers, garlic powder, onion powder, and pepper in shallow dish; toss until ingredients are mixed. Dip chicken pieces into egg mixture; roll in cracker-crumb mixture, coating on all sides. Place chicken bites in a single layer on baking sheet and bake 10 to 15 minutes until chicken is tender and cooked through. Serve with dipping sauce of choice. These can be eaten hot or cold; great for quick carbohydrate-protein snack!

Serves: 4

Shopping List:

1 lb. boneless, skinless chicken tenders, egg substitute, skim milk, cornflake crumbs, reduced-fat wheat crackers, garlic powder, onion powder, pepper, dipping sauce (of choice)

Nutrition per serving

calories:	226
total fat (13%):	3 g
carbohydrate:	21 g
cholesterol:	71 mg
dietary fiber:	1 g
protein:	27 g
sodium:	482 mg

Exchanges

1½ starch
3 very lean meat
½ fat

carbohydrate choice: 1½

***Put more emphasis on healthy foods
and downplay the "unhealthy" stuff.
Think moderation and limits, not
deprivation and avoidance!***

Grilled Tuna Sandwich

Easy

Ingredients:
2 6½-oz. cans tuna packed in water, drained
½ cup shredded carrot
¼ cup diced jicama
½ cup pineapple tidbits, drained well
2 tbsp. nonfat mayonnaise
2 tbsp. nonfat sour cream
2 tbsp. pineapple juice
1 tsp. Dijon mustard
½ tsp. Mrs. Dash extra-spicy seasoning
8 slices whole-wheat bread
4 slices tomato

Directions:
Combine tuna, carrot, jicama, and pineapple in medium bowl. Combine mayonnaise, sour cream, pineapple juice, mustard, and Mrs. Dash seasoning in a small bowl; mix until ingredients are well blended. Spoon mayonnaise mixture over tuna and mix well. Divide tuna mixture among four bread slices; top with slices tomato and remaining bread slices. Spray large nonstick skillet with cooking spray and heat over medium-high heat. Add tuna sandwiches and grill until lightly browned on both sides.

Serves: 4

Shopping List:
2 6½-oz. cans tuna packed in water, whole-wheat bread (sliced), tomato, shredded carrots, jicama, 8 oz. can pineapple tidbits, nonfat mayonnaise, nonfat sour cream, pineapple juice, Dijon mustard, Mrs. Dash extra-spicy seasoning

Nutrition per serving		Exchanges
calories:	307	2 starch
total fat (9%):	3 g	½ other carbohydrate
carbohydrate:	37 g	2 very lean meat
cholesterol:	17 mg	1 lean meat
dietary fiber:	7 g	
protein:	34 g	carbohydrate choice: 2½
sodium:	769 mg	

Beta-carotene, vitamins C and E, and selenium are the most essential antioxidant nutrients.

Mini–Meat Loaves
Easy — Do Ahead — Freeze

Ingredients:
¼ cup egg substitute
½ cup Quaker multigrain cereal
¼ cup wheat germ
1 tbsp. dried parsley
½ cup tomato paste
¼ tsp. Mrs. Dash seasoning
14 oz. Gimme Lean meat substitute
¼ cup barbecue sauce

Directions:
Preheat oven to 350 degrees. Line baking sheet with foil and spray with cooking spray. Combine all ingredients except barbecue sauce in medium bowl; mix until ingredients are completely blended. Shape into four mini–meat loaves. Bake 15 to 18 minutes; brush tops with barbecue sauce and continue cooking until browned and cooked through (10 to 15 minutes).

Serves: 4

Shopping List:
14 oz. Gimme Lean meat substitute, egg substitute, Quaker multigrain cereal, wheat germ, tomato paste, barbecue sauce, dried parsley, Mrs. Dash seasoning

ENERGY BOOSTING RECIPES

Nutrition per serving		Exchanges
calories:	223	½ starch
total fat (4%):	1 g	1½ other carbohydrate
carbohydrate:	34 g	2 very lean meat
cholesterol:	0 mg	
dietary fiber:	4 g	carbohydrate choice: 2
protein:	21 g	
sodium:	789 mg	

Soy foods contain high-quality protein, fiber, lecithin, and omega-3 fatty acids, in addition to B vitamins, vitamin E, calcium, zinc, and iron.

Tortilla Pizza

Easy

Ingredients:
4 low-fat flour tortillas (10-inch)
½ cup nonfat pasta sauce
1 tsp. Italian seasoning
1⅓ cups nonfat shredded mozzarella cheese, divided
2 cups frozen pepper strips, thawed, drained, and dried
2 cups frozen broccoli florets; thawed, drained, and dried
¼ cup diced red onion
¼ cup nonfat Parmesan cheese

Directions:
Preheat oven to 450 degrees. Line baking sheet(s) with foil and spray with cooking spray. Arrange tortillas on baking sheet(s). Spread each tortilla with 2 tablespoons pasta sauce; sprinkle with Italian seasoning and ⅓ cup mozzarella cheese. Top each tortilla with ¼ cup peppers, ¼ cup broccoli, and 1 tablespoon red onion; sprinkle with Parmesan cheese. Bake 5 to 7 minutes until lightly browned and crisp.

Serves: 4

Shopping List:
low-fat flour tortillas (10-inch), 16 oz. frozen pepper strips, 16 oz. frozen broccoli florets or cuts, red onion, 4 oz. nonfat pasta sauce, 6 oz. nonfat shredded mozzarella cheese, nonfat Parmesan cheese, Italian seasoning

Nutrition per serving		Exchanges
calories:	222	2 very lean meat
total fat (8%):	2 g	1 starch
carbohydrate:	29 g	3 vegetable
cholesterol:	0 mg	
dietary fiber:	5 g	carbohydrate choice: 2
protein:	21 g	
sodium:	434 mg	

Healthy snacks help maintain blood-sugar levels without providing unwanted calories, fat, sugar, and sodium.

Wholesome Hearty Veggie Burgers
Easy — Do Ahead — Freeze

Ingredients:
15 oz. can black beans, rinsed, drained, and mashed
½ cup shredded zucchini
½ cup shredded yellow squash
½ cup shredded carrot
½ cup chopped red onion
½ tsp. garlic powder
½ cup cooked brown rice, cooled
½ cup egg substitute
2 tbsp. seasoned bread crumbs
1½ tsp. Mrs. Dash seasoning
4 whole pita pockets (cut in half)
lettuce
tomato slices
honey mustard, barbecue sauce, ketchup, Dijon mustard, or other condiments of choice

Directions:
Preheat broiler on high heat. Line baking sheet with foil and spray with cooking spray. Combine beans, zucchini, squash, carrot, onion, and garlic powder; mix well. Add rice, egg substitute, bread crumbs, and Mrs. Dash seasoning; mix until ingredients are blended and hold together. Shape mixture into eight patties and arrange on baking sheet. Broil 5 to 6 minutes; turn over and broil another 5 to 6 minutes until browned and cooked through. Line each pita pocket with lettuce and sliced tomato; add condiments of choice. Place one patty in each pita pocket and serve (2 patties, 1 whole pita pocket per serving).

Serves: 4

Shopping List:
15 oz. can black beans, zucchini, yellow squash, shredded carrot, red onion, lettuce, tomato, brown rice, seasoned bread crumbs, large pita pockets, egg substitute, Mrs. Dash seasoning, garlic powder, condiments of choice

Nutrition per serving

calories:	272
total fat (3%):	1 g
carbohydrate:	52 g
cholesterol:	0 mg
dietary fiber:	6 g
protein:	14 g
sodium:	661 mg

Exchanges
3 starch
2 vegetable

carbohydrate choice: 3½

Beans canned in water are nutritionally similar to dried beans, except they may have higher sodium content. Rinse and drain canned beans before using them in recipes.

Cinnamon-Spice Popcorn

Easy — Do Ahead

Ingredients:

    8 cups hot-air popped popcorn, no oil
    1 tbsp. sugar
    1 tbsp. brown sugar
    2 tsp. water
    ½ tsp. cinnamon
    ¼ tsp. nutmeg
    ⅛ tsp. ginger

Directions:

Preheat oven to 350 degrees. Spray 9 x 13-inch baking dish with cooking spray; place popcorn in baking dish. Combine sugar, brown sugar, water, cinnamon, nutmeg, and ginger in a small bowl; mix well. Drizzle sugar mixture over popcorn and toss to coat. Bake 12 to 15 minutes, stirring once or twice. Spray large piece of foil with cooking spray; transfer popcorn mix to foil and let cool completely. Store leftovers in Ziploc bags or sealed container.

Serves: 4

Shopping List:

popcorn, sugar, brown sugar, cinnamon, nutmeg, ginger

Nutrition per serving		Exchanges
calories:	76	½ starch
total fat (0%):	0 g	½ other carbohydrate
carbohydrate:	17 g	
cholesterol:	0 mg	carbohydrate choice: 1
dietary fiber:	1 g	
protein:	2 g	
sodium:	1 mg	

Air-popped, unbuttered popcorn is one of the best snacks around; 32 cups of unbuttered popcorn contains the same number of calories (840) as a cup of peanuts; 3% of the calories in popcorn come from fat, while 76% of the calories in peanuts do.

Granola
Easy — Do Ahead

Ingredients:

3 cups rolled oats
¼ cup honey
¼ cup frozen orange juice
    concentrate, thawed
    (undiluted)
½ tsp. cinnamon

⅛ tsp. ginger
⅛ tsp. nutmeg
¼ tsp. almond extract
¼ tsp. vanilla extract
1 cup wheat germ
1 cup dried fruit

Directions:

Preheat oven to 350 degrees. Line baking sheet with foil and spray with cooking spray. Spread oats on baking sheet and bake until oats are toasted, turning frequently (about 8 to 10 minutes). Combine honey and juice concentrate in small saucepan; cook over low heat until mixture is blended smooth. Spray 9 x 13-inch baking dish with cooking spray; pour honey mixture into dish. Add cinnamon, ginger, nutmeg, almond extract, and vanilla to honey mixture and mix until blended. Add toasted oats and toss until coated. Bake oat mixture 5 to 6 minutes, stirring frequently, until lightly browned. Remove from oven and let mixture cool in pan. When oat mixture is cooled stir in wheat germ and dried fruit; toss to mix. Great as snack or cereal with skim milk, nonfat soy milk, or nonfat yogurt.

Serves: 12

Shopping List:

rolled oats, wheat germ, dried fruit, honey, frozen orange juice concentrate, cinnamon, ginger, nutmeg, almond extract, vanilla extract

Nutrition per serving

calories:	176
total fat (10%):	2 g
carbohydrate:	35 g
cholesterol:	0 mg
dietary fiber:	3 g
protein:	6 g
sodium:	3 mg

Exchanges

½ starch
1 fruit
½ other carbohydrate

carbohydrate choice: 2

Run measuring cup under hot water before measuring honey; it will pour more easily without sticking to the cup. The best honey is labeled "100% pure unfiltered," "raw," or "uncooked." This honey has not been nutrient depleted by heat processing.

Pumpkin Power Bars

Easy — Do Ahead — Freeze

Ingredients:

2 cups shredded apples, peeled
1 cup canned pumpkin
¼ cup corn syrup
½ cup brown sugar
¼ cup egg substitute
¾ tsp. vanilla

1½ cups all-purpose flour
¼ cup rolled oats
2 tbsp. wheat germ
1½ tsp. baking powder
1 tsp. cinnamon
¾ tsp. allspice

Directions:

Preheat oven to 350 degrees. Spray 9 x 13-inch baking dish with cooking spray. Combine apples, pumpkin, corn syrup, brown sugar, egg substitute and vanilla in a large bowl; mix until ingredients are blended. Add flour, oats, wheat germ, baking powder, cinnamon, and allspice to apple mixture; stir batter until all ingredients are blended. If dough is too sticky, add extra flour a tablespoon at a time. Spread batter into baking dish; bake 35 to 45 minutes until toothpick inserted in center comes out clean. Cool completely; cut into squares.

Serves: 18

Shopping List:

2 apples, 8 oz. can pumpkin, egg substitute, rolled oats, wheat germ, all-purpose flour, brown sugar, corn syrup, vanilla, baking powder, cinnamon, allspice

Nutrition per serving		**Exchanges**
calories:	96	1½ other carbohydrate
total fat (0%):	0 g	
carbohydrate:	22 g	carbohydrate choice: 1½
cholesterol:	0 mg	
dietary fiber:	1 g	
protein:	2 g	
sodium:	38 mg	

Researchers at the National Cancer Institute and the U.S. Department of Agriculture singled out pumpkin as an excellent source of beta-carotene, which cuts the risk of certain cancers.

Raspberry Oat Bars

Easy — Do Ahead — Freeze

Ingredients:

1 cup Quaker multigrain cereal
1 cup whole-wheat flour
¼ cup Grape Nuts cereal
⅔ cup brown sugar
1 tsp. cinnamon
¼ tsp. baking soda
½ cup nonfat vanilla yogurt
2 tbsp. egg substitute
10 oz. all-fruit red raspberry spread

Directions:

Preheat oven to 350 degrees. Lightly spray 9-inch baking dish with cooking spray. Combine multigrain cereal, flour, Grape Nuts cereal, brown sugar, cinnamon, and baking soda in medium bowl; toss ingredients to mix. Combine yogurt and egg substitute in a small bowl; whisk until blended. Add yogurt mixture to oat mixture; cut or mix in with fork, pastry blender or two knives. Mixture will be sticky and crumbly. Set aside ½ cup oat mixture for topping. Press oat mixture into bottom of baking dish; spread preserves evenly over crust. Sprinkle remaining oat mixture over top and bake 25 to 30 minutes until golden brown. Cool completely and cut into bars.

Serves: 16

Shopping List:

Quaker multigrain cereal, Grape Nuts cereal, 10 oz. all-fruit red raspberry spread, 4 oz. nonfat vanilla yogurt, egg substitute, whole-wheat flour, brown sugar, cinnamon, baking soda

Nutrition per serving		Exchanges
calories:	156	2 other carbohydrate
total fat (6%):	1 g	
carbohydrate:	35 g	carbohydrate choice: 2
cholesterol:	0 mg	
dietary fiber:	3 g	
protein:	3 g	
sodium:	36 mg	

Raspberries have Ellagic acid, which helps stall cancer-cell growth.

Snack Mix

Easy — Do Ahead

Ingredients:
30 mini–rice cakes (flavor of choice)
¾ cup Corn Chex cereal
¾ cup pretzels (sticks, nuggets, or goldfish mix)
¾ cup nonfat bagel chips, broken into bite-size pieces
¾ cup raisins
1½ tbsp. low-fat margarine, melted
1½ tsp. Worcestershire sauce
¾ tsp. Mrs. Dash extra-spicy seasoning

Directions:
Preheat oven to 300 degrees. Spray 9 x 13-inch baking dish with cooking spray. Combine rice cakes, cereal, pretzels, bagel chips, and raisins in baking dish; toss to mix. In a small bowl, combine margarine, Worcestershire sauce, and Mrs. Dash seasoning; mix well and drizzle over snack mix. Toss gently so snack mix is coated. Bake 15 to 20 minutes, stirring occasionally, until crisp. Cool completely before serving; store in Ziploc bags or tightly sealed container.

Serves: 8

Shopping List:
mini–rice cakes (flavor of choice), Corn Chex cereal, pretzels, nonfat bagel chips, raisins, low-fat margarine, Worcestershire sauce, Mrs. Dash extra-spicy seasoning

Nutrition per serving		Exchanges
calories:	126	1 starch
total fat (7%):	1 g	½ fruit
carbohydrate:	28 g	½ other carbohydrate
cholesterol:	0 mg	
dietary fiber:	1 g	carbohydrate choice: 2
protein:	2 g	
sodium:	132 mg	

Watch out for sodium in disguise! If you're concerned about sodium intake, watch out for hidden salts by reading labels: baking powder, baking soda, soy sauce, brine, garlic salt, onion salt, monosodium glutamate (MSG), sea salt, sodium chloride, sodium citrate, sodium nitrate, sodium phosphate, and sodium saccharin contain high concentrations of sodium.

DRINK
YOUR WAY
TO HEALTH

♦ ♦ ♦

DRINK your WAY to HEALTH!

Smoothies, Shakes, Health Drinks, Energy in a Cup—
souped-up superdrinks with the potential to increase brain power, detoxify your digestive tract, provide a day's worth of essential vitamins and minerals, satisfy your sweet tooth, cool you down on a hot summer day or simply fill you up with a multitude of ingredients!

The **BARE NECESSITIES:** blender, fruit, juice, ice

ABUNDANT ADDITIONS: nonfat yogurt, soy or dairy milk, sorbet, wheat germ, protein powder, flaxseed, and more

BEST time for a smoothie? **ANYTIME!**

Smoothie SMARTS . . .

- Choose nonfat yogurt—best nutrients at the lowest cost of calories and fat without losing flavor!
- They're not free—calorie- or cost-wise! Even "good ingredients" can take your caloric intake over the edge if you don't pay attention!
- Portion control—Supersized does not equal superhealth!
- For frostier smoothies . . . freeze your fruit!
- Skip sweetened frozen fruits—it's just extra sugar and calories!
- Don't wait—smoothies are meant to be slurped on the spot! You can freeze some smoothies for an "ice cream" texture, but leaving them in the refrigerator too long may cause some separation.

No IFS, AND, or BUTS about it . . .

- If your drink is too thick, add a little more juice.
- If your drink is too thin, add a little more fruit, yogurt, sorbet, or crushed ice.
- If you want a "smoother" smoothie, always use small ice cubes or crushed ice.
- If your drink is just a little too puckering tart, add more sweet fruit (berries, bananas, pineapple, etc.)
- If your sweet tooth isn't satisfied, add a drop or two or honey, maple syrup, or other natural sweetener.

- If your drink is too sweet, add a spoonful of lemon juice.
- If you can't tolerate the taste of nonfat dairy products, replace half the nonfat yogurt with low-fat and gradually adapt to the taste.
- If your stomach cringes at the thought of dairy, go for whole fruit smoothies or substitute lactose-free dairy products.
- If you saved some smoothie and it lost its creamy texture, blend it back up—it'll be as fresh as new!

Healthy Additive Knowledge for the Novice (or Experienced) Smoothie-Slurper:

- **aloe vera juice:** helps soothe upset stomachs
- **bee pollen:** contains eighteen amino acids, fourteen minerals, and B-complex vitamins (not recommended for those suffering from pollen allergies!)
- **brewer's yeast:** excellent source of vegetable protein, B vitamins, minerals, amino acids, and iron
- **calcium:** as the number one mineral in the human body, it never hurts to add a little more. Calcium not only aids in strengthening bones and teeth, guarding against osteoporosis, inhibiting colon cancer, and promoting hormone secretion, but also regulates heartbeat and muscle contractions, facilitates blood clotting and may help prevent hypertension.
- **ginseng:** energy booster that improves athletic performance, fights exhaustion, detoxifies your body, and increases the use of fatty acids that provide fuel and energy to your body.
- **flaxseed or flaxseed oil:** rich source of omega-3 fatty acids, antioxidants, phytochemicals, and fiber
- **protein powder:** promotes muscular development
- **vitamin C:** powerful antioxidant strengthens cells, promotes collagen formation, enhances immune function, maintains healthy connective tissue, helps wounds heal and aids in the absorption of calcium, iron and folic acid
- **wheat germ:** rich source of B vitamins, vitamin E, and protein
- **tofu:** excellent source of cholesterol-free protein and phytoestrogens, protecting against certain cancers and heart disease

Apple Spice Slush

Easy

Ingredients:
- ¾ cup nonfat yogurt, apple spice or vanilla
- ¾ cup diced apples
- ½ cup frozen apple juice concentrate
- ½ frozen banana
- ¼ tsp. cinnamon
- ⅛ tsp. nutmeg

Directions:
Combine all ingredients in blender and process until smooth and creamy.

Serves: 2

Shopping List:
6 oz. nonfat yogurt (apple spice or vanilla), apple, banana, frozen apple juice concentrate, cinnamon, nutmeg

Nutrition per serving		Exchanges
calories:	114	½ milk
total fat (0%):	0 g	1 fruit
carbohydrate:	25 g	
cholesterol:	2 mg	carbohydrate choice: 1½
dietary fiber:	2 g	
protein:	3 g	
sodium:	57 mg	

Americans eat approximately twenty-two pounds of apples per year per person. Apples contain 84% pure water, carbohydrates, protein, minerals, vitamins (A, B, C), iron, potassium, and other nutrients.

Banana-Berry "C-ful" Shake
Easy

Ingredients:
1 cup nonfat yogurt (banana, strawberry, or mixed berries)
¾ cup frozen unsweetened strawberries, raspberries or
   blueberries
¼ cup pineapple chunks, drained
¼ cup orange juice
1 banana, peeled and quartered

Directions:
Combine all ingredients in blender; process until smooth
and creamy. Garnish with fresh berries and sliced pineapple,
if desired.

Serves: 2

Shopping List:
8 oz. nonfat yogurt (flavor of choice); frozen strawberries,
raspberries, blueberries, or berry mix; 8 oz. can pineapple
chunks in juice, orange juice, banana

Nutrition per serving		Exchanges
calories:	150	½ milk
total fat (0%):	0 g	1½ fruit
carbohydrate:	34 g	
cholesterol:	3 mg	carbohydrate choice: 2
dietary fiber:	3 g	
protein:	5 g	
sodium:	72 mg	

**Orange juice is packed with the powerful antioxidant
vitamin C, which not only controls harmful free
radicals, but boosts immunity and helps
the body absorb iron from food.**

DRINK YOUR WAY TO HEALTH

B . . . B . . . B . . . Smoothie

Easy

Ingredients:
1 cup frozen blueberries
½ cup frozen blackberries
½ cup frozen boysenberries
1 cups nonfat mixed berry yogurt
½ cup grape juice

Directions:
Combine all ingredients in blender and process until smooth and creamy.

Serves: 2

Shopping List:
8 oz. nonfat mixed berry yogurt, frozen blueberries, frozen blackberries, frozen boysenberries, 4 oz. grape juice

Nutrition per serving		Exchanges
calories:	164	½ milk
total fat (4%):	1 g	2 fruit
carbohydrate:	36 g	
cholesterol:	3 mg	carbohydrate choice: 2½
dietary fiber:	6 g	
protein:	5 g	
sodium:	73 mg	

Blueberries, blackberries, and boysenberries are high in fiber, potassium, and vitamin C.

Berry-Almond Rich Power Shake

Easy

Ingredients:
½ cup skim milk
1 cup nonfat yogurt (flavor of choice)
½ banana, peeled and cut in half
¾ cup frozen mixed berries
2 tbsp. sliced almonds
2 tsp. flaxseed oil

Directions:
Combine all ingredients in blender; process until smooth and creamy. Great breakfast substitute!

Serves: 2

Shopping List:
4 oz. skim milk, 8 oz. nonfat yogurt (flavor of choice), frozen mixed berries, banana, sliced almonds, flaxseed oil (in the health food section of most grocery stores)

DRINK YOUR WAY TO HEALTH

Nutrition per serving

calories:	294
total fat (18%):	6 g
carbohydrate:	54 g
cholesterol:	4 mg
dietary fiber:	5 g
protein:	11 g
sodium:	104 mg

Exchanges

1 milk
2½ fruit
1 fat

carbohydrate choice: 3½

Flaxseed contains seventy-five times more lignans than any other plant food. Lignans have powerful antioxidant properties, reducing the damage caused by free radicals.

Blended Veggie Drink

Easy

Ingredients:
2 cups V8 juice
2 cucumbers, peeled and diced
½ cup canned beets, drained
1 red bell pepper, cut into chunks
½ cup shredded carrots
1 bunch parsley without stems
¾ cup broccoli florets without stems
½ cup ice cubes
2 to 3 drops Tabasco pepper sauce to taste
pepper to taste

Directions:
Combine all ingredients except Tabasco and pepper in blender; process until smooth and blended. Season with Tabasco and pepper to taste; add enough ice cubes until drink is consistency you desire.

Serves: 2

Shopping List:
16 oz. V8 juice, 2 cucumbers, red bell pepper, packaged shredded carrots, ½ lb. broccoli florets, bunch parsley, 8 oz. can red beets, Tabasco pepper sauce, pepper

Nutrition per serving

calories:	129
total fat (7%):	1 g
carbohydrate:	30 g
cholesterol:	0 mg
dietary fiber:	10 g
protein:	6 g
sodium:	933 mg

Exchanges
5½ vegetable

carbohydrate choice: 2

Making simple changes in diet and lifestyle can reduce your chances of getting cancer by up to 40%.

Cran-raspberry Smoothie

Easy

Ingredients:
1 cup nonfat vanilla yogurt
1 frozen banana
2 tbsp. frozen cranberry juice concentrate
⅓ cup frozen raspberries

Directions:
Combine all ingredients in blender and process until smooth and creamy.

Serves: 2

Shopping List:
8 oz. nonfat vanilla yogurt, banana, frozen cranberry juice concentrate, frozen raspberries

Nutrition per serving

calories:	170
total fat (0%):	0 g
carbohydrate:	38 g
cholesterol:	3 mg
dietary fiber:	3 g
protein:	5 g
sodium:	75 mg

Exchanges

½ milk
2 fruit

carbohydrate choice: 2½

DRINK YOUR WAY TO HEALTH

Cranberry juice may help control female bladder infections.

Dreamsicle Creamsicle Smoothie

Easy

Ingredients:
1 cup orange juice
1 cup nonfat vanilla yogurt

Directions:
Combine all ingredients in blender; process until smooth and creamy. For a slushier drink, add several ice cubes and blend. Garnish with orange slice, if desired.

Serves: 2

Shopping List:
8 oz. orange juice, 8 oz. nonfat vanilla yogurt

Nutrition per serving		Exchanges
calories:	146	½ milk
total fat (0%):	0 g	1½ fruit
carbohydrate:	30 g	
cholesterol:	2.5 mg	carbohydrate choice: 2
dietary fiber:	1 g	
protein:	6 g	
sodium:	71 mg	

Yogurt contains vitamin-B complex, which is essential for smooth, blemish-free skin.

"Kinango" Smoothie

Easy

Ingredients:
½ frozen banana, cut into 1-inch pieces
½ cup mangoes, peeled and sliced
½ cup kiwifruit, peeled and sliced
¼ cup frozen strawberries
¼ cup nonfat vanilla yogurt
¼ cup mango nectar
3 to 4 ice cubes

Directions:
Combine all ingredients in blender; process until smooth and creamy. Serve immediately; leftovers can be refrigerated and reblended the next day.

Serves: 2

Shopping List:
banana, mango, kiwifruit, frozen strawberries, nonfat vanilla yogurt, mango nectar

Nutrition per serving

calories:	142
total fat (6%):	1 g
carbohydrate:	35 g
cholesterol:	1 mg
dietary fiber:	5 g
protein:	2 g
sodium:	25 mg

Exchanges
1 fruit
1 other carbohydrate

carbohydrate choice: 2

Foods rich in soluble fiber bind with cholesterol and pull it out of the body, decreasing blood cholesterol and, therefore, reducing the risk of heart disease.

DRINK YOUR WAY TO HEALTH

Mango Colada Smoothie

Easy

Ingredients:

1 frozen banana, peeled and cut into 1-inch pieces
1½ cups sorbet (pineapple, coconut, or pina colada)
¾ cup canned pineapple chunks in juice, undrained
¾ cup ice cubes
¾ cup mango nectar
½ tsp. coconut extract (optional)

Directions:

Combine all ingredients in blender; process until smooth and creamy.

Serves: 2

Shopping List:

12 to 16 oz. container sorbet (flavor of choice), 8 oz. canned pineapple chunks in juice, 6 oz. mango nectar, banana, coconut extract (optional)

Nutrition per serving

calories:	208
fat (0%):	0 g
carbohydrate:	57 g
cholesterol:	0 mg
dietary fiber:	1 g
protein:	1 g
sodium:	5 mg

Exchanges

3 fruit
1 other carbohydrate

carbohydrate choice: 4

Bananas are potassium-rich to help muscles function properly and prevent cramps during workouts. Great preworkout food!

Mellow Mango Shake

Easy

Ingredients:
1½ cups frozen mango chunks
1 cup nonfat frozen vanilla yogurt
1 cup orange juice
1 cup ice cubes
¾ tsp. vanilla

Directions:
Combine all ingredients in blender and process until smooth and creamy. Garnish with orange slice, if desired.

Serves: 2

Shopping List:
frozen mango chunks, 8 oz. frozen nonfat vanilla yogurt, 8 oz. orange juice, vanilla

Nutrition per serving

calories:	299
total fat (3%):	1 g
carbohydrate:	70 g
cholesterol:	0 mg
dietary fiber:	6 g
protein:	6 g
sodium:	66 mg

Exchanges

4½ other carbohydrate

carbohydrate choice: 4½

DRINK YOUR WAY TO HEALTH

Mangoes are a real "powerfood" with a high content of vitamins A and C. They are also a good source of insoluble fiber. Mangoes contain as much vitamin C as an orange.

Melon-Berry Slush

Easy

Ingredients:
1 cup watermelon, seeded and diced
1 cup diced cantaloupe
1 cup frozen unsweetened strawberries
¼ cup strawberry sorbet

Directions:
Combine all ingredients in blender and process until slushy. Add several ice cubes if thicker consistency is desired.

Serves: 2

Shopping List:
seedless watermelon, cantaloupe, frozen unsweetened strawberries, strawberry sorbet

Nutrition per serving

calories:	105
total fat (9%):	1 g
carbohydrate:	27 g
cholesterol:	0 mg
dietary fiber:	3 g
protein:	2 g
sodium:	10 mg

Exchanges

1½ fruit
½ other carbohydrate

carbohydrate choice: ½

Whole melons can stay unrefrigerated for several days, but they must be covered and refrigerated once they are cut.

Melon Mix

Easy

Ingredients:
1 cup honeydew melon chunks
½ cup cantaloupe chunks
1 frozen banana
1 cup nonfat vanilla yogurt
½ cup crushed ice

Directions:
Combine all ingredients in blender and process until smooth and creamy.

Serves: 2

Shopping List:
honeydew melon, cantaloupe, banana, 8 oz. nonfat vanilla yogurt

Nutrition per serving

calories:	141
total fat (0%):	0 g
carbohydrate:	32 g
cholesterol:	3 mg
dietary fiber:	2 g
protein:	5 g
sodium:	83 mg

Exchanges

½ milk
1½ fruit

carbohydrate choice: 2

One-half cantaloupe provides more vitamin A (beta-carotene) and vitamin C than most other fruits. It is ranked just behind broccoli as a top ten fruit and vegetable in overall nutritional content.

Papaya-Berry Smoothie

Easy

Ingredients:

1 cup pineapple juice
1 cup frozen unsweetened strawberries
¾ cup diced papaya
1 frozen banana
ice

Directions:

Combine all ingredients in blender and process until smooth and creamy.

Serves: 2

Shopping List:

8 oz. pineapple juice, frozen unsweetened strawberries, papaya, banana

Nutrition per serving		Exchanges
calories:	164	3 fruit
total fat (0%):	0 g	
carbohydrate:	41 g	carbohydrate choice: 3
cholesterol:	0 mg	
dietary fiber:	3 g	
protein:	2 g	
sodium:	5 mg	

**Papaya breaks down uric and toxic acids,
unwanted substances in the body. Papaya is also
good for inflammation, heartburn, ulcers,
back pain and digestive system disorders.**

Paradise Smoothie

Easy

Ingredients:
¾ cup pineapple-orange juice
¼ cup canned crushed pineapple
¼ cup nonfat yogurt (pineapple, vanilla, strawberry-banana, or flavor of choice)
½ frozen banana, cut into pieces
1½ tsp. frozen pineapple juice concentrate (or berry-flavored)
¼ tsp. vanilla extract
¼ tsp. pineapple extract
¼ tsp. coconut extract
3 ice cubes

Directions:
Combine all ingredients in blender; process until smooth and creamy. Garnish with pineapple slice, if desired.

Serves: 2

Shopping List:
6 oz. pineapple-orange juice, 8 oz. can crushed pineapple in juice, nonfat yogurt (flavor of choice), banana, frozen juice concentrate (flavor of choice), vanilla extract, pineapple extract, coconut extract

Nutrition per serving

calories:	102
total fat (0%):	0 g
carbohydrate:	23 g
cholesterol:	1 mg
dietary fiber:	1 g
protein:	2 g
sodium:	20 mg

Exchanges
½ other carbohydrate
1 fruit

carbohydrate choice: 1½

A recent study published in the Journal of the American Medical Association indicated that people with a high risk for colon cancer may be able to reduce their risk by consuming at least 1,200 mg of calcium each day.

DRINK YOUR WAY TO HEALTH

Peach Melba

Easy

Ingredients:
1 cup chopped peaches
1 cup peach nectar
½ cup frozen raspberries
1 cup nonfat yogurt (peach or raspberry)
½ cup crushed ice

Directions:
Combine all ingredients in blender and process until smooth and creamy.

Serves: 2

Shopping List:
peach, 8 oz. peach nectar, frozen raspberries, 8 oz. nonfat yogurt (peach or raspberry)

Nutrition per serving		Exchanges
calories:	146	½ milk
total fat (0%):	0 g	1½ fruit
carbohydrate:	33 g	
cholesterol:	3 mg	carbohydrate choice: 2
dietary fiber:	2 g	
protein:	5 g	
sodium:	79 mg	

Although diets low in nutrition result in feelings of fatigue, only 23% of Americans eat the recommended five or more servings of fruits and vegetables each day. In 1995, the average American consumed twelve pounds of candy, up from ten pounds in 1983.

Peach 'n' Ginger Smoothie

Easy

Ingredients:
1 cup nonfat yogurt (peach or vanilla)
1 tbsp. honey
1 cup frozen peaches, chopped
1 piece crystallized ginger
¼ cup ice

Directions:
Combine all ingredients except ice in blender; process until smooth and creamy. Add crushed ice and process until frothy.

Serves: 2

Shopping List:
8 oz. nonfat yogurt (vanilla or peach), frozen peaches, crystallized ginger, honey

Nutrition per serving

calories:	144
total fat (0%):	0 g
carbohydrate:	32 g
cholesterol:	3 mg
dietary fiber:	6 g
protein:	5 g
sodium:	71 mg

Exchanges
½ milk
1 fruit
½ other carbohydrate

carbohydrate choice: 2

Ginger soothes stomach upset and improves digestion.

Peachy Clean Slushie

Easy

Ingredients:

2 cups sugar-free pink lemonade
1 cup ice cubes, divided
½ cup fresh strawberries, cut in half with stems removed
½ cup frozen sliced peaches

Directions:

Combine all ingredients in blender; process until smooth and creamy. Garnish glass with fresh strawberry or peach slice, if desired.

Serves: 2

Shopping List:

16 oz. sugar-free pink lemonade, fresh strawberries, frozen peach slices

Nutrition per serving		Exchanges
calories:	125	1 fruit
total fat (0%):	0 g	1 other carbohydrate
carbohydrate:	33 g	
cholesterol:	0 mg	carbohydrate choice: 2
dietary fiber:	2 g	
protein:	0 g	
sodium:	2 mg	

Strawberries are rich in anthocyanins, antioxidants that protect against cancer and the mental decline associated with aging. Good news: Frozen and dried varieties of berries are just as nutritious as fresh!

Piña Colada Smoothie

Easy

Ingredients:
 1 cup nonfat yogurt (pina colada or pineapple)
 1 banana, cut in pieces
 ¼ to ½ tsp. coconut extract to taste
 ice
 ½ cup pineapple juice

Directions:
 Combine all ingredients in blender; add enough ice to make smoothie the consistency you desire. Garnish glass with fresh pineapple slice, if desired.

Serves: 2

Shopping List:
 8 oz. nonfat yogurt (pina colada, pineapple, vanilla, or flavor of choice), banana, 4 oz. pineapple juice, coconut extract

Nutrition per serving		Exchanges
calories:	133	½ milk
total fat (0%):	0 g	1½ fruit
carbohydrate:	29 g	
cholesterol:	3 mg	carbohydrate choice: 2
dietary fiber:	1 g	
protein:	5 g	
sodium:	71 mg	

Yogurt has more than twice the calcium as cottage cheese and more calcium than milk. One cup yogurt provides 300 to 450 mg calcium (25 to 50% RDA).

DRINK YOUR WAY TO HEALTH

Pumpkin Spice Smoothie
Easy

Ingredients:
1 cup canned pumpkin, chilled
½ cup evaporated skim milk
1 cup pineapple juice
½ cup bananas, peeled and sliced
3 tbsp. brown sugar
½ tsp. cinnamon

Directions:
Combine all ingredients in blender; process until smooth and creamy. Sprinkle with cinnamon before serving, if desired.

Serves: 2

Shopping List:
8 oz. canned pumpkin, 4 oz. evaporated skim milk, 8 oz. pineapple juice, banana, brown sugar, cinnamon

Nutrition per serving		**Exchanges**
calories:	133	1½ fruit
total fat (0%):	0 g	½ other carbohydrate
carbohydrate:	31 g	
cholesterol:	1 mg	carbohydrate choice: 2
dietary fiber:	2 g	
protein:	3 g	
sodium:	44 mg	

Pumpkin, also known as the "king of squash," provides 16 milligrams of beta-carotene in a ½ cup serving.

Raspberry-Lemon Smoothie

Easy

Ingredients:
1 cup nonfat raspberry yogurt
½ cup orange juice
1 cup frozen raspberries
1 tbsp. lemon juice
½ cup crushed ice

Directions:
Combine all ingredients in blender; process until smooth and creamy.

Serves: 2

Shopping List:
8 oz. nonfat raspberry yogurt, 4 oz. orange juice, 10 oz. frozen raspberries, lemon juice

Nutrition per serving		Exchanges
calories:	204	1 fruit
total fat (0%):	0 g	1 milk
carbohydrate:	47 g	1 other carbohydrate
cholesterol:	3 mg	
dietary fiber:	6 g	carbohydrate choice: 3
protein:	5 g	
sodium:	72 mg	

Raspberries are a great source of vitamin C, an antioxidant that helps fight fatigue and depression.

Strawberry-Kiwi Slush

Easy

Ingredients:
1½ cups strawberries
1 kiwifruit, peeled and sliced
1 cup strawberry-orange juice
½ cup strawberry sorbet
½ cup crushed ice

Directions:
Combine all ingredients in blender and process until smooth and creamy.

Serves: 2

Shopping List:
1 pint strawberries, kiwifruit, 8 oz. strawberry-orange juice, 4 oz. strawberry sorbet

Nutrition per serving		Exchanges
calories:	162	2 fruit
total fat (6%):	1 g	1 other carbohydrate
carbohydrate:	41 g	
cholesterol:	0 mg	carbohydrate choice: 3
dietary fiber:	5 g	
protein:	2 g	
sodium:	4 mg	

One kiwifruit contains 46 calories and supplies more than twice the RDA for vitamin C, vitamin K, and potassium, which may help reduce high blood pressure. Two kiwifruit contain the same amount of fiber as 1 cup of bran flakes.

Strawberry Plus Smoothie

Easy

Ingredients:
- 1 cup frozen strawberries
- 1 banana, cut into 1-inch pieces
- 1 cup apple juice
- 1 tbsp. flaxseed meal
- 3 to 4 ice cubes

Directions:
Combine all ingredients in blender; process until smooth and creamy.

Serves: 2

Shopping List:
10 oz. frozen strawberries, banana, 8 oz. apple juice, flaxseed meal (can be purchased in the health section of most grocery stores)

Nutrition per serving		Exchanges
calories:	146	1½ fruit
total fat (12%):	2 g	½ other carbohydrate
carbohydrate:	33 g	
cholesterol:	0 mg	carbohydrate choice: 2
dietary fiber:	4 g	
protein:	2 g	
sodium:	10 mg	

According to the **Tufts University Health and Nutrition Letter,** *flaxseed is the number one nutritional fad, but also contains plant lignans that work as phytochemicals and antioxidants. Flaxseed is also an excellent source of fiber and omega-3 fatty acids, essential nutrients for forming cell walls and reducing the risk of heart disease.*

Tropical Mango Smoothie

Easy

Ingredients:
- ½ cup orange juice
- ½ cup canned pineapple chunks, drained
- 1 cup frozen strawberries
- 1 mango, peeled and cut into pieces
- 1 banana, cut in pieces
- 3 ice cubes

Directions:

Combine all ingredients in blender; process until smooth and creamy.

Serves: 2

Nutrition per serving		**Exchanges**
calories:	308	5 fruit
total fat (3%):	1 g	
carbohydrate:	80 g	carbohydrate choice: 5
cholesterol:	0 mg	
dietary fiber:	14 g	
protein:	2 g	
sodium:	8 mg	

Shopping List:

4 oz. orange juice, canned pineapple cubes in juice, 10 oz. frozen strawberries, mango, banana

Mangoes are high in vitamin A and contain beta-carotene. One serving (½ mango) provides 40% of the vitamin A your body needs each day for good health.

DRINK YOUR WAY TO HEALTH

DELECTABLE DESSERTS

Delicious
Enjoyable
Scrumptious
Savory
Enticing
Rich
Temptations

DESSERT . . . as American as apple pie! Now you can have
**your cake and eat it too! Desserts no longer need to be fat-laden,
calorie-dense, guilt-inducing indulgences. Try out some of these
savory sweets you can create with simple substitutions. Use these
tips throughout the year—cut the fat without cutting the flavor!
All you'll miss are the calories and fat!**

- Use fruit-based substitutes (applesauce, apple butter,
  pureed prunes, etc.) in place of butter or margarine in most
  cookie, muffin, and cake recipes. Substituting ¼ cup
  applesauce for ¼ cup butter will save 350 calories and 45
  grams of fat!

- Substitute nonfat ricotta cheese, cream cheese, or cottage
  cheese when preparing cheesecakes. Save 92 to 560 calories,
  10 to 80 fat grams per cup!

- Substitute nonfat yogurt or 1 cup skim milk + 1½
  tablespoons lemon juice in place of buttermilk. Save 13
  calories, 2+ fat grams per cup (savings based on cultured
  fluid buttermilk and skim milk).

- Frost nonfat cakes with marshmallow cream instead of high-
  fat frosting and save 26 calories, 5 fat grams per OUNCE!

- Create flavorful piecrusts by combining nonfat cookie
  crumbs, graham cracker crumbs, cornflake crumbs, or
  crushed granola with low-sugar preserves, Butter Buds, or
  nonfat yogurt.

- Substitute egg whites or nonfat egg substitute for whole
  eggs. Use ½ cup egg substitute or 2 egg whites per egg and
  save 30 to 38 calories and 4 grams of fat per whole egg.

- Substitute dried fruits, nonfat granola or GrapeNuts cereal
  for nuts in baked goods and save yourself 72 calories and
  18 grams of fat per OUNCE!

- Use almond extract to give a nutty flavor to cookies, muffins, and cakes. If a recipe calls for 1 teaspoon vanilla, substitute ¾ teaspoon almond extract, and ¼ teaspoon vanilla.
- Use nonfat dessert syrup to make delicious ice cream or frozen yogurt desserts. Try nonfat versions of chocolate, butterscotch, or chocolate-raspberry sauce over your favorite frozen treat; top with maraschino cherries, sliced bananas, or fresh berries for a low-cal sundae special.
- Use 1 cup undiluted evaporated skim milk in place of light cream; save calories, 28 fat grams per cup. If a recipe calls for whole cream, substitute 1 cup powdered nonfat nondairy creamer + 1 cup hot water.
- Skip the whipped cream and substitute whipped, chilled evaporated skim milk or easy-prep nonfat Cool Whip; save 54 calories and 11 grams of fat per H cup!)
- Add chocolate flavor with unsweetened cocoa powder, chocolate extract, or a sprinkling of reduced-fat chocolate chips.

BAKERS BEWARE . . .
Not all ingredients are created equal! For successful baking . . .

- Try one substitution at a time in a recipe or substitute only half of an ingredient for another.
- Don't assume a fat-free counterpart of an ingredient will guarantee the same result! Many nonfat ingredients are enhanced with extra water or gelatin that may break down when heated.
- To maintain soft, moist texture, use cake flour (it doesn't absorb as much water as high-protein or all-purpose flour).

Almond Biscotti

Average — Do Ahead — Freeze

Ingredients:

2 cups flour
1 tsp. baking powder
1¼ cups sugar, divided
2 egg whites
¼ cup + 1 tbsp. egg substitute

1 tsp. almond extract
2 tsp. cinnamon
butter-flavored cooking
   spray

Directions:

Preheat oven to 350 degrees. Line baking sheet with foil and spray with cooking spray. Combine flour and baking powder in a large mixing bowl; mix well. Combine 1 cup sugar, egg whites, egg substitute, and almond extract in medium bowl; beat with electric mixer at high speed until mixture is frothy. Make a well in the center of the flour mixture; pour egg mixture into center and mix until ingredients are moistened. Knead the dough to hold together. Divide dough in half. Shape into two logs and place on baking sheet about 1 inch apart. Bake 25 to 30 minutes, until golden brown. Remove from oven and let cool for 10 minutes. Using a serrated knife cut the logs into ⅜-inch-thick slices. Arrange in single layer on baking sheet. Combine cinnamon and remaining sugar in small bowl; mix well. Lightly spray cookies with butter-flavored cooking spray; sprinkle with cinnamon-sugar mixture. Bake 10 minutes; turn cookies over, sprinkle, and bake an additional 5 to 10 minutes until lightly browned. These cookies can be stored in tin for several weeks or frozen for several months.

Serves: 12

Shopping List:

flour, sugar, baking powder, whole eggs, egg substitute, almond extract, cinnamon, butter-flavored cooking spray

Nutrition per serving		Exchanges
calories:	159	2½ other carbohydrates
total fat (0%):	0 g	
carbohydrate:	37 g	carbohydrate choice: 2½
cholesterol:	0 mg	
dietary fiber:	1 g	
protein:	3 g	
sodium:	46 mg	

By substituting a recipe with egg whites or egg substitutes you save 10 grams of fat and 400 milligrams of cholesterol.

Amaretto Baked Alaska

Average — Do Ahead — Freeze

Ingredients:
4 slices Entenmann's nonfat golden loaf cake (1-inch slices)
¼ cup amaretto liqueur
2 cups nonfat cherry-vanilla frozen yogurt
4 egg whites
½ cup sugar
4 maraschino cherries

Directions:
Line baking sheet with foil. Arrange cake slices 4 inches apart on baking sheet; brush each slice with amaretto. Place 1 large scoop frozen yogurt in center of each cake slice. Freeze several hours or overnight. (If freezing overnight, cover with plastic wrap after 1 to 2 hours.) Preheat oven to 450 degrees. In a large bowl, beat egg whites with electric mixer until soft peaks form. Gradually beat in sugar until meringue forms stiff, shiny peaks. Divide meringue among yogurt-topped cake slices, covering yogurt completely. Swirl meringue with back of spoon for decorative design. Bake 3 to 5 minutes until meringue is lightly browned. Top each serving with maraschino cherry and serve immediately.

Serves: 4

DELECTABLE DESSERTS

Shopping List:
Entenmann's nonfat golden loaf cake, 1 pint nonfat frozen yogurt (cherry-vanilla or flavor of choice), eggs, sugar, 2 oz. amaretto liqueur, maraschino cherries

Nutrition per serving		Exchanges
calories:	449	6 other carbohydrate
total fat (0%):	0 g	
carbohydrate:	92 g	carbohydrate choice: 6
cholesterol:	0 mg	
dietary fiber:	1 g	
protein:	12 g	
sodium:	365 mg	

Fewer than 8% of all cases of colorectal cancer are genetically related—most are diet-related!

Apricot-Peach Soufflé

Average

Ingredients:
    16 oz. canned peaches in syrup, drained
    16 oz. canned apricots, drained
    2 tbsp. cornstarch
    2 tbsp. skim milk
    3 egg whites
    ½ cup sugar

Directions:
    Preheat oven to 400 degrees. Place peaches and apricots in food processor or blender; process until smooth (set aside 2 to 2½ cups pureed fruit). Combine cornstarch and milk in medium bowl; mix until paste forms. Add reserved pureed fruit and blend. In a separate bowl, beat egg whites with electric mixer until soft peaks form; add sugar and continue beating until peaks are stiff and glossy. Carefully fold half the egg whites in the fruit mixture; fold fruit mixture back into remaining egg whites. Spoon batter into six custard cups. Set the cups in a deep baking pan and pour hot water (about 1 inch) into the pan. Bake 25 to 30 minutes until soufflés are puffy; serve immediately.

Serves: 6

Shopping List:
    16 oz. canned peaches in syrup, 16 oz. canned apricots, cornstarch, skim milk, sugar, eggs

DELECTABLE DESSERTS

Nutrition per serving		Exchanges
calories:	198	2 fruit
total fat (0%):	0 g	1 other carbohydrate
carbohydrate:	50 g	
cholesterol:	0 mg	carbohydrate choice: 3
dietary fiber:	2 g	
protein:	3 g	
sodium:	35 mg	

Apricots are power packed with carotene, the plant form of vitamin A. Three raw apricots provide half the RDA for carotene. With little or no fat, sodium, and cholesterol, apricots are good for your heart.

Banana Split with Mixed Berry Sauce

Easy — Do Ahead

Ingredients:
1 cup frozen unsweetened mixed berries
2½ tbsp. sugar
1½ tsp. cornstarch
1½ tsp. lemon juice
2 bananas, cut in half lengthwise
2 cups nonfat frozen yogurt (flavor of choice)

Directions:
Combine frozen berries, sugar, cornstarch, and lemon juice in small saucepan; bring to a boil over medium-high heat, stirring frequently. Remove from heat; pour berry sauce into glass or plastic bowl and refrigerate 15 to 20 minutes before serving. Place 1 banana slice in each dessert dish; top with ½ cup frozen yogurt and drizzle with mixed berry sauce.

Serves: 4

Shopping List:
1 pint nonfat frozen yogurt (flavor of choice), 10 oz. package frozen mixed berries, 2 bananas, sugar, cornstarch, lemon juice

Nutrition per serving		Exchanges
calories:	210	1 fruit
total fat (0%):	0 g	2 other carbohydrate
carbohydrate:	49 g	
cholesterol:	0 mg	carbohydrate choice: 3
dietary fiber:	2 g	
protein:	5 g	
sodium:	61 mg	

Bananas are known for their high levels of potassium, but they are also a good source of calcium and magnesium, essential minerals for proper nervous system and muscular function.

Berrrrry Shortcake

Easy

Ingredients:
6 oz. nonfat Cool Whip, thawed
1 cup sliced strawberries
1 cup raspberries
1 cup blueberries
8 slices nonfat Entenmann's nonfat golden loaf

Directions:
Spoon dessert topping into medium bowl; add berries and toss lightly until mixed. Place one slice pound cake on each dessert plate; top with fruit dessert topping. Repeat layers.

Serves: 4

Shopping List:
Entenmann's nonfat golden loaf, 8 oz. nonfat Cool Whip dessert topping, ½ pint strawberries, ½ pint raspberries, ½ pint blueberries

DELECTABLE DESSERTS

Nutrition per serving		Exchanges
calories:	512	7 ½ other carbohydrate
total fat (0%):	0 g	
carbohydrate:	114 g	carbohydrate choice: 7 ½
cholesterol:	0 mg	
dietary fiber:	5 g	
protein:	9 g	
sodium:	494 mg	

Raspberries and blueberries rank among the top three fruits highest in fiber: 1 cup raspberries contain 5.5 grams of fiber; 1 cup blueberries contain 4.00 grams of fiber.

Berry-ful Cheesecake Pie

Easy — Do Ahead

Ingredients:
- 1 cup sliced strawberries
- 1 cup raspberries, rinsed and dried
- 2 tbsp. sugar
- 1 low-fat graham cracker crust
- 1 cup nonfat cream cheese, softened
- ¾ tsp. almond extract
- 2 cups cold skim milk, divided
- 3⅜ oz. sugar-free instant vanilla pudding mix

Directions:
Combine strawberries, raspberries, and sugar in a medium bowl; toss until fruit is coated and spoon into piecrust. Combine cream cheese, almond extract, and ½ cup milk in mixing bowl; beat until creamy and smooth. Add pudding mix and remaining milk; beat until blended smooth. Pour cheese mixture over fruit; cover and refrigerate several hours or overnight before serving.

Serves: 8

Shopping List:
low-fat graham cracker crust, ½ pint strawberries, ½ pint raspberries, 8 oz. nonfat cream cheese, 16 oz. skim milk, 3½ oz. sugar-free instant vanilla pudding mix, sugar, almond extract

DELECTABLE DESSERTS

Nutrition per serving		Exchanges
calories:	173	2 other carbohydrate
total fat (5%):	1 g	
carbohydrate:	35 g	carbohydrate choice: 2
cholesterol:	1 mg	
dietary fiber:	4 g	
protein:	8 g	
sodium:	605 mg	

Eight strawberries provide more vitamin C than an orange; 20% of the RDA for folic acid; and 50 calories per serving without cholesterol or fat.

Blueberry Lemon Cake

Average — Do Ahead — Freeze

Ingredients:

1½ cups flour
1½ cups cake flour
2 tsp. baking powder
1½ cups sugar
½ cup brown sugar
1 tbsp. grated lemon zest
1⅓ cups egg substitute

½ cup unsweetened
   applesauce
2½ tsp. lemon extract,
   divided
1½ cups + 2 tbsp. skim
   milk, divided
2 cups blueberries, pureed
1 cup powdered sugar

Directions:

Preheat oven to 350 degrees. Spray Bundt pan with cooking spray. In a large mixing bowl, combine flour, cake flour, baking powder, sugar, brown sugar, and lemon zest; mix until ingredients are blended. Add egg substitute, applesauce, lemon extract, and 1½ cups milk to flour mixture; mix well. Remove 1 cup cake batter and place in medium bowl. Add blueberry puree and blend well. Spoon half the remaining cake batter into Bundt pan; top with half the blueberry mixture. Swirl batters with a knife. Alternately spoon remaining plain and blueberry batters into Bundt pan; swirl through. Bake 60 to 80 minutes, until toothpick inserted in center comes out clean. Remove from oven and cool completely. Combine powdered sugar with 2 tablespoons milk and ½ teaspoon lemon extract; blend until smooth and creamy. Drizzle lemon glaze over cooled cake.

Serves: 12

Shopping List:

16 oz. skim milk, 12 oz. egg substitute, 4 oz. unsweetened applesauce, 1 pint blueberries, flour, cake flour, sugar, brown sugar, powdered sugar, baking powder, grated lemon zest, lemon extract

Nutrition per serving		Exchanges
calories:	306	5 other carbohydrate
total fat (0%):	0 g	
carbohydrate:	71 g	carbohydrate choice: 5
cholesterol:	.5 mg	
dietary fiber:	1 g	
protein:	6 g	
sodium:	110 mg	

Blueberries have been found to prevent urinary tract infections. One-half cup blueberries a day is sufficient.

Blueberry Rice Pudding

Easy — Do Ahead

Ingredients:
1 cup short grain rice, uncooked
1¾ cups water
½ cup sugar
½ cup evaporated skim milk
1 cup fresh blueberries, rinsed and dried

Directions:
Combine rice and water in a small saucepan; bring to a boil over medium heat. Reduce heat to low, cover, and simmer 15 to 18 minutes until tender. Add sugar and evaporated milk; cover pan and simmer over low heat 8 to 10 minutes. Remove pan from heat and fold in blueberries. Let pudding stand at room temperature 1 to 2 hours.

Serves: 4

Shopping List:
short grain rice, ½ pint blueberries, 4 oz. evaporated skim milk, sugar

Nutrition per serving		**Exchanges**
calories:	304	2 starch
total fat (3%):	1 g	1 fruit
carbohydrate:	70 g	1½ other carbohydrate
cholesterol:	1 mg	
dietary fiber:	1 g	carbohydrate choice: 4½
protein:	6 g	
sodium:	41 mg	

__Blueberries have been ranked number one in antioxidant activity compared with forty other fruits and vegetables.__

Brown Rice Pudding

Easy — Do Ahead

Ingredients:
2 cups cooked brown rice
1 cup skim milk
¾ tsp. ground nutmeg
¾ tsp. cinnamon
2 tbsp. wheat germ
⅓ cup dried fruit
2 tbsp. brown sugar

Directions:
Combine cooked rice, milk, nutmeg, cinnamon, wheat germ, and dried fruit in a medium saucepan; simmer over medium-low heat until heated through. Sprinkle with brown sugar and toss lightly. Serve hot or cold.

Serves: 4

Shopping List:
8 oz. skim milk, brown rice, dried fruit (dates, raisins, apricots, apples, or mixed fruit), brown sugar, wheat germ, ground nutmeg, cinnamon

Nutrition per serving

calories:	213	
total fat (8%):	2 g	
carbohydrate:	46 g	
cholesterol:	1 mg	
dietary fiber:	2 g	
protein:	6 g	
sodium:	36 mg	

Exchanges
½ milk
1½ starch
1 fruit

carbohydrate choice: 3

Dried fruits are excellent substitutes for foods high in refined sugar—the fiber helps slow down absorption of sugar into the blood and helps stabilize blood-sugar levels.

Caramel Bread Pudding

Easy — Do Ahead

Ingredients:
6 slices day-old French bread, cut into ½-inch cubes
1 cup brown sugar
1 cup hot water
1 cup egg substitute
2 cups skim milk, warmed
½ cup sugar
¾ tsp. vanilla
¾ tsp. cinnamon
¼ tsp. nutmeg

Directions:
Preheat oven to 350 degrees. Spray 2- or 3-quart baking dish with cooking spray. Place bread cubes in baking dish; combine brown sugar and hot water in medium bowl and mix until sugar dissolves. Pour sugar mixture over bread. Combine remaining ingredients; pour into dish and bake 45 to 60 minutes, until knife inserted in center comes out clean. Serve with nonfat Cool Whip, whipped cream, or frozen yogurt, if desired.

Serves: 6

DELECTABLE DESSERTS

Shopping List:
French bread, 8 oz. egg substitute, 16 oz. skim milk, brown sugar, sugar, vanilla, cinnamon, nutmeg

Nutrition per serving		Exchanges
calories:	343	4 other carbohydrate
total fat (5%):	2 g	1 starch
carbohydrate:	74 g	
cholesterol:	1 mg	carbohydrate choice: 5
dietary fiber:	1 g	
protein:	9 g	
sodium:	300 mg	

The Surgeon General's Report states, "For two out of three adult Americans who do not smoke and do not drink excessively, one personal choice seems to influence long-term health prospects more than any other: what we eat."

Cinnamon-Sugar Fruit Compote

Easy — Do Ahead

Ingredients:
29 oz. can peach halves in juice, drained
20 oz. can pineapple chunks in juice, drained
16 oz. can pear halves in light syrup, drained
½ cup maraschino cherries
½ cup brown sugar
1½ tsp. cinnamon

Directions:
Preheat oven to 350 degrees. Combine fruit in 9 x 13-inch baking dish. Combine brown sugar and cinnamon in a small bowl; mix well. Sprinkle sugar mixture over fruit and bake 35 to 45 minutes until bubbly and hot. Serve warm.

Serves: 6

Shopping List:
29 oz. can peach halves in juice, 20 oz. can pineapple chunks in juice, 16 oz. can pear halves in light syrup, maraschino cherries, brown sugar, cinnamon

Nutrition per serving		Exchanges
calories:	250	2½ fruit
total fat (0%):	0 g	1½ other carbohydrate
carbohydrate:	64 g	
cholesterol:	0 mg	carbohydrate choice: 4
dietary fiber:	1 g	
protein:	1 g	
sodium:	37 mg	

Peaches provide modest amounts of vitamins A and C while low in fat and sodium.

Craisin-Raisin Sour Cream Bars

Easy — Do Ahead — Freeze

Ingredients:

2 tbsp. reduced calorie margarine, melted
2 tbsp. cinnamon applesauce
⅔ cup sugar
1½ tsp. vanilla
1 cup nonfat sour cream
2 egg whites

¼ cup egg substitute
1½ cups flour
¾ tsp. baking soda
¾ tsp. baking powder
½ cup raisins
¼ cup Craisins

Directions:

Preheat oven to 350 degrees. Spray 8-inch baking dish with cooking spray. Combine melted margarine, applesauce, sugar, vanilla, sour cream, egg whites, and egg substitute in a large bowl; mix until ingredients are creamy. Add flour; sprinkle baking soda and baking powder into flour and mix lightly. Stir flour mixture into creamy mixture until well combined. Fold in raisins and Craisins. Spoon batter into prepared pan and bake 25 to 35 minutes, until toothpick inserted in center comes out clean. Cool completely before cutting into squares.

Serves: 8

Shopping List:

8 oz. nonfat sour cream, egg substitute, eggs, reduced-calorie margarine, cinnamon applesauce, flour, sugar, vanilla, baking soda, baking powder, raisins, Craisins

Nutrition per serving

calories:	224
total fat (4%):	1 g
carbohydrate:	47 g
cholesterol:	0 mg
dietary fiber:	1 g
protein:	6 g
sodium:	181 mg

Exchanges

3 other carbohydrate

carbohydrate choice: 3

Dried fruits are a good source of beta-carotene, which prevents cancer and heart disease, and boosts vision, healthy skin, bones, and teeth.

Cran-Apple Crumble

Easy — Do Ahead

Ingredients:

¾ cup low-fat granola
¾ cup fresh cranberries
3 tbsp. maple-flavored syrup
3 tbsp. honey
¾ tsp. vanilla

3 apples, peeled, cored,
 and sliced
¼ cup brown sugar
¾ tsp. cinnamon

Directions:

Preheat oven to 375 degrees. Spray 8- or 9-inch baking dish with cooking spray. Combine granola and cranberries in food processor; process until crumbly (best to pulse pulverize so you don't overprocess). Pour granola mixture into large bowl. Combine syrup, honey, and vanilla in a small saucepan; simmer over medium heat, stirring constantly, until ingredients are heated through. Gradually pour syrup mixture over granola, mixing with hands to moisten and crumble. Place apple slices in baking dish; sprinkle with brown sugar and cinnamon. Top with granola mixture and bake 15 to 25 minutes until top is lightly browned and apples are soft. Top with nonfat Cool Whip or frozen yogurt, if desired.

Serves: 6

Shopping List:

3 apples, fresh cranberries, low-fat granola, maple-flavored syrup, honey, vanilla, brown sugar, cinnamon

Nutrition per serving

calories:	179
total fat (0%):	0 g
carbohydrate:	46 g
cholesterol:	0 mg
dietary fiber:	2 g
protein:	1 g
sodium:	15 mg

Exchanges

1 fruit
2 other carbohydrate

carbohydrate choice: 3

Two apples a day can cut cholesterol by 10%

Decorative Petit Fours

Easy — Do Ahead — Freeze

Ingredients:
1 Entenmann's nonfat golden loaf, frozen
1½ lb. powdered sugar
½ cup water
3 tbsp. light corn syrup
2 tsp. almond extract
decorative gel icing, sprinkles, mini candies, etc.

Directions:
Trim frozen cake on top to make flat surface; trim crust from sides. Cut cake in half horizontally; cut into squares or simple shapes with cookie cutters (you should have about twenty pieces). Arrange cake slices on waxed paper. Combine powdered sugar, water, corn syrup, and almond extract in medium bowl; blend until smooth and creamy. Spoon frosting over cake pieces to cover tops and sides; decorate petit fours with icing, sprinkles, candy, etc., if desired. Let cake set 30 to 45 minutes

Serves: 10

Shopping List:
Entenmann's nonfat golden loaf, 1½ lb. powdered sugar, light corn syrup, almond extract, toppings of choice (decorative gel, candies, sprinkles, etc.)

Nutrition per serving

calories:	435
total fat (0%):	0 g
carbohydrate:	107 g
cholesterol:	0 mg
dietary fiber:	1 g
protein:	3 g
sodium:	197 mg

Exchanges
7 other carbohydrate

carbohydrate choice: 7

Someone dies of cardiovascular disease every thirty-three seconds in the United States— reduce your risk by watching what you eat!

Devil's Apples

Easy — Do Ahead

Ingredients:

1½ cups cran-apple juice
½ cup sugar
½ tsp. cinnamon
1½ tsp. lemon juice
4 apples, peeled (leave whole with stem on)
1 tbsp. cinnamon red hots

Directions:

Combine cran-apple juice, sugar, cinnamon, and lemon juice in a medium saucepan; bring to a boil over medium-high heat, stirring constantly, until sugar is dissolved. Set apples in syrup; cover and cook 8 to 10 minutes until apples are tender. Using a slotted spoon, transfer apples to serving dish. Boil syrup to reduce to 1 cup; pour hot syrup over apples and sprinkle with cinnamon red hots. Let cool slightly before serving.

Serves: 4

Shopping List:

12 oz. cran-apple juice, 4 large apples, sugar, cinnamon, lemon juice, cinnamon red hot candy

Nutrition per serving		Exchanges
calories:	233	2 fruit
total fat (4%):	1 g	2 other carbohydrate
carbohydrate:	61 g	
cholesterol:	0 mg	carbohydrate choice: 4
dietary fiber:	3 g	
protein:	0 g	
sodium:	6 mg	

Apples are a rich source of soluble fiber, preventing sharp swings in blood-sugar levels.

Flan

Average — Do Ahead

Ingredients:

⅓ cup sugar
1½ cups evaporated skim milk
½ cup egg substitute
2 egg whites
2 tsp. vanilla

Directions:

Preheat oven to 350 degrees. Place sugar in small saucepan; cook over low heat, stirring constantly, until sugar is melted and golden brown. Divide sugar evenly among 4 custard cups; tilt cups to coat bottoms. Let stand at room temperature 5 minutes until hardened. Combine milk, egg substitute, egg whites, and vanilla in a medium bowl; mix until blended and frothy. Divide mixture among custard cups. Place cups in square baking dish; pour very hot water into dish within ½ inch of tops of cups. Bake 45 to 50 minutes, until knife inserted in center comes out clean. Remove custard cups from baking dish; unmold and refrigerate 4 to 6 hours before serving.

Serves: 4

Shopping List:

12 oz. can evaporated skim milk, 4 oz. egg substitute, whole eggs, sugar, vanilla

Nutrition per serving		**Exchanges**
calories:	163	1 very lean meat
total fat (0%):	0 g	½ milk
carbohydrate:	28 g	1½ other carbohydrate
cholesterol:	4 mg	
dietary fiber:	0 g	carbohydrate choice: 2
protein:	11 g	
sodium:	178 mg	

Evaporated skim milk has a thick, creamy consistency, similar to that created with heavy cream. Switch from heavy cream to evaporated skim milk and save 40 grams of fat and 300 calories for every ½ cup.

Frosted Banana-Date Cake

Easy — Do Ahead — Freeze

Ingredients:

1½ cups mashed bananas
⅓ cup unsweetened applesauce
¼ cup egg substitute
2 egg whites
½ cup sugar
¾ cup brown sugar
⅓ cup skim milk
1 tsp. lemon juice
1½ tsp. vanilla extract, divided

1½ cups all-purpose flour
1 cup whole-wheat flour
1½ tsp. baking powder
¼ tsp. baking soda
1½ cups chopped dates
8 oz. nonfat cream cheese, softened
⅓ cup powdered sugar

Directions:

Preheat oven to 350 degrees. Spray 9 x 13-inch baking dish with cooking spray. Combine bananas, applesauce, egg substitute, egg whites, sugar, brown sugar, milk, lemon juice, and 1 teaspoon vanilla in a large bowl; mix until creamy. Add flour, whole-wheat flour, baking powder, and baking soda to cream mixture; stir until ingredients are moistened and mixed. Fold in dates. Spread batter into prepared pan and bake 30 to 40 minutes, until toothpick inserted in center comes out clean. Cool cake completely. While cake is baking, prepare frosting: combine cream cheese, powdered sugar, and remaining vanilla in a medium bowl. Blend with electric mixer until smooth and creamy. Spread over cooled cake; store leftovers in refrigerator.

Serves: 24

Shopping List:

3 bananas, 8 oz. nonfat cream cheese, chopped dates, skim milk, egg substitute, whole eggs, unsweetened applesauce, lemon juice, all-purpose flour, whole-wheat flour, sugar, brown sugar, powdered sugar, vanilla extract, baking powder, baking soda

Nutrition per serving

calories:	148
total fat (0%):	0 g
carbohydrate:	34 g
cholesterol:	0 mg
dietary fiber:	2 g
protein:	4 g
sodium:	101 mg

Exchanges

2 other carbohydrate

carbohydrate choice: 2

Bananas contain vitamin B$_6$ important for protein, fat, and carbohydrate metabolism.

Fruitful of Surprise Yogurt Pops

Easy — Do Ahead — Freeze

Ingredients:
2 cups canned apricots packed in juice, drained
1 cup nonfat vanilla yogurt
2 tbsp. dried fruit pieces

Directions:
Combine apricots and yogurt in food processor or blender; process until smooth. Divide ½ the mixture evenly among 4 Popsicle molds or paper cups; sprinkle dried fruit pieces and top with remaining yogurt mixture. If using paper cups, insert craft stick in center of pop. Freeze until firm, about 3 to 5 hours.

Serves: 4

Shopping List:
16 oz. can apricots packed in juice, 8 oz. nonfat vanilla yogurt, dried fruit pieces

Nutrition per serving		Exchanges
calories:	113	½ milk
total fat (0%):	0 g	1½ fruit
carbohydrate:	26 g	
cholesterol:	1 mg	carbohydrate choice: 2
dietary fiber:	2 g	
protein:	4 g	
sodium:	40 mg	

DELECTABLE DESSERTS

***Apricots are a great source of vitamin A—
one apricot contains 18% of the
Recommended Daily Allowance for vitamin A.***

Granny's Fresh Apple Crumb Cake

Average — Do Ahead — Freeze

Ingredients:

1½ cups all-purpose flour
1 cup whole-wheat flour
1 cup brown sugar
½ cup sugar
1½ tbsp. cinnamon, divided
1 tsp. nutmeg
½ cup reconstituted Butter Buds
  (liquid form)

1 tsp. baking powder
1 tsp. baking soda
3 Granny Smith apples,
  peeled, cored, and
  chopped
½ cup egg substitute
1 tsp. vanilla
powdered sugar

Directions:

Preheat oven to 350 degrees. Spray 9 x 13-inch baking dish or 9-inch springform pan with cooking spray. Combine both flours, brown sugar, sugar, 1 tablespoon cinnamon, and nutmeg; mix well. Gradually drizzle Butter Buds into flour mixture; mix with hands after each addition until coarse crumbs form. Remove ½ cup crumb mixture; add remaining cinnamon and mix lightly. Set crumb mixture aside. Add baking powder, baking soda, apples, egg substitute, and vanilla to flour mixture. Mix until ingredients are blended. Batter will be thick. Spread batter in baking pan. Sprinkle reserved crumb mixture over batter. Bake 45 to 50 minutes until toothpick inserted in center comes out clean. Cool cake before removing from pan. Just before serving, sprinkle with powdered sugar.

Serves: 8

Shopping List:

3 Granny Smith apples, 4 oz. egg substitute, all-purpose flour, whole-wheat flour, sugar, brown sugar, powdered sugar, Butter Buds mix, baking powder, baking soda, cinnamon, nutmeg, vanilla extract

Nutrition per serving		Exchanges
calories:	336	4½ other carbohydrate
total fat (3%):	1 g	½ fruit
carbohydrate:	78 g	
cholesterol:	0 mg	carbohydrate choice: 5
dietary fiber:	4 g	
protein:	6 g	
sodium:	174 mg	

Apples contain quercetin, which helps prevent blood clots, reducing the risk of heart disease.

Melon-Berry Freeze

Easy — Do Ahead — Freeze

Ingredients:

2 cups cantaloupe cubes or balls
1 cup water
⅓ cup sugar
½ cup frozen strawberries
1 tbsp. lemon juice

Directions:

Place cantaloupe cubes in shallow dish; cover with plastic wrap and freeze 3 to 4 hours. Combine water and sugar in small saucepan; bring to a boil over medium-high heat and cook until mixture thickens (about 1 minute). Pour into small glass dish and refrigerate. Combine frozen cantaloupe, strawberries, sugar syrup, and lemon juice in blender; process until smooth and slushy. Garnish with fresh strawberries, if desired.

Serves: 4

Shopping List:

1 cantaloupe, frozen strawberries, sugar, lemon juice

Nutrition per serving

calories:	95
total fat (0%):	0 g
carbohydrate:	25 g
cholesterol:	0 mg
dietary fiber:	1 g
protein:	1 g
sodium:	8 mg

Exchanges

½ other carbohydrate
1 fruit

carbohydrate choice: 1½

DELECTABLE DESSERTS

Melons are a good source of soluble fiber, important for keeping the colon healthy.

Monkey's Favorite Frozen Yogurt
Easy — Do Ahead — Freeze

Ingredients:
1 envelope unflavored gelatin
⅓ cup cold water
⅓ cup honey
1 cup mashed bananas
1 tbsp. lemon juice
1 cup nonfat vanilla yogurt
2 tbsp. egg substitute
1 egg white

Directions:
Combine gelatin and cold water in a small saucepan; let stand without stirring 1 minute. Cook over medium heat, stirring constantly, until gelatin is dissolved. Stir in honey; remove from heat. Add bananas, lemon juice, and yogurt; mix until blended. Pour mixture into freezer-safe dish; freeze several hours until firm. Spoon mixture into large bowl; add egg substitute and egg whites. Beat on high speed with electric mixer until fluffy and smooth. Spoon back into freezer dish; freeze several hours before serving.

Serves: 6

Shopping List:
unflavored gelatin, 3 bananas, 8 oz. nonfat vanilla yogurt, egg substitute, whole egg, honey, lemon juice

Nutrition per serving		Exchanges
calories:	98	1½ other carbohydrate
total fat (0%):	0 g	
carbohydrate:	22 g	carbohydrate choice: 1½
cholesterol:	1 mg	
dietary fiber:	0 g	
protein:	3 g	
sodium:	37 mg	

Bananas, a low-sodium food, are heart-healthy, and fiber- and potassium-rich.

Orange Gingerbread Squares

Easy — Do Ahead — Freeze

Ingredients:

¾ cup all-purpose flour
½ cup whole-wheat flour
2 tsp. pumpkin pie spice
½ tsp. baking soda
½ tsp. baking powder
¼ cup cinnamon applesauce
¼ cup sugar
¼ cup brown sugar

½ cup orange juice
⅓ cup dark molasses
¼ cup egg substitute
¾ tsp. vanilla extract
½ cup chopped dates
½ cup nonfat Cool Whip

Directions:

Preheat oven to 375 degrees. Spray 8- or 9-inch baking dish with cooking spray. Combine flour, whole-wheat flour, pumpkin pie spice, baking soda, and baking powder in a medium bowl; mix well. Combine remaining ingredients except dates and Cool Whip in a large bowl; mix until blended smooth. Gradually pour flour mixture into large bowl and mix until all ingredients are moistened. Fold in dates. Spread batter into baking dish and bake 25 to 30 minutes, until toothpick inserted in center comes out clean. Let cool 10 to 15 minutes. Cut into squares and serve warm with a dollop of Cool Whip topping.

Serves: 8

Shopping List:

all-purpose flour, whole-wheat flour, sugar, brown sugar, dark molasses, pumpkin pie spice, baking powder, baking soda, vanilla extract, cinnamon applesauce, 4 oz. orange juice, egg substitute, chopped dates, nonfat Cool Whip

DELECTABLE DESSERTS

Nutrition per serving

calories:	203
total fat (0%):	0 g
carbohydrate:	48 g
cholesterol:	0 mg
dietary fiber:	2 g
protein:	3 g
sodium:	99 mg

Exchanges

3 other carbohydrate

carbohydrate choice: 3

Applesauce is a good substitute for fat in baked goods, low in calories and virtually fat-free.

Parfait with Powerful Punch

Easy — Do Ahead

Ingredients:
3 tbsp. nonfat granola cereal
1½ cups nonfat yogurt (pineapple, vanilla, or pina colada)
½ cup cantaloupe chunks, chopped
½ cup strawberries, chopped
½ cup kiwifruit, peeled and chopped

Directions:
Alternate layers of granola, yogurt, and fruit in parfait glasses or goblets, beginning and ending with granola cereal.

Serves: 2

Shopping List:
12 oz. nonfat yogurt (pineapple, vanilla, pina colada, or flavor of choice), cantaloupe, strawberries, kiwifruit, nonfat granola cereal

Nutrition per serving		Exchanges
calories:	142	½ milk
total fat (0%):	0 g	1 fruit
carbohydrate:	29 g	½ other carbohydrate
cholesterol:	4 mg	
dietary fiber:	3 g	carbohydrate choice: 2
protein:	7 g	
sodium:	311 mg	

Kiwifruit, also known as "Chinese gooseberry," is rich in vitamin C and potassium, which helps to keep blood pressure levels down.

Peach Melba Granola Crisp

Easy — Do Ahead

Ingredients:
1¼ cups nonfat or low-fat granola
¼ cup brown sugar
½ tsp. cinnamon
1 tbsp. reconstituted Butter Buds (liquid form)
4 cups canned raspberry-flavored peaches in light syrup,
   reserve 1¼ cups syrup
1⅓ tbsp. cornstarch
1 cup raspberries, fresh or frozen

Directions:
Preheat oven to 350 degrees. Spray square baking dish or pie plate with cooking spray. Combine granola, brown sugar, and cinnamon in a small bowl; drizzle with Butter Buds and mix lightly with fingers until slightly moistened and crumbly. Pour reserved syrup into a small skillet; add cornstarch and stir to blend. Bring to a boil over high heat, stirring constantly. Remove from heat; stir in peaches and raspberries. Spoon into baking dish; top with granola topping and bake 8 to 10 minutes until golden brown. Serve hot or cold.

Serves: 6

Shopping List:
nonfat or low-fat granola, 2 15½-oz. cans raspberry-flavored peaches in light syrup, ½ pint raspberries (fresh or frozen), brown sugar, cinnamon, cornstarch, Butter Buds

Nutrition per serving		Exchanges
calories:	187	2 fruit
total fat (0%):	0 g	1 other carbohydrate
carbohydrate:	48 g	
cholesterol:	0 mg	carbohydrate choice: 3
dietary fiber:	1 g	
protein:	2 g	
sodium:	12 mg	

**Peaches provide modest levels of vitamin A
and C, while low in calories and fat.**

"Pine-a-cot" Angel Cake

Easy — Do Ahead

Ingredients:
2½ cups crushed pineapple, undrained
1 tbsp. apricot or orange marmalade
2 tbsp. sugar
1 tbsp. cornstarch
1 angel food cake, sliced

Directions:
Combine pineapple, marmalade, sugar, and cornstarch in a small saucepan; bring to a boil over high heat. Immediately reduce heat to low and simmer, uncovered, stirring constantly until sauce thickens. Cool 5 to 10 minutes and serve over angel food cake slices.

Serves: 12

Shopping List:
20 oz. can crushed pineapple, apricot or orange marmalade, angel food cake (or mix), sugar, cornstarch

Nutrition per serving		Exchanges
calories:	185	3 other carbohydrate
total fat (0%):	0 g	
carbohydrate:	43 g	carbohydrate choice: 3
cholesterol:	0 mg	
dietary fiber:	0 g	
protein:	4 g	
sodium:	143 mg	

Pineapple is rich in manganese, a trace mineral that is needed to metabolize protein and carbohydrate.

Raspberry-Almond Bundt Cake

Easy — Do Ahead — Freeze

Ingredients:

3 tbsp. reduced calorie
margarine, melted
2 tbsp. applesauce
¾ cup sugar
¼ cup brown sugar
¼ cup egg substitute
2 egg whites
1 tsp. almond extract

½ cup nonfat vanilla yogurt
½ cup nonfat raspberry
yogurt
2 cups cake flour, divided
1¼ tsp. baking powder
½ tsp. baking soda
powdered sugar
2 cups fresh raspberries

Directions:

Preheat oven to 350 degrees. Spray Bundt pan with cooking spray. In a large mixing bowl combine melted margarine, applesauce, sugar, brown sugar, egg substitute, egg whites, almond extract, and yogurt; mix until smooth and creamy. Add 1 cup flour; sprinkle baking powder and baking soda over flour and mix into yogurt mixture. Add remaining flour and mix until smooth. Spread batter into prepared pan; bake 30 to 40 minutes, until toothpick inserted in center comes out clean. Let cool 10 minutes; invert pan on platter or rack and let cake cool completely. Sprinkle with powdered sugar; spoon fresh raspberries into center of cake and serve.

Serves: 8

Shopping List:

reduced-calorie margarine, egg substitute, whole eggs, nonfat vanilla yogurt, nonfat raspberry yogurt, applesauce, cake flour, sugar, brown sugar, powdered sugar, baking powder, baking soda, almond extract, 1 pint fresh raspberries

Nutrition per serving		Exchanges
calories:	275	4 other carbohydrate
total fat (7%):	2 g	
carbohydrate:	59 g	carbohydrate choice: 4
cholesterol:	1 mg	
dietary fiber:	2 g	
protein:	7 g	
sodium:	206 mg	

Raspberries are a good source of fiber, which reduces the time that cancer-causing chemicals are in your system, thus preventing colon cancer and other related diseases.

Rhubarb Crisp

Easy Do Ahead

Ingredients:

3 cups rhubarb, fresh or frozen, diced
½ cup flour, divided
½ cup sugar
1½ tsp. cinnamon
½ cup brown sugar
½ cup nonfat granola
1 tbsp. Butter Buds dry mix
water

Directions:

Preheat oven to 350 degrees. Spray 8-inch baking dish with cooking spray. Combine rhubarb, 1 tablespoon flour, sugar, and cinnamon in baking dish; toss until coated. Combine remaining flour, brown sugar, and granola in a medium bowl; mix well. Sprinkle Butter Buds mix over flour mixture. Sprinkle with water to moisten; toss mixture with hands until crumbly. Add several drops of water at a time (do not soak). If mixture becomes too moist, add small amounts of flour, sugar, and granola until crumbly. Sprinkle over rhubarb mixture; bake 35 to 40 minutes until lightly browned and bubbly. Serve with nonfat vanilla ice cream or frozen yogurt, if desired.

Serves: 6

Shopping List:

1½ lb. rhubarb (fresh or frozen), flour, sugar, brown sugar, nonfat granola, cinnamon, Butter Buds

Nutrition per serving		**Exchanges**
calories:	205	3½ other carbohydrate
total fat (0%):	0 g	
carbohydrate:	51 g	carbohydrate choice: 3½
cholesterol:	0 mg	
dietary fiber:	<.5 g	
protein:	2 g	
sodium:	9 mg	

Rhubarb provides fiber and potassium, prevents high blood pressure, and aids digestion.

Simpler Than Simple Sorbet

Easy — Do Ahead — Freeze

Ingredients:
    2 16-oz. cans fruit packed in juice (peaches, pears, apricots or other fruit of choice)

Directions:
    Freeze unopened cans of fruit in freezer overnight (at least 12 hours). While frozen, remove fruit from can, place in blender, and process until smooth. Serve immediately. Refreshing midday or late-night snack.

Serves: 4

Shopping List:
    2 16-oz. cans fruit packed in juice (fruit of choice)

Nutrition per serving		Exchanges
calories:	100	½ other carbohydrate
total fat (0%):	0 g	1 fruit
carbohydrate:	26 g	
cholesterol:	0 mg	carbohydrate choice: 1½
dietary fiber:	0 g	
protein:	1 g	
sodium:	10 mg	

Fruit is an excellent source of insoluble fiber, preventing colon cancer and diverticulosis.

Strawberry-Almond Dessert Treat

Easy — Do Ahead

Ingredients:
4 cups strawberries, stemmed and sliced
¾ tsp. almond extract
¼ cup powdered sugar
¼ cup nonfat Cool Whip, thawed (optional)

Directions:
Combine all ingredients except Cool Whip in a medium bowl; toss until coated and sugar is dissolved. Cover and refrigerate at least 3 hours before serving. Top each serving with 1 tablespoon Cool Whip, if desired.

Serves: 4

Shopping List:
2 pints strawberries, powdered sugar, almond extract, nonfat Cool Whip (optional)

Nutrition per serving		Exchanges
calories:	79	1 other carbohydrate
total fat (7%):	.6 g	
carbohydrate:	19 g	carbohydrate choice: 1
cholesterol:	0 mg	
dietary fiber:	4 g	
protein:	1 g	
sodium:	3 mg	

Strawberries are a good source of beta-carotene, lutein, lycopene, and vitamin C, which may help prevent osteoarthritis (especially of the knees).

Strawberry-ful Clafouti

Easy — Do Ahead

Ingredients:
¼ cup + 2 tbsp. flour
½ tsp. baking powder
¼ cup egg substitute
2 egg whites
⅓ cup sugar
2½ cups frozen strawberries, quartered, thawed, and
    drained (reserve ½ cup syrup)
powdered sugar (optional)

Directions:
Preheat oven to 375 degrees. Spray 8-inch baking dish with cooking spray. Combine flour and baking powder in medium bowl. Combine egg substitute and egg whites in a small bowl; blend until frothy. Add egg mixture, sugar, and reserved juice to flour mixture; stir until ingredients are blended. Fold in strawberries. Spread batter into pan and bake 35 to 45 minutes until lightly browned. Cool slightly before sprinkling with powdered sugar, if desired. Great served hot, cold, or at room temperature.

Serves: 4

Shopping List:
20 oz. package frozen strawberries, egg substitute, whole eggs, flour, baking powder, sugar, powdered sugar (optional)

DELECTABLE DESSERTS

Nutrition per serving		Exchanges
calories:	228	2 fruit
total fat (0%):	0 g	1½ other carbohydrate
carbohydrate:	55 g	
cholesterol:	0 mg	carbohydrate choice: 3½
dietary fiber:	3 g	
protein:	5 g	
sodium:	90 mg	

**Strawberries are a great source of ellagic acid,
one of the most potent cancerfighters.
Ellagic acid may prevent cellular changes
that can lead to cancer.**

Tiramisu

Average — Do Ahead

Ingredients:
¼ cup + 1½ tsp. Kahlúa
2½ tbsp. sugar, divided
1 tbsp. water
2 tsp. instant espresso powder, divided
3 tbsp. nonfat nondairy creamer (hazelnut or vanilla)
½ cup nonfat cream cheese
¾ cup nonfat Cool Whip
½ Entenmann's nonfat golden loaf, cut into 8 slices
unsweetened cocoa (optional)

Directions:
In a small cup or bowl, combine Kahlúa, 1½ teaspoons sugar, 1 tablespoon water, and espresso; mix until sugar and espresso are completely dissolved. In a mixing bowl or food processor, combine 1 tablespoon of the espresso mixture, creamer, remaining sugar, and cream cheese. Mix with electric mixer or blender until mixture is smooth and creamy. Fold in Cool Whip (do not mix!). Place 1 cake slice in wine glass or custard cup. Brush each slice generously with half the remaining espresso-Kahlua mixture. Spread cheese mixture over cake and top with other cake slice. Repeat layering until all ingredients are used. Sprinkle with unsweetened cocoa powder, if desired. Serve immediately.

Serves: 4

DELECTABLE DESSERTS

Shopping List:
Kahlua, instant espresso powder, Entenmann's nonfat golden loaf, 4 oz. nonfat cream cheese, nonfat Cool Whip, nonfat nondairy creamer (hazelnut or vanilla), sugar, unsweetened cocoa powder (optional)

Nutrition per serving		Exchanges
calories:	530	7½ other carbohydrate
total fat (0%):	0 g	
carbohydrate:	111 g	carbohydrate choice: 7½
cholesterol:	0 mg	
dietary fiber:	2 g	
protein:	12 g	
sodium:	685 mg	

According to the National Cancer Institute, dietary change can prevent 70 to 75% of most major cancers.

CHARMING
CHOCOLATES

Chocolate, Chocolate . . .
How Do I Love Thee?

Enough to jog an extra mile, forgo the nearest elevator, or skip a coffee break—nothing is quite as gratifying as CHOCOLATE! When the craving strikes . . . nothing but CHOCOLATE fits the bill! Weigh the good, the bad, and the historical facts about chocolate—now you can have your chocolate and enjoy it too!

Where does this "tastes delicious, crave it, shouldn't have" food come from anyway?

Blame it on Hernando Cortez! Brushed off by King Ferdinand and Queen Isabella, the great Spanish explorer Hernando Cortez saw great value in the small cocoa beans. During his conquest of Mexico, Cortez discovered the Aztec Indians preparing the royal *chocolatl* drink for Emperor Montezuma, who consumed as much as fifty glasses a day. Treated as a "food for the gods," *chocolatl* was presented in golden goblets to Montezuma's Spanish guests, who found the bitter drink repugnant. Hernando Cortez to the rescue! Cortez not only conceived the idea of sweetening the once-bitter chocolate with cane sugar, but also discovered the endless commercial possibilities the bean offered. From Spanish monks to the Court of France; from English Chocolate Houses in Great Britain to pre-Revolutionary New England, chocolate became recognized as an invaluable asset. From Hernando Cortez to the space program, chocolate has proven its worth—as a nation we consume **2,478,000,000 pounds** of gooey, fudgy, creamy chocolate each year!

THE ANNUAL STATISTICS:
- **11.7 pounds** consumed per person per year
- **3.1 BILLION** pounds in total consumption
- **7.6 BILLION** dollars worth of chocolate manufactured
- **11.7 BILLION** dollars in retail sales

So, now that we know that chocolate tastes good, is there anything in it that's good for you? Let us count the ways!

1. **Chocolate** is rich in cancer-fighting antioxidants.
2. **Chocolate** contains tannin, a phenol in cocoa that blocks the oxidation of LDL (bad) cholesterol.
3. **Chocolate** will not clog your arteries! The primary fatty acid in chocolate is stearic acid, a saturated fat that does not increase the blood-cholesterol level the same way

other types of saturated fats do. (Source: Southwestern University Medical Center in Dallas, Texas; Pennsylvania State University study; Center for Human Nutrition at the University of Texas)

4. **Chocolate** contains copper, an essential mineral for red blood cells to carry oxygen through your body.

5. **Chocolate** contains phenylethylamine and tyramine, chemicals that produce feelings of love and contentment.

6. **Chocolate** contains magnesium, a mineral involved in manufacturing serotonin (the mood stabilizer).

7. A 1.4 ounce milk **chocolate** bar contains: 3 grams of protein; 15 percent of the Recommended Daily Allowance for riboflavin; 9 percent of the Recommended Daily Allowance for calcium; and 7 percent of the Recommended Daily Allowance for iron.

8. **Chocolate** is not an acne activator. You are more likely to "break out" from the stress of "denial" than eating chocolate.

9. **Chocolate** can lift your spirits! One-half ounce of chocolate releases serotonin (for calming) and endorphins (for energy).

10. One ounce of **chocolate** only contains as much caffeine as 1 cup of *decaffeinated* coffee!! You would have to eat ten to twelve Hershey's milk chocolate bars (over 2,300 calories with 130 to 150 grams of fat) to equal the amount of caffeine in one-cup of regular coffee!

11. **Chocolate** does not deserve the bad rap it has received for promoting tooth decay. Research at the Forsyth Dental Center in Boston and at the University of Pennsylvania School of Dental Medicine has shown that cocoa and chocolate can actually offset the acid-producing potential of the sugar they contain. A study conducted at the Eastman Dental Center in Rochester, New York, found that milk chocolate and chocolate chip cookies were among the snack foods that contributed least to dental decay.

12. **Chocolate** is not the headache-trigger food some thought it to be. A study at the University of Pittsburgh found promising results that headache sufferers can enjoy chocolate without the fear of it causing headaches.

13. **Chocolate** is not addictive! Ranked as the single-most craved food in the United States, people love the taste, scent, and texture of chocolate, but it is NOT addictive!

You can love your chocolate and eat it too . . . IN MODERATION.

Cherry-Chip Brownie Treat

Easy — Do Ahead

Ingredients:

1 (17 oz.) package nonfat brownie mix
2 tbsp. miniature semisweet chocolate chips
21 oz. can cherry pie filling, divided
2½ cup nonfat Cool Whip

Directions:

Prepare brownie mix according to package directions; fold chocolate chips into batter. Pour batter into two 9-inch round cake pans and bake according to package directions. Cool completely before removing from pans. Place one "brownie cake" on large serving platter; top with ½ the Cool Whip and ½ the cherry pie filling. Repeat layers, cut, and serve.

Serves: 12

Shopping List:

1 17½-oz. package nonfat brownie mix, 21 oz. can cherry pie filling, 20 oz. nonfat Cool Whip, miniature semisweet chocolate chips

Nutrition per serving		Exchanges
calories:	245	4 other carbohydrate
fat (4%):	1 g	
carbohydrate:	0 g	carbohydrate choice: 4
cholesterol:	0 mg	
dietary fiber:	0 g	
protein:	2 g	
sodium:	236 mg	

Good news: Chocolate contains the compound catechin, a flavonoid that reduces LDL (bad) cholesterol oxidation and suppresses lipoxygenase activity, reducing the risk of atherogenesis and heart disease.
Bad news: Chocolate is still high in calories and saturated fat!

Chocolate-Almond Cake Surprise

Average — Do Ahead — Freeze

Ingredients:

1 cup sugar, divided
1 cup nonfat cream cheese, softened
1 cup egg substitute, divided
2 tsp. almond extract, divided
2 cups flour
¾ cup brown sugar

½ cup unsweetened cocoa powder
½ cup applesauce
1 cup + 2 tbsp. skim milk
1¼ tsp. baking powder
1 tsp. baking soda
1 cup powdered sugar

Directions:

Preheat oven to 350 degrees. Spray 12-cup Bundt pan with cooking spray. Combine ½ cup sugar, cream cheese, ½ cup egg substitute, and 1 teaspoon almond extract in a medium bowl; beat at low speed with electric mixer until smooth and creamy. Combine flour, sugar, cocoa, applesauce, 1 cup skim milk, remaining egg substitute, baking powder, baking soda, and remaining almond extract in a large mixing bowl. Beat at high speed with electric mixer until all ingredients are blended and smooth. Pour 3 cups batter into Bundt pan; top with cream cheese filling and remaining cake batter. Bake 45 to 60 minutes, until toothpick inserted in center comes out clean. Cool in pan 30 minutes; remove from pan and cool completely. Combine powdered sugar and 2 tablespoons skim milk in a medium bowl; mix until smooth and creamy. Drizzle glaze over cooled cake; let stand at room temperature until glaze hardens.

Serves: 16

Shopping List:

8 oz. nonfat cream cheese, 8 oz. egg substitute, 9 oz. skim milk, flour, sugar, brown sugar, unsweetened cocoa powder, powdered sugar, applesauce, almond extract, baking powder, baking soda

Nutrition per serving		Exchanges
calories:	201	3 other carbohydrate
total fat (4%):	1 g	
carbohydrate:	45 g	carbohydrate choice: 3
cholesterol:	0 mg	
dietary fiber:	1 g	
protein:	6 g	
sodium:	200 mg	

CHARMING CHOCOLATES

One more good reason to choose low-fat dairy products: Fat inhibits calcium absorption!

Chocolate-Banana Shake

Easy

Ingredients:
1 cup skim milk
2½ tbsp. chocolate syrup
½ cup nonfat chocolate sorbet
2 frozen bananas
2 tsp. vanilla

Directions:
Combine all ingredients in blender and process until smooth and creamy.

Serves: 2

Shopping List:
8 oz. skim milk, 4 oz. nonfat chocolate sorbet, chocolate syrup, 2 bananas, vanilla

Nutrition per serving		Exchanges
calories:	249	½ milk
total fat (4%):	1 g	2 fruit
carbohydrate:	57 g	1½ other carbohydrate
cholesterol:	2 mg	
dietary fiber:	2 g	carbohydrate choice: 4
protein:	6 g	
sodium:	77 mg	

Consumption of low-fat milk has increased while consumption of whole milk (containing 65% saturated fatty acids) has dramatically decreased (from twenty-six gallons per person in 1970 to nine gallons in 1994).

Chocolate-Cherry Custard Cake

Easy — Do Ahead

Ingredients:
  1 angel food cake, cut into bite-size pieces
  5.1 oz. package instant chocolate pudding mix
  1½ cups cold skim milk
  1 cup nonfat sour cream
  21 oz. cherry pie filling

Directions:
  Place angel food cake pieces in 9 x 13-inch baking dish. Combine pudding mix, milk, and sour cream in a medium bowl; beat with electric mixer until smooth, creamy, and thick. Spread mixture over cake pieces; top with pie filling. Cover and refrigerate several hours before serving.

Serves: 12

Shopping List:
  1 angel food cake (or mix to prepare), 5.1 oz. package instant chocolate pudding, 12 oz. skim milk, 8 oz. nonfat sour cream, 21 oz. cherry pie filling

Nutrition per serving		**Exchanges**
calories:	430	6½ other carbohydrate
total fat (4%):	2 g	
carbohydrate:	99 g	carbohydrate choice: 6½
cholesterol:	1 mg	
dietary fiber:	5 g	
protein:	10 g	
sodium:	230 mg	

*Milk is an excellent source of calcium;
1 cup skim milk contains more than
300 milligrams calcium, almost one-third of
the Recommended Daily Allowance.*

CHARMING CHOCOLATES

Chocolate-Chocolate Cake

Average — Do Ahead — Freeze

Ingredients:

2½ cups flour
¾ cup sugar
¾ cup brown sugar
1¾ cups unsweetened
  cocoa powder, divided
1½ tsp. cinnamon
1½ tsp. baking soda
1 cup skim milk
1 cup nonfat vanilla yogurt

⅔ cup unsweetened
  applesauce
½ cup egg substitute
1 tbsp. vanilla extract
2 cups nonfat cream cheese,
  softened
1½ cups powdered sugar
½ cup chocolate chips

Directions:

Preheat oven to 350 degrees. Spray two 9-inch-round cake pans with cooking spray. In a large mixing bowl, combine flour, sugar, brown sugar, cocoa, cinnamon, and baking soda; mix well. Add skim milk, yogurt, applesauce, egg substitute, and vanilla; mix until blended. Divide cake batter and spread in cake pans. Bake 40 to 45 minutes, until toothpick comes out clean. Remove cakes from oven and cool completely. In a medium bowl, combine cream cheese, ½ cup cocoa, and powdered sugar. Beat mixture until smooth. Fold in chocolate chips. Cut each cake in half horizontally (you will have four sliced cakes). Arrange one cake slice on serving platter; frost with cream cheese frosting. Repeat layers using all cake slices and frosting.

Serves: 16

Shopping List:

8 oz. nonfat cream cheese, 9 oz. skim milk, 8 oz. nonfat vanilla yogurt, 4 oz. egg substitute, unsweetened applesauce, flour, sugar, brown sugar, ½ lb. powdered sugar, 4 oz. reduced-fat chocolate chips, unsweetened cocoa powder, cinnamon, baking soda, vanilla

Nutrition per serving		Exchanges
calories:	278	4 other carbohydrate
total fat (10%):	3 g	
carbohydrate:	59 g	carbohydrate choice: 4
cholesterol:	1 mg	
dietary fiber:	1 g	
protein:	10 g	
sodium:	318 mg	

Hernando Cortez discovered the value of small cocoa beans and is credited with creating CHOCOLATE!

424

CHARMING CHOCOLATES

Chocolate Chocolate-Chip Biscotti

Average — Do Ahead — Freeze

Ingredients:

1 cup all-purpose flour
1 cup whole-wheat flour
¼ cup unsweetened cocoa
    powder
1 cup sugar
½ cup brown sugar

½ tsp. baking soda
¾ cup egg substitute
1 egg white
2 tsp. vanilla
¼ cup miniature
    chocolate chips

Directions:

Preheat oven to 325 degrees. Line baking sheet with foil and spray with cooking spray. Combine flour, whole-wheat flour, cocoa, sugar, brown sugar, and baking soda in a large bowl; mix until ingredients are blended. Combine egg substitute, egg white, and vanilla in a medium bowl; whisk until frothy. Pour egg mixture into flour mixture and mix until ingredients are blended. Fold in chocolate chips. Shape dough into 2 logs; place several inches apart on baking sheet. Bake 35 to 40 minutes until toothpick inserted in center comes out clean. Remove from oven and let cool 10 to 15 minutes. Slice logs diagonally into ½-inch pieces; arrange pieces cut side down on baking sheet. Bake 10 to 15 minutes; turn biscotti over and bake 10 to 15 minutes until crisp. Cool completely before storing in sealed container.

Serves: 24

Shopping List:

6 oz. egg substitute, eggs, all-purpose flour, whole-wheat flour, unsweetened cocoa powder, sugar, brown sugar, baking soda, vanilla, miniature chocolate chips

CHARMING CHOCOLATES

Nutrition per serving

calories:	101
total fat (9%):	1 g
carbohydrate:	22 g
cholesterol:	0 mg
dietary fiber:	1 g
protein:	2 g
sodium:	32 mg

Exchanges

1½ other carbohydrate

carbohydrate choice: 1½

Powdered carob can be substituted for cocoa powder in equal amounts, reducing the amount of caffeine in the recipe.

Chocolate Chocolate-Chip Pudding

Easy — Do Ahead

Ingredients:
1 cup sugar
¼ cup cornstarch
3 tbsp. unsweetened cocoa powder
2 cups skim milk
¼ nonfat Cool Whip
2 tsp. miniature chocolate chips

Directions:
Combine sugar, cornstarch, cocoa powder, and skim milk in a medium saucepan; cook over medium heat, stirring frequently, until mixture starts to thicken. Spoon into bowl or 4 dessert dishes; refrigerate at least 15 to 30 minutes until pudding sets. Top each serving with 1 tablespoon Cool Whip and sprinkle with ½ teaspoon chocolate chips.

Serves: 4

Shopping List:
16 oz. skim milk, sugar, cornstarch, unsweetened cocoa powder, miniature chocolate chips, nonfat Cool Whip

Nutrition per serving
calories:	281
total fat (3%):	1 g
carbohydrate:	67 g
cholesterol:	2 mg
dietary fiber:	0 g
protein:	5 g
sodium:	68 mg

Exchanges
4½ other carbohydrate

carbohydrate choice: 4½

According to Judith Stern, ScD, RD, professor of nutrition and internal medicine at the University of California, Davis, nonfat milk, combined with a low-fat diet rich in fruits and vegetables, has been shown to lower blood pressure as well as any single prescription drug.

Chocolate-Coated Banana Wrap

Easy — Do Ahead

Ingredients:
butter-flavored cooking spray
4 low-fat crepes*
2 bananas, peeled and cut in half lengthwise
1½ tbsp. lemon juice
¾ tsp. ground cinnamon
¼ cup sugar
⅓ cup nonfat chocolate syrup
2 tsp. sliced almonds

Directions:
Preheat oven to 350 degrees. Line baking sheet with foil and spray with butter-flavored cooking spray. Lay crepes on flat surface; place 1 banana half on each crepe. Brush bananas with lemon juice. Combine cinnamon and sugar in small cup; mix until blended. Reserve 2 tablespoons cinnamon-sugar; sprinkle remaining mixture over bananas. Roll crepe around banana and place seam side down on baking sheet. Lightly spray with butter-flavored spray and sprinkle with reserved cinnamon-sugar. Bake 3 to 5 minutes until golden brown. Drizzle with chocolate syrup, sprinkle with almonds (½ teaspoon per crepe) and serve.

Serves: 4

Shopping List:
2 bananas, low-fat crepes (e.g., Melissa's French crepes: 1-800-588-0151 or www.melissas.com), sugar, ground cinnamon, lemon juice, nonfat chocolate syrup, sliced almonds, butter-flavored cooking spray

Nutrition per serving		Exchanges
calories:	271	1 fruit
total fat (3%):	1 g	1 starch
carbohydrate:	65 g	2 other carbohydrate
cholesterol:	0 mg	
dietary fiber:	3 g	carbohydrate choice: 4
protein:	5 g	
sodium:	354 mg	

Bananas are the powerfood of potassium, which plays an important role in controlling blood pressure.

Chocolate-Chip Glazed Coffeecake

Easy — Do Ahead — Freeze

Ingredients:

2 cups flour
2 tsp. baking powder
½ tsp. baking soda
⅛ tsp. cinnamon
⅛ tsp. nutmeg
1 cup nonfat vanilla yogurt
½ cup sugar
¾ cup brown sugar
¼ cup egg substitute

1 egg white
1 tbsp. skim milk
5 tsp. vanilla, divided
½ cup mini chocolate chips
1 cup powdered sugar
2 tbsp. unsweetened cocoa
   powder
1½ tbsp. hot water

Directions:

Preheat oven to 350 degrees. Spray 10-inch baking dish with cooking spray. Combine flour, baking powder, baking soda, cinnamon, and nutmeg in a Ziploc bag; shake until ingredients are blended. Combine yogurt, sugar, brown sugar, egg substitute, egg white, milk, and 4 teaspoons vanilla in a large bowl; mix until blended smooth. Gradually add flour mixture, stirring until ingredients are moistened. Fold in chocolate chips. Spoon batter into pan and bake 35 to 45 minutes, until toothpick inserted in center comes out clean. Let cool in pan 10 minutes; remove from pan and cool completely. Combine powdered sugar, cocoa powder, 1 teaspoon vanilla, and hot water in a small bowl; mix until creamy smooth. Drizzle chocolate mixture over cake; let sit 45 to 60 minutes before serving.

Serves: 12

Shopping List:

8 oz. nonfat vanilla yogurt, skim milk, egg substitute, whole eggs, flour, sugar, brown sugar, powdered sugar, unsweetened cocoa powder, vanilla extract, baking powder, baking soda, cinnamon, nutmeg, reduced-fat chocolate chips

Nutrition per serving		Exchanges
calories:	242	3½ other carbohydrate
total fat (7%):	2 g	
carbohydrate:	53 g	carbohydrate choice: 3½
cholesterol:	0 mg	
dietary fiber:	1 g	
protein:	4 g	
sodium:	123 mg	

Chocolate contains theobromine, a feel-good compound.

Chocolate-Marshmallow Cupcakes

Easy — Do Ahead

Ingredients:
¾ cup egg substitute
¼ cup sugar
½ cup brown sugar
1 tbsp. vanilla
¾ cup flour
⅓ cup unsweetened cocoa powder
1 tsp. baking powder
1½ cups + 2 tbsp. marshmallow cream, divided
powdered sugar (optional)

Directions:
Preheat oven to 325 degrees. Spray muffin tin with cooking spray. Combine egg substitute, sugar, brown sugar, vanilla, flour, cocoa, baking powder, and 1½ cups marshmallow cream in a large bowl; mix until ingredients are completely blended. Divide batter among muffin cups and bake 20 to 25 minutes, until toothpick inserted in center comes out clean. Cool cupcakes; remove from muffin tin and let cool completely. Using a serrated knife, carefully cut a small circle in the center of each cupcake. Carefully remove cake and set aside. Fill cupcakes with 1-teaspoon marshmallow cream and replace cutout cake. Sprinkle with powdered sugar, if desired.

Serves: 6

Shopping List:
6 oz. egg substitute, marshmallow cream, sugar, brown sugar, flour, unsweetened cocoa powder, baking powder, vanilla, powdered sugar (optional)

CHARMING CHOCOLATES

Nutrition per serving		Exchanges
calories:	179	3 other carbohydrate
total fat (5%):	1 g	
carbohydrate:	42 g	carbohydrate choice: 3
cholesterol:	0 mg	
dietary fiber:	0 g	
protein:	4 g	
sodium:	84 mg	

Most people can get all the vitamins and minerals they need from a well-rounded diet; vitamin and mineral supplements cannot replace food or turn a junk-food diet into a healthy one.

Chocolate-Mint Smoothie

Easy

Ingredients:
  1 cup nonfat vanilla yogurt
  1 frozen banana
  3 tbsp. chocolate syrup
  ½ tsp. mint extract
  ⅔ cup crushed ice

Directions:
  Combine all ingredients in blender and process until smooth and creamy.

Serves: 2

Shopping List:
  8 oz. nonfat vanilla yogurt, banana, chocolate syrup, mint extract

Nutrition per serving

calories:	163
total fat (6%):	1 g
carbohydrate:	38 g
cholesterol:	3 mg
dietary fiber:	1 g
protein:	5 g
sodium:	86 mg

Exchanges

½ milk
1 fruit
1 other carbohydrate

carbohydrate choice: 2½

Adults purchase over 50% of all chocolate sold in the United States.

CHARMING
CHOCOLATES

Cookies 'n' Cream Yogurt Pops

Easy — Do Ahead — Freeze

Ingredients:
2 cups nonfat vanilla yogurt
½ cup cookie crumbs (from reduced-fat Oreo cookies)
4 tsp. chocolate sprinkles

Directions:
Spoon 2 tablespoons yogurt into each of four Popsicle molds or paper cup. Sprinkle with cookie crumbs; top with remaining yogurt. If using paper cups, insert craft stick in center of pop. Freeze 1 to 2 hours until pops are slightly firm. Remove from freezer; roll in chocolate sprinkles until coated. Freeze 2 to 4 hours until completely firm.

Serves: 4

Shopping List:
16 oz. nonfat vanilla yogurt, reduced-fat Oreo cookies, chocolate sprinkles

Nutrition per serving

calories:	132
total fat (7%):	1 g
carbohydrate:	26 g
cholesterol:	3 mg
dietary fiber:	0 g
protein:	6 g
sodium:	102 mg

Exchanges

1½ other carbohydrate
½ milk

carbohydrate choice: 2

Yogurt is an excellent low-fat source of calcium and protein. Lack of calcium can lead to osteoporosis, which affects one in four postmenopausal women.

CHARMING CHOCOLATES

"Devilishous" Frosted Brownies

Easy — Do Ahead — Freeze

Ingredients:
2 18-oz. packages nonfat fudge brownie mix
1 oz. unsweetened chocolate, melted in microwave
5½ tbsp. evaporated skim milk, divided
2¾ cups powdered sugar
3 tbsp. unsweetened cocoa powder
1 tsp. vanilla

Directions:
Prepare brownie mix according to package directions. Bake in 9 x 13-inch baking dish; cool completely. Place unsweetened chocolate in medium-size microwavable bowl; microwave on high power 45 to 60 seconds, stirring until smooth. Immediately stir in 3 tablespoons milk to thin, stirring until completely blended. Combine powdered sugar and cocoa in medium bowl; mix well. Gradually add sugar mixture to melted chocolate, beating well until smooth. Add remaining milk and vanilla; beat until completely smooth and creamy. Let frosting stand 5 to 10 minutes; spread over brownies. Cut and serve; top with nonfat frozen yogurt, if desired.

Serves: 16

Shopping List:
2 18-oz. packages nonfat brownie mix, evaporated skim milk, powdered sugar, unsweetened cocoa powder, unsweetened chocolate, vanilla

Nutrition per serving
calories:	321
total fat (3%):	1 g
carbohydrate:	75 g
cholesterol:	0 mg
dietary fiber:	0 g
protein:	3 g
sodium:	366 mg

Exchanges
5 other carbohydrate

carbohydrate choice: 5

Chocolate is not an acne activator. You are more likely to "break out" from the stress of "denial" than from eating chocolate.

Fruit 'n' Yogurt Sundae

Easy

Ingredients:
2 cups nonfat frozen chocolate yogurt
1½ cups canned fruit packed in juice
½ cup chocolate syrup
½ cup nonfat or low-fat granola

Directions:
Scoop ½ cup frozen yogurt into each of four dessert dishes. Spoon fruit on top. Drizzle with chocolate syrup and sprinkle with granola.

Serves: 4

Shopping List:
1 pint nonfat frozen chocolate yogurt, 15 oz. can fruit packed in juice (cinnamon-flavored peaches, pears, etc.), 4 oz. chocolate syrup, nonfat or low-fat granola

Nutrition per serving		Exchanges
calories:	255	½ milk
total fat (0%):	0 g	3 fruit
carbohydrate:	61 g	½ other carbohydrate
cholesterol:	0 mg	
dietary fiber:	0 g	carbohydrate choice: 4
protein:	6 g	
sodium:	86 mg	

According to a new report by Dutch researchers, cocoa has an important health benefit: large amounts of catechins, powerful antioxidant compounds that may protect the body against cardiovascular disease and cancer. Chocolate contains four times the amount of catechins as tea.

CHARMING CHOCOLATES

Fudge-Brownie Smoothie

Easy

Ingredients:
1 cup nonfat vanilla yogurt
1 cup frozen sliced strawberries
4 brownies prepared from nonfat brownie mix
2 tbsp. skim milk

Directions:
Combine all ingredients in blender; process until smooth and creamy.

Serves: 2

Shopping List:
8 oz. nonfat vanilla yogurt, 10 oz. package sliced frozen strawberries, skim milk, nonfat brownies (or mix to prepare)

Nutrition per serving		Exchanges
calories:	133	½ milk
total fat (0%):	0 g	½ fruit
carbohydrate:	27 g	1 other carbohydrate
cholesterol:	3 mg	
dietary fiber:	2 g	carbohydrate choice: 2
protein:	5 g	
sodium:	969 mg	

Chocolate is not addictive! Ranked as the single most-craved food in the United States, people love the taste, scent, and texture of chocolate, but it is NOT addictive! You can love your chocolate and eat it too . . . in moderation!

Guilt-Free Brownie Pie
Easy — Do Ahead

Ingredients:
18 oz. nonfat fudge brownie mix
2½ cups skim milk
2 3⅞-oz. packages nonfat instant pudding mix (chocolate or vanilla)
nonfat Cool Whip, thawed
2 tbsp. miniature chocolate chips

Directions:
Prepare brownie mix according to package directions. Spray glass pie plate with cooking spray; spread batter evenly and bake according to package directions. Cool completely. Pour skim milk into medium bowl; add pudding mix and beat until completely smooth and slightly thickened. Spread mixture over brownie crust. Spoon Cool Whip over pudding layer and sprinkle with chocolate chips. Refrigerate until ready to serve.

Serves: 8

Shopping List:
18 oz. package nonfat fudge brownie mix, 20 oz. skim milk, 2 3⅞-oz. package nonfat instant pudding mix (chocolate or vanilla), nonfat Cool Whip, miniature chocolate chips

Nutrition per serving		Exchanges
calories:	398	6 other carbohydrate
total fat (5%):	2 g	
carbohydrate:	89 g	carbohydrate choice: 6
cholesterol:	1 mg	
dietary fiber:	2 g	
protein:	6 g	
sodium:	110 mg	

CHARMING CHOCOLATES

"Guilt-Free Brownie Pie" is a great alternative to chocolate, which is high in saturated fat, increasing the risk of heart disease in women.

Jumbo Chocolate-Cherry Surprise Muffins

Easy — Do Ahead — Freeze

Ingredients:
½ cup egg substitute
½ cup skim milk
¼ cup applesauce
½ cup sugar
½ cup brown sugar
1 tsp. vanilla
1 cup all-purpose flour

½ cup whole-wheat flour
½ cup unsweetened
 cocoa powder
1 tbsp. baking powder
6 tbsp. cherry pie filling
powdered sugar (optional)

Directions:
Preheat oven to 325 degrees. Spray jumbo muffin tin with cooking spray. Combine egg substitute, milk, applesauce, sugar, brown sugar, and vanilla in a large mixing bowl; mix until creamy and smooth. Add flour, whole-wheat flour, cocoa powder, and baking powder; mix until ingredients are blended. Fill muffin cups half full with batter; top with 1 tablespoon cherry pie filling and cover with remaining batter. Bake 20 to 25 minutes until toothpick inserted in center comes out clean. When muffins are cooled, sprinkle with powdered sugar, if desired.

Serves: 6

Shopping List:
4 oz. egg substitute, 4 oz. skim milk, applesauce, all-purpose flour, whole-wheat flour, unsweetened cocoa powder, sugar, brown sugar, baking powder, vanilla, cherry pie filling, powdered sugar (optional)

Nutrition per serving
calories:	297
total fat (4%):	1 g
carbohydrate:	69 g
cholesterol:	0 mg
dietary fiber:	2 g
protein:	7 g
sodium:	226 mg

Exchanges
4½ other carbohydrate

carbohydrate choice: 4½

Don't overcrowd your oven when baking; if heat cannot circulate freely, foods will not bake evenly.

Mini Chocolate-Cherry Cheesecakes

Average — Do Ahead

Ingredients:

1½ cups graham cracker crumbs
1 cup nonfat sour cream
2 tbsp. + ½ cup sugar, divided
2 tsp. vanilla, divided
¼ cup unsweetened cocoa powder
2 cups nonfat cream cheese, softened
½ cup egg substitute
¼ cup cherry pie filling

Directions:

Preheat oven to 325 degrees. Line muffin tin with foil baking cups. Sprinkle 2 tablespoons graham cracker crumbs in each muffin cup; spray very lightly with cooking spray. Combine sour cream, 2 tablespoons sugar, and 1 teaspoon vanilla in a medium bowl; blend until creamy and smooth. Set mixture aside. Combine ½ cup sugar, cocoa, cream cheese, egg substitute, and 1 teaspoon vanilla in a medium bowl; blend with electric mixer until creamy and smooth. Divide batter among muffin cups (filling about three-quarters full). Bake 25 to 30 minutes; remove from oven and spoon 1 to 1½ tablespoons sour cream mixture over each mini cheesecake. Bake an additional 8 to 10 minutes until topping is set. Remove from oven and cool completely; arrange cheesecakes on serving platter; spoon about 2 teaspoons cherry pie filling on top, cover with plastic wrap, and refrigerate until firm (about 1 to 2 hours). Store any leftovers in refrigerator.

Serves: 12

Shopping List:

16 oz. nonfat cream cheese, 4 oz. egg substitute, 8 oz. nonfat sour cream, graham cracker crumbs, sugar, unsweetened cocoa powder, vanilla, cherry pie filling

Nutrition per serving		Exchanges
calories:	123	1½ other carbohydrate
total fat (7%):	1 g	
carbohydrate:	22 g	carbohydrate choice: 1½
cholesterol:	0 mg	
dietary fiber:	0 g	
protein:	8 g	
sodium:	298 mg	

When you're craving sweets, add a dessert to the end of your meal rather than having the treat as a meal or snack.

Mini Chocolate-Chip Meringues

Average — Do Ahead

Ingredients:
3 egg whites
1 cup sugar
1 tbsp. vanilla
6 tbsp. unsweetened cocoa powder
3 tbsp. miniature chocolate chips
powdered sugar

Directions:
Preheat oven to 250 degrees. Line baking sheet with foil and spray with cooking spray. Place egg whites in medium bowl; mix with electric mixer until soft peaks form. Gradually add sugar and vanilla, beating until stiff peaks form. Gently fold in cocoa powder and chocolate chips. Drop dough by teaspoonfuls onto baking sheet; bake 25 to 30 minutes, until cookies are lightly browned and crisp. Cool completely; sprinkle lightly with powdered sugar.

Serves: 12

Shopping List:
eggs, sugar, unsweetened cocoa powder, vanilla, miniature chocolate chips, powdered sugar

Nutrition per serving		Exchanges
calories:	60	1 other carbohydrate
total fat (15%):	1 g	
carbohydrate:	14 g	carbohydrate choice: 1
cholesterol:	0 mg	
dietary fiber:	0 g	
protein:	1 g	
sodium:	10 mg	

CHARMING CHOCOLATES

Americans consume approximately $3.4 billion worth of candy per year and 1.3 billion pounds of chocolate candy bars.

Mocha-Berry Sundae
Easy

Ingredients:
2 cups nonfat frozen coffee yogurt
¼ cup nonfat chocolate syrup
¼ cup low-fat granola
1 cup raspberries

Directions:
Place ½ cup yogurt in each of four dessert dishes (or small bowls). Drizzle each dessert with 1 tablespoon chocolate syrup; sprinkle with 1 tablespoon granola and 2 tablespoons raspberries.

Serves: 4

Shopping List:
16 oz. nonfat frozen coffee yogurt, nonfat chocolate syrup, low-fat granola, ½ pint raspberries

Nutrition per serving

calories:	133
total fat (14%):	2 g
carbohydrate:	26 g
cholesterol:	3 mg
dietary fiber:	2 g
protein:	5 g
sodium:	95 mg

Exchanges
2 other carbohydrate

carbohydrate choice: 2

Save 173 calories, 15 grams fat, 82 milligrams sodium, and 10 grams of sugar per cup of granola by switching from regular granola to a low-fat version.

CHARMING CHOCOLATES

Mocha-Blend Masterpiece

Easy

Ingredients:
1 tsp. coffee powder
2 tbsp. nonfat chocolate syrup
1 frozen banana
1 cup nonfat vanilla yogurt
¼ tsp. cinnamon
½ cup crushed ice

Directions:
Combine all ingredients in blender and process until smooth and creamy.

Serves: 2

Shopping List:
8 oz. nonfat vanilla yogurt, banana, nonfat chocolate syrup, coffee powder, cinnamon

Nutrition per serving		Exchanges
calories:	140	½ fruit
total fat (0%):	0 g	½ milk
carbohydrate:	32 g	1 other carbohydrate
cholesterol:	3 mg	
dietary fiber:	1 g	carbohydrate choice: 2
protein:	5 g	
sodium:	81 mg	

Yogurt consumption in the United States rose from one pound per person per year in 1970 to four pounds per person in 1994.

Secret Surprise Mocha Cake

Easy — Do Ahead

Ingredients:
1 cup flour
⅔ cup sugar, divided
½ cup brown sugar
6 tbsp. unsweetened cocoa powder, divided
1½ tbsp. instant coffee granules
2 tsp. baking powder
½ cup skim milk
3 tbsp. unsweetened applesauce
1 tsp. vanilla
1 cup boiling water
2 tbsp. powdered sugar (optional)

Directions:
Preheat oven to 350 degrees. Spray 8-inch square baking dish with cooking spray. Combine flour, ⅓ cup sugar, brown sugar, 4 tablespoons cocoa, coffee granules, and baking powder in a medium bowl; mix until ingredients are blended. Add milk, applesauce, and vanilla to dry ingredients. Mix until blended and moistened. Spread batter in baking dish. Combine remaining sugar with remaining cocoa powder and mix well; sprinkle mixture over batter. Pour 1 cup boiling water over batter; do not mix. Bake 25 to 30 minutes, until cake springs back when touched in center. Cool cake and sprinkle with powdered sugar, if desired.

Serves: 8

Shopping List:
flour, sugar, brown sugar, unsweetened cocoa powder, vanilla, baking powder, powdered sugar (optional), 4 oz. skim milk, unsweetened applesauce, instant coffee granules

Nutrition per serving		Exchanges
calories:	195	3 other carbohydrate
total fat (5%):	1 g	
carbohydrate:	47 g	carbohydrate choice: 3
cholesterol:	0 mg	
dietary fiber:	1 g	
protein:	3 g	
sodium:	98 mg	

According to the American Chemical Society, chocolate and cocoa contain heart-protective and anticancer benefits.

CHARMING CHOCOLATES

"Simply Mahvelous"
Chocolate-Mallow Pie

Easy — Do Ahead

Ingredients:
1 cup nonfat cream cheese, softened
2 cups skim milk, divided
3⅞ oz. nonfat instant chocolate pudding mix
1½ cups miniature marshmallows
2 tbsp. miniature semisweet chocolate chips
1 low-fat graham cracker crust

Directions:
Combine cream cheese and ½ cup milk in food processor, blender, or large mixing bowl; process or beat with electric mixer until creamy. Add remaining milk and pudding mix; mix until blended and smooth. Fold in marshmallows and chocolate chips. Pour into prepared crust; cover and refrigerate several hours before serving.

Serves: 8

Shopping List:
low-fat graham cracker crust, 8 oz. nonfat cream cheese, 16 oz. skim milk, 3⅞ oz. nonfat instant chocolate pudding mix, miniature marshmallows, miniature semisweet chocolate chips

Nutrition per serving		Exchanges
calories:	214	3 other carbohydrate
total fat (8%):	2 g	
carbohydrate:	43 g	carbohydrate choice: 3
cholesterol:	1 mg	
dietary fiber:	2 g	
protein:	8 g	
sodium:	351 mg	

Switching to low-fat milk (especially skim)
can save you more than 6 grams of fat per cup:
1 cup whole milk = 8.9 fat grams;
1 cup 2% milk = 4.7 fat grams;
1 cup 1% milk = 2.6 fat grams;
1 cup skim milk = <.5 fat grams!

TWO-WEEK
MENU PLAN

Two Week Menu Plan

DAY ONE

Breakfast: Cinnamon Apple Puffy Pancakes
page 31
1 cup grape juice

Lunch: Apricot Baked Chicken
page 109
Quick-Pick-Me-Up Carrot-Apple Salad
page 343
Pepper Topped Crostini
page 16

Dinner: Chicken, Broccoli, and Noodle Casserole
page 304
1 cup chunky homestyle applesauce

DAY TWO

Breakfast: Cheese Egg'l
page 335
orange

Lunch: Crispy Chicken Bites
page 347
Green Beans Parmesan
page 285
1 cup nonfat yogurt + 1 cup raspberries

Dinner: shrimp cocktail (4 cooked shrimp +
¼ cup cocktail sauce)
Rainbow Angel Hair Pasta
page 321
1 slice crusty bread sprinkled with Butter Buds,
garlic powder, nonfat Parmesan cheese

DAY THREE

Breakfast: Fantabulous Smoothie
page 216
English muffin

Lunch: Turkey 'n' Cheese Tortilla Wraps
page 106
1 cup fruit cocktail (packed in juice)

Dinner: "Squashly" Mostaccioli
page 251
sourdough bread roll
1 cup Romaine lettuce + 2 tbsp. Creamy
Caesar Salad Splash
page 93

DAY FOUR

Breakfast: Banana-Berry-Orange Blast
page 334
½ whole-wheat bagel

Lunch: Snappy Vegetable-Beef Soup
page 65
English muffin sprinkled with Butter Buds
1 cup red grapes

Dinner: Marinated Turkey Roast
page 122
"Double Up" Sweet Potatoes
page 223
tossed salad with 2 tbsp. nonfat salad dressing

DAY FIVE

Breakfast: Cinnamon-Spice Oatmeal
page 32
1 cup skim milk
½ grapefruit

Lunch: Asian Chicken Soup With Snow Peas
& Noodles
page 55
1 slice bread, roll, ½ bagel, or pita
pear

Dinner: Honey Dijon Chicken
page 120
Vegetable Couscous
page 253
1 tomato sliced, drizzled with 1 tbsp. nonfat
Italian salad dressing

TWO-WEEK
MENU PLAN

DAY SIX

Breakfast: Date-Bran Muffin
page 193
1 cup nonfat cottage cheese mixed with
    ½ cup pineapple tidbits
¾ cup calcium-fortified orange juice

Lunch: Baked Potato topped with ½ cup nonfat chili
2 tbsp. nonfat cheese
tossed salad with 2 tbsp.nonfat salad dressing
apple

Dinner: Teriyaki Snapper
page 156
Shiitake Mushrooms and Brown Rice
page 267
Citrus-Splashed Baby Greens
page 75

DAY SEVEN

Breakfast: 1 cup bran flake cereal + ¾ cup skim milk
¾ cup blueberries
¾ cup calcium-fortified orange juice

Lunch: No-Cook Chicken-Cheddar Wraps
page 100
1 cup canned peaches (packed in juice)

Dinner: Vegetarian Burger Pizza
page 327
Crunchy Coleslaw
page 76
1 cup canned pineapple slices (packed in juice)

DAY EIGHT

Breakfast: Wholesome Hearty Pancakes
page 37
½ cup nonfat yogurt (plain, vanilla, or berry)
¾ cup sliced strawberries

Lunch: Chicken Caesar Pita Pocket
page 98
1 cup cauliflower and broccoli florets +
    ½ cup nonfat Ranch salad dressing
1 cup red grapes

Dinner: Seafood Stew
page 324
2 slices whole-wheat bread + 2 oz. Swiss
cheese slice

DAY NINE

Breakfast: ½ toasted whole-wheat bagel + ¼ cup
nonfat ricotta cheese
2 tbsp. raisins + 1 tsp. cinnamon
¾ cup red grape juice

Lunch: Bountiful Bean and Corn Salad
page 73
low-fat flour tortilla

Dinner: Grilled Tuna with Pineapple-Orange Salsa
page 135
½ cup brown rice
1 cup steamed green beans

DAY TEN

Breakfast: 4 egg whites cooked with ½ cup cooked spinach
1 oz. nonfat cheese
1 slice whole-wheat toast + 2 tsp. all-fruit spread
¾ cup calcium-fortified orange juice

Lunch: Tossin' It Creamy Veggie Salad
page 91
1 oz. nonfat bagel chips

Dinner: 2 slices Hawaiian Ham Pineapple Pizza
page 315
Cabbage and Cucumber Dill Salad
page 74

DAY ELEVEN

Breakfast: Overnight French Toast Casserole
page 35
2 tbsp. powdered sugar
1 oz. lite maple syrup
1 cup mixed berries
1 cup skim milk

Lunch: Shredded Barbecue Chicken and
Slaw Sandwich
page 103
2 dill pickle spears
celery sticks and cucumber slices with
½ cup nonfat Ranch salad dressing

Dinner: 3-Step Minestrone Meal
page 66
1 slice Italian bread
tossed salad with 2 tbsp. nonfat salad dressing

DAY TWELVE

Breakfast: ½ English muffin with ½ cup egg substitute +
½ cup chopped broccoli + 2 tbsp. nonfat
shredded cheese
1 cup cantaloupe cubes

Lunch: Zesty White Bean Chili
page 70
Cheese-Pleasin' Cornbread
page 42
½ cup chunky homestyle applesauce

Dinner: Barbecue Meat Loaf
page 163
Cheesy Mashed Potatoes
page 222
1½ cup frozen vegetable medley

DAY THIRTEEN

Breakfast: Apricot-Ginger Bread (1 slice)
page 39
1 cup nonfat yogurt
1 banana

Lunch: Tropical Blend Gazpacho
page 67
1 oz. baked tortilla chips
½ cup nonfat bean dip (or refried beans)

Dinner: Vegetarian Sloppy Joes
page 207
Home Fries
page 224
Jicama, Carrot and Pepper Slaw
page 79

DAY FOURTEEN

Breakfast: Berry Berry Muesli
page 27
¾ cup calcium-fortified orange juice

Lunch: Grilled Tuna Sandwich
page 348
carrots, celery, jicama sticks with ½ cup salsa
kiwi fruit

Dinner: Steak Fajitas
page 178
Red and Green Rice Veracruz
page 264

Menu Substitutions and/or Food Choices

Breakfasts:

Kinango Smoothie
page 367
2 slices whole-wheat toast
   with 1 tbsp. diet margarine

Blueberry Blintzes
page 27
½ cup calcium-fortified orange juice
3 oz. Healthy Choice Ham

Lunches:

Seafood Stuffed in Sun-Dried Tomato Wraps
page 19
Butternut Squash Soup
page 56
Melon Berry Slush
page 370
Spinach Chicken Salad
page 84
Now THAT'S a FRUIT SALAD!
page 82
Crustless Spinach Quiche
page 280
Peach 'n' Berry Summer Soup
page 62
Fruitful of Surprise Yogurt Pop
page 402
Salmon Burger
page 145
Tropical Blend Gazpacho
page 67

Dinners:

Oven-Fried Crunchy Parmesan Fillets
page 141
Mushroom Risotto
page 261
Oriental Almond Green Beans
page 289
Poached Salmon
page 142
Thyme-Roasted Potatoes
page 231
Honey-Coated Baby Carrots
page 286

TWO-WEEK
MENU PLAN

Snacks . . . Why do we eat them?

Crunchy, creamy, salty, or sweet—snacks taste great; they're "quick to pick," they satisfy our cravings, and keep us fueled with energy! Plan ahead—incorporate snacks into your meal plans—don't use them as substitutes for meals!

Snacks under 100 calories and < 2 grams fat per serving:
- 1 cup cherries
- ¼ cantaloupe topped with ½ cup nonfat vanilla yogurt
- 1 medium kiwifruit
- 1 cup strawberries
- 6 large strawberries dipped in nonfat chocolate syrup
- 3 small plums
- 2 medium tangerines
- 4 prunes
- orange
- 2 slices fresh pineapple
- 1 oz. raisins or dried berries
- banana
- 1 small apple
- 25 fresh or frozen grapes
- 10 dried apricot halves
- ½ cup chunky-style applesauce
- ½ cup lemon nonfat yogurt mixed with ½ cup fresh blueberries
- ½ cup peach nonfat yogurt mixed with ½ cup fresh raspberries
- ½ cup zucchini slices topped with 2 tablespoons salsa
- 1 celery stalk stuffed with 1 tablespoon nonfat garden-vegetable cream cheese
- 1 cup vegetable-juice cocktail flavored with a dash of Worcestershire sauce and lemon juice; serve with celery stalk
- 3 medium carrots
- 2 cups raw broccoli or cauliflower florets + ¼ cup nonfat Ranch salad dressing

- 1 kosher dill pickle (high sodium)
- 2 oz. water-packed tuna with 1 teaspoon nonfat mayonnaise
- 3 oz. surimi (imitation seafood) with cocktail sauce
- 2 oz. low-fat turkey breast slices wrapped around 4 melon balls
- 1 mini-bagel with 1 tbsp. nonfat cream cheese
- 1 cup dry unsweetened cereal
- 1 shredded wheat biscuit drizzled with 1 tbsp. honey
- 8 baked tortilla chips with ¼ cup salsa
- 100 thin (2¼-inch nonfat pretzel sticks or 1 hard pretzel
- 3 cups 94% fat-free microwave popcorn with 1 tablespoon nonfat Parmesan cheese
- 2 nacho-flavored rice cakes with 2 tbsp. salsa
- 2 caramel rice cakes
- 1 slice reduced-calorie whole-wheat bread with 2 tsp. all-fruit spread
- Three 2½-inch graham cracker squares
- 10 animal crackers
- 1 fortune cookie
- 1 frozen nonfat fudge bar
- Two 100% fruit frozen-juice bars
- 4 oz. frozen nonfat sorbet
- ½ cup chocolate nonfat frozen yogurt with 1 tbsp fresh raspberries
- 1 cup sugar-free cocoa with 2 large marshmallows
- ½ cup vanilla instant sugar-free fat-free pudding with 1 tbsp. nonfat Cool Whip
- 10 jelly beans
- 2 nonfat Fig Newton cookies
- 4 Bagel Chips with ¼ cup Garlic Herb Spread*
- ½ cup Garlic Aioli Dip* with 1 cups Fresh Cut-up Vegetables (carrots, celery, jicama, cucumber slices, zucchini or yellow squash, broccoli, cauliflower)
- 3 Mini Rice Cakes with ⅓ cup Tofu-Cheese Spread*
- 1 cup Quick-Pick-Me-Up Carrot Salad*
- 2 cups Cinnamon Spice Popcorn*
- (1) Pumpkin Power Bar*
- (1) Chocolate-Chocolate Chip Biscotti*

Snacks containing 100 to 150 calories/<2 grams fat:
- Apple Spice Slush* (114 calories/0 grams fat)
- Banana Berry "C-Ful" Shake* (150 calories/0 grams fat)
- Blended Veggie Drink* (129 calories/1 gram fat)
- Paradise Smoothie* (102 calories/0 grams fat)
- Peachy Clean Slushie* (125 calories/0 grams fat)
- ¾ cup Snack Mix* (126 calories/1 gram fat)
- Cookies 'n' Cream Yogurt Pop (132 calories/1 gram fat)
- Fudge Brownie Smoothie (133 calories/0 grams fat)
- 2 Mini Chocolate Chip Meringues* (120 calories/2 grams fat)
- 2 large marshmallows dipped in nonfat chocolate syrup (120 calories/0 grams fat)

For additional "snacks" and "treats" refer to the Dessert and Chocolate Sections of the Cookbook. Plan to indulge every now and then. Just remember . . . it's a treat, not a meal!

References

"Age Buster Food Plan." Prevention Magazine a Rodale Publication. September 1999, Rodale Inc. All rights reserved.

American Diabetes Association Complete Guide to Diabetes, 2nd edition.

Bader, Dr. Myles H. 6001 Food Facts and Chef's Secrets. Northstar Publishing Co., Las Vegas, Nevada, 1995.

Balch, James F. and Phyllis A. Balch, C.N.C. Prescription for Dietary Wellness: Using Foods to Heal

Cedar, D. Phytochemicals. www.wellweb.com/nutri/phytochemicals.

Clark, Nancy, MS, RD. Sports Nutrition Guidebook. Human Kinetics, 1990.

Complete Book of Vitamins and Minerals. Publications International, Ltd., Lincolnwood, Illinois, 1996.

Craig, W. "Phytochemicals: Guardians of Our Health." www.andrewscdu/NUFS/phyto.

Craig, W. Phytochemicals: New Frontiers in Disease Prevention. "The Soy Connection." Volume 4, Number 3, Summer 1996.

Drozd, Shelley. "The Top of the Food Chain." Men's Health, September 2000.

"Eat it Today—Tomatoes." http://www.welltopia.com/eatit.

Eftekhar, Judy Lin. Eating Right! Globe Communications Cc . 2000.

Fanz, M. Exchanges for All Occasions, 4th edition.

Guide to the Foods You Eat. Black Dog & Levent' . Publishers, Inc., New York, New York, 1998.

Houck, Catherine. "Cut Your Cancer Risk by   Percent." Good Housekeeping. August 1999.

"If Forced to Choose, America Would I , Sweet Tooth." 2000 Reuters.Ltd.

Jibrin, Janis R.D. "The New Super Foc .' Woman's Day Magazine, August 2000.

Liebman, B. "Antioxidants Repor. ,ets Ceilings." Nutrition Action Newsletter, June 2000.

"Lycopene: A good reason to eat tomatoes." Mayo Clinic Health Letter, September 1998.

McDonald, Arline, PH.D., R.D. Complete Book of Vitamins and Minerals. Publications International, Ltd., Lincolnwood, Illinois. 1996

Monson, E. Dietary Reference Intake for the Antioxidant Nutrients: Vitamin C, Vitamin E, Selenium, Carotenoids. Journal of American Dietetic Association, Volume 100, Number 9, June 2000.

Murphy, Franklin L., M.D. "What You Don't Know Can Hurt You." www.preventivehealthcenter.com/education/fiber.

Natow, Annette B., Ph.D., R.D., and Jo-Ann Heslin, M.A, R. D. The Fast Food Nutrition Counter. Pocket Books, New York, 1994.

"Nutrition Action Healthletter." Center for Science in the Public Interest, Washington, D.C.

Pennington, J. Bowes & Church's Food Values of Portions Commonly Used. 16th edition. Philadelphia, Pennsylvania. J.B. Lippincott Co., 1994.

"Phytochemicals." www.phytolink.net/phyto_main.

Polunin, Miriam. DK Living: Healing Foods, DK Publishing, New York, New York, 1999.

Smith, Pamela R.D. The Energy Edge

Somer, E. The Essential Guide to Vitamins and Minerals. Harper Paperbacks, New York, New York, 1992.

The Merck Manual. Table 1-2, Chapter 1
www.merck.com/pubs/mmanual/tables/1tbs.

Tufts University Health and Nutrition Letter. Volume 18, Number 4. June 2000.

Van Straten, Michael. Healing Foods: Nutrition for the Mind, Body and Spirit. Welcome Rain Publishers, New York, New York, 1999.

Web M.D. Health, Vitamins, Carotenoids and Phytochemicals; mywebmd.com/content/dmk_article_40088.

"Wellness Made Easy." University of California, Berkeley Wellness Letter, 1990.

Yeager, Selene. The Doctors Book of Food Remedies. Rodale Press, Inc., Pennsylvania, 1998.

Zimmerman, M. Phytochemicals: Nutrients of the Future.
www.realtime.net/ant/phytonut.

Index